TERRY PRATCHETT
A LIFE WITH FOOTNOTES

www.penguin.co.uk

TERRY PRATCHETT

A LIFE WITH FOOTNOTES

ROB WILKINS

doubleday

TRANSWORLD PUBLISHERS

Penguin Random House, One Embassy Gardens,
8 Viaduct Gardens, London SW11 7BW
www.penguin.co.uk

Transworld is part of the Penguin Random House group of companies
whose addresses can be found at global.penguinrandomhouse.com

First published in Great Britain in 2022 by Doubleday
an imprint of Transworld Publishers

A CIP catalogue record for this book
is available from the British Library.

ISBNs 9780857526632 (hb)
9780857526649 (tpb)

Typeset in 11.75/14.5 pt Bembo Pro by Jouve (UK), Milton Keynes
Printed and bound in Great Britain by Clays Ltd, Elcograf S.p.A.

The authorized representative in the EEA is Penguin Random House Ireland,
Morrison Chambers, 32 Nassau Street, Dublin D02 YH68.

Penguin Random House is committed to a sustainable
future for our business, our readers and our planet. This book
is made from Forest Stewardship Council® certified paper.

INTRODUCTION

Five months before he died, Terry Pratchett wrote five letters, sealed them in envelopes and locked them in the safe in his office to be opened after his death. This was the one he addressed to me.

Wiltshire
4th October 2014

Dear Rob,

So. I have gone. There were days when I felt I had already gone and so all I wish for now is a cool, quiet room and some peace to gather my addled thoughts. I think I was good, although I could have been better, but Terry Pratchett is dead and there are no more words.

Look after Lyn, please. Have those fine pieces of jewellery cast to my design and give them with my love. Choose a gift every Christmas and birthday. Send flowers. Have a big dinner each year, more if necessary or if a celebration is required, and raise a brandy to my memory and to happy days.

Look after the business and it will look after you. For all you have done, for all of the little things and all of the much bigger things and for the burying of the bodies . . . I thank you.

Learn to fly. Do it now.

And mind how you go.

Strive!

Terry

Just to be clear from the outset: there were no actual bodies in need of burying during my years of working with Terry Pratchett. Terry could get quite exasperated with people sometimes, and certainly did not (as people often found themselves saying about him) suffer fools gladly. But he never got *that* exasperated. So, for fans of exhumation and cold-case detective mysteries – the book you are holding is not that kind of book.

However, there is no question that a lot went on during Terry's life that I was in a unique position to witness and be involved with – 'all of the little things and all of the much bigger things', to quote Terry's letter – and the plan is that this will be very much *that* kind of book.

And just to be clear about something else, the pages that follow attempt to cover the whole of Terry's life-story, not just the part of Terry's life-story that I was around for. And they are certainly not an attempt to tell *my* life-story. But I probably do need to spend a little time here at the beginning to explain who I am, how I came to be in the room with Terry in the first place and how I come to be writing this biography of him.

So, by way of background: my name is Rob Wilkins and I was meant to be a lady from the village. At least, to the extent that he had a particular type of person in mind, those seemed to be the lines along which Terry was thinking when he decided it was time he got a personal assistant.

She would be someone who might respond to a card in the window of the village shop: someone, most likely retired, who was in a position to come in for a few days a week to help with the admin, do some filing, maybe turn her hand to a VAT return – perhaps, with a bit of luck, ensure there was milk in the office fridge for cups of tea so that Terry, who kept forgetting that detail, didn't have to get up from his desk and walk all the way back down to the house for it.

She would be someone (and this was important) who wasn't a big reader of Terry Pratchett's books, who might then have questions or, worse than that, suggestions. Or, worse than *that*, opinions. Because, without wishing to sound ungrateful, that could be distracting, which would defeat the point.

2

The fact that Terry was thinking about personal assistants at all . . . well, this, I think we can allege, was substantially Jilly Cooper's fault. These two stellar British authors, Jilly and Terry, had collided amid the canapés at a publishing event in London, as stellar authors sometimes will. And during the conversation Terry's ears had pricked up at Jilly's casual references to 'my PA' – a woman called, it seemed, Amanda, whom Jilly warmly described as 'heavenly' and 'wonderfully kind' and whom she unhesitatingly declared to be 'the best in the business'.

Now, Terry, who was largely indifferent to the world's trappings, nevertheless had, like most writers, a thin but steely competitive streak that ran through him like a piano string, and which could occasionally be plucked. This appears to have been one of those occasions. If the author of such bestselling works as *Riders*, *Rivals* and *Score!* was officially a novelist in need of personal assistance, then didn't it follow that Terry, who at this point had sold around 50 million books in 29 languages, was in need of personal assistance too?*

Whatever, the hymning of Amanda reverberated with Terry, and continued to reverberate with him as, entirely unassisted personally, he drove himself back home to Wiltshire that night.

This was in the year 2000. Terry was 52. He was living in what he called a 'Domesday Manorette' outside Salisbury. He had spent a decade as Britain's best-selling author, a title he had only recently conceded, with some reluctance, to a writer called J. K. Rowling. The Discworld series was now 25 novels long, on its way to the eventual total of 41, and he had written a string of books outside it, too, including an enormously successful strand of work for younger readers. A prodigious creator, who appeared never to have experienced so much as two minutes of writer's block (and was accordingly rather contemptuous of that concept and those who complained of it), Terry was producing two books per year and occasionally finding room to squeeze in a third. The popularity of his work was immense, and its ubiquity was legendary: it was frequently said that no train anywhere in Britain was permitted to

. . . .

* At the time of writing, in 2021, that sales total is bobbing around 100 million books.

3

run until it was established that at least one passenger on board was reading a Terry Pratchett.*

Inevitably success at such dizzying levels brought with it burdens on Terry's time over and above the pressure to deliver further novels. Principally there was the business that came with, as Terry dryly put it, 'being a *nauthor*'. The business of being a *nauthor* was, as Terry would explain, different in important ways from the business of being a writer. Indeed, *nauthorship* essentially comprised the obligations that kept a writer from doing any writing: in Terry's case, the two long and phenomenally well-attended book-signing tours per year in Britain and the others abroad for which he would don his black fedora, black Levi's leather jacket and black Hugo Boss jeans ('taking the album on the road', as he referred to it), and the appearances, similarly clad, at packed-out talks and conventions and festivals, all of which occasions were at this point absorbing an increasing amount of his time and energy.

But the burden of being a *nauthor* necessarily followed Terry home to his desk, too. It followed him in the form of the post – whole sacks of it. Readers of Terry's books were not just remarkable for their numbers, they were remarkable for the strength and depth of their attachment to his work, and many of them felt drawn to write to him. And on top of that were the more formal requests, frequently for advice or money or, in the case of the really forward correspondents, advice *and* money. It had reached the stage where just reading and responding to that mail in the manner that Terry felt honour-bound to do would have been a full-time job on its own, leaving him no room in the working day to get on with anything else he might want to do, such as, for example, write a book. Or, in Terry's case, write several books at once. He liked to have two, or even three, on the go, and with the outlines of a fourth often beginning to take shape somewhere in the gloaming.

....

* It was also frequently said that Terry had the honour of being Britain's most shoplifted author, an allegation made lightly on one occasion which then followed him around for ever. No reliable statistics are available in this area, but either way, Terry didn't especially mind. By the time people were in a position to shoplift them, he felt he had been paid for the books already.

Then there was the constantly ringing office phone – people calling up on matters regarding those books, those tours, those festivals, or for interviews or comment, or for contributions to what Terry referred to as the 'My Favourite Spoon' slots in the newspaper supplements. And Terry, whose background was in journalism – first on papers, and then, from the other side of the barbed wire, as a press officer – was constitutionally incapable of leaving a ringing phone unanswered. Miss a phone call, miss the story. (Terry's schooling on papers informed much of his approach to work, as we shall see.)

And on top of all *that* there was the merchandising. This was by now a significant sideline, yet Terry insisted on having the final sign-off on any licensed Discworld product, from figurines to candles, from tea towels to doorplates, from postcards to pendants. The way Terry saw it, these things were an extension of the world he had created in his books and he didn't want anybody getting things wrong or taking unsanctioned liberties which caused that world to be misrepresented, thereby disappointing or, even worse, ripping off his readers. This was a noble position to take, especially when you learned how much money – 'eye-wateringly large sums' was Terry's phrase for it – companies of various kinds were dangling in front of Terry to remove the Discworld franchise from his grip. But those high principles were bound to exact a heavy toll in terms of admin. As Terry said in an interview with the Science Fiction Book Club in 1996, 'If your Mickey Mouse ears fall off, that nice Mr Disney is not unduly perturbed. If someone buys a Discworld T-shirt and the colours run in the wash, I am the person who gets the email.'*

So, what with one thing and another, Terry had reached that precarious point where the business of being Terry Pratchett was threatening to prevent him from doing the thing that had made him Terry Pratchett in the first place. Meanwhile, what had started out as, literally, a cottage

....

* Or as he put it in an interview with David Langford for *Ansible* in 1999: 'When the tip drops off your *Star Wars* light-sabre, George Lucas never hears about it. But if a candle's the wrong colour, it's me that gets the bloody emails.' Different franchise, same point, albeit with additional swearing.

industry – with Terry in the side-room he had turned into a study at his and Lyn's small house in Somerset, determinedly tapping 400 words into an Amstrad CPC 464 in the evenings after work – had grown beyond anything its founder had dared anticipate to become a multi-million-pound international business. And yet a multi-million-pound international business in which the slightly haphazard spirit of the cottage industry was still a dominant strain.

For example, Terry was, in those days, in the habit of writing onto floppy disks and, at the end of the working day, before walking from his office back down to the house for supper, ejecting those disks from his computer and slipping them into the top pocket of his shirt for safe-keeping. But, in the way of these things, that shirt might then end up in the laundry basket. And then from the laundry basket it might reasonably make its way to the washing machine. Accordingly it had been by no means unknown for £1 million-worth of novel-in-progress to pass precariously through a 60-degree hot wash and full spin cycle.

Then there was the time a royalty cheque for just south of a quarter of a million pounds arrived in the post, got put down somewhere and somehow vanished into thin air before it could be banked. But we'll get to the full story of that one in due course.

For now, let's just say it was clear to Terry what he needed. He needed a lady from the village.

Instead he got me. I wasn't from the village (I was living about 70 miles from Salisbury in Cheltenham at the time), and I didn't identify as a lady. Nor had I ever filled out a VAT return; it hadn't come up at all in my earlier roles. Nor was I retired: I was 29. What's more, on top of these other key disqualifiers – and potentially the biggest red flag of them all – I was definitely a reader of Terry Pratchett. An avid one, in fact – one whose appearances in the queue at Pratchett book signings since 1993 (WH Smith, Oxford, for *Johnny and the Dead*) had been so conspicuously consistent that he had on his shelves a copy of the 1997 novel *Jingo* signed to 'one of the sad gang'.

I had also come to be working on what we might call the outer inner-edges of the Pratchett operation. I had met Colin Smythe, who was Terry's agent and the man on whom Terry had first thrust an unpublished typescript back in 1968 in search of a response. (Colin's response had been to publish it, which was not a decision he had ever had cause to regret.) Because my background was in tech, Colin had asked me, in 1998, to come and work for him as technical director at Colin Smythe Publishing, where it was chiefly my task to digitize the hitherto defiantly analogue business that Colin had been running from his house in Gerrards Cross.

In this role, I found myself sometimes answering the phone to Colin's most successful client. And when Terry acquired his first CD-burner and was struggling to get it to function, the operation's chief, and indeed sole, tech guy was dispatched to Salisbury for the day on secondment.

I parked, walked down the slope to the house and found a note stuck to the kitchen door. 'Rob: in Chapel.' I followed the helpful hand-drawn map, tapped at the door, and for the first time was admitted to the inner sanctum, the epicentre of Discworld on Roundworld: a purpose-built writing room with a big stone-mullioned window, a huge wood-burning stove, a long wall of bookshelves and a powerful smell of beeswax polish, where, at a large, leather-topped desk and just about visible beyond a mountain of books, magazines, pieces of paper and general *stuff*, sat the author.

I was twenty years younger than Terry. I was also, on account of my love for the Discworld novels, in awe of him, which I realized that he quite liked. But it emerged that we had some common ground. We had both, during our teenage years, known the joy of motor scooters; and we had both known the great good fortune of having fathers who were happy to spend their evenings and weekends teaching us how to fix up those motor scooters. We had both cultivated an interest in hobby electronics – had read the same magazines, bought the same components from the same mail order companies, embarked on the same home-build projects.

'Ah,' said Terry. 'So you know the unique pain of splashing hot solder on nylon socks.'

I did.

Furthermore, we were both people whose first instinct, upon taking delivery of any new piece of electronic hardware, was to sweep aside the instruction manual, unopened, rip off the side-panel, peer into the innards of the machine and see what modifications we could perform which the manufacturer would probably rather we didn't. At some point in the eighties we had both taught our early Sinclair ZX81 computers to talk – albeit that Terry had taught his to say good morning to him and report the overnight high and low temperatures in his greenhouse, whereas I had taught mine to say rude words for the amusement of my friends. Still, it was a bond. It certainly impressed Terry that I knew what a General Instrument SPO256 integrated circuit was.* And it impressed him equally that I could easily and swiftly sort out his new CD-burner. I now rejoiced under the Terry-given nickname of Captain Capacitor – the first of a succession of names that Terry would find for me. Other secondments to Wiltshire for similar tech-based missions followed. In December 2000, when Terry heard that I was finishing at Colin Smythe Publishing, he rang me and asked if I would consider coming to work for him as his PA.

I thought it might be fun for a little while, not least given my love for Terry's books. At the same time, it wasn't my idea of a job for the long-term. I figured it was something I might do for a year, and then eventually be able to tell my grandchildren about it. 'You know that Terry Pratchett? Well . . .'

I was still working for him a decade and a half later in 2015 when he died, and I'm still working for him now.

The job turned out to be engaging in ways I hadn't thought about. I had not, for instance, envisaged being in any way witness to Terry's creative process, even as his PA. I thought the actual writing of the books would take place privately and silently behind a closed door while I sat elsewhere and attended to other things: the post, the VAT, the milk. And, indeed, I did attend to those things. But that was not exclusively how Terry saw my role, a fact which became apparent one day when, at the end of a morning's writing, he stood up from the screen and put on his jacket.

. . . .

* Essentially, the guts of a rudimentary speech synthesizer. But I probably don't need to tell you that.

'I've got to pop out,' he said. 'Tidy that up for me, would you?'

A Terry Pratchett first draft, I now discovered as I nervously slid into Terry's seat, was a highly eccentric document, featuring randomly shifting font sizes and even randomly shifting font *colours*. But imagine the thrill of this task for someone who had drummed his fingers between publication dates waiting for new words from Terry Pratchett. I had devoured Terry's writing and to be in the room, and even at the keyboard, where those novels were taking shape, and not just standardizing their fonts but, in due course, reading them back to the author so he could reappraise them, talking about them with him, and eventually taking them down as dictation as they flowed from his brain (a tactic it had suited Terry to adopt even before the last years when he lost the ability to operate a keyboard) . . . well, this was a rare privilege.

As for Terry, I think he very quickly became comfortable with the idea of himself as a person who had 'staff', although he never would have admitted it. One day, he was on the phone to a newspaper – not a 'My Favourite Spoon' piece this time, but that close relative of the 'Favourite Spoon' genre, a 'Q & A' interview. At one point, he lowered the receiver to his collar bone and called across the office.

'Rob, what's my biggest indulgence?'

I had about a second to think about it before Terry cut me off.

'Never mind. It's you.'

In my first tentative weeks in the job, Jilly Cooper and her 'best PA in the business' were held over my head on a fairly frequent basis. There were several threats (rhetorical, I'm sure – or were they?) to send me to Gloucestershire for a week of schooling at the hands of Jilly and Amanda. I was also fired many times over, although one quickly learned that Terry, being a writer, had an experimental interest in saying things to see what they sounded like, and that if you adopted an experimental approach yourself, and simply turned up the next day, it would normally turn out that you hadn't been fired at all.

In his foreword to *A Slip of the Keyboard**, Neil Gaiman arguably

. . . .

* Terry's collected non-fiction, published in 2014.

changed the shape of Pratchett studies for ever by definitively taking issue with the public perception of Terry as a 'jolly old elf' – mostly, perhaps, a misunderstanding arising from the beard and Terry's general stature. (He was five foot eight on a good day.) This well-meaning sentimentalization of Terry, Neil pointed out, overlooked, among many other things, the anger in him. 'The anger is always there,' Neil wrote, 'an engine that drives.'

Well, I came to know that anger in all its 57 varieties, as we'll see. But I also came to know (as Neil had come to know, too) how generous Terry could be, how spectacularly funny he was and what brilliant company. During an average working week in the Chapel, a vast amount of writing would get done, yet somehow, while the work was percolating in Terry's mind, there also seemed to be plenty of time for activities that could only be filed under A for 'Arsing Around'. There were, for example, the days spent devising ever more intricate and unnecessary ways to automate the office. There were the hours passed feeding the tortoises, or up at the local garden centre. There were the times we took lunch down to the shepherd's hut that Terry had restored by the river, and then carried on working out there for the rest of the afternoon.* There were the evenings we sat up in the copper-roofed observatory Terry had built in the grounds, having a beer and looking at the stars, prior, very often, to heading back across the grass to the Chapel and knocking off the day's last words.

The early weeks passed and the threats to pack me off to Jilly Cooper for disciplining gradually subsided. Indeed, I can remember the last time the subject came up. Following some sin of omission on my part, the details of which I can no longer remember, talk had again surfaced of a period of detainment at Jilly's pleasure. After a couple of days spent working hard to redeem myself, and rather needily seeking reassurance that things were now straight between us, I wondered aloud whether I should be getting ready to leave for Gloucestershire.

Terry didn't raise his eyes from the screen in front of him. 'You don't

* An authentic shepherd's hut, I should add: this was long before David Cameron, the former Tory Prime Minister, ruined for ever the image of hut-based literary endeavour.

need to go there now,' he said casually. 'She has the *second* best PA in the business.'

Once I had earned Terry's trust, the hours for which I seemed to be needed started to expand. The call might come in the evenings or at weekends: 'Do you fancy coming up and doing a little light work?' I joined him on the road and ended up being alongside him wherever it was that work took him. The relationship deepened and broadened and soon it clearly wasn't just work but also a friendship.

After Terry was diagnosed with Posterior Cortical Atrophy, a rare form of Alzheimer's Disease, in 2007, at the cruelly early age of 59, the job of being his PA necessarily expanded again. As illness unsentimentally eroded Terry's ability to cope from day to day, he became a person in need of assistance in ways that neither of us could have prophesied. I began to accompany him during public appearances, reading for him when he no longer could, helping him through interviews on stage as 'keeper of the anecdote'. We became, of necessity, a sort of double act. Starsky and Hutch? Laurel and Hardy? You be the judge. But if the point of the job had always been to clear the space around Terry to enable him to do the thing that made him Terry Pratchett, then now, with the clock running, it became only more urgently so.

There were, inevitably, grim and testing times in those years, and it was sometimes hard to revisit them for this book. I spent a lot of that period, I retrospectively realize, in denial about the full gravity of what was unfolding, which seemed to me the easiest (and most English) way to deal with it. Yet Terry, of course, was doing exactly the opposite, reacting to the news of his imminent demise with bravery, with unsparing thought, with a determination to confront his condition head on in public, with a bold mission to force the topic of assisted dying into the national conversation, and most of all (being Terry) with work – with three television documentaries and seven more bestsellers.

And, of course, he met it with humour – and humour of an abidingly Terry kind. Late on, Terry said to me, 'It appears we now share a brain.' I was very flattered.

But, of course, with Terry, there was nearly always the delayed depth-charge.

'And if you put the two of us together,' he went on, 'you might make one half-decent human being.'

★ ★ ★ ★ ★

Terry often talked about 'doing' his autobiography. In the years before he was ill, he talked about it almost exclusively to dismiss the idea. What could possibly be interesting for a reader, he would argue, in the tale of a bloke who got up, had breakfast, wrote some words, had lunch, wrote some more words, had supper, watched a film or some television with his wife and went to bed (possibly having sat up a little longer to write a few more words)?

He didn't seem persuaded that there was anything in the story of the journey that took a kid from a council house in Beaconsfield to a knighthood and a mansion near Salisbury by the sheer power of his imagination alone; or in the tale of how a boy with, as Terry put it, 'a mouthful of speech impediments' became one of his generation's most popular communicators; or how someone who left school with five O levels could also go on to be someone with an honorary professorship at Trinity College Dublin, and so many honorary doctorates that he began to lose count.

And besides, there were always other things waiting to be written – bigger stories in which far more outlandish and arresting things were free to happen.

Earlier in 2007, Jacqueline Wilson, a writer whom Terry greatly admired, had published a memoir, *Jacky Daydream*, which was the story of her childhood, a choice that intrigued Terry. Jacqueline was 62 at that point, a couple of years older than Terry. Why now, he had asked her, and why just that section of her life? Jacqueline replied, with tongue in cheek, 'Because everyone who could check the facts is now dead.' After this, Terry, too, briefly drew the conclusion that he could only really comfortably write his memoir when everybody who appeared in it was no longer alive enough to object. Which was, of course, another way of punting the project so far into the long grass that we could no longer see it.

But now that Terry's memory itself was under an explicit threat, the prospect of a memoir felt different. Even in the car driving back together from Addenbrooke's hospital in Cambridge that awful December afternoon when the devastating diagnosis had been given to him, Terry started talking about his autobiography – about how he needed to get going on it, and how the clock was running.

Yet we had no clear idea how long we had. One year? Two years? How should we apportion that time? What should he concentrate on? We had more time than we knew, in fact; it would be seven years before Terry's last day at work in the Chapel. Yet, when it came down to it, the priority was always the novels – first *Nation*, which was the book Terry was working on at the time of the diagnosis, and then *Unseen Academicals*, *I Shall Wear Midnight*, *Snuff*, *Dodger*, *Raising Steam*, *The Shepherd's Crown* . . . All through this period he was chasing to get those stories down.

However, there would be days, when the mood was right, when Terry would tell me to close the file from whichever novel we were working on and open the memoir file, and he would do an afternoon on the autobiography, him dictating, me typing. He began, conventionally, with memories of his childhood and worked forwards, and sometimes it came easily and sometimes it didn't. At the point at which we ran out of time, we had reached 1979, with Terry putting on a suit (a rare event in his life) to go for an interview in Bristol with the Central Electricity Board, south-west division. The file had grown to just over 24,000 words, rough-hewn, disjointed, awaiting the essential polish that Terry would never be in a position to give them. He was intending to call the book *A Life with Footnotes*.*

It goes without saying that those words were an invaluable source for the chapters ahead, and you will find them liberally quoted from. Of course, it's a pertinent question: was the Terry of 2014 an entirely reliable documenter of his own life? Perhaps not. But was the Terry of any age? For a person who was bracingly committed to honesty and

. . . .

*   Terry loved a footnote.

openness in his everyday dealings, Terry was also a great believer in not letting the truth stand in the way of a good story, and especially a good *funny* story. We may detect in this instinct the influence of his mother who, Terry said, 'was inclined to polish up a fact to make it shine brighter'. But Terry also imputed a way with the story-polish to his grandfather on his father's side. And one of his uncles seems to have conjured an entire *Boy's Own* story of unflagging Second World War derring-do from a campaign actually spent boxing up fruit in Kent. Terry admired him hugely for that.

And when you think about it, story-polishing, genetic or otherwise, was Terry's whole business. Indeed, his three chosen professions – first journalism, then public relations, then written fiction – were all vocations in which the truth was, shall we say, up for negotiation at the very least. Certainly for Terry there was a kind of story that fell into the category 'too good to check'. And it was always possible, of course, that the story that was 'too good to check' might, in the broader scheme of things, cut through to a greater truth about life than the less good, checked story.

Still, this approach to anecdotes presents something of a challenge to the biographer, who has a certain formal duty to hold the claims that things happened against the evidence that they actually did so. And, complicating things still further, sometimes the mere fact of whether or not something actually happened proved to be less interesting, from my point of view, than the fact that Terry claimed it did. Suffice it to say that in any contentious areas in the pages that follow, I have done my best to uphold the establishable truth, while at the same time endeavouring not to come over as a killjoy and (more importantly) while trying not to crush the indisputable entertainment value of a well-polished fact.[*]

The plainest – and saddest – truth of all, of course, is that his autobiography has to take its place on the long list of books by Terry Pratchett that a merciless degenerative brain disorder harshly denied us

....

[*] Footnotes will be our friend in this area – somewhere to position corrections and alternative readings without completely knocking the shine off the original story.

the opportunity to read. That was the loss for which those of us who loved Terry ended up grieving, on top of our grief at the loss of Terry himself, and there is simply no mending either of those gaps. But here, offered with all humility, is my portrait of him, drawing on my own memories, on the memories of Lyn and Rhianna, on the memories of Dave Busby and Colin Smythe and of so many others who knew him so well, and on Terry's own memories in so far as he wrote them down or made them known to us.

And I will try to imagine that the Terry who is at my shoulder as I set down my contribution to this tale isn't always saying, 'Rubbish! It was nothing like that at all!' and is at least sometimes saying, 'Hmm. Well, I suppose it was a *bit* like that . . .'

PART ONE

I

DANGEROUS SLATES, A CLOTHED MOLE AND THE ESCAPE FROM ENFORCED GOATHOOD

It was never just imagining things. Sometimes, Terry said, the products of his childhood mind were so vivid to him, so entirely real, that they were closer to hallucinations than imaginings, as solidly located in the space in front of his eyes as his parents were, or his house, or the village he first lived in.

Like the time when, tramping through the disused chalk pit near home, he saw the skeletons of fish swimming in the ground below his feet – presumably a connection in his mind with the micro-fossils which he'd recently learned about at school or, more likely, read about in a library book, yet somehow now reanimated and actually squirming and darting around underneath him in the chalk dust.

Or like that time, aged five, when he was taken to see Father Christmas at Gamages department store in London, and wandered dreamily away from his mother, only to be found by her later riding the escalators and voyaging solo through the festive decorations with head upturned in a state of rapt awe, entirely oblivious to the panic he had caused.

Seeing Father Christmas that day had been important and memorable, too, of course, although Terry confessed that he hadn't actually had the courage to meet the great man's gaze, because, as Terry related it, 'you cannot look on the face of a god'. But the flight to the North Pole aboard the wooden aeroplane, the painted clouds on canvas cranking squeakily past the plane's windows, the team of elves in the reception party – that had all burned itself into Terry's imagination, too. It's just that it hadn't burned itself as strongly as the glittering universe under one roof which was the department store itself, dressed for Christmas.*

And what about the train that had brought them to the city that day? Those trains seemed friendly enough when you were inside them, and riding in them, but from outside, on the platform, their roar, their thunder, their billowing blackened steam, the way they seemed to try to suck you up behind them as they smashed through the station at speed . . . those things were clearly alive and altogether demonstrably *demons*, weren't they? The five-year-old Terry thought so.

He wasn't being entirely metaphorical, many years later, when he described himself in interviews as 'hallucinating gently for a living'. He seems to have discovered very quickly that there were things within things, worlds within worlds, wholly visible, practically tangible, and certainly available for story-telling, if you could only be allowed a bit of space and time to see them.

★ ★ ★ ★ ★

Home, at first, was the small, undistinguished and, indeed, easily driven-through hamlet of Forty Green, which sat in a hollow near the Chiltern Hills in Buckinghamshire – 'a sort of Lark Rise to Beaconsfield's

. . . .

* Gamages in High Holborn, which closed in 1972, clearly pulled all the stops out for a fifties Christmas – 'LAUGHS, SCREAMS and THRILLS all day long,' as the flyers said, referring not just to the plane-borne grotto experience, but also to the 800-foot model railway installed for the season and featuring a minutely rendered day/night scenario. They also had a very good hardware department, apparently, though Terry never mentioned that.

Candleford', as Terry described it in the notes he made towards his autobiography, 'not so much a place as an area in the fields and forests containing about 36 people and one telephone box'.*

And also, we should note, containing a village shop, a pub – the Royal Standard of England – and, for at least a short while, according to Terry's recollections, a sweet shop. 'I know there was a sweet shop,' Terry insisted, 'because I bought aniseed balls there, and black jacks and sherbet fountains and pink shrimps for prices as low as a farthing. Heaven knows how the place survived at all.'

Indeed, there seem to have been scarcely enough children around Forty Green to keep a sweet shop in business, even in the short term; Terry recalled a gang of about half a dozen residents his own age or thereabouts, during his shorts-wearing years, forming 'a sort of ever-changing cloud of kids, arguing, exploring, fighting', stomping about in the chalk pits, the woods and the fields, and generally thumbing their noses in advance at later anxieties surrounding children and safe play. 'We fell out of trees,' Terry wrote, 'climbed them again and fell out more interestingly this time.'

Forty Green was so small and tight a community that if one mother called her child in for tea, everybody seemed to run home. And, far more significantly than children, that population of 36 contained, in Terry's recollection, 'elderly and leathery professional gardeners with flat caps and pipes, who every morning sedately pedalled their black sit-up-and-beg bicycles to the more prosperous village of Knotty Green, a mile or so away' and then, in the evening, 'pedalled just as sedately back, quite often with something strapped onto the handlebars, such as a bundle of cabbage seedlings.'

It was a slow, quiet and essentially countrified place, then. And it was here that the Pratchetts lived in a small, rented cottage, where the facilities were so basic that Terry always struggled to talk about it without sounding as though he was auditioning for a part in the Four Yorkshiremen

....

* Unless indicated otherwise, the quotations from Terry in these pages are from his unfinished autobiography.

sketch.* (*'Corridor? I used to dream of living in a corridor. That would have been a palace to us . . .' etc.*)

There was, for instance, no running water chez Pratchett: each morning Terry's father dragged a hose to a standpipe on the property next door and drew off water into a metal drum in the scullery for extraction throughout the day. There was, by extension, no flushing loo, either; there was a 'little room' in a lean-to out the back of the house, bombarded with disinfectant by Terry's mother and containing an Elsan chemical lavatory which needed to be up-ended periodically in a freshly dug hole in the garden. (This was officially the worst domestic chore of the week, although apparently the tomatoes greatly benefited.)

A tin bath hung from a hook on the outside wall of the 'little room' and would be hauled inside on bath night. Gas for the cooker came off a visiting lorry in giant replacement Calor canisters which had to be rolled into the living room, and the radio (no television for the Pratchetts at this point) was powered by a loaned-out rechargeable battery the size and weight of a house-brick, lugged to and from the branch of Radio Rentals in Beaconsfield every month on a home-made metal trolley. If you wanted to listen to *Down Your Way* and *Family Favourites* in those days, which the Pratchetts clearly did, you had to put the effort in. And although there was a scullery, which sounds faintly grand, there was no kitchen attached to it, which made that room, as Terry put it, a bit like 'a cart with no horse'. That cramped, dark and slightly damp space did the work of both utility room and kitchen.

Still, say whatever else you like about it (and the spirit of the Four Yorkshiremen can't help but loom again here), the house at least offered a roof over the Pratchetts' heads – and British roofs in general had taken a bit of a pounding during the period between 1939 and 1945, so this was not to be sneered at. True, that roof was not entirely stable and shed its tiles under the lightest encouragement from the wind, creating a

* Which is often casually referred to as 'Monty Python's Four Yorkshiremen sketch', and, indeed, the Python team did perform a version of it in live shows, but the sketch was originally written and performed by John Cleese, Tim Brooke-Taylor, Graham Chapman and Marty Feldman for the 1967 television revue series *At Last the 1948 Show*.

kind of sniper's alley effect for people leaving or approaching the house. 'If you heard the sliding of a slate,' Terry wrote, 'you didn't attempt to run, you just pressed yourself against the wall and watched the errant tile fly out of the eaves and smash into sharp little fragments a short way in front of you. It wasn't even noteworthy; it was just something you did automatically.'

Factor in the continuing rationing of food (butter, meat, cheese, tea, jam), the long strings of washing hung out to dry on Thursdays and the complete absence of teenagers, who hadn't been invented yet, and Forty Green would have supplied a fairly textbook model of semi-rural, working-class British austerity in the immediate post-war years. And it was into these modest, and in certain aspects clearly downright dangerous, circumstances that David and Eileen Pratchett introduced their new-born son, Terence David John, delivered at the Magellan Nursing Home, Beaconsfield, on 28 April 1948. ('I was a Taurean but slightly cuspal,' Terry observed of his birth-date, 'which I believe is why I can never get trousers that fit me.')

The baby was three days overdue and the product of a long and arduous labour which apparently capped a complicated pregnancy. It is perhaps unsurprising, then, that, handed her offspring in the delivery room, Eileen welcomed Terry to the world with the words, 'About time,' and later claimed to have resolved right there never to put herself through anything like *that* again.* It was a promise to herself that she kept. Terry shared the family home with, at various times, an almost entirely brainless spaniel, a tortoise named Pheidippides, after the original marathon runner, and a budgerigar called Chhota, but no further small Pratchetts joined them.

'Shortly after that,' wrote Terry, of the initial moments after his

....

* Terry lived in mortal fear of being late for things. It was something he simply couldn't tolerate – in himself far more than in others. Left to his own devices, he would get to an airport so far in advance of his scheduled flight that he would technically be on time for the previous one. Would it be fanciful to link this anxiety to the lateness of his original arrival, and the family legend which that lateness grew into? Possibly, but Terry certainly did so.

protracted birth, 'I was introduced to my father, although I have no recollection of that first meeting.' In due course, in more convenient
circumstances for both of them, Terry would learn more about his dad,
including the important detail that he worked as a mechanic at the Old
Town Garage in Beaconsfield. David Pratchett was small, slim, completely bald, wore a thin moustache and was 'a genius with a busted car',
according to his son. The Second World War had very recently provided
him with the opportunity to hone his mechanical skills in the RAF.
David had been posted to India and, at least as he recounted it to Terry,
seemed to have enjoyed a relatively un-harrowing war, appreciating the
warm sun, casually collecting good names for budgerigars* and impressively rising to challenges such as fixing the wing commander's car
in the middle of nowhere by rewinding the starter motor by hand.
He then brought his talents back to Beaconsfield, where they seem to
have gone down well.

'I swear, if there is such a thing as the horse whisperer,' Terry wrote,
'then my father was the man that listened to cars. He would put one
end of a large spanner against the side of his face and let the other end
touch the engine block and the metal beast would open its soul. Owners of quite posh cars, with good English marques such as Bentley and
Jaguar, took their cars to the Old Town Garage so that he could listen
to them intently.' In a time when money was short, it was a useful reputation to have. Terry recalled his father coming home in the evenings
and standing with his oily and greasy arms in a bowl of soapy water,
recounting to Eileen the tips for good service he had been slipped by
wealthy patrons.

David could also bring a near-scrapper back from the dead, so,
unusually for families in their position, the Pratchetts always had a car
to travel in, including at one time 'a rather spiffy streamlined Rover
P4 – the poor man's Rolls-Royce', complete with cigarette lighter and
leather upholstery. David sold it on to a collector in the end, and, for all

....

* As well as being a decent approximation of the noise budgies make, 'Chhota' is a Hindi
word meaning 'little'.

its spiffiness, Terry wasn't entirely sad to see it go. 'I was always sliding around on the back seat and on long journeys to the seaside the interior stank like a dead cow.'

Terry's other abiding memory from those long summer drives to (invariably) the Cornish coast: the passage of the car through 'clouds of smoke and flashes of flame' as it threaded its way through the August stubble-burning.

Terry's mother, Eileen Pratchett, née Kearns, was of Irish descent and had been raised in London's East End. She was employed as a secretary by Easton and Roll, a Beaconsfield department store, and was a highly efficient accountant who, according to Terry, could tot up a stack of numbers upside down more quickly than most people could do it the right way up. Her character in these days was lively, a touch mischievous; she loved dancing and socializing and drinking and was a raconteur. Late in her life, when a stroke deprived her of the power of speech, Dave Busby, Terry's close friend who knew Eileen and David well, observed that 'it was as if a malicious god had taken from her what was most precious to her'.

But she was also a formidable and dominant wife and mother and very emphatically the head of the household. David, on to whom she seemingly fastened at the age of seventeen, was entirely under her thumb, cheerfully admitted as much and appeared entirely content to be so. Terry, meanwhile, as an only child often does, would come to know both the blessings and the drawbacks of having his mother's undivided attention, and the pressure of being the sole repository of her post-war hopes and ambitions.

'Both my parents were hoping for a better world,' wrote Terry. 'My mother, though, most definitely considered that you progress in *this* one, and although I did not know it at the time, I suspect that the vehicle for her progress was me. The space race was a little way off, but already she was preparing to sling me into a higher orbit – by my ears if necessary.'

The first evidence of those wider ambitions perhaps came when, at the age of three, Terry was deposited at a rather superior nursery school in one of the leafier parts of Beaconsfield. Run by two elderly and genteel ladies, it struck Terry, when he came to recall it, as some sort of throwback to the old Dame Schools of the 1930s – a place chiefly designed to equip the better class of child with social accomplishments and, above all, with manners. Given the age of Terry's group, this was to a great extent a basic matter of teaching the children to put up their hands when they needed the loo, but also on the toddler curriculum apparently was calisthenics and (Terry shivered to recall this) folk dancing.

And then there was flower-sniffing, to which Terry, for one, seems to have responded with enthusiasm.

'One day one of the ladies brought in from her garden some magnificent roses and gave each of us one to sniff deeply while reciting:

I wonder, I wonder, if anyone knows,
Who lives in the heart of this velvety rose.
Is it a pixie or is it an elf?
Or is it the queen of the fairies herself?

I have no idea what she was on, but I was off my face with the scent of roses. Heaven knows what it did to me, but I have one or two clues.'

Who knows how things might have panned out if Terry's education had continued in this rarefied line. That it did not is perhaps botany's loss, and maybe folk dancing's. But Terry soon reached the age of four and was automatically wrenched from that perfumed sitting room and lobbed into the more conventional state-funded environment of Holt-spur Primary School, a mile and a half's walk away from home, in Cherry Tree Road, on the western edge of Beaconsfield.

He arrived a day late. His parents had booked the family's summer holiday in Cornwall and were not inclined to cut it short for something as unimportant as their child's first day in a new academic institution. Terry later claimed that this casual decision put him out of step with his peers from day one – which was day two, of course, in everybody else's case. What it certainly did was ruin his options when it came to coat pegs. Every child's peg in Terry's infant class had a picture above it, for ease of recognition. Instead of being on a level playing field to lay claim to the cowboy hat or the elephant or the tank, he was left with the only peg remaining, which sat witheringly beneath a lame drawing of a pair of cherries.* 'I could have been a contender . . .' Terry wrote ruefully.

Even once settled under the evidently kindly care of Mrs Smith, his infant-class teacher, Terry struggled with school. Nothing came easily. He would start out writing with his left hand and, halfway down the page, switch to his right.† He was, at least at first, reluctant to read. He appeared to be more keen on finding ways to climb on his desk than to sit at it. He seemed overall to lack the ability to concentrate – or at any rate to concentrate on the things the teachers wanted him to concentrate on, and at the times in the day when the teachers wanted him to do so. 'I could hang upside down in the hazelnut tree in our garden for hours at a time,' Terry noted, with the slightly hurt tone of someone whose talents had not been given their due. But school was demanding more of him than an ability to hang upside down and he hadn't yet quite worked out how to respond.

The point, though, about this particular child – 'he of the scabby knees and the permanent sensation of low-level fear', as Terry now painted himself – was that he was clearly bright. Indeed, in some respects he seemed ahead of the game. He obviously thought about things. Why, he asked his mother one day, was that legendary run made by Pheidippides known as a Marathon? Surely, on the principle that buses bore their destinations on their front plates, not their places of origin, it should technically have been known as an Athens. His mother didn't really have an answer to that.

And he definitely knew stuff. It seems to have stung him early and hard that, when the class was asked where rain came from, and Terry immediately slung up his hand and answered, 'The sea,' this earned a burst of mocking laughter from his peers and a gentle correction from

....

* And here, surely, one might find a firmer psychological source for Terry's lateness phobia (should one be searching) than in his tardy appearance in the delivery room, even though he favoured the latter in his own analysis.

† This issue resolved itself in time and Terry became an entirely right-handed writer. However, even as an adult, if the cutlery was ever set the 'wrong' way round at the table, he would pick up the knife and fork without really noticing and plough on regardless.

the teacher, who was looking for the answer 'the clouds'. But Terry *knew* he was right. That was how precipitation worked. So what was this place in which people were rewarded for working out the answer the teacher wanted them to give, rather than the right answer?

The headmaster at Holtspur was a man named Henry William Tame. With thick-rimmed glasses, a moustache and carefully lacquered hair, H. W. Tame was a big presence in his own school – the writer and the producer of the annual school pantomime in which he himself liked to take a role, frequently as a giant. He gave that school 31 years of his career. He was also a revolutionary figure, in some ways, and greatly to be admired. Tame was a significant advocate for the then controversial idea that sex education should be given in schools, and specifically to children in their last year at primary school.*

Unfortunately, where he earned the unending contempt of the Pratchetts was, not in his pioneering attitude to sex education, but in his decision to sort the pupils in his school into two streams – those who were deemed to be on track to pass the eleven-plus examination in their final year and take places at the area's better secondary schools, and those who were not. On the one side of the divide were the sheep, as Terry saw it, and on the other the goats. According to Terry, this separation of the Holtspur flock happened when the children were just six. And to his, and more particularly Eileen's dismay, Terry found himself herded in with the goats. Interpreted as evidence of Tame's 'vicious dislike' of him, this premature assessment of Terry's likely ability was, I don't think it's any exaggeration to say, the source of a whole lifetime of bitter resentment. It seemed to confirm Terry's worst suspicions that school was not about encouraging you to become something so much as it was about keeping you where you were, holding you in your allotted place – a suspicion shared, with reason, by Terry's father, who had

....

* In the 1960s, Tame wrote two key tuitional texts in this area, *Time to Grow Up* and *Peter and Pamela Grow Up*. Sample sentence from the latter: 'If the boy is healthy and takes part in games and other forms of rigorous exercise the sperms will be reabsorbed into the body and the wet dreams will not be very frequent.' Perhaps nothing ages quite so fast as radical sexual education advice.

turned up for his own eleven-plus exam, back in the day, and found himself confronted by questions on subjects that his teachers had quite simply never taught him.

Asked, in 2011, to contribute a few words for the school's sixtieth anniversary celebrations, Terry gamely obliged but chose not to gild it too thickly. 'In all truth, I cannot say that my memories of Holtspur School were of the warmest,' he wrote. He then equally gamely took the blame upon himself: 'but possibly that was entirely because I was an absolutely quintessential example of a twit and dreamer.' I don't think he believed for one moment that the fault was truly his, though. It was a lifelong position of Terry's that schools would be far better places if they took special care to look out for and nurture the twits and the dreamers.

With her son relegated to the B-group, Eileen stepped up. If the school had a low-grade mould prepared for her only offspring, then she was going to ensure that he overflowed it. That mile and a half walk to school in the morning became an additional tuition period, an opportunity to impart what she knew and push Terry in a way the school had obviously decided not to.

'She dispensed learning as if it had a sell-by date,' wrote Terry. 'She told me about kings and knights and Robin Hood and camels. She told me that monks live in monasteries and that monkeys live in trees, and that it was important not to get that the wrong way round. She told me that America was so far away it would cost a thousand pounds to get there. She also sang songs and passed on the stories told to her by her Irish grandfather, which included the revelation that bees were really fairies, an observation which I considered erroneous. Would I have even known what the word meant at the time? With my mum you never knew.'

More firmly, to encourage him in his reading, Eileen proposed an arrangement whereby she paid him a penny for a page well read. Terry, who knew that pennies could be traded for Black Jacks, responded to the challenge. 'I wasn't dumb,' he said. 'I could drone my way through a text with enough accuracy to keep my head above the water. But I had no great enthusiasm for reading. I got along. Surely that was enough. Mum thought otherwise.'

As the eleven-plus exam neared, Eileen started putting past papers in front of Terry at home in the evenings. And when she saw him struggling with them, she paid for him to go every week to the house of a retired teacher for extra tuition. Terry wouldn't fail, whatever the system had decreed. Eileen wasn't going to let him.

★ ★ ★ ★ ★

Contrary, perhaps, to modern perception, Britain after the war was not a particularly church-going place. In 1948, just 15 per cent of respondents told Gallup that they had been to a church service the previous Sunday. Only one in ten participants in a Mass Observation survey conducted in London at about the same time indicated that they attended church 'fairly regularly', and an Archbishops' Committee reported that '90 per cent of our people seldom or never go to church'.* David and Eileen Pratchett, then, would have been firmly among the majority in having decided that institutionalized religion was largely irrelevant to their lives. Consequently Terry was able to say of his parents, in his inaugural professorial lecture at Trinity College Dublin in 2010: 'They raised me with kindness and, where appropriate, a side order of brief and effective sternness and – may they be for ever blessed for this final consideration – without any religious upbringing whatsoever.'

Eileen had grown up a Catholic but, by the time Terry was born, had long since stopped practising as one, and her decision to marry an Anglican in an Anglican church evidently divorced her from a large swathe of her family. On account of the shockwaves emanating ever afterwards from this rift, there were a number of aunts and uncles on the Kearns side whom Terry simply never knew. Christianity does not seem to have featured very much as a topic for discussion at home. Aged six, Terry happened innocently on the sole relic of Eileen's Catholicism – a small, cheaply produced wooden crucifix on the

....

* Sources: *Religion in Great Britain, 1939–99: A Compendium of Gallup Poll Data* by Clive D. Field; and that superb history book *Austerity Britain, 1945–51* by David Kynaston.

dressing table in his parents' bedroom – and he gathered it up and carried it to her with the immortal line, 'Mum! I've found a stick with an acrobat on it.'

Even then, Eileen's corrective explanation was apparently so circumspect that Terry barely gave this strangely suspended and wounded figure in his loincloth another thought. However, that crucifix was to find an unobtrusive but safe spot in every house in which Eileen lived, including the room in the care home in Salisbury where she spent her final days. After she died Terry and I went through everything looking for it and he was filled with despair when it didn't show up. When I eventually found it, tucked away behind some other ornaments, Terry's relief was palpable. The little crucifix went back to the Chapel with him and he had it in his hand when he was dictating some lines about this time in his life.

'I do not know what solace she found in the tiny, stricken face,' Terry said, 'but now I see the face of a humble carpenter who was moved to tell people to be kind to one another – the golden rule of so many wise men – and for his pains was tortured to death by a tyrant at the behest of zealots. Perhaps the message may be to ignore tyrants and tumble zealots.'

Similarly, the message of Christ, Terry liked to point out, was not really so far from the message of Bill and Ted in *Bill & Ted's Excellent Adventure*: be excellent to each other. And, the way Terry saw it, why would anybody want to pick an argument with that fine message?

However, there was definitely no church-going for Terry and neither did the family seem all that impressed with their local clergyman, the Reverend Oscar Muspratt, the Anglican vicar of Holy Trinity church in Penn. Tall, thin and forever known to Terry, through a childhood misunderstanding, as the Reverend Muskrat, the Revd Muspratt seems to have riled David and Eileen right away through his habit of addressing his parishioners – 'or certainly the working class ones', Terry darkly suggested – by their surnames alone.

The vicar further lost the support of the family during a teatime drop-in on their home one day by referring to the small ornamental brass statue of the Buddha which squatted in the sitting room (it had been brought back from India by Terry's father) as 'a pagan idol'. Apparently this slur caused Eileen to show the Revd Muspratt the door directly – to 'put him out on the pavement', even, in the most vivid versions of this tale. With what exact levels of violence the vicar was ejected, we will now never know, but certainly no further tea-dates followed. When Terry's father returned from work that evening and the details of this encounter were relayed to him, he promptly branded the vicar 'a sanctimonious old fart'. 'I had never heard the word "sanctimonious" before,' Terry said, 'and saved it for future use.'

A shame it ended that way, perhaps. Instinctively suspicious of institutional authority, Terry and his parents appear to have somewhat underestimated the Revd Oscar Muspratt. At any rate, Terry's future newspaper, the *Bucks Free Press*, found enough extraordinary in this man's life to run a three-part tribute to him in 1988 in its series 'Interesting Vicars of Penn'. As an army chaplain in wartime, the Revd Muspratt saw action at El Alamein and the siege of Malta and in Normandy on D-Day; he was invited to Washington in 1962 to lead a service of Anglican prayers during the Cuban Missile Crisis; and officiated at the necessarily secret burial of the spy Donald Maclean in 1983. All in all he sounds like exactly the kind of vicar that Terry would have been interested in chatting to. Alas, though, he called David Pratchett 'Pratchett' instead of 'Dave' and (allegedly) was culturally insensitive about their Buddha ornament, so it wasn't to be.

In 1957, when Terry was nine, the family left the rented cottage and moved a mile south, to 25 Upper Riding in Holtspur – one from the end of a nine-house strip of new-build terraced council houses on the western edge of Beaconsfield, a short walk from Terry's primary school. In a significant upgrade, the Pratchetts now had access to the luxuries of running water (cold *and* hot), a real kitchen rather than a scullery, a roof with firmly attached tiles and (greatest blessing of them all) a bathroom with a flushing lavatory.

Being on the edge of the development, the new house also enjoyed unbroken views of the adjacent countryside. Indeed, Terry could look out from the kitchen window and retrace in its entirety his former walk to school and take in a view beyond that as far into the distance as Penn.

Also included within this panorama was the rectory of the maligned Revd Muspratt, which was apt to catch the light on a bright day, opening up a running joke for Terry's father who would always remark, in a suitably baleful tone: 'The sun is shining on the righteous.' Terry sensed his parents were initially a little sad to leave their old house, killer slates and all, and make the move. 'But after a couple of baths they were less so.' This would be the house he lived in until he got married.

By this time, Terry's interests had begun to expand beyond hanging from trees. If school struggled to engage him, things outside school most certainly did not. On one occasion his father invited Terry to join him in making a crystal radio set – a battery-free wireless that he could listen to in his bedroom. Together they scoured dusty boxes in the garden shed for an old set of headphones and the wherewithal to construct an aerial. 'That evening,' Terry remarked, 'I became a nerd without knowing it.'

The commercial coil on that first crystal set bore the legend, 'What are the wild waves saying?' Terry, who could never part with a piece of hardware, still had it in his possession, packed away in a box, at the end of his life. Given that the radio signal that swung first into clarity would tend to be the BBC Third Programme, with its earnest roster of serious talks and highbrow classical music, the wild waves were normally filled with the sound of Dr Leon Roth lecturing on 'Myth, Science and Religion', or Alfred Brendel playing Busoni. But Terry sat and listened, enthralled, in any case, because soundwaves borne from the world directly into your bedroom without batteries were a form of magic however you cut it. At mealtimes, his parents would get used to having to go to his bedroom to pull him out from under his headphones.

Under his father's influence, he would eventually begin to gravitate towards the pages of *Practical Wireless* – 'Practically Wireless', as they renamed it – the monthly bible (price, 1s 3d) for disciples seeking life-changing enlightenment, via carefully wrought wiring diagrams, regarding the construction of, say, an anti-interference aerial or a shipping and medium wave band receiver.

He would learn too the careful husbandry of precious components on a limited budget. Terry could recall going with his father to the television repair shop in Beaconsfield, handing his coppers across the counter and proudly leaving the premises with one solitary transistor the size of a thumbnail in a paper bag. Further along the line, he also bought a transistor socket so that he could more easily transport that precious, solitary transistor between different projects without damaging its tiny, fragile legs. And he would learn that electricity could be fun, not least if you knew how to jury-rig the shed door handle to a magneto to give your father an electric shock. Once the feeling had returned to his fingers, his father was apparently proud of him for that.

Meanwhile there was space. This was a very good time to be interested in the night sky – the mid to late 1950s – with America and the Soviet Union ramping up their competing exploratory plans, and the news full of talk of rockets of imponderable power and satellites and the prospect (how soon?) of manned spaceflight. Terry, certainly, was enthralled, and notably aided and abetted in his enthralment by the Brooke Bond tea company.

In 1956, when Terry was eight, members of the wider family and all other acquaintances found themselves being urged to speed up their tea consumption, if they didn't mind, so that Terry could complete his collection of the Brooke Bond tea cards series 'Out Into Space'. The album for the cards (sixpence) had a blue cover which bore the impressive label, 'A series of 50 picture cards on astronomy approved by A. Hunter PhD, Secretary of the Royal Astronomical Society'. Terry marvelled at the coloured drawings of the planets, drank in the information on the backs of the cards, collected them all. It awoke in him an enthusiasm for astronomy that never abated.

Many years later, his original collection having long since disappeared, Terry conceived a sudden desire to own that Brooke Bond album again, just to see whether it retained any of its magic. Work in the Chapel paused while we fired up eBay.

It turned out that the series had been issued twice, in 1956 and in 1958. The 1956 edition was rarer and had the words 'Issued with Brooke Bond Choicest and "Edglets" Teas' on the reverse of each card, rather than, as in 1958, 'Issued in packets of Brooke Bond "Choicest", "PG Tips" and "Edglets" teas'. To the purist, such distinctions matter. The more coveted 1956 version which Terry would have originally owned was available for £300, the 1958 version for £60 – and I know which one the avid collector in *me* would have gone for, in Terry's position. But Terry, who was no fool with his money even when he could afford to be, bought the £60 one. And fair enough: it did the trick. When the package arrived in the post, he unwrapped it gently and tentatively turned its pages. The image on card number nine in the series, 'Planets & Their Moons', which was the first he had laid eyes on as a child, now once again exerted its own particular gravitational pull and seemed to cause the years to melt away. 'Like that bloke Proust,' Terry suggested, in mid-reverie. 'He eats a biscuit and goes back in time.' Indeed.*

Witnessing the emergence of this new interest and keen, as ever, to encourage anything that might pave the way to a future of pioneering, impressive and potentially even world-changing employment, Terry's mother took him to see the light show at the London Planetarium, beneath its famous pale green dome on the Marylebone Road. They must have been there not long after it first opened for business in March 1958 and the trip handed Terry another overwhelming and formative experience of utter absorption. More than fifty years later he could still recall the 'velvet hush as the light streamed and the projector growled into life and the heavens opened on earth'. Afterwards his mother asked him if he would like to step next door and tour the famous waxworks at Madame Tussaud's – practically a rite of passage for most children in the second half of the twentieth century. But Terry said he would much rather go back around and watch the Planetarium light show all over again, so they did that instead.

With the help of Brooke Bond tea's marketing department and the special effects team at the Planetarium, Terry quickly found himself in a position of precocious expertise on matters astronomical. Indeed, while still very much a tyke in shorts, one morning, over breakfast, he spotted an error in the description of the planet Mars on the back of a

....

* A madeleine cake was Marcel Proust's sensory portal, in fact, which Terry, of course, knew perfectly well, but it's funnier if you say biscuit, and you sound a bit less pretentious.

packet of Kellogg's Corn Flakes and (either egged on by his mother or entirely off his own precocious bat, it's not clear which) duly wrote to the manufacturers to point out their mistake.

Alas, the mistake was, in fact, Terry's: the mass of Mars was exactly as Kellogg's had printed it. Even so, he got a nice reply from Kellogg's and, better still, several complimentary boxes of Corn Flakes – thereby earning the admiration of his father, whose own effort to snag free product Terry had just comprehensively outclassed. David Pratchett once wrote to a razor blade company to inform them that he had managed to make one of their blades last an entire year, a glowing testimonial he felt quietly confident would yield dividends. A few days later, a disappointingly small envelope arrived, containing a solitary new blade and a note to the effect that the company were delighted to hear about the durability of their product, 'and please find herewith another year's supply'.

In the spirit of yet further encouragement, his parents bought Terry a telescope. It was not a particularly good one; through its foggy gaze, Jupiter was 'a wobbly ball of rainbows'. But what was your imagination for if not to provide for exactly this kind of shortfall? Terry stood in the dark in a garden on the edge of Beaconsfield and learned to navigate his way around the moon.

★ ★ ★ ★ ★

And then suddenly in Terry's world there was this book with a badger in it, and a water rat, and a toad that could drive cars.

'If there was any sense of theatre in the universe,' Terry wrote, 'at that moment there should have been an audible *ping!*, quite possibly played on a harp.'

This was all along, for Terry, the pivotal point, the coin-drop moment, the minute at which the scales fall away, the machinery clicks into gear and his life sets off at speed in a wholly new direction. He was with his mother and father, visiting a family friend in London, Donald Gibbons. And Terry at least entertained the possibility later that his mother might have had a word with Donald in advance – that this whole thing might have been a set-up from the beginning, another of Eileen's galvanizing ploys. It didn't matter. The effect was the same. Before Terry and his parents left that day, Donald Gibbons went to the bookshelf, took down Kenneth Grahame's *The Wind in the Willows* and handed it to him.

Up to this point, as we have seen, reading had been something that Terry was reluctant to involve himself in without naked bribery on his mother's part. Maybe his resistance had been quietly dissolving. He had certainly picked up a few comics of his own volition, and was introduced to Superman by one of them, which led to a period of going about the place with a red towel knotted around his neck to form the all-important superhero cape. And he had quite enjoyed it at school when his teacher read the class Eve Garnett's 1930s working-class classic *The Family from One End Street*. There was plenty to recognize there.

But this? This was something on another plane altogether.

'There was a mole,' wrote Terry, 'but this one was spring cleaning! Moles and rats and toads all walking around like human beings, with clothes on? This was El Dorado – even though I didn't yet know what El Dorado was.* As the latest of my father's cars drove me home again along the Western Avenue, I read; I read by the light of the street lights, which were never designed to illuminate the literary epiphany of a small boy on a back seat, which is why my eyesight was a bit wobbly by the time we crunched along the flint lane to home.

'If there had been a watcher, they would have seen, in the south-facing bedroom, a very faint light go on. It was faint because it was under the bedclothes.'

Terry finished the book the next day. And that was it. He was reading, for free. Reading, for pleasure. 'It got inside your head in a strange way; after a while, without you noticing. After all, how big was the toad? Ones at the bottom of our garden you could hold in your hand; this toad, *while still being a toad*, could drive a car! Nobody in the book expressed any amazement about the fact. So, to enjoy it, you had to pretend the world was slightly different. That was good enough for me.'

....
* Not the doomed British soap opera (1992–93); the South American legend pertaining to the discovery of a city of gold.

The Wind in the Willows set him going. And, as we shall see, the transformation was nothing less than startling. Having been mostly reluctant to read anything, Terry would now apply himself to the project of reading *absolutely everything*.

Moreover, in other news, confounding the doomy predictions of H. W. Tame and entirely vindicating the active work behind the scenes of Eileen Pratchett, Terry had passed his eleven-plus – the only pupil, allegedly, in the class of goats to do so. When we next see him he will be wearing a pair of long trousers. And, of course, reading.

2

BORROWED BOOKS,
MIDDLE EARTH IN A DAY AND
NEWS OF BOB MONKHOUSE

It's the spring of 2017 and Terry's daughter Rhianna and I have been invited to attend the unveiling of a plaque which Beaconsfield town council has commissioned to mark Terry's connection with Beaconsfield Library – a lovely idea and an entirely fitting tribute because, as we shall shortly see, if you were going to pick one building in Terry's home town that would help to explain him, then Beaconsfield Library would be the place.

On the way there in the car, though, the pair of us are feeling more than a little apprehensive. This is the first time we have accepted an invitation to do anything publicly 'in Terry's name' since the memorial event at the Barbican in 2016 and neither of us quite knows how we are going to feel about it or quite what our roles should be. During that time, in the still raw absence of her father, Rhianna has come under a lot of pressure to become what the pair of us have started referring to as 'an emergency pop-up Pratchett', and it has seemed only fair to protect her from that. And what, to use the business jargon, are the 'public-facing aspects' of my own role now that Terry is gone? At this point, I am still only beginning to work that out.

It also happens to be the week of the second anniversary of Terry's death, a thought which is inevitably subduing us both. And going back to Beaconsfield Library is causing memories to resurface of the two other, wildly contrasting occasions that brought me there, when Terry was alive.

There was that time in March 2004, when Terry pitched up to give a talk and a reading. Any event involving librarians was all right by Terry, and an event involving librarians on his old home turf was doubly so. He enthusiastically spent an hour and a half working behind the front desk, checking out people's library books — so enthusiastically, in fact, that they practically had to prise the rubber stamp from his grip at the end of the stint. He then spent another chunk of time signing copies of his own books for anyone who had brought one along — and signing anything else for that matter, in keeping with Terry's long-standing and firmly adhered to philosophy on these occasions, which was, essentially: 'If it belongs to you and you want me to write on it, I will.' He was on top form that day, in the phase when he was going everywhere at 100mph and I, normally carrying the bags, would be struggling to keep up with him in the street and breaking into a run sometimes over the final yards. As his assistant, I thought I should be the first of us through the door wherever we were going, but it was often a fight.

And then, starkly different, there was the visit we made on a sweltering day in the summer of 2013. Beaconsfield-based librarians meant no less to Terry than they had always done, but that day, before we set out from the Chapel to attend what was going to be a fund-raiser for the library, Terry had been really struggling. It was getting on for six years at this point since the PCA diagnosis, years in which, by and large, through a combination of Terry's extraordinary determination and the development of an elaborate system of work-arounds, he had been able to forge onwards — to carry on as normal for the most part, and then, on those occasions when carrying on as normal simply wasn't an option, at least to give the impression of carrying on as normal.

But it was getting harder. Terry had started experiencing bouts — debilitating and frightening — in which the external world suddenly became almost entirely overwhelming. His visual and spatial awareness would desert him and he would be unable to negotiate a path through the disorientating messages that his brain was sending him. And in the face of those bouts, even a determination as steely as Terry's was starting to find that there were limits.

Not long before this, Terry had cancelled an appointment to go to Windsor Castle to present some Duke of Edinburgh gold awards – a signal moment, as it felt to me. It was something that he had been 100 per cent looking forward to – which I cannot pretend was always the case, even at the best of times, with the commitments that took Terry away from his desk and didn't involve librarians. 'We should put something in the diary every week that we can cancel,' Terry used to say, brightly. 'It's like gaining a free day.' And it was true: if an appointment got knocked out for whatever reason, unexpected hours would suddenly open up for writing and recreation in the Chapel, and what was almost a holiday atmosphere would prevail. Going to Windsor Castle to present the Duke of Edinburgh awards, however, definitely had not fallen into the category of 'something in the diary we can cancel'.*

Yet that morning the car and driver stood waiting on the drive . . . and carried on waiting. Terry couldn't make it out of the house. He stayed at home with Lyn. I called and sent his apologies. He took the rest of that day off and all of the following day. That was unheard of. And then he rallied again. But I realized with a sinking heart that there would always be a question mark now over everything that we arranged. Nothing in the diary could be written in ink any more.

Soon after that episode, on the morning of the Beaconsfield Library talk, Terry was again having trouble. I couldn't really see how there was any way that we would be able to go – the lure of Beaconsfield and its librarians notwithstanding. Yet somehow he got out of the Chapel and into the car. I'm still not sure how. He slept a lot on the way, while I sat there and worried about how he might be when we arrived. I need not

....

* Terry greatly approved of the Duke of Edinburgh awards, with their encouragement to young people to get outdoors, roam in the wild, pitch tents, get rained on, and generally try things beyond the normal classroom curriculum. He considered them, as he once put it, 'a fundamental part of the "Make a Human Being" kit'. True, he was not a noticeably keen camper himself, but anything that promised to loosen the grip of school on young people's minds seemed to be fine by Terry.

have done. By the time he got out of the car and into the library, warmly greeting people along the way, he seemed to have the world under control again. I sat alongside him in front of the audience in my latter-day role as 'keeper of the anecdote', ready to try and plug the gaps if the conversation faltered. But the conversation didn't falter. There was laughter, which was guaranteed in any audience with Terry Pratchett. Speaking about the importance of a library in a child's life, Terry assured the room that all he had learned at school was 'how to spit and fight', which might not have been straightforwardly accurate but which went down well anyway. He revealed that the model for Nanny Ogg, a witch from the Lancre coven on Discworld, had been a resident of Beaconsfield Old Town – a friend of his parents called Mrs Plumridge and known as Mrs Plum.*

And he spoke about the 'Black Mill' – his analogy for the writer's often coldly dispassionate mindset, that material-seeking part of their brain which never quite clocks off, no matter the circumstance: 'When my father was dying and my mother was weeping and I was comforting her,' Terry told the audience, 'there was even then a part of my brain that was going, "So, this is what this is like . . ." It's all grist to the Black Mill. It will be used at some point.'

The manuscript of *Raising Steam* had just been turned over to the publishers and, because Terry was no longer in a position to do so himself, I read a couple of pages from the file on my phone – the part where the residents of Sto Lat gather to witness the inaugural journey of Discworld's first ever steam train. And then we left, as Terry always did, in a gale of applause and good wishes.

In the car he went back to sleep again and I picked over my conflicting feelings. There was intense relief that all had gone swimmingly after

....

* Terry wrote about Mrs Plum in the notes towards his autobiography. A fixture in his childhood, and a regular drinking companion of David and Eileen's, she was a cheerful, highly optimistic woman 'with a dirty laugh like the gurgle of a plug-hole in a high class bordello'. Her annual Christmas gift to Terry's father was a mildly salacious nude calendar – without which, history would seem to confirm, no car mechanic's garage wall would have been complete in those days.

all. There was awe that this man with a degenerative brain disorder had pulled it off once again. And there was sadness and anxiety because how many more of these days could there possibly be?

And now it's 2017 and Terry is gone, and I am back in Buckinghamshire, with Rhianna, pulling up outside the library again, with no real idea what to expect. The first surprise is all the cars. We have hardly dared to speculate whether anyone will turn up for this unveiling. Do people leave their homes for plaques? Yet, as well as the official library party and their guests, and a sprinkling of press photographers, fans have come, and not just from the area – from places as far away as Leeds and Swansea too, apparently. The place is thronged and the atmosphere is almost carnival-like, which you don't necessarily expect at the unveiling of a smallish round ornament on the wall of a provincial library. The Mayor of Beaconsfield is there in his elaborate chain of office, some of the fans have dressed as Discworld characters, and also present is Beaconsfield's town crier, Richard 'Dick' Smith, in his splendid green and gold . . . well . . . crying outfit, I suppose you would call it, replete with medals and a black feathered admiral's hat that Terry would have very much approved of, and possibly even worn if given half a chance.

And finally there is the plaque itself, which, when the velvet cover duly comes off it, is in gold relief lettering on a dark brown background and is formal but touching and somehow entirely appropriate. It reads, 'Terry Pratchett woz ere.'

OK, not really. It reads, 'Sir Terry Pratchett, OBE. Born in Beaconsfield 28th April 1948. World Famous Author of the Discworld novels and many other literary works. 1948–2015.'*

Rhianna is completely on top of the event, which makes me both proud and extremely grateful, while for me, in no small measure on account of the amount of costuming going on, the next couple of

....

* Of course, Terry had already satirized this kind of thing in the 1987 novel *Equal Rites*: 'Often there is no more than a little plaque to reveal that, against all gynaecological probability, someone very famous was born halfway up a wall.'

hours go by in something of a surreal haze, which by no means lessens when a man comes up and introduces himself as a former agent of the late Bob Monkhouse. He then tells me how much the comedian and erstwhile host of *The Golden Shot* had liked Terry's writing and how Bob had been the proud owner of at least one personally signed Discworld novel. As a long-standing admirer of Bob Monkhouse, and indeed the owner of a copy of his autobiography, *Crying with Laughter: My Life Story*, I am more than delighted to learn this.*

An extension has been added to one of the wings; the letters spelling 'BEACONSFIELD BRANCH LIBRARY' have been taken down from the wall; and the space in front of the building has been converted for car parking. But otherwise the building is almost exactly as it would have appeared to Terry in 1959: a spanking new but unimposing provincial block of bricks, fronted by a mini concrete plaza with a couple of council-ordained planters on it.† Inside, a single barn-like room with a high ceiling, housing an array of modular shelving units, which in turn housed the starter motor for Terry Pratchett's writing career.

I imagine him taken there by his mother, out shopping one Saturday – this formerly indifferent eleven-year-old who would once have needed dragging to a room full of books, of all things, but who was now woken by the power of *The Wind in the Willows* and actually

· ·

* As I recall, we got into a conversation about the parallels between Bob Monkhouse's approach to comedy (his habit of filling books with jokes and possible frameworks for jokes wherever he found them) and Terry's approach to collecting material for novels, concluding that the two of them shared a permanently switched-on and ultimately scientific view of their craft. Maybe some of that stands up. It certainly occurs to me now that you could quite successfully organize a game of 'Monkhouse or Pratchett?' using their respective catalogues of possibly purloined one-liners: 'A miniature village in Bournemouth caught fire and the flames could be seen from three feet away' (answer: Monkhouse); 'Build a man a fire and he'll be warm for a day; set a man on fire and he'll be warm for the rest of his life' (answer: Pratchett), and so on.

† I feel fairly confident in asserting that Beaconsfield Branch Library was in no literal way the inspiration for the library of the Unseen University on Discworld. The latter is perhaps best envisaged as an M. C. Escher drawing, full of vertiginous book stacks, dizzyingly swerving shelves and disappearing horizons; the former was clearly designed to operate very much within the usual three dimensions.

thirsty for books. Moreover, being this particular eleven-year-old, he was abruptly on a mission to read *everything*, and although it would have become rapidly apparent on first entry that Beaconsfield Branch Library didn't have everything in stock, it clearly did have a lot of things, and it also seemed to know where it could lay its hands on a decent amount of the rest of it.

There was so much to read, and so much to be discovered about how reading worked, and here was a room, smelling of paper and glue and vacuumed carpet, where that discovering could be done. His father had told him that, as a boy, he had enjoyed Richmal Crompton's *Just William* series, so maybe Terry would, too. Two William books seem to have been his first library borrowings, taken to the desk and freshly stamped with their return dates, three weeks hence, and noted against the new card with his name on, because libraries clearly had their hallowed administrative rituals – and even that carried a certain thrill for the novice.

And those borrowed books worked for him straight away, perhaps in part because the William stories chimed a little with the days of Forty Green as Terry had romanticized them – that roving gang of interchangeable kids at a blissful loose end, knocking about in search of ways to scab their knees and pass the time – and partly because they were nothing like his life at all, and that was also clearly what reading could supply you with: transport to other places and other people.

And then a neighbour whose son had grown out of them handed over a whole batch of William books which Terry could keep in his bedroom and call his own, and now he was in deep.

'I fell under the spell,' Terry said, about reading Crompton. 'I couldn't explain it then, but I know now that I was experiencing irony, a verbal wink that made the reader wonderfully complicit in the action. This was heady stuff! You could play games with the words!'

On his next visit to the library, and again at his father's suggestion, he took out some of Capt. W. E. Johns's Biggles stories. Planes! Dogfights! Explosions! And so much of it! By the time Terry got through the door of Beaconsfield Library in 1959, Capt. W. E. Johns had written

65 books starring his heroic airman, on his way to a total of 98.* *Biggles Flies West, Biggles Flies North, Biggles Flies South, Biggles Goes Home* . . . A boy could be months getting through the library's extensive selection of those – unless he was Terry, that is, in which case he would be merely days. And then he was on to T. H. White's *Mistress Masham's Repose* (1946), about a ten-year-old orphan girl who finds Lilliputians in Northamptonshire and that was spellbinding, too, because it suggested a world in which another fictional world – that of Swift's *Gulliver's Travels* – was real. Oh, and while he was at it, he'd better read Swift's *Gulliver's Travels*, too.

'I wasn't looking for ideas, techniques or, that terrible word, tips,' Terry wrote, many years later, 'I simply absorbed.' Or as he told the audience at that 2013 talk, 'I read until my head was full to bursting.' And never mind picking them up and worming your way through them, it even occurred to him that there might be something to be gained from just being *near* books. 'Somehow,' Terry wrote in the notes towards his autobiography, 'it seemed to be that just being inside a library was very nearly enough, as if everything in the books would permeate your skin by some kind of osmosis, and I'm not certain even now that I was wrong.'

All of which would conveniently explain why his Saturday morning trips to the library began to elongate. After a certain point he wasn't just going there to return his books and choose some new ones, he was hanging out around the shelves for whole hours at a time. Indeed, Terry seems to have hung around Beaconsfield Library at the weekends in the same way other people might stand in a guitar shop on a Saturday afternoon – just to be there, in the vicinity of the thing you were passionate about, among your tribe.

And somehow, from all this hanging out, emerged something in the shape of actual employment. By the age of twelve, Terry found himself

. . . .

* Biggles, rather like Roy of the Rovers, proved unusually impervious to the traditional effects of ageing, presenting as fresh a cheek and as keen an eye in 1968, at the conclusion of his adventures, as he had at their beginning, in 1932.

incorporated into the library workforce as a Saturday boy. Had the library actually advertised any such vacancy? Did the library even have 'Saturday boys' before this? It seems that Terry simply graduated from hanging out to helping out, unasked, and that the role grew from there. At first, he mostly returned books to their shelves. Later he would sit at a table with a pile of damaged volumes and help repair them, applying the glue and the Sellotape, wielding the scissors and the scalpel.* At some point he was given a briefing on the miracles of the Dewey Decimal classification system. At no point was he paid.

But here was the sweetness of the deal: in return for his labours, the small but useful and certainly persistent kid with the glasses was the beneficiary of an unspoken agreement whereby the management turned a blind eye to how many tickets he was writing himself for his own borrowings. Terry's estimates of the number of tickets he held at his borrowing peak varied, but 67 was the figure he frequently returned to. Nobody seemed to mind too much that whole shelves of books which by rights belonged to the people of Beaconsfield and its surrounding area had been temporarily removed to Terry's bedroom.

Occasionally browsers would buttonhole him for guidance. 'People coming into the library,' Terry remembered, 'would stop the strange but inoffensive kid carrying stacks of books all over the place and ask questions like, "What have you got that is suitable for a child with a reading age of eight?" And I would say, "The book for a child with a reading age of twelve," because it always seemed to me that parents who have to ask the librarians for information never really understand how kids who like reading actually read. Who would want to read a book that is *suitable* for you? Not me, for one. I wanted the unsuitable books.'

Was *The Specialist* by Charles 'Chic' Sale unsuitable? This was another of Terry's father's recommendations. For David Pratchett this

....

* When I think of Terry competently mending library books, I reflect on the times when I would be kneeling on the Chapel floor, wrapping up his Christmas gifts for him while he stood above me with his arms folded, saying, 'I'm always deeply suspicious of a man who can wrap a present well.' He knew far more in this area, clearly, than he let on.

work stood among the most wonderful literary creations of all time, and he may have had a point. Sale was an American vaudeville actor and his short book, written in 1929, was the tale of a builder of outdoor lavatories, a man in love with his craft who is always willing to offer people the benefit of his wisdom on privy placement. Terry found it on the library shelves, took it home and swallowed it whole. What seems to have caught him was the way in which the book was funny without containing anything that you could define as a joke. There was a real art to that, clearly, and Terry would later, in 2004, in an essay for Waterstones' in-house publication *Books Quarterly*, hymn that slim volume as 'a gentle education in the nature of humour. That stuff needs deep soil,' Terry wrote, adding caustically, 'You can grow wit on a damp flannel.'

Or what about the library's bound copies of old *Punch* magazines? Were those unsuitable? Those dark red, slightly fusty volumes, dating all the way back to the turn of the century and rather intimidatingly consuming whole yards of shelf space, perhaps weren't specifically aimed at the 12–14 age-group. Yet the young Terry filleted these, reading them all, and everything in them, he claimed: not just falling on the cartoons and the H. M. Bateman drawings – although they must have been a part of the inspiration for Terry starting to draw cartoons of his own at around this time – but steeping himself in the articles and thereby receiving a peerless introduction to the art of comic prose.

In those bound *Punch* volumes he came across pieces by P. G. Wodehouse, Joyce Grenfell, Kingsley Amis, Quentin Crisp, Basil Boothroyd, Somerset Maugham; Geoffrey Willans and Ronald Searle, who sent him off to the Molesworth books; and R. J. Yeatman and W. C. Sellar, whose history spoof *1066 and All That* Terry now also devoured, along with their less celebrated works *And Now All This*, *Horse Nonsense* and *Garden Rubbish* . . .

Punch brought Mark Twain into his life, too, and Jerome K. Jerome, so he could work outwards from there, also. And reading *Punch* meant he read columns by Patrick Campbell who later, like Alan Coren (another *Punch* writer and newspaper columnist whom Terry would come to adore, and also to pillage openly for gags), became famous as a team captain on the BBC word quiz *Call My Bluff* but who would always be famous to Terry, first and foremost, as a *Punch* writer.* Those bound magazines were essentially an encyclopaedia of influences that would shape, in the first instance, Terry's journalism, but would for ever after feed his writing beyond that.†

And it was in *Punch* that he first came across the name Henry Mayhew, which led him to another shelf in the library where he turned, mesmerized, the pages of Mayhew's masterpiece of Victorian journalism, *London Labour and the London Poor*. Mayhew combed the capital, talking to everyone he met about their work, from 'the Queen's rat and mole destroyer' cheerfully rising above the vicious bites which were the hazards of his trade, to the 'pure finders' collecting up dog faeces to sell to the tanneries, and every shade and stripe of street-market vendor in between, so that the book itself teems, as the London streets did, with people and the sounds of their voices. Mayhew's great work would eventually feed directly into Terry's 2012 novel *Dodger*, but you could argue that it had already peopled the streets of Ankh-Morpork long before then, and the corners of Terry's imagination long before that.

And then, late in 1961, when Terry was thirteen, one of the Beaconsfield librarians pushed across the table to the Saturday boy three volumes,

. . . .

* When Terry appeared on *Call My Bluff* in November 1997, along with Alan Coren, Barry Cryer and Sandi Toksvig, it was the fulfilment of a lifelong dream. It was only a shame that, by then, Bob Holness had replaced Robert Robinson as presenter, because Robinson was someone else whom Terry had revered, first and foremost, as a writer. Of his experience on the show, Terry told the fan forum alt.fan.pratchett, 'Better to slit your wrists than to drive a weak bluff into the combined skills of Alan Coren and Barry Cryer.' But he acquitted himself well enough. His further remark: 'Coffee adverts next, I expect.'

† When we went back in 2013, Terry lamented loudly to the librarians that those *Punch* volumes were no longer on the shelves and he suggested that the proceeds from the ticket sales that day, which were being donated to the library, be used to reacquire them. He wasn't entirely kidding, though I believe the library graciously exercised their absolute right to ignore him.

tied together with string, and said something to the effect of, 'I think this might be of interest to you.'

'That damn book was a half-brick in the path of the bicycle of my life,' Terry said later of *The Lord of the Rings*.* Tolkien's great work wasn't exactly hot off the press at this point: those three volumes had been published across a year, from 1954 to 1955, and completed even earlier, in 1949. Other kids at school had already been there and the book had already been a topic of conversation. So, no particular urgency, then. Terry set it aside for a couple of weeks – until New Year's Eve, in fact, when he had the task of babysitting for some friends of his parents. And then, alone in the sitting room of someone else's house, he opened up volume one.

The presence of a map in the endpapers instantly struck the young Terry as a good sign. A map at the front of a book was often an indication of quality in the product, wasn't it? It promised you were going places. He wasn't to be disappointed. Years later he could still recall the sixties sofa he was sitting on, the bareness of a slightly chilly front room (the heating eventually went off – a notorious babysitting hazard), and the sense, as he read, that 'at the edges of the carpet, the forest began. I remember the light as green, coming through the trees. I have never since then so truly had the experience of being inside a story.'

He read through the evening. Midnight arrived, followed by 1962, but Terry was still reading. Then, when the parents returned from their party, he went home and continued to read in bed until 3.00 a.m. He woke up on New Year's Day with the book on his chest, re-found his place and carried on reading. And later that night, somewhere between, by Terry's calculations, 23 and 25 hours after starting, he had finished all three volumes. And when he reached the end of volume

. . . .

* He said that in 'Why Gandalf never married', a talk he gave in Coventry at Novacon, the science fiction convention, in 1985.

three, he turned back to the beginning of volume one and started again.

If *The Wind in the Willows* was one harp-pluck moment in the movie of Terry's life, then *The Lord of the Rings* was another, with perhaps the harp plucked even more firmly. It was his initiation into the genre of 'fantasy writing' – and by extension his first occasion to pause and wonder whether that label really made any sense, or as much sense as people clearly thought it did. (Wasn't all fiction, by definition, fantasy to some degree? Terry would spend much of his adult life waist-deep in this debate.) And it was his first immersion in a kind of teenage fandom he would eventually outgrow until only the deepest-set and most persistent traces remained. Terry was, of course, by no means alone in spending some of his young years regarding *The Lord of the Rings* as right up there among the greatest achievements of humanity. But for Terry, in his uniquely privileged position at the Beaconsfield Library coalface, it seems to have been not just about what the book itself was, but also about what that book opened up beyond itself, the way it sent him to whole other thus far untravelled regions of the library: the mythology section, the ancient history shelves, the history shelves, the archaeology shelves . . . It was an earthquake that sent cracks running off across the surface in multiple directions.

Six years later, Terry would find himself writing to Tolkien regarding the novella *Smith of Wootton Major*, about a blacksmith's son who swallows a token hidden in a festival cake and finds himself admitted to 'the Land of Faery'. The book was published on 9 November 1967, and Terry was onto it pretty quickly: his letter to the author is dated 22 November. Tolkien, for his part, was onto Terry's letter pretty quickly, too: his reply is dated 24 November, so therefore came almost by return of post. Written when he was nineteen, Terry's letter, sent from 25 Upper Riding, doesn't mention that he's a journalist (nearly two years into his first stint at the *Bucks Free Press*), nor that he's an aspiring author who has, by this point, had his first story published and has the manuscript of a novel for children tucked away. He writes, seeking nothing back, purely as a fan, expressing gratitude.

Dear Professor Tolkien;
This is simply a letter of appreciation. I have just read 'Smith of
Wootton Major'. To tell the truth, when I ordered it I expected a
light tale akin to 'Farmer Giles of Ham'* – instead I read and re-read
it with awe.

I don't know what there was in it that moved me to write this
letter. It was something that 'The Lord of the Rings' never
possessed except in very short measure, that feeling of recognition.
You said something in 'Smith' which I hope I grasped, and there
was a feeling almost of recognition. An odd feeling of grief
overcame me when I read it. I cannot explain my feelings any
clearer. It was like hearing a piece of music from way back, except
that it was nearer poetry by Graves's definition.† Thank you very
much for writing it.

Now I await the Silmarilion,‡

Yours faithfully,
Terence Pratchett

Tolkien's reply was brief – possibly even a bit of a brush-off – but, in
four crisp sentences, he remarked that this was the first fan mail he had
received about *Smith of Wootton Major*, and added, 'You evidently feel
about the story very much as I do myself. I can hardly say more.' Let us
not ask whether Tolkien could, in fact, despite his protestation to the

. . . .

* Tolkien's 1937 comic medieval fable in which an unpromising farmer accidentally
  becomes a local hero by seeing off a partially-sighted giant with a blunderbuss and is then
  expected to deal with a more properly terrifying visiting dragon.

† Robert Graves (1895–1985), the author most famously of the war memoir *Goodbye to All
  That* and the fictional autobiography of the Roman emperor *I, Claudius*, and also of
  numerous volumes of poetry, into which Terry had clearly been dipping.

‡ Terry would have to wait a while. The collection of stories comprising *The Silmarillion*
  (misspelled by Terry in his letter), which Tolkien had been working on since 1917, was
  eventually stitched together by Tolkien's son Christopher, and published posthumously in
  1977, four years after the author's death.

contrary, have said more. It didn't really matter. Far more importantly, the fact of that correspondence, along with its swiftness, and the sense it allowed, rightly or wrongly, of Tolkien, not as some lofty, remote figure, but as an accessible mortal with a typewriter, directly answering to his readers, left a lasting impression on Terry.

And, again, it all threaded back to Beaconsfield Library and those string-tied volumes pushed across the desk. That this 'twit and dreamer' (Terry's phrase again) who found possibilities for himself in a library went on to become the author of books that themselves ended up in libraries, where they could be found by other twits and dreamers in search of possibilities for themselves . . . I would maintain that the circularity of this outcome satisfied Terry more lastingly and more deeply than any other of the outcomes of his professional success.

'It's hard to imagine an author who is not a reader first,' Terry once wrote. And I can almost see him, eleven going on twelve, cross-legged on the floor by the children's fiction section, his head lowered over the book open on his lap, several others on the floor beside him and his path already opening out in front of him. Or, as Rhianna unimprovably put it in her speech when the plaque on the wall was unveiled, 'Dad was born in Beaconsfield but Terry Pratchett the author was born in Beaconsfield Library.'

3

SMUTTY MAGAZINES, UNFINISHED CUSTARD AND THE SCHOOL UNIFORM OF SATAN

Two things to which Terry Pratchett was introduced by his grandmother:

1: the writings of G. K. Chesterton.
2: smoking.

Maybe we should deal with the smoking first.

Granny Pratchett, Terry's paternal grandmother, rolled her own cigarettes. Then, having smoked them, she would take the butts from the ashtray, pick the paper apart and return any strands of unburnt tobacco to the tin where she kept her supply. Waste not, want not. As Terry wrote in a short essay about her in 2004, 'As a child this fascinated me, because you didn't need to be a mathematician to see that this meant there must have been some shreds of tobacco she'd been smoking for decades, if not longer.'

During school holidays, while his parents were at work, Terry would be packed off to Granny Pratchett's council flat in Beaconsfield for the day.* And it was there on one such occasion that he made the mistake

. . . .

* This was the flat in which Terry claimed to have looked up from whatever he was playing with on the floor at the time to see the figure of Death engaged in conversation with

of crafting in front of his grandmother a mock pipe from a hollowed potato and a drinking straw. While he worked, he explained aloud his growing curiosity about what smoking might taste and feel like. He would have been about eight years old.

Now, a less tactically astute guardian than Granny Pratchett – or perhaps just a more modern guardian – might well at this point have dashed the potato from the small boy's hands and instructed him to turn his young mind to building something more wholesome instead, like a gun. But Granny Pratchett clearly operated on a different level from other guardians. Leaving Terry to complete the project, she silently fetched a little tobacco from her tin, placed it in the bowl of Terry's improvised pipe, helped him to light it . . . and then looked on in silence as he drew on the straw and turned a deathly shade of pale green. Still without comment, she then presented him with a glass of lemonade to aid his recovery.

Job done. With what Terry referred to, without further elaboration, as 'a few understandable aberrations in the 1960s', he was a lifelong non-smoker from that day on.

And then, about three years after this, when Terry was eleven, there was G. K. Chesterton. Here, again, Granny Pratchett's tactic seemed to be a form of immersion therapy, but this time with more immediately pleasant results. There was, in her flat, a single filled bookshelf, the largest volume on which was probably the *Crossword Puzzle Solver's Dictionary*. (Granny Pratchett was a committed and capable doer of crosswords.) But there was a selection of fiction, too, and one day while Terry was with her, she pulled out Chesterton's 1904 fantasy *The Napoleon of Notting Hill*, which is set in 1984* in a London adjusting to the ascent of a king with a taste for jokes.

. . . .

someone on the television. It was, in fact, a scene from Ingmar Bergman's 1957 fantasy film *The Seventh Seal* and the Death in question struck Terry as a rather amiable figure for a Grim Reaper, and not very grim at all, as it happened. He appears to have filed that idea away for later use.

* Like a certain George Orwell book. Indeed, some believe that choice of date was a homage to Chesterton by Orwell.

'I read it while my granny listened,' wrote Terry. When he was finished with that, his grandmother tried him on *The Man Who Was Thursday*, a book that Terry later said he thought everybody in politics should be made to read.

But it wasn't just about supplying the books. Granny Pratchett was also in a position to inform Terry that Chesterton, who died in 1936, was a former resident of Beaconsfield, and someone she had actually come across, knocking about the place, back in the day. He was, she informed Terry, a 'big man with a squeaky voice'. This (the fact that he had lived there, rather than the fact that he was big and had a squeaky voice) suddenly explained to Terry why the patch of grass opposite Granny Pratchett's flat was known as Chesterton Green.

And then came the following gleaming anecdote: Granny Pratchett recalled the day a train was held at Beaconsfield station so that it could take down to London the article for the *Strand* magazine that the great author was a little late in finishing.

The superhero-like power of G. K. Chesterton to stop trains was in itself something to wonder at, but what seems to have grabbed Terry most firmly in these revelations was the way they located this famous writer on entirely familiar ground – in Beaconsfield, at the same train station where Terry had but recently laid coins on the tracks for passing trains to crush. In that sense, this news of Chesterton was arguably similar in weight to the moment a handful of years later at a science fiction convention in London, when Terry, who was there as a fan, found himself next to Arthur C. Clarke at the urinals. It brought with it the realization that, for all that one might very easily form grander ideas about them, authors were flesh and blood and moved among us – indeed, in the case of Arthur C. Clarke, emptied their bladders alongside us. And if that were the case, then perhaps it wasn't so outlandish, in the long run, to believe that one might oneself even *become* an author.

Terry took his interest in Chesterton to the library. There, he would eventually find him defending fairy stories against the claim that they were unsuitable for impressionable children. 'The objection to fairy stories is that they tell children there are dragons,' Chesterton wrote, in sentences that, from this end of the telescope, can look highly Pratchett-like. 'But children have always known there are drag-ons. Fairy stories tell children that dragons can be killed.'

And he would in due course take from Chesterton the notion that 'far more grotesque and wonderful than any wild, fantastical thing was anything that was every-day and un-regarded, if seen unexpectedly from a new direction' – a sentiment which was a clear touchstone for Terry's own writing. Many years later, asked to nominate guests for his 'dream' writers' dinner party, Terry chose G. K. Chesterton, Mark Twain and Neil Gaiman, adding that he chose Chesterton and Twain for their literary prowess and the likely brilliance of their conversation, and that he chose Gaiman because he could be relied upon to locate good sushi. Terry and Neil would dedicate their co-written novel *Good Omens* to Chesterton – 'a man who knew what was going on'.

So Granny Pratchett gave Terry G. K. Chesterton and everything that followed from that gift, and Terry, by way of return, gave Granny Pratchett science fiction. This was the section of Beaconsfield Branch Library in front of which Terry had started spending an increasing amount of his time, and it only seemed right to him that he should share his literary findings from there with his grandmother, as she had shared her literary findings with him. Thus he would arrive at the flat bearing volumes from the *Cities in Flight* series by James Blish – *Earthman Come Home* (1955), *They Shall Have Stars* (1956), *A Clash of Cymbals/The Triumph of Time* (1959) – and Brian Aldiss's collections of short sto-ries, *Space, Time and Nathaniel* (1957), *The Canopy of Time* and *No Time Like Tomorrow* (both 1959). And Granny Pratchett, ever encouraging, would take them from him enthusiastically and read them avidly after he had gone.

'Or so she said,' Terry wrote. 'You could never be quite sure with Granny.'

To the determined steering of his mother, then, one needs to add the influence on Terry's developing mind – more gently administered but equally profound – of Granny Pratchett. Florence Pratchett, née Hunt, was a small woman, seemingly withdrawn and perhaps even a little put-upon, yet, Terry would come to realize, self-contained and powerfully wise. Also adventurous when she was permitted to be. She had gone into service after leaving school, but then had taught herself French and had set off to take a job as a lady's maid in France.

This was during the First World War. Young women then were encouraged to write to soldiers at the front and, according to Terry, Florence drew from the hat of potential 'lonely Tommy' penfriends the name of William Pratchett. Their correspondence turned into a relationship when William became one of no fewer than three Pratchett brothers who returned from service in the Great War with their lives. 'It was like *Saving Private Ryan*,' Terry remarked, anachronistically, of his family's mass rush to the front. 'Except that all the privates survived.' Family legend proudly insisted that Terry's great-grandfather and great-grandmother had been in receipt of a letter from the King, expressing gratitude for their triple-strength contribution to the war effort.

Terry always felt that his grandmother had married slightly beneath her. Not that William Pratchett – variously described by Terry as resembling Winston Churchill, the band leader Billy Cotton, and a grumpy potato – wasn't a decent man and a loyal husband. He was also a high quality grandfather, in a position to regale Terry with eye-widening tales of the First World War, of his exploits at some point as a poacher, and of various things he had been asked to do as a little boy, including urinating onto a car's acetylene lamp because the carbide crystals had gone dry and weren't producing the gas on which the car depended for its night vision. 'That was *proper* nostalgia,' Terry recounted in the notes towards his autobiography, 'not like the nostalgia you get today.'

But there was nothing intellectual about William Pratchett, whose interests included cheating to a wonderful degree at pontoon and dominos, and who rather sneered at books and reading, which meant that Granny Pratchett had to indulge those interests slightly furtively and not a little defensively. Still, she undemonstratively read everything she could lay her hands on – give or take, perhaps, the odd book by James Blish – and jealously guarded that bookshelf of hers, whose riches she offered to the openly receptive Terry.

Grandad Pratchett, incidentally, was to live to the grand old age of 92, while believing himself to be at the even grander old age of 94. After Florence died, he soldiered on stoically alone, surrounded by 'bubbling carboys of home-made wine', Terry remembered, and learn-ing belatedly to look after himself in ways that men of his generation frequently never had to. One day he settled down to a robust solo lunch of shepherd's pie followed by prunes and custard, felt unwell in the middle of the meal, and banged on the wall for his neighbour, who called an ambulance. Grandad Pratchett died on the way to hospital, and the family legend, propagated in particular by Terry's father, was that William Pratchett's last words on this earth were an anguished cry of, 'I haven't had my custard yet.'

File under 'too good to check'.

* * * * *

We know how it goes. You start out just borrowing a few books from the library, or your grandmother, and thinking you've got it under control and that you can handle it – they're just loans, after all, so what's the fuss about? And the next thing you know, you're moving on to the harder stuff – second-hand books from second-hand bookshops, and actually paying for them with your own money and taking them home with you to own, putting them on a shelf in your bedroom, even. And at that point, most likely, it's all over and you'll be on to brand new books before you realize it, and almost certainly an addict for the rest of your life.

And so it was that the young Terry Pratchett, on his bicycle, one weekend when he wasn't in the library, found himself on the threshold of The Cottage Bookshop down the road from home in the village of Penn. The shop was well named. The building had seen service as a fish and chip shop and a branch of Barclays Bank before someone put a handful of old hardbacks in one of the windows, priced at a few pence each, and a new business was born. But it was still, to all appearances, more of a little house than a shop.

However, readers of the Discworld books will be familiar with the concept of 'L-space', and anybody else need only consult *The Discworld Companion* under 'Libraries, nature of': 'Even big collections of ordinary books distort space and time, as can readily be proved by anyone who has been around a really old-fashioned second-hand bookshop, one of those that has more staircases than storeys and those rows of shelves that end in little doors that are surely too small for a full-sized human to enter.' In The Cottage Bookshop, the laws of L-space clearly applied; indeed, its various little rooms piled high and wedged tight with books of every type and vintage were possibly the first place in which Terry was brought to consider those laws. They were by no means the last.

The first book Terry bought in The Cottage Bookshop was a used but good-condition copy of *Brewer's Dictionary of Phrase and Fable*. In the introduction he was invited to write for that golden reference work's Millennium edition – and that was a proud career milestone, by his own definition* – Terry began to describe it as 'a compendium . . . of myth, legend, quotation, historical byways, and slang'. But then he gave up, and said instead, 'A better description would be an education.' It was, of course, a place where he could look things up: as he put it in a speech at Noreascon in 2004, 'When I needed to find out exactly how you build a clock of flowers in order to tell the time by the open- ing and closing of the blooms, I turned first to *Brewer's Dictionary of Phrase and Fable* and there it was.' However, that was not how he under- stood the book at first. Knowing no better, and seeing no reason not to, he simply opened his copy at the beginning and read it through to the end, as though it were a novel.†

He used it more conventionally later in life, but even then, for Terry, that book's particular magic wasn't just in the way it could slake an obscure curiosity; it was, on the contrary, in the way it made obscure curiosity lead to further obscure curiosity, carving idiosyncratic journeys for the mind through its pages. He adored the serendipity it embodied and encouraged, the way that, within those covers, things just led natur- ally to other things. Trying to read just one entry in *Brewer's* was, he felt,

---

* It was arguably greater even, in Terry's eyes, than the come-on-down to appear on *Call My Bluff*.

† It would be some time before Terry heard spoken aloud some of the words he encountered in *Brewer's*. He told me that for many years, until enlightenment arbitrarily came his way, it remained his belief that the word 'ogre' was pronounced 'oggree'.

as doomed to failure as 'trying to eat just one salted peanut'. It was, in that sense, from Terry's point of view, the perfect reference work.

And then there was The Cottage Bookshop's shelf of used sci-fi and fantasy novels. It's easy to forget, at this distance and in the age of global online shopping, just how hard this stuff was for a new enthusiast to lay hands on at the beginning of the 1960s. Once you had exhausted the local library's supply, science fiction had to be sniffed for and rooted out. Terry's best bet in those days would have been the plastic carousels of cheap paperbacks that stood in newsagents and tobacconists and chemists, periodically restocked by visiting reps and carrying motley selections of British and US editions. Any new town would need to be scoured for those stands. Mostly the slots would be occupied with bodice-rippers, war stories and westerns, but occasionally, if his luck was in, he would happen on little nuggets of gold: an Isaac Asimov, an Arthur C. Clarke, a Hal Clement, an A. E. van Vogt.

But, as Terry now discovered, a well-stocked second-hand bookshop could be your best friend in this regard, too. And just as the gardeners of Forty Green would pedal home in the evenings unreasonably bur-dened with vegetables, Terry now steered his way back to Upper Riding with the handlebars of his bike perilously weighed down by carrier bags stuffed with cheap but precious books. If Terry Pratchett was born in Beaconsfield, and Terry Pratchett the author was born in Beacons-field Library, then Terry Pratchett the book accumulator was born in The Cottage Bookshop in Penn.

There, and also in The Little Library, Terry's second major discovery in this line, and a place which barely qualified as a shop, and certainly not as a library, being just a wooden shack on an as yet unrestored bombsite in the Frogmoor district of High Wycombe. One afternoon after school, aged around thirteen and with his school satchel still slung over his shoulder, Terry boldly parted this ostensibly unpromising estab-lishment's beaded curtain and entered within.

Had he been taller, or had enough confidence to raise his eyes, he would have been confronted by what was possibly Buckinghamshire's leading collection of printed pornography. And at that point, the shopkeeper – an elderly lady who sat behind the counter, knitting – might have suggested this schoolboy had come to the wrong place and told him to leave.

As it was, Terry's eyes were lowered to the floor where, occupying half the room, were cardboard boxes filled with British and American science fiction magazines. He flipped through them in amazement. Here were back numbers of British publications like *New Worlds Science Fiction* and *Science Fantasy*. And here were periodicals from America, and therefore instantly exotic: copies of *The Magazine of Fantasy and Science Fiction* with fabulous full-colour cover art; *Galaxy Science Fiction* where you could read Cordwainer Smith or Harlan Ellison; and the pleasingly squat and thick *Astounding Science Fiction*, going since 1930, with, if you were lucky, long tales by Robert Heinlein and James Blish. And here were copies of *Vector* magazine, a rudimentary, typed-up, black and white fanzine in form, yet the monthly critical journal of something called the British Science Fiction Association, which Terry immediately knew he needed to learn more about. He would eventually find himself in The Little Library two or three times a week and each time he would depart, several shillings poorer, with a bursting satchel.

Terry had the strong impression that he was the only regular customer for the contents of the boxes on the floor. The knitter behind the counter became used to his visits, even offering him a cup of tea from time to time, and, when Terry asked her from where she was acquiring these pearls, as he saw them, she simply answered, 'People drop them in.' As for the main plank of her business . . . well, Terry's eyes must have drifted to the upper shelves eventually, but what he saw there was, he insisted, entirely soft-core and practically innocent by later standards – 'giggles and garters', as Terry defined the genre. That said, Terry did witness some goods being withdrawn from under the counter and handed over to the occasional, inevitably raincoated customer in discreet brown envelopes without further comment and, as Terry observed, it seemed unlikely that these were rare science fiction magazines.

However unfortunate it was, the proximity of these sci-fi treasures to shelves of smut did seem to be telling a story of sorts about science fiction's general standing in British culture at this point in history – a sense that there was something slightly tawdry and embarrassing about it. Science fiction in those days was clearly many things, Terry would have been realizing, but respectable was not automatically one of them.

Still, they couldn't touch you for it. One day, as he trawled the boxes, Terry was joined in the hut by a gentleman whose haircut and narrow-eyed demeanour seemed to suggest a plain-clothes policeman on duty. 'What's *he* doing in here?' the man immediately wanted to know, gesturing at the minor on the floor.

The woman with the knitting replied, magnificently, and to Terry's lasting delight, 'Onny swar key marley ponce, Geoffrey.'* The policeman had no answer to that and left.

The Little Library disappeared in due course under the forecourt of a car dealership, but not before it had furnished the teenage Terry with stacks of material to squirrel away in his bedroom and marvel at in his own time. More grist to the mill. A lot of this stuff was sub-par or mere hack-work, dashed down and rushed out, and Terry knew it.† But even the pulpiest piece of sci-fi or fantasy could provide what he called 'an exercise bicycle for the mind: it might not take you anywhere but it tones the muscles that can.' And a kind of fiction which was constantly pondering alternative horizons and reflecting on previously unimagined futures was never going to be only corrosive in its effects, was it? 'It's hard to read a lot of science fiction and be a bigot,' Terry claimed. And in his own case, he wasn't wrong.

* * * * *

Of course, he couldn't be reading *all* of the time. There was also school to find room in his day for. In the September of 1959, having managed,

....

* The French maxim 'honi soit qui mal y pense', here translated into the Bucks dialect, and meaning, 'shame on the one who thinks ill of it'.

† See also the brusque reflection of John Baxter, the sci-fi writer and biographer of J. G. Ballard, in his memoir about book collecting, *A Pound of Paper*, upon his own excited discovery of a trove of sci-fi magazines in the garage of a schoolfriend: 'I'd stumbled on the great rule of science fiction: 90 percent of it is crap.' Terry would have agreed wholeheartedly. And yet . . .

thanks to Eileen's active work in the background, a borderline pass in his eleven-plus, Terry politely skirted Beaconsfield Secondary Modern and caught the bus instead to Wycombe Technical High School, wearing the regulation uniform, freshly acquired from the Hull, Loosely and Pearce department store in High Wycombe, and including not just a tie and a blazer but also (this being 1959) a cap in black with yellow trim – 'the colours of Satan, I remember reading later,' Terry observed.*

Ignoring that connection, we can still conclude that Wycombe Tech was an atypical place, at least in one sense. Intended to sit in the middle ground between secondary moderns at the bottom of the eleven-plus divide and the grammar schools at the top of it, technical schools were supposed to provide a traditional, rounded, grammar-style education but with a practical emphasis which leaned towards eventual emergence into a trade or business or some kind of vocation deemed 'useful'. Thus Terry's standard school equipment included a woodwork apron and a set of metalwork tools and the school facilities featured an unusually high quota of well-equipped workshops, in addition to a Fives court. In practice, though, this educational middle ground proved harder to occupy than the Butler Education Act of 1944 imagined it would and in the end very few secondary technical schools got off the ground. At best, only between 2 and 3 per cent of UK schoolchildren ever found themselves at a 'Tech'. Terry's schooling had at least a rarity value.

No doubt both Terry's parents would have approved of the school's practical bent – though not necessarily strongly enough, it seems, to get their son there for the first day. That September, as before with Holtspur Primary, the Pratchetts once more appear to have balked at cutting short their hard-won summer holiday, and Terry was again obliged to report for his new school a whole day after everybody else had done so. This time, at least, there was no psychologically damaging indignity relating to pictures on pegs, but Terry claimed ever afterwards, in tones

....

* Obscure but not untrue. Medieval frescoes in a church in Bessans in France depict Satan in black and yellow on a background of red flames. They do not, however, depict him wearing a cap, nor catching a bus to High Wycombe.

as adamant as they were unconvincing, that that first day was the one on which the maths teacher had covered algebra and that this was why he had never been able to get his head around quadratic equations.

Having eventually orientated himself, and having located his locker — and also having come to the realization that every locker key at Wycombe Technical High opened not just its designated locker, but all of the others as well — Terry seems to have quickly settled down into being an almost entirely middling student, unlikely to catch the eye and thereby, for the most part, able to stay out of the limelight at one end and out of trouble at the other. 'High enough not to be squashed but low enough not to be shot,' was how Terry would eventually describe what he thought of as the happy student's optimum position in an educational setting, and it was a position he seems to have rapidly and lastingly attained.

He was diligent: his mother would have made sure of that. His homework certainly got done. But in the formal ways in which the school wanted to measure him, he was not exceptional. Apart from the algebra, he coped with maths well enough.* He was interested in history, but not necessarily in the history that was being taught to him and on the day that it was being taught. His woodworking and metalworking were a little above average. He was good at art, though he favoured cartoons and caricatures over the formal approaches demanded by the coursework. Short and slight, he was bad at games, with the exception of hockey at which he was both 'bad and very dangerous', although he did like the fact that 'they gave you a weapon'. There is no record of whether or not Terry ever attempted Fives, which is possibly just as well. But he was obliged with the rest of his year to participate in cross-country running. Here, he would contentedly adopt a position at the back of the pack with a friend, Mick Rowe, and, as they jogged compliantly but uncompetitively round the boating stream and into the woods of

. . . .

* He was still suffering with it many years later when his friend Professor Ian Stewart attempted to give Terry a private lesson in the solution of quadratic equations. Many napkins were filled with numbers and brackets, but Terry remained none the wiser and equally convinced that the whole thing was a conspiracy to defraud him in Greek. 'I must lack an enzyme or something,' Terry concluded, non-mathematically.

Wycombe Rye, engage in lively conversation and observations about their surroundings. One day, by the waterfall, they paused to observe vast numbers of tiny, recently spawned froglets that were hopping around in the grass. Their delight was short-lived. 'Looking down at our feet,' Mick recalled, 'we suddenly realized that we were standing on a layer of dead froglets. The trail of runners ahead of us had trodden on literally hundreds of these little critters as they ran past, turning the path into a carpet of flattened corpses.' Mick and Terry jogged on, slightly horrified.*

In the classroom, left to his own devices and beyond the reach of his mother, Terry does not seem to have been especially concentrated or particularly tidy in any of his work.

Among the handful of his surviving exercise books, the cream front cover of Terry's English and Maths notebook, which was made to serve him in both 3C and 4A, is a thick blizzard of doodles and scribblings in red and blue biro amid which the interested viewer may discern the following: some lengths of twisted railway track, a bicycle, two misshapen pirates in tricorn hats, a guillotine with a severed, crowned head looking a touch unhappy underneath it, a sign on a stake reading 'RHUBARD PATCH', a long set of footprints, and various think-bubbles containing phrases such as, 'THINKS: RHUBARD, RHUBARB, RHUBARB, RHUBARB . . .', 'THINKS: OW!' and 'THINKS: I THOUGHT MY FACE WAS RED UNTIL I SAW YOURS'. Terry has also perhaps unhelpfully crossed out his name and written above it, 'MY NAME IS ON THE BACK PAGE'.

Meanwhile, for no apparent reason the inside of his German exercise book contains the lines, 'Do you smoke? No, but I burst into flames sometimes', and experimental drawings abound of little figures labelled 'SNARGS' – each one of them consisting almost entirely of a beard and a nose – who will later make a fuller appearance in Terry's first novel, *The Carpet People*. In another drawing – a full-page one this time – a

---

* Shades here of the skeletal fossils that Terry felt were below his feet during his childhood walks on the chalk. The possibility of carnage underfoot would again detain Terry when he wrote *The Carpet People*.

cigar-shaped alien craft plummets towards Earth, trailing smoke. Of actual German, there is not a great deal.

Without setting academe alight – but also, importantly, without setting the school alight, which should always be accounted a plus – Terry was wending his way fairly unremarkably towards the five solid O level passes that would grant him a passage into the sixth form and a shot at some A levels, which in turn might stand him in good stead to become the first member of his family ever to go to university. Not that the prospect of higher education seemed at any stage to engage Terry's imagination, nor especially that of his parents who, although they probably wouldn't have ruled it out, were mostly keen to see Terry settled as soon as reasonably possible into steady, decently paid and preferably pensionable employment.

Terry was clearly sparky, and he had interests, but they were mostly things he was doing outside school. Adventures in home electronics with his father continued, opening out gradually as Terry got older into adventures in home mechanics. In David Pratchett, Terry had the great good fortune of a father who encouraged him to play with things that more cautious parents might have kept him away from: hot solder, live wires.* The pair of them devoted some time to the construction of an electric Noughts and Crosses game, built from radio valves, which enabled the player to pit himself against the machine.† And, under the joint radio call-sign

. . . .

* According to Terry, his father's hands were so thickly callused from his labours as a mechanic that they were 98 per cent insulated against electric shocks, meaning he could happily test live wires by the generally unrecommended approach of laying a finger on them. Surprise electric shocks administered by his son via the shed door-handle and a magneto were another matter, though.

† This contraption must have sat in Terry's bedroom alongside his Magic Robot. 'Well, we all had one, didn't we?' as Terry said in a 1987 speech at Beccon, referring to the legendary 1950s robotic quizmaster, with his boxy metal head and limbs, who, by the miracle of magnetism, would whirl and direct his pointer at the correct answer to ANY question asked of him, as long as it was one of the ones on the board. 'And when we got fed up with the smug way he spun around on his mirror getting all the right answers,' Terry went on, 'we cut them out and stuck them down differently for the sheer hell of it. Gosh, weren't we devils?'

'Home-brew R1155', they joined the Chiltern Amateur Radio Club, who met weekly in a public hall five miles up the road in High Wycombe.

In the February 1962 issue of the Wycombe Technical High School magazine, *Technical Cygnet*, the notes for Form 3C give 'Pratchett' a nod for this interest, declaring him to be 'a very keen radio enthusiast' who 'owns his own amateur receiver'.* But, of course, as Terry would insist, all this was going on elsewhere rather than as part of a flourishing and varied school life. In a photo taken at a Chiltern Amateur Radio Club meeting in 1962 or 1963, Terry beams out from under a floppy fringe in the middle of a large group of grown men in ties, jackets and cardigans. Among his Technical School classmates, however, he seems to have been less clubbable: he was a bookworm, clearly, but when his head was out of a book he was smart and given to sharp comments or surreal improvisations, slightly alienating, a little difficult to befriend, something of a loner – in Terry's own formulation, 'a bit weird'. Mick Rowe recalls how he and Terry would gravitate towards each other for conversations at break times. Terry had his 'mouthful of speech impediments', as he referred to it, and Mick a stutter. 'Subliminally, we may have bonded as fellow sufferers of a speech disorder,' Mick suggested, 'but we never discussed it.' They certainly shared a maverick, beyond-the-curriculum interest in their favourite subjects – Terry's in creative writing, Mick's in metalwork.† Terry drew caricatures of Mick hammering at an anvil, and presented them to him along with a typewritten draft of a satirical sci-fi story called 'Hail, Analogue', on which he sought Mick's opinion. He also gave him a detailed map he had drawn: 'The Isle of Doodles'. 'It was as though he already knew he needed to lay down a territory where his stories could be enacted,' Mick said. The pair of them often discussed Terry's idea for an all-embracing volume called 'The Book of All Known Facts'. 'It came up again and again. Would *this* get

. . . .

*   Indeed – an army-surplus D-65 HRO communications receiver with a giant black and silver dial at its centre, sourced by Terry's dad in *Exchange & Mart* and capable of eavesdropping on every station in Europe.

†   Michael Rowe was the first student at Wycombe Technical High to take metalwork to A level. He became Professor of Metal Art & Design Jewellery at the Royal College of Art in London.

into the book? Would *that* get into the book?' But they never went to each other's houses. If there were closer friendships formed at school, Terry never spoke about them. For a few years here, as Terry tended to paint it, he was more comfortable making things at home with his dad, or crafting things entirely alone, than rubbing along with his classmates.

However, that Terry wasn't entirely a disengaged oddball lingering awkwardly on the fringes of school life is suggested by his appointment as 3C's 'form representative', his widely lauded, lisp-defying performances in the debating society, somewhat later in his school career, which we will come to, and eventually, in the Lower Sixth, by his promotion to the giddy heights of deputy librarian – a minor role in the school's power network, it would appear, and one which mostly seems to have gained Terry the doubtful privilege of staying behind after school on Thursdays in order to do cataloguing or repair damaged books, wherein Terry's skills with the glue and Sellotape, carefully cultivated at Beaconsfield Branch Library, could come into their own again. Still, his perceived fitness for the role suggests that Terry didn't exist entirely outside the warm regard of the school's authorities.

And then there was his relationship with the teachers. Readers of *Mort*, Terry's 1987 Discworld novel, will remember how Mr Keeble, the job broker, tries to find new employment for Death who, being essentially a skeleton in a cloak, doesn't automatically present well at interview. 'It would seem that you have no useful skill or talent whatsoever,' Mr Keeble says. 'Have you thought of going into teaching?' It's a broad swipe – too broad, of course, which is partly where the humour lies. Yet asked by a reader one time whether that line came 'from the heart', Terry replied, without pausing, 'It certainly came from the brain.'

One might assume from such a sentiment that Terry had it tough from the staff at Wycombe Technical High. And it's true that there were disciplinarians among his teachers who were quick to anger – the throwers of chalk, and indeed, more recklessly, of wooden-backed blackboard rubbers. For Terry and his classmates, the flinging of a blackboard rubber was a corrective tactic common enough that they had given it its own name: 'incurable brain damage'. Terry himself never seems to have come under enraged bombardment with the classroom equipment, but he was in the room when one of the most ruthless of his masters allegedly beat a boy ('a likeable lad with a grin like an air raid siren', Terry reported) so hard with the boy's own T-square that it broke – causing the teacher to put the hapless pupil in detention for a week in the woodwork shop until he had made a new one.

'Oddly enough, I don't think there were many hard feelings,' Terry wrote. But then, up to a point, corporal punishment was merely expected in those days: if you had read your William books or your Billy Bunter stories, or if you had only leafed through the pages of Beano and Dandy, you would have grown accustomed to the idea of schools as places where the cane was as much a part of the furniture as the desks and the canteen tables. This fact enabled Terry for the rest of his life to depict school as a forbidding place, 'a survival course' through which the more sensitive child, such as himself, was condemned to drag his anxious limbs.

Even then, though, Terry would concede that there were teachers who clearly loved their subjects and reached out to their pupils to teach them assiduously, without the application of violence or the misapplication of blackboard rubbers, and whom he remembered, accordingly, 'with some fondness'. These included, Terry admitted, 'the science teacher who loaned me Darwin's *Origin of Species*, fortuitously the day before I fell prey to a terrible bout of flu. Notwithstanding, I read through it doggedly because it all made sense, it *really* did.' And Terry was fond enough of his history teacher, Stan Betteridge, to make someone of that name a member of the Guild of Historians in Ankh-Morpork in the Discworld fable *The Last Hero*. Furthermore, while he was taking Terry for technology lessons, Mr Stibbons probably did not imagine that he would one day, in a parallel, flat world, ascend to the role of Head of Inadvisably Applied Magic at Unseen University, having assumed the form of the well-liked wizard Ponder Stibbons.*

* *

* We first meet Ponder Stibbons as a student in *Moving Pictures* (1990) and we should note that he was one of the few wizards in the Unseen University who was regarded as having his head anywhere near screwed on.

However, once again, in a repeat of the fate of H. W. Tame at Holtspur Primary, the headmaster of Wycombe Technical High School, as the institution's ultimate authority figure, was doomed to occupy a permanent place in Terry's personal pantheon of villains. Harry Ward, who arrived in the school at more or less the same time as Terry, seems from time to time to have put Terry in mind of Arthur Lowe playing Captain Mainwaring in *Dad's Army* – a comically thwarted figure, in other words, rather than a cruel and exacting tyrant. But that was before they crossed each other. After that, Terry had another role in mind for the head: Harry Ward was doomed, in *The Last Hero*, to become Evil Harry Dread – a piece of delayed literary vengeance, it would seem, for a blazing row that Ward had with Terry over (and this is a detail which we will probably have no choice but to label 'very Terry') the *Encyclopaedia Britannica*.

Specifically, it was over the old, battered 24-volume edition of the *Encyclopaedia Britannica* in the school library which the passing of time, plus many years of consultation by the students of Wycombe Tech, who weren't always gentle with the bindings and didn't always have clean hands, had rendered obsolete. Or so thought Mr Ward, who one morning had all 24 volumes taken off the shelves and dumped in one of the school's industrial-waste skips.

Upon discovering this act of cultural vandalism – vandalism which had taken place while his back was turned, on his own patch – the deputy librarian was incensed. The destruction of any book was, to Terry's mind, an unconscionable desecration, but the destruction in particular of the *Encyclopaedia Britannica* . . . well, that was an offence against, literally, everything we know. As deputy librarian – and also simply as Terry – he could not stand idly by and allow this barbarism to go unchecked.

Accordingly, Terry retrieved all 24 of those volumes from the skip, returned with them to the library and then allegedly, over the course of the next week, devoted his breaktimes, lunch-hours and free periods to mending the books and restoring them to a serviceable condition. Terry told me, in all sincerity, how proud he was of that work when it was finished – as good a job of book restoration, he reckoned, as he had ever turned his hand to. He imagined that Mr Ward would look upon these labours and have no option but to praise him for his ingenuity and craftsmanship, not to mention his fashion-forward commitment to recycling, and admit that his own decision to dump the sum of human knowledge on the grounds that some of it was a bit dog-eared had been premature.

But no. On confronting the rejuvenated *Encyclopaedia Britannica*, Mr Ward saw only insubordination and had the whole lot removed to the skip again. At which point Terry (and this probably *was* insubordinate, to be fair) again decided to liberate the books and return them once more to the library. And during that liberation, in the most colourful of Terry's renditions of this tale, a kind of chase scene ensued, with Terry haring away from the skip in the direction of the library, clutching at least one and possibly several volumes of the *Encyclopaedia Britannica*, and with a furious and presumably red-faced headmaster in hot pursuit.*

Whether or not this caper element of the story is true, it was certainly the case that Mr Ward eventually hunted Terry down, gave him the worst telling off he had ever endured and removed him from the list of prospective prefects.† And it's also true that Terry, who despised irrational abuses of power as much as he despised anything, held a glimmering resentment about this episode for the rest of his life, along with a lingering contempt for the school system.

Still, it was undoubtedly within that school system, rather than in spite of it, that Terry got his first break as a writer. He was soaking up so much from all that reading he was doing that it was inevitable that some of it would begin leaking out into his compositions for English. Perhaps the earliest evidence of this process in action was when Terry produced

. . . .

* Add your own brandished cane and cries of 'Come back here, boy!' and 'Why, you . . .' to taste.

† Terry, in his notes towards an autobiography, explained that he regarded the role of prefect as 'a Quisling position, handed down from the occupying forces of the headmaster: in reality, this heady power consisted largely of being able to report boys who ran in the corridors and other transgressions of that nature, and was as useful as a rubber spanner.' Yet, however token, the position would have been his by default as acknowledgement of his role in running the library, so he could regard himself as having been unfairly and maliciously thwarted.

a Jane Austen fantasy pastiche, which featured Orcs attacking a vicarage. Alas, no trace of that possibly epochal piece survives, nor the teacher's response to it, although Terry always claimed this bold, and one might almost say reckless bringing-together of genres earned him some kudos from his amused classmates, and you can see why it might have done.

What do survive, however, are five pieces of Terry's creative writing, done, similarly, as English exercises, in various years at Wycombe Technical High, including one he produced at the age of fourteen which proved to be pivotal.

One day, with the English master off sick, the school's Technical Drawing and Art teacher, Janet Campbell-Dick (the only female teacher in the school, known affectionately to everyone as 'Mrs C-D'), stood in for the lesson and gave the class the task of composing a short story. Terry set to and came up with a piece of writing which he titled 'Business Rivals'.

Herein, the Devil, materializing on earth loudly in a puff of sulphurous smoke, visits a successful advertising agency executive called Crucible and asks him to put together a campaign for Hell, on the grounds that business has dried up a little down there in the last two thousand years, besides a visit from Dante, and they're having trouble putting bums on seats. Crucible complies, Hell booms, Satan prospers, Crucible grows rich. Orpheus and Cerberus are fleetingly, and jokingly, alluded to. Along the way there are pastiches of adverts for dog food and cigarettes, given a suitably hellish twist. Ultimately there is comeuppance and divine intervention, of a sort, in the form of thunder and blinding light in a denouement in which, along the way, a bust of Charles Darwin gets shattered.

The piece is loud, showy, precocious, and altogether rather remarkable. 'It was by no means a great story,' Terry conceded, 'but it was certainly the best one written in the schoolroom that day.'

Mrs C-D agreed. She gave Terry 20 out of 20 for it and showed it to the returning English teacher who put the piece forward for the school magazine. 'Business Rivals' duly appeared in *Technical Cygnet*'s December 1962 edition, a tale of hellish depravity bylined, rather sweetly, 'T. Pratchett 3C'.

Terry was to write four more stories which made it into the pages of *Technical Cygnet*: 'Look for the Little – Dragon?', 'The Searcher', 'The Picture' and 'Solution', the blue-ink draft of which, for some reason, is found in Terry's Economic History exercise book, overlaid with pencil drawings of bats and mushrooms. Those stories would be variously bylined 'T. Pratchett, 5A' and 'T. Pratchett L6A'.

But it was 'Business Rivals' by T. Pratchett 3C that stood out – and stood out far enough that Terry could conceive an audacious plan to tout the story to the wider world and see what happened. Was he egged to do this by his teachers, his mother, or his peers? Or did he decide to do so entirely off his own bat? It's not clear. Perhaps all of those individual forces nudged him along in some way. In any event, Terry, having carefully composed an accompanying letter, sent a copy of the pages from *Technical Cygnet* to the office of John Carnell, who, as Terry well knew from his trawlings in The Little Library, was the editor of both *New Worlds Science Fiction* and *Science Fantasy*.

This unsolicited submission was, it goes without saying, a long shot. Both *New Worlds* and *Science Fantasy* were in a position to draw from an extensive roster of already published and celebrated sci-fi authors, British and American, and neither publication explicitly declared itself to be in the market for schoolwork, whether from people in 3C or anywhere else. Consequently, Terry can't have been all that surprised when, a month later, an envelope arrived at 25 High Riding containing his story, returned to him.

However, the story was accompanied by a letter from Carnell, who clearly felt he had happened upon something and that this matter should be pursued a little further. 'He suggested a few alterations,' Terry wrote, 'and said I should do another draft.' Terry did as requested, working on the piece at home in the evenings after school. The story received a tauter opening and grew in length. When he was satisfied with it, he enlisted, with the help of his ever-watchful mother, a friend of the family who owned a typewriter to tap out the new, handwritten draft and he resubmitted it.

Carnell, openly acknowledging in an editorial the undeniable truth that the story was 'not perfectly written by any means', nevertheless placed 'The Hades Business'* in *Science Fantasy*, Volume 20, Number 60, the issue that came out in August 1963. And Terry, who had now turned fifteen, was suddenly a published author.

As well as giving it a warm mention in his editorial, Carnell introduced the story with an above-the-title editor's note in italic: 'While we often receive material from would-be young writers, we seldom find a story from one of them which merits publication – remembering, however, that writers like Ray Bradbury and our own John Brunner first broke into print at the age of seventeen, we are always on the lookout – hence, Terry Pratchett this month, who is even younger and shows great promise for the future.'

On the back of a piece conceived and written at the age of fourteen, Terry now found himself in heady company. *Science Fantasy* may have had a relatively small circulation (around 5,000), but it was the home, as Carnell mentioned, of Bradbury and Brunner, and also of sci-fi scions such as J. G. Ballard and Thomas Burnett Swann. Terry's name appears on the contents page next to that of Mervyn Peake, already famous as the author of the Gormenghast books, who has a short story in the same issue and is himself the subject of an appreciation, beginning on page 53, by Michael Moorcock. Soon after this the magazine would start publishing stories by Brian Aldiss, Keith Roberts and James Blish, all writers that Terry admired and drew inspiration from, and, as a result of this monumentally early breakthrough, could consider himself as sharing turf with. This was a resounding vote of confidence for a young schoolboy to receive. And at the first attempt.

For his first completed sale of a work of fiction, Terry received a cheque for £14. That would be the equivalent, in 2021, of about £250 – a by no means negligible lump of spending money for a fifteen-year-old. It was a very early lesson that fiction, like crime, pays – although only if you get it right. Terry wisely decided to invest his new wealth in a second-hand typewriter, a stout, loudly clattering, British-built

....

* It's not clear whether the decision to retitle the story in a more arresting manner was Terry's or Carnell's.

Imperial 58. With that on his desk at home, he could not only look like a proper writer, he could sound like one, too. His mother, meanwhile, looking on at these developments and always capable of identifying a learning opportunity, signed Terry up for a course of touch-typing lessons at the house of a private tutor in Beaconsfield, reasoning, it seems, that if her son was getting mad ideas in his head about wanting to be a professional writer, he might at least acquire a skill that could be repurposed in the real world when it all inevitably went wrong.

Terry, meanwhile, took to his Imperial 58 almost immediately to fire off a letter to the editor of *Vector*, that journal of the British Science Fiction Association which had attracted his curiosity in The Little Library. In a recent issue of that publication, in an article titled 'Science Fiction in Schools', Ron Bennett, a fanzine editor who also taught English Literature, had argued that, contrary to the prevailing scornful thinking, there was no reason why science fiction shouldn't feature in the curriculum or be deemed suitable as work for the imagination in composition exercises. Deferentially signing himself 'Master Terry Pratchett', the fifteen-year-old Terry wrote in to agree. 'I think Ron Bennett's pupils are dead lucky in having a Master who is interested in Science Fiction,' he observed. 'All we get at my school are the same old dreary titles "My Pets" or "A Day at a Railway Station".'*

Clearly, despite the enthusiastic endorsement of his 'Business Rivals' story by the school magazine and the acclaim and the typewriter that it had already earned him, Terry could still feel himself to be operating without the blessing of the establishment and in the face of a general snootiness about his favourite kind of fiction. This would certainly not be the last time he had that perception. Meanwhile, beneath the letter, the editor of *Vector* gently and quite fairly pointed out that both the titles 'My Pets' and 'A Day at a Railway Station' would happily lend themselves to sci-fi treatments if you used the right kind of pet, the right kind of railway station and the right kind of day. More for Terry to ponder.

. . . .

* Terry's letter appeared in the September 1963 issue of *Vector*.

In the same publication, Terry would soon be staring longingly at adverts for the next annual UK National Science Fiction Convention, for which tickets were about to go on sale. It was going to be taking place in Peterborough over the Easter weekend of 1964, and it seemed to be promising talks, readings, stalls, appearances by famous authors . . . He would have loved more than anything to have gone and to have mingled with the like-minded people he was sure he would find there – mingle with them, indeed, as a published author, albeit a startlingly young one. But that would involve setting off on his own to stay in a hotel for three nights, and realistically his mother would be more likely to let him ride a muddy motorbike round and round the sitting room of an evening than allow him to do that.

That said, maybe he could try to persuade her.

4

ABSENT WAFFLES, PIPE SMOKERS AND AN OUTBREAK OF FELT-TIP NIPPLES

Writing for the May issue of *Vector* magazine, Jim Groves declared the 1964 UK National Science Fiction Convention to have been 'the best I have yet attended'. The only dark spot on an otherwise unblemished occasion, in that reporter's opinion, was the presence of 'a few "herberts" who apparently get their kicks by screaming up and down the corridors'.

Who can he possibly have meant? Not registrant number 85, Terry Pratchett, we can be sure. Not T. Pratchett of 5A in his jacket and tie – still a month shy of his sixteenth birthday and coming up to his O level exams. Not Master Terry Pratchett of 25 Upper Riding, Beaconsfield, who had only recently and extremely narrowly won a protracted argument with his mother regarding his attendance at this convention, chiefly by selling it to her as an entirely anodyne, serious-minded and indeed virtually *academic* proposition – indeed, practically, for an ambitious published author such as himself, a jobs fair.

Not that Terry hadn't been, shall we say, *around* while the herberts did their herberting. He was certainly aware that, in the small hours of that weekend, packs of sci-fi fans had roamed the two upstairs floors of the Bull Hotel in Peterborough, clanking rhythmically on bottles and chanting a message for attendees who were long abed, but not necessarily with their partners: 'Go back to your wives! Go back to your wives!'

And he had certainly heard the tale of the drunken late-night party in somebody's over-stuffed room which was finally interrupted by an angry pounding on the door.

'Do you know what time it is?' a voice in the corridor had shouted.

'Yes,' came the helpful reply. 'It's twenty to three.'

He had heard about all of that, and found it amusing enough. But was he at the forefront of it – in the thick of the herberty action? It appears not.

And as for the incident that we'll come to shortly, where Terry and another delegate innocently walked into the room of a published sci-fi author and caught him *in flagrante* with another registrant . . . Well, yes, that really had been an eye-opener for all concerned, but at the same time accidents happen, and maybe the published sci-fi author in question should have been more careful to lock the door.

The truth is that although mischief was definitely got up to at the 1964 UK National Science Fiction Convention, and although herberts were most certainly at large, Terry, at fifteen – and this can't be overstressed – was in Peterborough that Easter for one thing and for one thing only: the sci-fi.

He went alone, knowing nobody – but at the same time with the advantage of knowing that people would know *him*. At any rate, he knew that if he dropped into conversations the detail that he was the author of a story that had been published the previous summer in *Science Fantasy*, this would handily place him straight away among this particular company, and even grant him some kudos. And him just fifteen, too! He had a calling card.

So, on Good Friday in 1964, Terry got off a train in Peterborough and walked confidently from the station to The Bull, a two-star hotel in the centre of the town, next door to the Golden Heather Buttery. The previous Eastercon had been held at this venue, too, opening an unmissable opportunity for the organizers to christen this year's event 'RePetercon'. Terry made his way to the convention registration desk – a table with hand-painted paper draped over it. On the wall behind it a 12-foot papier-mâché and card mural depicted an underwater scene with a sub-marine, rocks, a shark and a treasure-filled sea trunk – themed in tribute to the convention's Guest of Honour, E. C. 'Ted' Tubb. Terry gave his name at the desk and was issued with his badge – an orange disc featuring a drawing of a spaceman availing himself of a jet-pack to blast skywards. Except that the badges were late arriving, so a growing cluster of registrants sat around in reception for a while and waited.* A member of the Liverpool contingent, spotting a captive audience, put on a tape-recorded sci-fi play they had made entitled *The March of Slime*.

There were 120 registrants like Terry, making, with speakers and guests, a gathering of around 150 in all – too many for the Bull Hotel alone to accommodate, so some attendees found themselves decamping up the road to The Angel. In attendance was a large group from London, and an even larger quorum from Birmingham (instantly nicknamed 'the Easter Brummies'), plus the aforementioned Liverpool contingent, who had gone to the trouble of making and distributing 'quote cards' around the venue for the attendees to find once they had checked in – tucked into picture frames, slipped under beer mats, wedged into the towel-dispensers in the lavatories. Written on them were conversation openers, ranging from the more or less straightforward ('You don't like Weetabix', 'You can't spell amateur') via the openly flirtatious ('You have sexy feet'), to the outright surreal ('You have eyes in your hair and are frightened by crippled moths', 'You played with spaghetti in a Hieronymus machine', 'You appreciate the turgid turmoil of a torn soul').

All of which, in addition to the opportunistic early broadcasting of *The March of Slime*, could strongly imply that the fifteen-year-old Terry had just plunged himself into the middle of some kind of sixties 'happening'. And, true enough, there was a strong core of young fans and writers present – agitators for science fiction's 'new wave', with their taped plays and their home-made sci-fi cine films ready for the scheduled Saturday afternoon screening session, and, indeed, with their scattered quote cards

. . . .

* When the badges did arrive, there was no means for people to attach them to themselves. Easy oversight.

('You slobber'). And yet also present in even greater numbers were representatives of the old school – veteran sci-fi writers and long-time aficionados, predominantly male, suited or in tweed sports jackets and cardigans, some of whom were war veterans and many of whom, in between sessions as the weekend unfolded, were to be found seated round tables in the bar or on the hotel landings, playing cards and smoking pipes.

A snapshot of a moment in time, then: it's 1964, a national 'youthquake' is underway, the Beatles and the Stones are in the charts (Peter and Gordon have just ended 'Can't Buy Me Love's month in the top spot and 'Not Fade Away' is holding steady at number eight) and a general unbuttoning is taking place – but not everywhere and not really at the 15th BSFA Convention in the Bull Hotel, Peterborough, where the vast majority of attendees are, like Terry, wearing ties.

In the notes towards his autobiography, Terry issued the following advisory regarding the eventually 'swinging' sixties, in particular as they affected High Wycombe and its environs: 'Don't believe everything you read. In the UK the sixties happened to about 250 people in the vicinity of Carnaby Street who did wonderful things with Mars Bars while the world watched, or at least, while the police did. The rest of us listened to the music while doing our homework.' Terry's conclusion was that 'on the whole the sixties didn't come to me until around, oh, the seventies.' And they certainly didn't come to him in Peterborough, at Eastercon 1964.

What did come to him on that occasion, however, was a meeting with Dave Busby. Impressively tall, thin and with dark curly hair, Dave had arrived from Wokingham on a Lambretta, frozen practically solid by an icy end-of-March wind and wearing a helmet, goggles and a grey suit with, over it, a Gannex raincoat of the type forever associated with Harold Wilson. Also like Harold Wilson, Dave smoked a pipe. Unlike Wilson, he was seventeen and set to be Terry's close friend for the rest of his life.[*]

....

[*] By contrast, in 1964, Harold Wilson, who would be Prime Minister that October, was the grand old age of 48. Dave's premature pipe-adoption was a source of 'hilarity' for Terry, according to Dave.

These two seem to have latched on to each other very quickly – probably during the first evening's 'meet and greet' session, a drawn-out affair at which a long list of attendees were invited to stand and say a few words about themselves while a committee member at the front helpfully held up signs saying 'SILENCE' and 'APPLAUSE'. Dave and Terry clearly had a lot in common. Not height, perhaps. And not age either, really, Dave being the best part of two years older than Terry at a time in their lives when a gap that size could seem gulf-like. But in this case the gap was irrelevant because they shared so many other things, not least the experience of provincial sci-fi fandom. Dave, too, had optimistically twirled the plastic book-carousels in small-town shops in the unpromising hunt for sci-fi treasure among the bodice-rippers and garish true crime tales. Dave, too, knew the intellectual unease of publicly declaring yourself a sci-fi aficionado and being met not with warm recognition but a look of horror or, worse, of sympathetic embarrassment.

And Dave, too, had started writing fiction. A month after Terry's 'The Hades Business' had appeared in *Science Fantasy*, 'No Ending' by David Busby had found a home in another John Carnell-edited publication, *New Worlds* (September 1963). They were two published authors, then, with a precociously early breakthrough behind them, and both of them were looking for a kindred spirit which they quickly found in each other.

In each other – but not necessarily in the rest of the convention. And that was something else that Terry and Dave shared: a certain kind of ironic detachment that, for all their passionately sincere fandom, tended to transport them to the edge of things, from where they could look on with a slightly arched eyebrow and a ready supply of teenage cynicism. This attitude they could indulge to the hilt in Peterborough, to their mutual glee, peering askance at some of the gaucheness surrounding them, alert to all traces of undue seriousness and pomposity, making it very clear to everybody else that they were in it, but not entirely of it.

Back in 1957, the great J. G. Ballard had been persuaded to attend a sci-fi convention – the 15th Worldcon, held at the King's Court Hotel in London. He swore he would never do so again. 'It's possible he resented the clique-ish atmosphere,' wrote John Baxter in his biography of Ballard, 'with old hands such as John Wyndham, Sam Youd, Tedd Tubb and even the teetotal Arthur C. Clarke clustering in the bar, discussing everything except science fiction. Nor would he have relished the fans in costume, waving raygun-like water pistols and sporting beanie caps topped with a propellor.'[*]

Either way, Ballard left after one evening and later claimed that the experience had left him unable to write anything whatsoever for a whole year afterwards.

'We were closer to Ballard's attitude,' said Dave. 'We were amused, but disapproving.' So, for example, there was the traditional costume contest on the Saturday night with prizes. Somebody came as a space rocket, somebody else as a nurse, but the prize for 'Most Authentic SF Outfit' went to Ian and Betty Peters from London who turned up as Fafhrd and the Grey Mouser from the stories of Fritz Leiber. It did not occur to Terry or Dave to costume up; it did occur to them to turn cold at the prospect. Dave thinks they might have performed a high-minded pass, too, on the Saturday-night performance by skiffle group The Bellyflops (lead vocalist and harmonica player, Michael Moorcock).

'The would-be writers,' Dave said, 'like myself, Terry, Chris Priest *et al.*, wanted only to have earnest conversations about writing, SF, science, society, the future of the world . . .'

There was plenty of scope for that over the weekend, between the skiffle and the dressing-up and the corridor-roaming. Brian Aldiss, alas for Terry, was not present for consultation – summoned on business to Yugoslavia, apparently. But there was a panel discussion: 'Does Fandom Need Science Fiction?'. E. C. 'Ted' Tubb, as advertised and celebrated in the lobby in papier mâché, spoke, read and took questions. Wally Weber had flown in from Seattle. The American husband-and-wife writing team Edmond Hamilton and Leigh Brackett were on hand to discuss the advantages and perils of being an American husband-and-wife

. . . .

[*] *The Inner Man: The Life of J. G. Ballard*, by John Baxter, 2011.

writing team.* On the Sunday, an event was organized to celebrate Nova Publications and John Carnell and his support for young writers, to which both Terry and Dave were in a position to attest.

And then, perhaps most valuable of all, there were the conversations that it was possible to fall into between the events. Archie Mercer, a figure on the sci-fi fan scene since the fifties, seems to have buttonholed Terry at one point to talk about 'The Hades Business'. He put it to Terry that, on the evidence of that story, he had to be an Oliver Anderson fan, and Terry confirmed that he was. And then, as Dave Busby looked on, Mercer and Terry began to discuss their passionate attachment to a book that Dave had never heard of, called *The Lord of the Rings*. ('It was clearly part of Terry's DNA by then,' said Dave, who was never to be persuaded by Tolkien, 'and it remained so.')

'It sounds theatrical,' Dave said, 'but there was a feeling then amongst all of us that we were rather special. We were in touch with the future, the possessors in some sense of secret knowledge. The internet, pandemics, climate change, manned space travel, artificial intelligence . . . these things were the currency of our conversation when we came together back then. And we weren't discussing their likelihood, we were discussing their timeline. We knew these things were on the way and we considered ourselves a part of it all.'

True, there were more down-to-earth strands of conversation, too, such as how much John Carnell was paying for a thousand words and how, exactly, one broke into the US market where they seemed to pay ten times more. But even these grubbier considerations didn't alter the sense a convention-goer could have of themselves as part of, as Dave put it, 'an invisible sect whose devotees were like secret agents, emerging occasionally at conclaves as if part of a subversive conspiracy'.

'If this all sounds a bit snooty and pretentious,' Dave added, 'that's because in those days Terry and I *were* a bit snooty and pretentious.'

. . . .

* As a screenwriter with credits on the Bogart/Bacall movie *The Big Sleep* and the Hawks/ Wayne film *Rio Bravo* (and eventually on Robert Altman's *The Long Goodbye*), Leigh Brackett would have had some claim to be regarded as the most distinguished writer gracing the convention, though one senses that it wasn't quite framed that way.

So it would have been entirely in pursuit of enlightening conversation that Terry and Dave went looking one evening for an author with whom they had newly acquainted themselves, opened the door of his hotel room and found him naked on the bed, accompanied by someone else, also naked, and very much not occupied in discussing the future of the world.

The woman looked at the two intruders levelly and said, 'Do you mind?' Terry and Dave turned and left.

As the convention drifted to a slightly bleary end on the Sunday evening, E. C. Tubb and others, possibly in a state of advanced refreshment, organized an impromptu 'humming and swaying' ritual – a pagan rite which involved the mock slaughter and then reanimation of a virgin girl, a role filled, apparently perfectly happily and with unscripted giggling, by a delegate called Nell Goulding. Meanwhile, a roomful of other delegates closed their eyes and hummed and swayed to order. According to a report of this moment written for a fanzine by Charles Platt, 'Mike Moorcock didn't help when he . . . slipped and fell over amidst the sound of breaking glass, and E. C. Tubb in shirt sleeves, a bottle in one hand and a glass in the other, did not exactly add to the tone of the ceremony.'

'The hum and sway was actually quite strange,' Dave said. 'Both Terry and I talked about it over the years, remembering it as an almost hypnotic happening, like the ritual of some bizarre cult.'

The next morning, Terry, his overnight bag weighed down with magazines and fanzines and paperbacks acquired at the convention bookstall, caught the train back to Beaconsfield. And shortly after that he went back to school.

★ ★ ★ ★ ★

In May, when *Vector* 26 arrived in the post, containing Jim Groves's report on the 1964 Eastercon and, for the first time in the history of this rudimentary publication, a set of accompanying black and white photographs, Terry felt another letter to the editor coming on and duly strapped himself in at the Imperial 58.

'Vector' 27* struck me as a rather 'bitty' issue [Terry typed], but since it is the first under new management perhaps it is to be expected. The electro-stencils improved the layout no end; let's have more! The photos were a surprise too; but why did the Guest of Honour appear only once, in the back-background of one photo?

'It *was* rather unfortunate that Ted Tubb didn't appear in the photo section,' conceded *Vector*'s new editor, Roger Peyton, in his reply below Terry's letter, 'but I was unable to obtain a good photo of him – he was too busy dashing around trying to get people to join the British Science Fiction Association!'

His experiences in Peterborough would continue to occupy Terry's imagination well into the new term at Wycombe Technical High – would go some way, you might even suggest, to eclipsing what school seemed to be offering him at this juncture. He completed his O levels, got his five passes to no particular fanfare, and chose his A level subjects: English, History and Art. But the greater part of his concentration now seemed to be officially elsewhere.

Dave Busby and Terry had left Peterborough vowing to keep in touch and they duly did so. Every fortnight, on a Saturday afternoon, Dave would head over from Wokingham on his Lambretta and visit Terry at home in Beaconsfield, a twenty-mile journey. Dave had been to a middle-class prep school, Holme Grange in Wokingham,† until he was thirteen. But then circumstances at home changed and he found himself transferred to a local secondary, where his interest in schooling and exams swiftly evaporated. He left at fifteen with very little in the way of qualifications but with 'an unbeaten record for low attendance'. Since then he had done a variety of jobs: answering the phone for a taxi company based in a railway yard for £4 a week, going down to £3 a week; in the inspection department of a printed circuit factory; as a printing machine

....

* It was *Vector* 26. *Vector* 27 was the issue in which Terry's letter appeared.

† Its headmaster was John Graves, who was the younger brother of the poet Robert Graves, to whom Terry alluded in his letter to Tolkien.

operator in the warehouse of a women's retail chain. He was worldly by comparison with Terry who now, on Dave's first visit, experienced the mild mortification of seeing his home at 25 Upper Riding and his circumstances through his older visitor's eyes. There was, Terry was newly aware, a considerable amount of orange in the Pratchett décor. On the wall above the fireplace in the sitting room – and somehow more prominent than it had ever been before – was a framed paint-by-numbers picture of a log cabin in a wood. As his eyes took it in on that first visit, Dave could sense Terry slightly squirm with embarrassment.

Not that any of it bothered Dave. The two of them already knew what they had in common, and now the friendship grew. Partly they messed about and filled time, like any other loose-end teenagers. They made tanks out of cotton reels, bits of candle and matches, and waged tank wars. They went outside and flew planes powered by elastic bands. They pored over copies of *Mad*, the US satirical magazine, an item considered so darkly corrupting that Terry had a copy confiscated when he made the mistake of taking it into Wycombe Technical High. But mostly they sat in Terry's tiny bedroom, where cartoons he had drawn decorated the walls, and had long conversations about sci-fi. 'We were proto science fiction writers, talking shop,' Dave said. They showed each other stories they were writing. 'I was a bad one for typos,' Dave admitted, and Terry (who was no one to talk, frankly) apparently got a lot of mileage out of the fact that the phrase 'cheese and wine' had appeared in one of Dave's typescripts as 'cheese and wind'. They shared and discussed the latest things they had found by their favourite writers – Fritz Leiber, Larry Niven, A. E. van Vogt, Keith Roberts. These Saturday conversations could occupy them for hours at a time. Sometimes it would be four in the morning before Dave got back on his scooter and left to return to Wokingham.

What they didn't talk about was Terry's school. His subjects, his schoolwork – those topics simply never arose. It was as if, in Dave's company, Terry had already moved on.

Getting published and attending the Peterborough convention had opened up a little place for both of them in the insular and self-absorbed but nevertheless thrilling world of sci-fi. But when it came to pushing further into that world, Dave had age, transport and independence on his side; Terry, for all that he determinedly failed to mention it, was still a schoolboy and had his mother to contend with. It was one thing, clearly, to convince Eileen of the professional, contact-building advantages of convention attendance. It was another to sell her on the idea of Terry going to a party for sci-fi writers and their friends at Charles Platt's tenement house in Notting Hill. Which is why, when the invitation was there for Terry in February 1965, Eileen – a former Londoner who, rightly or wrongly, would have had a view about Notting Hill and what went on there – put her foot down and Dave went alone.

And so it was that sixteen-year-old Terry missed out on a bohemian, libertarian spectacular, with vodka, hashish and other substances allegedly in evidence, and wild dancing on an upper floor that caused the ceiling above the drinkers on the storey below to bow ominously; and with an appearance by J. G. Ballard, 'the Seer of Shepperton'. Dave, fresh from skittering around the streets of Notting Hill on his Lambretta in search of an off-licence that would sell him Smirnoff, didn't approach this special guest, being overawed by his air of avant-garde intellectual sophistication and feeling gauche by comparison. But he would forever recall standing at a top-storey window, looking down into the dark street and, as if in a scene from an unmade black and white spy film, watching Ballard leave and climb into an Austin A90 Atlantic, a fifties model with an element of Dan Dare futurism about it. Terry, unlike Dave, was no fan of Ballard's writing, but he feasted on these stories, even as he quietly resented missing out on the occasion.

Eventually Dave's slight seniority would start to work to Terry's advantage. Once Eileen had got over her initial suspicion of his middle-class vowels, and realized that he was fundamentally sensible despite the Lambretta, she could regard Dave as a trustworthy chaperone for her son. Accordingly, a couple of months after the Notting Hill party, Terry relatively easily secured permission to attend the 1965 Eastercon, held at the Midland Hotel in Birmingham. By comparison with Peterborough, the convention felt a little flat. The turnout was low – just 70 people. Indeed, it was so low that the costume prize, for which Terry and Dave again had less than no intention of competing, could not be awarded.

However they met, and felt a certain amount of condescension coming from, John Brunner, a decade and a half their senior and altogether smoother than your average sci-fi writer, with his goatee beard and predilection for white cable-knit polo necks. Did he actually smoke using a long cigarette holder, or did they add that detail later? Either way, it would have seemed in keeping.

And they met, at last, Brian Aldiss, who was kind to them and who on these occasions seemed to have a kind of double act going with his fellow Brummy Harry Harrison. Terry and Dave themselves would quickly develop a reputation in these circles as a duo: Terry, the impish and impudent one, Dave the lanky straight man, both of them affecting a slightly haughty distance from the fray. Even in Birmingham it had already reached the stage where, if Terry was found alone, people would inevitably say, 'Where's your mate?' and the same if Dave was without Terry. In her convention report, Beryl Henley notes that she met Terry in the course of the weekend and observed him 'doing something incredibly funny in a corner, only I can't remember what'. A photo of the emergent double act in the audience at one of the events in Birmingham shows Terry with his head in a book and, next to him, Dave looking off to one side, more than faintly bored. It may not be entirely insignificant that they are seated in the back row, which is one of the most efficient ways to attend a fan event and express your scepticism about it at the same time.

The duo had certainly – and probably as early as the Peterborough convention – already attracted the attention of Ella Parker, who had black hair, swept back under an Alice band, and horn-rimmed glasses and who ran a kind of sci-fi writers' 'salon' at her home in London – if 'salon' isn't too posh a word for the cake, coffee and wine-fuelled discussion evenings which Parker hosted in her eleventh-floor tower-block flat in the East End of London. Either way, the hostess was impressed enough by Terry and Dave to start inviting them to some of those gatherings and in due course, with Eileen appeased (this would be an important networking opportunity, obviously), the pair would be heading into Marylebone on the train on Friday evenings and then catching the tube across the city to join the group of fifteen or so mostly male writers that Parker had collected up for that week's soirée. On one such evening, Dave remembers

Terry crossing swords with Charles Platt after Terry stated a belief in the fantastical imagination which seemed to stray from the sci-fi orthodoxy. Dave also recalls producing a critique of J. G. Ballard and coming up against Michael Moorcock in an argument about it. 'I know Jim personally,' Moorcock said, clinchingly, at one point – 'A pretty good put-down,' Dave conceded.

'Do you remember Fred?' Terry, quite late in his life, suddenly asked Dave out of the blue one day. Fred was Ella Parker's poor brother who was banished to his bedroom and given strict instructions to remain there while these meetings of minds took place.

One of the reasons that numbers were down for the Eastercon in Birmingham was that members of the sci-fi community were saving themselves and their money for the summer when, for only the second time in its 23-year history, the big one, the World Science Fiction Convention, would descend on London, bringing greater glamour and a higher quotient of recognizable American names. Dave and Terry each paid their 60 shillings, including room, and, on the Bank Holiday weekend of August 1965, checked in to the Mount Royal Hotel in Marble Arch.

Dave's recollections of this event would be for ever impaired by the loss of one whole day to what he described as 'a hangover of epic proportions. Terry reported that when I first emerged my complexion was a hideous green, shading gradually through yellow to merely deathly pale.' It's possible that Dave had taken to strong drink in response to the stress of having appeared on a fan panel in one of the convention's scheduled events on the Saturday afternoon. In a discussion of fanzines and what people felt they had gained from reading and contributing to them, Dave did not hold back. 'I'm not sure the strength of my opinions was entirely welcomed,' he said, having shredded the pretensions of a number of these publications to offer either readers or contributors anything very much at all. Terry sat in the audience, royally amused.

Still, it was all a significant step up from Peterborough and Birmingham in terms of the accommodation and the standard of the hotel food. Not that all the guests were satisfied. Terry and Dave were enormously pleased to overhear the American writer James Blish complain bitterly at the breakfast buffet over the lack of waffles. Thereafter, 'Waaaaaffles,' said loudly and plaintively in an American accent, became one of the pair's catchphrases.

It was also at the Worldcon that Terry found himself at an adjacent urinal to Arthur C. Clarke and gained, as we have mentioned before, the lasting realization that even greatness must relieve itself in public from time to time. However, there was a possibly even more levelling moment subsequent to this, when Terry and Dave eavesdropped on a conversation that Clarke was having, most likely with a journalist, on the subject of his writing – and promptly concluded that it was the most pretentious exchange they had ever heard.

Back in the room, Clarke gave a talk titled 'How I Learned to Stop Worrying and Love Stanley Kubrick', during which he spoke about a new collaboration between himself and that film director. The initial working title for this project had been *Journey Beyond the Stars* but they had just had a better idea: *2001: A Space Odyssey*. It sounded promising. Clarke also brought with him a nail allegedly from HMS *Bounty*, of eighteenth-century mutiny fame, and a piece of heat shield from a Mercury spacecraft, and he held them up in order to make the point emphatically that only two hundred years separated these two items and that both technology and the future crept up on you fast.*

In other events, the now familiar battle lines were drawn. Harry Harrison featured on a panel with the title 'SF: The saviour of the modern novel', and boldly argued that the non-sci-fi novel was dead, adding, uncompromisingly, 'Don't be afraid to say that we were right and they were wrong.' And the convention's 'mystery guest' was revealed to be Robert Bloch, the American author of *Psycho*, on which the Hitchcock film is based. Terry wasn't sure the novel was up to much, but Bloch delivered some smart lines that day, referring to Westminster Abbey as 'the poor

* Terry's frequently used version of this time-collapsing trick was to point out that his father, in only slightly different circumstances relating to geography, could very easily have shaken hands with Wyatt Earp.

man's Forest Lawn', announcing that 'relatives run in my family' and declaring, 'I've made my peace with God; he surrendered two weeks ago.'*

As for the kind of riotous behaviour that had been seen in Peterborough and Birmingham, it's possible that the greater grandeur of the Worldcon occasion had a calming effect on at least some of the 'herberts'. But not, clearly, on all of them. Somebody drew nipples in red felt tip on many of the Victorian women depicted in the hotel's freshly hung wallpaper. (The Mount Royal may have regretted timing its refurb to directly precede rather than follow the Worldcon.)

Apparently Christopher Lee made an appearance at some point, but Terry and Dave didn't see him and wouldn't have been impressed if they had. At this point, as far as Terry and Dave were concerned, Lee was the embarrassing face of entirely naff Hammer Film productions and not the revered national treasure that he would become.[†] Similarly, they skirted the convention-closing *Dr Who*-themed event that Penguin Books staged at the Planetarium, at which at least one actual Dalek was present. Daleks and Dr Who were not Terry and Dave's idea of proper science fiction. Those things were for kids.[‡]

It was the end of August. Just as he had done after the Peterborough convention in 1964, Terry went home and then straight back to school. But to say his heart wasn't really in it now would be an understatement. Before the month was out, still only seventeen, he would have abruptly abandoned full-time education and joined Dave in the world of work.

. . . .

* As if it wasn't enough to have your book converted into a classic movie by Alfred Hitchcock, after the rights were secured the director also, apparently, bought every copy of Bloch's *Psycho* that he could find in order to keep as many people as possible from discovering the story. Double win.

† By 2008, when Lee voiced the part of Death for Sky TV's adaptation of *The Colour of Magic*, that shift in the actor's status was long since complete and Terry was more than thrilled to have him on board – and also thrilled when Lee turned up at Terry's 50th birthday party.

‡ Terry remained immune to the appeal of *Dr Who*. Although he loved David Tennant without reservation, the Doctor's conveniently crisis-dissolving 'sonic screwdriver' was, for Terry, a prominent embodiment of the 'with one bound he was free' solution to fictional dilemmas that Terry regarded as a) creakingly old-fashioned and b) an absolute cop-out, imagination-wise.

5

NOVELTY VEGETABLES,
THE MAGISTRATE'S KNICKERS
AND HELL'S OWN SCOOTER

One day in the Chapel, Terry and I were devoting a few hours to making some headway with the mail. This was a task which could frequently match painting the Forth Bridge for circularity, but periodically we would stake out some time and do our best – me reading aloud, Terry dictating his replies.

There were a couple of important ground rules. Rule number one was that any letter arriving which began, 'I have an idea for a story which I really think you could use . . .' would have to be quietly set aside, unheard by Terry. That was no reflection on the likely quality of the story-idea, whether zinger or stinker. It was, however, a reflection on the likely duration and cost of the legal action that might ensue further down the line if the sender of the idea tried to claim that Terry had taken them up on it. For the same reason, any unsolicited package with a covering note beginning, 'I have written a novel set on Discworld which I would love you to read . . .' would be subject to the identical statutory avoidance clause.*

. . . .

* Someone did once claim to have handed Terry the idea for the 1998 novel *The Last Continent*. Unfortunately for the strength of that claim, at the point at which their letter

And rule number two was that anything edible would not be eaten. This edict was set in place following the arrival at the Chapel of a delicious-looking fruit cake which Terry and I had gratefully made short work of one afternoon, washed down with cups of tea. We would have thought nothing more of it, except that, over the next 24 hours or so, both of us independently had the mild but persistent sensation that we were ever so slightly hallucinating. Now, Terry often said the act of imagining things was, for him, sometimes close to hallucinating. But not like this. This was a vague sense of unease accompanied by a slight feeling that things needed to be looked at a little bit harder than normal to be absolutely sure that they were what they seemed to be. What was actually in that fruit cake – apart from fruit and cake – we never found out, for the obvious reason that we had destroyed the evidence. But 'Don't eat fan food' was a precautionary mantra from that day forward.

At one point in this latest mail session, in the absence of edible goods, suspicious or otherwise, I opened and read aloud to Terry a letter from a student journalist who said how much she had always loved Terry's books and added that she was required to interview somebody for her coursework, and if Terry would possibly agree to talk to her, then it would be not only the fulfilment of a long-held ambition, but also extremely useful to her. Terry got a lot of letters of that nature and normally he wrote to wish the sender well with their course and the future, and left it at that. This time, though, he had another idea.

'Is there a phone number on there?'

There was. I passed the letter over and Terry picked up the phone.

'Hello,' I heard him say, crisply. 'This is Terry Pratchett. You want to interview me.'

. . . .

arrived, generously furnishing Terry with the broad notion of an Australian-themed Discworld adventure, Terry's finished manuscript was already at the printers. It often struck me that sending ideas for stories to someone who was famous for having ideas for stories, and whose job, indeed, was to have ideas for stories, was a slightly counter-intuitive thing to do, like sending Paul McCartney a helpful snatch of melody. But people obviously disagreed with me. And maybe people send Paul McCartney helpful snatches of melody, too.

Terry was silent for a little while after this, and listening. From the other side of the room, I tried to imagine the small bomb of panic that he had probably just set off in that poor student's world, and the flap that would now be ensuing. I actually found myself wincing on the girl's behalf. After all, it's one thing to contemplate interviewing a favourite novelist at a mutually agreed juncture, with time to prepare, and another to be cold-called by that novelist in the middle of some random Tuesday.

'OK, then,' Terry said eventually, and matter-of-factly. 'I'll give you the number.'

He did so and then he hung up.

'She said she needed to get her tape machine,' Terry said. 'She's going to call me back.'

We returned to going through the post, but Terry was distracted now, and glancing at his watch. How long could it take a person to find a tape machine? Fifteen minutes passed. There was no return call from the student journalist.

Terry picked up the phone again. Clearly he was not going to let this lie. This student had requested an interview and she was going to damn well get one, whether she wanted it or not.

Terry sat holding the receiver while somewhere in Britain in a student's room the phone rang. And rang. Terry let it ring for a very long time. Then he put the receiver down.

'That's why you'll never see her name on the front page of *The Times*,' he said.

Well, you never know, I guess. She must have stopped wincing at some stage, just as I did. And who knows where her career might have taken her then, once she had fully recovered? But there it was. In all Terry's dealings with journalists, whether student or otherwise, something was always in play: the fact that he was an ex-journalist. He liked that to be known. He liked journalists to be aware that, when it came to journalism, he had paid his dues, and, moreover, that he retained the trade's skills – that he knew why certain questions were being asked, that he understood how lines were taken and how articles got written, and that he knew at least as well as they did how their business worked. It could lend his encounters with journalists who came to interview him down the years a competitive edge – even a combative edge, sometimes. What, he might abruptly ask his interlocutor, were the five defences for defamation of character?* Could they do shorthand? How fast? What about touch-typing?

He liked, in short, to let them know that he *knew their game*. Which he undeniably did.

★ ★ ★ ★ ★

In September 1965, at the beginning of his second year of sixth form and with his thoughts necessarily turning to life beyond school, Terry composed a letter to Arthur Church, the editor of the *Bucks Free Press*. As the local weekly paper, based in High Wycombe, and regally in business since 1856, the *Press* was an institution without which, as Terry put it, 'a sizeable part of south Buckinghamshire, from Amersham to Beaconsfield, through the very heart of High Wycombe itself and across such outlying dependencies as Lacey Green, Loosely Row and, of course, Speen, would not be able to be properly born, married, buried, sentenced in court or feted as the grower of the most humorous turnip in the fruit and vegetable show'. Terry explained to the editor that he would be leaving Wycombe Technical High the following summer having completed three A levels. Was it likely that there would be any jobs going that he could apply for at that point?

It wasn't that Terry had abandoned all thought of being a writer of fiction. On the contrary, as he went back to school that autumn, he was in the process of concluding his second professional sale. Having talked it over with Dave Busby in their continuing weekend get-togethers, Terry had recently finished a short story called 'Night Dweller', written in the first person and taking the form of a captain's log from a craft travelling 40 million miles beyond Pluto. It was a fairly conventional piece of science fiction, dark, meditative and, unusually for Terry,

....

* Truth, honest opinion, publication as a matter of public interest, absolute privilege, innocent dissemination. But I had to look it up.

entirely without jokes. 'Space is an ocean,' it began portentously. 'I remember that now as I watch the armada of blue Nisphers sailing down against the solar wind. They are heading for the sun, to bask safely in the golden shadows. Even they flee from the storm.' Terry submitted the story to Michael Moorcock, who had taken over from John Carnell as the editor of *New Worlds Science Fiction* magazine, and Moorcock accepted it, ultimately running it in the November issue.*

Nevertheless, even while flush with the £14 that John Carnell had paid him for 'The Hades Business', and even with a similar fee just around the corner from Moorcock, Terry had worked out one thing very quickly about writing stories: the number of people who made a living from doing so was vanishingly small. Just looking around the room at those science fiction conventions, he could tell that the writers who were actually and consistently putting food on their tables with their writing were a minority compared with those who either had funding from somewhere else or were broke. Accordingly, it was entirely reasonable to conclude that the three main things you needed in order to become a writer were a facility with words, a well-stocked imagination and another source of income.

For some time Terry had wondered whether that source of income might be librarianship – a perfectly pleasurable prospect as far as he was concerned, indeed the equivalent, he felt, of 'putting a monkey in charge of a banana plantation'. But then the idea of applying to Beaconsfield Branch Library began to give way to the idea of journalism which, Terry reasoned, was quite a lot like writing, with the notable difference that you actually got paid a living wage for doing it. It might not be where his heart really lay, but it seemed, at the very least, an avenue worth exploring.

....

* It would eventually appear over six pages in what was a special edition for new and young writers. Michael Moorcock's editorial note said, 'Terry Pratchett, who made his debut in *Science Fantasy* at the age of 14, publishes his second story (he is now 16), which describes outer space in a new and somewhat poetic light.' Right about the story; wrong about Terry's age. He was fifteen when that issue of *Science Fantasy* came out, and seventeen at this point.

His letter of application to Arthur Church, as Terry was fond of point-ing out, itself contained some promising traces of journalistic skill, 'being accurate without being entirely true'. Yes, as he told Church, he would have *completed* three A levels by the conclusion of the current school year, but how many of them would he have actually passed? Terry could by no means have confidently put a figure on it at this stage. English? Probably. Art? Maybe, although there was a lot of work still to do. History? That one could go either way . . . Anyway, whether or not the editor recog-nized in that sleight of hand the work of a potential journalistic master, or simply because Terry had timed it right, Church wrote back and asked Terry to come and see him in his office.

Church was already a figure of renown at the *Bucks Free Press* – a true newspaper man, and a true *one* newspaper man. Having joined the *Press* as a cub reporter at the age of sixteen, he had already worked there for 37 years by the time Terry walked through his office door, and he would still be writing a column for the paper in 2000, the year before he died at the age of 89. Church's commitment to the cause of local journalism and his belief in its importance were absolute, and he had no time for the argu-ment that local papers were something that journalists 'graduated' from, on their way to the supposedly giddier heights of the nationals. On the contrary, Church considered that, if you were doing it properly, local papers were themselves the pinnacle.

Prominent among the tales Terry told fondly of Arthur Church was the time in 1969 when the editor was instructed by the owners of the *Bucks Free Press* to take advantage of the paper's new colour press by splashing across the front page a view of Earth from the Moon, as sent back by the Apollo mission. Church, who bridled at being given any instruction from above regarding his front pages, and who was certainly not keen to run non-local stories in his paper's precious shop window, responded dryly, 'It's not really in our circulation area.' Eventually, after a long wrangle with his conscience, he could just about persuade himself of the picture's merit as local news, explaining to the news room, 'I sup-pose the moon shines on High Wycombe too.'

Here, seated in front of this Titan of the local paper scene, Terry explained that he had already had a story published in *Science Fantasy* and had just sold another one, and that he could type. Church, who was not noticeably an aficionado of obscure science fiction journals – because 40 million miles beyond Pluto really *was* outside his circulation area – was probably more impressed by the typing than the fiction-writing, although it would quickly turn out that the paper had scope for Terry's talents as a fiction writer, too. Whatever, after a few more questions, Church ultimately told Terry, 'I like the cut of your jib, young man' – thereby becoming, Terry always felt, the last person in Britain ever to use that expression unironically in a conversational setting – and explained that he had a vacancy there and then for an apprentice reporter if Terry wanted to consider it.

A general enquiry about the future had suddenly become something more pressing and Terry now had to go home and set this all out in front of his parents. The good news: he'd been offered a job. The bad news: but only if he abandoned school immediately. The quandary seems momentarily to have divided them. David was unhesitatingly in favour of the idea, as he would have been in favour of anything, Terry realized, which spared his son a life of lying under cars, or similar. But Eileen was troubled, as David was not, by the prospect of Terry not completing his A levels, having come that far. At the same time, the day-release element of his apprenticeship would enable Terry to finish his A level in English, at least, so he *was* continuing his education in a sense. And salaried employment as, eventually, a staff journalist satisfied two of his mother's main criteria, being, if not entirely respectable, then at least a steady and certainly a pensionable occupation. Plus, there was a career path here, wasn't there? There were prospects beyond this two-year apprenticeship. Terry was convinced that it flashed into his mother's mind that, within a decade or two, if he put his mind to it, he could be editing *The Times*. And that *would* be respectable. Or, if not respectable, then certainly grand. Either way, it seems that Eileen, too, came round to the idea eventually.

What never seems to have been discussed was the possibility of Terry finishing his A levels and going on to university to do a degree. There was no precedent for that in the Pratchett family and no feeling, either, that it was a course of action with much to recommend it. A levels at least marked definitively the distinction between blue-collar opportunities and white-collar opportunities, so they were something worth aspiring to in terms of 'getting on'. But tertiary education was, surely, just wasting your time and everybody else's – a step too far. And the truth is that Terry himself, at this point in his life, would not entirely have disagreed. 'I don't believe that university would have been for me,' he wrote in the notes towards his autobiography, adding his sense that 'it would have rolled over the top of me, somehow. On the other hand,' he went on, 'the university of local journalism offered travel, sometimes all the way to Speen, the acquisition of a number of questionable tricks of the trade, education in the nature of humanity and a window onto the commonality of mankind in all its facets.'*

No contest, then. Terry accepted Church's offer, getting his father to go along to the office with him and countersign the indenture forms – 'a medieval-looking document' – because he was still legally a minor. He was also now legally an ex-schoolboy, and to underline the fact, Terry walked into Wycombe Technical High to return his books, experiencing a flush of pride at being in his own clothes on those premises rather than in uniform, which even the sixth formers were obliged to wear in those days. 'Then, for the first and last time, I walked out of the school through the entrance that only the teachers and visitors were allowed to use and went up the road to begin a life of putting words together in their proper order.'

Clearly he did not weep to leave. Did the school, for its part, weep to see him go? There is no record of the headmaster dropping to his knees and pleading with Terry to think again. But there is evidence that his exit was mourned in at least one area of school life: the debating society. Reflecting on his absence in *Technical Cygnet* that winter, the society's secretary lamented that 'the premature departure of Pratchett has meant the loss of one of our great characters' and warmly recalled his performance in a debate from May that year, on the proposition,

. . . .

* The 'commonality of mankind' was an enormously important phrase for Terry and one that we'll have cause to return to.

'This House believes that the Government should bend to the needs of the motorist.' It had been 'one of the most memorable debates of the year', the secretary declared, adding, 'Pratchett rose magnificently to the occasion and put on a performance that the arch Goon Spike Milligan would have found difficult to emulate. It was during this debate that Pratchett added another meaning to the word "autocracy", that is, "government by autos".'

A glowing review, then – the best of Terry's life so far. And it wouldn't by any means be the last time that he was praised for his facility with a pun. But it wasn't enough to make him change his mind.

★ ★ ★ ★ ★

As Terry wrote in his inaugural professorial lecture at Trinity College Dublin: 'The conditions of a trainee newspaper reporter in the mid-sixties were somewhere just above slavery; you could live at home and not be beaten with chains.' Other pluses: you got days off in lieu, although Terry always swore that those turned out, in practice, to be entirely mythical; and you were on a wage of £8 10s per week, which was modest but more, historically, than slaves tended to get.

Still, it's beyond question that the *Bucks Free Press* worked its apprentices hard. Because even local news didn't straightforwardly conform to a nine-to-five schedule, Terry's hours were long, irregular and frequently antisocial – altogether a shock to the system for someone who, only the previous week, had been a schoolboy taking things at his own pace. And then in addition to the landslide of new tasks and challenges coming his way at the paper, on one day each week he would be sent to various colleges for lessons towards his National Council for the Training of Journalists proficiency course, learning the law in relation to newspapers, the workings of local government and, not least, shorthand, 'because,' Terry wrote, 'one day there would be a test of your skills and you would not be allowed to sit it unless you had acquired one hundred words per minute in Pitman's shorthand.' And there were A level studies in English on top of that.

'The newspaper owned me,' Terry would say. 'My life was not my own and it was accelerating very quickly.'

On a Monday morning in late September 1965, wearing what he described as 'a terrible new coat', and 'with the taste of school dinners still in my mouth', Terry had reported for duty at the offices in High Wycombe and had been introduced to his new colleagues. There was George Topley, the chief reporter, 'the best natural journalist I have ever met', Terry maintained. A conscientious man with strong political opinions, Topley boasted the magnificent and almost certainly apocryphal back-story of having, as a young man, stowed away on a boat in the south of England with the intention of travelling to Spain and fighting in the Civil War, only to pick the wrong boat and end up going north to Hull. File, again, under 'too good to check'. 'Arthur Church instilled journalistic ethics into me,' Terry said, 'while George gently taught me that sometimes they were not enough.'

Then there was Johnny Howe, 'the chief, and to tell the truth, the only sub-editor', who was 'blessed with a wonderfully dirty mind' and an extremely well-tuned ear for double entendres, and who proudly shared with Terry the story of a report he had once allowed into print about a streaker at a Women's Institute flower, fruit and vegetable show in which the naked invader was depicted 'causing disarray among the tarts before he was caught by the gooseberries'. Howe was cheerful, short and rotund – so short and rotund that he was, according to Terry, 'only a little way away from being globular'. This distinguished him significantly from Ken 'Bugsy' Burroughs, the *Bucks Free Press* news editor, who was thin and saturnine. 'When the two of them headed off down to the pub at lunchtime,' Terry recalled, 'it looked like the number 10 going for a walk.'

And then there was Alan Hunt, a senior reporter, who was instructed by Arthur Church to take the new boy under his wing and show him how the news-gathering operation worked. After a few days of acclimatization in the office, Hunt eventually took Terry, now tremblingly equipped with a brand new notebook and pen, on his first trip out into the field, whereupon Terry found himself standing in a farmyard and face to face for the first time in his life with a corpse.

Talk about a baptism of fire – or, actually, to be more accurate, a baptism of slurry. All three emergency services were in attendance and the retrieved body had been laid out in the yard. 'Right in front of us,' Terry recalled, 'was a dead man in various colours of nastiness. He had jumped off a tractor in the yard and landed right on top of a well that nobody alive knew was there any more. It had been capped once upon a time with wooden boards which had become one with their surroundings and rotted, so the man, landing heavily, had gone right through and drowned in the mud below.'

Terry's senior guardian professionally busied himself talking to the police and the luckless owner of the farm. 'I, meanwhile, was trying to take it all in while keeping my breakfast down. I wondered who would have to tell his mother, and if he had a girlfriend.' As Terry said, the university of local journalism provided a crash course in life, but it was also clearly offering a subsidiary module in death.

That particular branch of his education continued, once or twice each week, with his duties at the coroner's court, where Terry listened to and queasily took down the coroner's minutely detailed descriptions of a wide range of people's final and frequently sticky moments. Murders were rare – this was south Buckinghamshire, after all, and not the Bronx – but suicides were less so. As Terry wrote in his Dublin lecture, 'Pierrepoint the executioner knew how to hang a man swiftly, and knew how long the rope should be and where on the neck the knot should lie to ensure a merciful end. Most people don't.' From that time onwards, the notion of 'a peaceful death' was always one that Terry was sceptical about.

And then, sometimes no less grimly, there were the magistrates' courts, where 'justice had to be seen to be done, and therefore a stalwart from the *Bucks Free Press* had to sit there in his cheap jacket and write it all down in impeccable Pitman's'. Here, two things immediately struck the young Pratchett: first, the sight of 'crooks, policemen and lawyers all in the same place, laughing and joking and sharing cigarettes while the jury or the magistrates consulted. And somehow your eyes watered and they all looked the same, the only exception being the bewildered man who had had his greenhouse smashed or his car set on fire and was wondering why the man involved was chatting companionably with a copper.'

And second there was the sight of the formidable 'dowager lady magistrate' who was frequently presiding, and who favoured navy blue underwear – a detail that Terry did not have to sleuth journalistically to uncover because the dowager lady uncovered it herself, to everyone present in court, by sitting legs apart on the bench in the absence of a modesty panel. 'Every person summoned to give evidence did so while staring up at the ceiling,' observed Terry, who wondered whether her inability to hold people's gaze ever caused the woman to wonder.

Less dramatically, there were the long evenings at the meetings of the Urban District Council whose seemingly endless proceedings were democratically open to both the public and the press, although Terry would frequently find himself in there alone, playing both roles and living in dread of the inevitable councillor who, even as the interminable session was finally winding up, would rise from his chair to say, 'Mr Chairman, if I could just raise one more matter under Any Other Business . . .'

And then there were the choirs, the bands and the amateur dramatic societies to be kept abreast of, and, of course, the village shows and the novelty fruit and veg circuit, when it was in season. And couples celebrating the milestone of a golden wedding anniversary were always deemed newsworthy enough to get a home visit from the cub reporter and a paragraph or two under a smiling photo in the next edition. It was, Terry realized, an assignment that had its creative limits; the only question to be asked on these occasions was about the secret of a long and happy marriage. 'Generally speaking, I could have written the answers in advance,' Terry wrote, 'consisting as they did of the importance of give and take, kindness and understanding, etc. But I remember one where the husband piped up cheerily with, "Well, we had a lot of sex, and we still do." And his beaming wife shamelessly chimed in with, "That's very true, oh dear, yes. You young people think you invented sex, but it's amazing what we got up to in the blackout." And the husband added happily, "And on a bicycle, dear. That lady's bicycle without a crossbar was a friend to me." And so it went on until, like a good journalist, I made my excuses and left in search of a cold bath.'*

Thursday was press day, the most hectic day of the week in the office, but Friday, when the paper came out, was relatively calm. Terry's first task on those days was to clear the spike, the viciously sharp, pointed instrument on a wooden base on which the week's discarded stories had been slapped down, whence they could always be retrieved if needed later – 'kind of a waste paper basket with a restore facility', as Terry put it.† And once the spike was cleared he was under orders to settle down and become, for an hour or two, Uncle Jim.

'*Nobody* wanted to do Uncle Jim's corner,' according to Terry. In the *Bucks Free Press*, 'Children's Circle' was the segment of a page ring-fenced every week for younger readers, a world of birthday announcements, as requested by parents, and short stories, sometimes featuring a talking rabbit called Boo Boo Bunny or, if not, a talking stoat called Peter Piper, and all presided over by the mythical Uncle Jim, who was in reality just the staff member who was the holder of what was regarded as the office's shortest straw. After all, on the scale of hard news assignments, this was about as soft as it got – way out beyond even novelty fruit and veg on the journalistic hardness scale.

And as if that wasn't bad enough, the assignment was also potentially a trap. 'The incumbent Uncle Jim had to have their wits about them,' Terry wrote, 'because every jokester in the area would try their best to get something dirty into the newspaper in the guise of an innocent child's name, the bastards. How can I put this delicately? Well, if your name genuinely was R. Sitch, then I apologise for electing not to notify

....

* I'm not sure I entirely trust the detail about the lady's bicycle in this anecdote. Then again, I wasn't present when the conversation took place.

† Many were the editors who, attempting to add a laconic flourish to their spiking of a story, ended up spiking parts of their own hands, in particular the little web of skin between the thumb and forefinger. According to Terry, clearing the spike at the end of a more than averagely hectic news-week could often involve sifting through pages spattered with considerable quantities of dried blood.

Buckinghamshire of your birthday that time, because I didn't let that one through, at least.'*

As the staff's most recently recruited lackey, who had no power to resist, it quickly fell to Terry to put on Uncle Jim's less than mighty mantle. But actually, in due course, he wasn't interested in complaining about it. Uncle Jim's less than mighty mantle turned out rather to suit him.

It's fair to say that 'Children's Circle' was revolutionized by the presence of Terry Pratchett. Nobody in the history of the *Bucks Free Press* had Uncle Jimmed quite like Terry could Uncle Jim. His first weeks in the role saw, by comparison with what had been passing muster in this slot, a tsunami of creativity. It was instantly the end of the road for Boo Boo Bunny and Peter Piper: on Terry's watch, Buckinghamshire's children would hear no more from either of them. Instead, they would be treated to the infinitely more compelling spectacle of Professor Whelk building a rocket intended to fly him to Mars, making sure to hang curtains in its windows and put a large brass knocker on its front door. Or they would join post-Roman invaders under General Hangdoge from the country of Tropnecia in the Tosheroon Islands as they staged a failed invasion of the British Isles. ('That was how things were done in history,' the narrator helpfully explains. 'As soon as you saw a place, you had to conquer it, and usually the English Channel was full of ships queuing up to come and have a good conquer.') Or they would watch a gang of gnomes set off through treacherous seas in a submarine fashioned from a walnut and driven by an elastic band. Or they would see the Pied Piper arrive in the town of Blackbury during a dustmen's strike and lead the town council away – 'except for Mr Patel, as he was hiding in the weeds at the edge of the river, trying to breathe through a reed, which isn't as easy as it sounds in stories'.

Readers also found Wales transformed into a kind of British Wild West, rendered rich, crazy and dangerous by, not a gold-rush, but a coal-rush, and were invited to meet and journey with Bedwyr, 'the handsomest

. . . .

* Others, allegedly, made it under the radar. Happy birthday, Hugh Janus.

of all the shepherds, and his dog, Bedwetter, the finest sheepdog in all Wales'.

What's clear from these endeavours, short and youthfully raw though they undoubtedly are, is how much of the classic Pratchett machinery is already polished up and hard at work. Only seventeen, Terry has already latched on to the idea of adopting received and dusty storytelling formalities, perking them up by instantly under-mining them, and then arranging for the whole fantastical set-up to be involved in a head-on collision with the modern world in all its colloquial glory. So, a story might open: 'Once upon a time – that's always a good start – there was a young prince . . .' And before long a bird in a tree will be conversationally informing that young prince, 'The girl is Princess Selena, but if you want to marry her you'll have to woo her. Chocolates and flowers and so on.' The apprentice journalist is already on his way to mastery of the mock-heroic, cheekily loosening the nuts and bolts of conventional storytelling to see what laughs might follow.

From Terry's point of view, there was a convenient aspect to being given the 'Children's Circle' beat, too: it was a natural space into which to inject short extracts from an as yet unfinished project he was tinkering with at home. This was a story for young readers that Terry was building around an idea which appears to have owed itself to a chance remark in the sitting room of Dave Busby's mother's house.

Terry's friend had by now exchanged the Lambretta for a leather-lined Rover 2000, bought with the help of a small inheritance 'which should have been used to avoid a day job for a little longer and concentrate on writing,' Dave confessed, 'but the temptation proved too great.' This meant that, instead of always hanging out at 25 Upper Riding on Satur-days during those weekend get-togethers, Dave could now sometimes pick up Terry and drive him back to Wokingham.

During one of these exchange visits, to emphasize a point in the mid-dle of a particularly animated debate, Dave found himself stamping down on the patterned Axminster in the living room.

'Careful,' Terry said. 'You'll disturb the carpet people.'

The who? The carpet people, of course – those microscopic families eking out an existence between the carpet fibres, among the crumbs, dust-mites and detritus, permanently at risk of ruinous strikes from the unknown vastness above them. Or so it emerged as Terry began to unpack this idea and write it up. Maybe there would be a book in it eventually, but in the meantime it would certainly go well in episodes in 'Children's Corner'. Terry's first outing for this material in that space focuses on a crisis brought down upon the tiny tribe by some idly flicked cigarette ash. The tale seemed to go over well, and he kept it coming.*

So, there was the budding journalist, a few months into his two-year apprenticeship, honing a skill that would stay with him for ever: 'the ability to apprehend a topic and write a coherent, informed and readable column about it within half an hour, possibly with the help of one telephone call and a newspaper clipping'. Sharpening his talent for children's fiction via a miniature world in the threads of a carpet hadn't necessarily been part of the bargain, but he'd take that, too.

★ ★ ★ ★ ★

Dave Busby's newly acquired Rover 2000 could carry the pair of them in unprecedented luxury to the 1966 Eastercon, which was held in Great Yarmouth, 160 miles away on the Norfolk coast. So, at the beginning of April, Terry booked a rare weekend off and he and Dave joined a hundred or so other sci-fi aficionados checking into The Royal Hotel on the seafront, where – a detail which would not have been lost on Terry – Charles Dickens had stayed while writing *David Copperfield*, doing so, presumably, without the distraction of three separate science fiction auctions, a costume parade and late-night disturbances by herberts in the corridors. No doubt to the relief of the Norfolk police force, bad weather damped down the weekend's other attraction: an informal

---

* An obvious point, but worth making: nearly two decades before *The Colour of Magic*, Terry was already experimenting with the creation of a self-contained world on a flat plane.

convention of mods and rockers. The notorious pitched battles on the beaches of Easter Monday 1965 were not repeated.*

They were old hands now, familiar with this world and familiar within it. Terry's badge declared him to be conventioneer number 108 – and, the programme instructed, 'PLEASE WEAR YOUR BADGES AT ALL TIMES – EVEN ON YOUR PYJAMAS (OR NIGHTGOWN AS THE CASE MAY BE).' The programme also contained an advertisement taken out by the publishers Victor Gollancz, touting the upcoming publication on 21 July of a novel by Frank Herbert (a more reputable kind of Herbert, clearly) entitled *Dune*, which both Terry and Dave felt it might be worth exploring in due course.

Unlike in Birmingham the previous year, this time there were enough participants to justify awarding the fancy dress prize, which meant that Ina Shorrock could receive her dues for taking the trouble to pitch up as 'the Constellation Andromeda'. But perhaps most significantly, on Saturday at 10.30 a.m., a sizeable 'new authors' panel was staged, featuring Langdon Jones, Keith Woodcott, Paddy O'Halloran, Ramsey Campbell, James Colvin, Hank Dempsey . . . and David Busby and Terry Pratchett. Dave, of course, was already a veteran of the Con panel, but this would have to be accounted Terry's first official public appearance as an author. Neither the records nor the memories of those involved reveal whether the Busby/ Pratchett double act distinguished or disgraced themselves, or whether they were content to fly under the radar during the discussions that followed. But one thing was growing clear: maybe because their experiences at Worldcon in 1965 had permanently made Eastercons seem a little parochial and second-best, or maybe because the demands of work were creeping up, or maybe for other reasons entirely, the novelty of convention-going was wearing off for both of them.

Driving back to Buckinghamshire in the Rover 2000, Terry and Dave decided that you could only do these things so many times before

....

* Coincidentally, Terry's future personal assistant won the Most Outstanding Scooter award at Great Yarmouth in Easter 1986 for his customized Vespa 50 Special. There was no rioting that year, either.

they started to lose their shine and agreed that it looked like they had burned through that convention-going phase of their lives and were out the other side. If it occurred to either of them that, 38 years after this conversation, Terry would be the Guest of Honour at the 62nd World Science Fiction Convention and be getting hailed by 6,000 attendees in Boston, Massachusetts, neither of them mentioned it. Terry wouldn't go to another convention until 1985, by which time, still a 'new author' as far as many people were concerned, he had some books to sell.

In the meantime, Terry was clearly in need of some means of getting around the place that wasn't south Buckinghamshire's patchy bus service or Dave Busby's Rover 2000. And so it was that the *Bucks Free Press*'s apprentice reporter found himself taking possession of his grandfather's old, battered and no longer needed Dunkley S65 Whippet scooter – much to the amusement of Dave, who, as a former Lambretta owner, was only ever withering about this clunky, fifties-era British attempt to ape Italian style.

Fair enough, too. Never widely admired for its looks, the Dunkley S65 was, as Terry conceded, 'surrounded by metal like a medieval knight in armour'. Moreover, to perform even the simplest act of maintenance on this vehicle, its hapless owner would have to force that armour high up into the air and hastily stop it from crashing back by deploying a flimsy stay. Operating on this bike in a high wind, or even a relatively light breeze, posed a radical risk to your fingers from its falling outer skin. Yet it was a risk that Terry and his father were constantly obliged to take, as the Dunkley – 'cantankerous', in Terry's estimate of its character – shed its chain apparently for its own amusement and played up in every other way, large and small, that it could think of.*

As Terry wrote, 'My dad, being a Dave, had automatic contact with the secret fraternity of Daves who dispensed antique spares from junk

---

* Terry's grandfather had clearly wildly over-driven the Whippet during his period of ownership – had thrashed it to within an inch of its life, in fact. It was very much a 'rescue' Whippet, in that sense.

yards and garages and strange and secret sheds under railway arches. Yet even he found it hard to keep the Dunkley on the road.' But for Terry that Whippet was transport, and transport represented freedom. Well, more or less. 'I rode the bastard hither and yon through the Buckinghamshire countryside,' Terry wrote, 'in a fragrant cloud of unburnt fuel and with an ever-present apprehension of what it would find to go wrong next.' The scooter did him a couple of years' intermittent service before it was eventually sent to its grave – and without too much in the way of mourning from its final owner. 'They say the Dunkley Whippet is a collectable,' Terry later wrote. 'Well, you can collect mine from the bottom of a hole in a farm on the Mendip Hills, but don't you dare dig it up because hell will follow after.'

Still, before it was put out to pasture, that terrible and deranged scooter would valuably assist Terry in the execution of a whole new project that he was about to embark upon: courting.

6

PRAWN COCKTAILS, POISONOUS BUBBLE CARS AND A DEAD MOUSE IN THE GOBSTOPPERS

'A young man finding himself accidentally in possession of a young lady's jewellery is honour-bound to return it to her. I'm pretty sure that Jane Austen said something about this.'

So wrote Terry in the notes towards his autobiography. And whatever thoughts Jane Austen might or might not have expressed in this area, the facts as we have them are these: that one night, after a party, as he undressed for bed in his bedroom at 25 Upper Riding, something soft and sparkly fell out of the top pocket of Terry's jacket and revealed itself on closer inspection to be a large magenta and mauve earring which did not belong to him.

Fate had just smiled on Terry as warmly as it ever had, and as warmly as it ever would.

The party had been thrown one weekend by Joanna, one of Terry's work colleagues, at her family's house in Princes Risborough, a town which Arthur Church would no doubt have defined as sitting at the extreme western end of the *Bucks Free Press*'s circulation area and which Terry would no doubt have defined as eighteen anxious miles from Beaconsfield by Dunkley Whippet. And for all that some people had evidently gone home at the end of the evening with other people's jewellery in their pockets, it hadn't actually been as wild a night as that might imply. On the contrary, Terry, aged eighteen going on nineteen, and in his best shirt, had found himself sitting among his newspaper co-workers, holding a small glass of Guinness and chatting, when, out of nowhere, as he wrote, 'a beautiful blonde girl wearing large, dangly earrings, fell into my lap, looked up at me and said, "Are you Wayne Fontana?" Seizing my chance, I said, "No."'

Well, he didn't lie: Terry was, indeed, not the lead singer with the Manchester-based pop group The Mindbenders, nor had he scored a major chart smash in 1965 with the hit 'The Game Of Love'. But maybe, in a crowded sitting room which was atmospherically lit, and seen through half-closed eyes, and after enough wine from the bring-a-bottle selection in the kitchen, he could almost have passed for someone who might just about, at a stretch, have been Wayne Fontana. As it was, despite this barn-door conversational opening, pretty much all he had managed to learn before the hostess, Joanna, led the interloper away – giving Terry, he felt, 'a meaningful look' as she did so – was that the girl in his lap had been called Lyn. Almost immediately after that the party began to break up.

Terry left in a thoughtful mood. 'The Dunkley toiled a bit on the way home, and it rained and I ploughed through the puddles, gloomily, despairing of a chance not taken.'

It would not be overstating it to suggest that Terry's adventures in the realms of dating had been fairly limited up to this point, and that he had yet to have the chance to put many of Jane Austen's maxims on love and attraction to the test. It was certainly the case that incidents in which girls dropped into his lap at parties and asked him if he was a pop star had thus far been happening to him with no regularity whatsoever. He had had a crush for a while on a girl in the office at the *Bucks Free Press*, soon after he started working there, but that turned out to be unrequited. Then one time he saw a girl on a train – a blonde girl who was reading *The Lord of the Rings*, which, quite apart from the fact that she was very pretty, would have got Terry's attention fairly quickly. But she didn't look up and he hadn't had the courage to talk to her. Imagine if, a couple of weeks later, *that* girl had just dropped into his lap at a party and asked him if he was Wayne Fontana.

The thing was, she just had. The girl at the party and the girl on the train were one and the same. Coincidence of coincidences. Later, when they started going out together and he got round to telling her that he had already admired her from afar, Lyn assumed Terry was spinning her a line. But it was true. Lyn was travelling into London each day to work at Selfridges, the department store, and Terry, who was heading to a college in East London on day release for his journalism studies, had seen her one morning with her head buried in a volume of Tolkien.* He had seen this girl on a train and wondered about her, and now that same girl had landed in his lap from a clear blue sky, or at least from a magnolia-painted ceiling in a sitting room in Princes Risborough. And he, the fool, had failed to capitalize on the moment.

Yet the magenta and mauve earring had ended up in his jacket pocket. Never mind Jane Austen, this was more like Thomas Hardy country, and if this turn-up wasn't actually some indication of larger forces at work attending to the intended order of things, it was at least, for Terry, a shot at redemption.

At work, trying to sound casual about it and entirely failing, Terry asked Joanna for Lyn's phone number, under the pretext of returning her earring to her. Blowing his cover still further, he also asked a lot of other questions, by way of background, and was somewhat daunted by what he heard. Apparently, Lyn's family, the Purveses, lived in Gerrards Cross – a well-to-do neck of the Buckinghamshire woods to which it was, and remains, practically obligatory to apply the word 'leafy'. You didn't *have* to be posh to live in Gerrards Cross, but it certainly helped. Worse than that, the Purveses owned a Bentley. Worse than that, they owned a boat and a country house in Dorset. With each of these class-defining details, Terry's heart sank further. What hope, batting in this league, for a council house boy on a measly apprentice journalist's wage?

. . . .

* It need not surprise us that Lyn did not notice Terry in this circumstance, his resemblance to Wayne Fontana notwithstanding. Lyn found *The Lord of the Rings* extremely absorbing. She was so absorbed by that book, in fact, that on one evening commute she ended up several stops down the wrong branch line.

Still, if there was one thing journalism taught you, it was to be bold about picking up the phone to people you didn't know, even rich ones. Moreover, there had been – Terry was sure – an encouraging glint in Joanna's eye as she passed on Lyn's number which gave Terry added heart for his mission. That evening he rang the Purves household.

'The phone was answered by an older woman,' Terry recollected, 'quite probably, I suspected, a Duchess. I asked to speak to Lyn, and she bustled off cheerfully enough without, to my surprise, asking my intentions or what my father did for a living. Eventually Lyn came to the phone. She sounded nice, and indeed grateful when I volunteered dropping the earring in the next time I was passing. The truth was, I was never passing Gerrards Cross, having no cause to. But tomorrow I would be passing it, that was for sure.'

So, at some point the following evening, Terry-who-just-happened-to-be-passing arrived at the given address in Dukes Wood Drive. It was, indeed, a very nice house: single-storey, modern, in a lovely garden. At the same time, it didn't have a two-mile drive, peacocks and a maze, and the door wasn't opened by a liveried flunkey, so Terry didn't feel entirely outclassed – only partly outclassed, although that can sometimes feel worse. Terry returned the earring, as Jane Austen might or might not have wished him to. And then with see-through nonchalance, he asked Lyn if she would like to go out for dinner with him sometime, and Lyn said yes.

So now the challenge for Terry was to find a suitable venue in which he could attempt the towering task of revealing that what he lacked by failing to be Wayne Fontana he could more than make up for by being Terry Pratchett. It didn't take him long to come up with somewhere. By this time, the sixties were swinging so hard in Buckinghamshire that someone in Beaconsfield had opened a Chinese restaurant. What woman could resist that? On a research trip, Terry stood outside this bogglingly exotic destination, consulting the menu in the window and doing some mental arithmetic. His calculations suggested that a meal for two could just about be stretched to without completely setting fire to his wallet. Moreover, the place appeared to serve that most Asian of dishes, the prawn cocktail. Class, then, as well as affordability. He booked a table.

That left the tricky issue of transport on the night. A pillion ride for his date on the Dunkley would be a high-risk enterprise in circumstances of doubtful dignity and even more doubtful legality – quite apart from the fact that that increasingly unreliable machine could hardly cope with the weight of one man and his toolbox, let alone two adults. A taxi, clearly, was the thing. But a taxi from Beaconsfield to Gerrards Cross, and then back to Beaconsfield, returning to Gerrards Cross at the end of the evening before again heading back to Beaconsfield . . . that would be at least twenty miles in total with the meter running and would therefore induce carnage, financially speaking. So, after much strategic cogitation, Terry arrived at a plan which included an especially cunning cut-price car element.

He would book a taxi to arrive at Lyn's parents' house. Then he would use the Dunkley to get himself from Beaconsfield to Gerrards Cross, concealing the battered scooter, along with his helmet and overalls, in a field around the corner. Then, with the taxi now idling in the road, he would walk nonchalantly up the drive as if the car had borne him the whole way. By this ruse, he reckoned on saving himself, at the very least, the cost of both prawn cocktails, while also presenting himself, to Lyn and any other member of the Purves family who might witness the moment, not as a desperate corner-cutter with a cheap British-made scooter, but as a man of means and style and, by extension, a genuine prospect.

Amazingly enough, the first part of the Dunkley-to-taxi transfer ploy went off smoothly. The taxi bore them into town and Terry was soon seated across a table from Lyn at Beaconsfield's premier, and indeed only, Szechuan-influenced dining emporium. Better still, the prawn cocktails were barely out of the fridge before the pair of them had fallen into easy conversation and before a swift and, as it turned out, eternal meeting of minds had got underway. Lyn, Terry now discovered, loved art and had studied illustration at Chelsea Art School. For one exercise, her college class had been required to design a jacket for a favourite novel. Pretty much everyone else had chosen *Brideshead Revisited*. Only Lyn chose to work on a cover for *A Sour Apple Tree*, a 1958 novel by the British thriller writer and 'Master of Horror' John Blackburn. Terry's kind of art student, clearly.

As for the poshness . . . well, there was reassuring news from Terry's point of view. Lyn's father was an executive engineer for what is now British Telecom, rather than a landed Duke. 'The boat was a two-berth motor boat rather than a gin palace,' Terry wrote, 'the cottage in Dorset was a derelict building that Lyn's father was in the process of doing up, by himself, and the Bentley, while it did exist, was almost like a four-wheel version of the Dunkley by now and confined to the garage.'*

In addition to these confidence-boosting revelations, Terry was staggered when, at the end of the meal, upon the arrival of the bill, Lyn reached for her purse and offered to pay her share. 'It was a concept that was totally alien to me at that point,' Terry wrote. Some instinctive notion of chivalry kicked in, though, and he gallantly refused Lyn's offer, instead resigning himself to a week of penury before his next pay cheque. Not just for that reason, Lyn's strongest and most abiding first impression of Terry was of his kindness. By the time the taxi was bearing them back to Dukes Wood Drive, it was clear that there would be other dates.

'After a gentle kiss on the doorstep of her home,' Terry wrote, 'I walked away into the gloom and the friendly taxi driver opened and shut the passenger door to make it seem as though I had climbed in. I then walked a bit further up the road and retrieved the Dunkley from its bush. True to its character, it gave up the ghost for the umpteenth time outside the Bell Inn on the A40, halfway home, and it rained as I pushed the damn thing the rest of the way back. But I had a song in my heart and water in my boots.'

What with Lyn's job in London and Terry's long and irregular hours at local journalism's coalface, clear nights for dating were harder to come by than either of them would have liked. Also, one night of the week, normally Thursday, was blocked out by Terry for writing this

....

* This is not fair on the Bentley, according to Lyn, which was certainly, like most other roadworthy vehicles including agricultural appliances, more reliable than the Dunkley, and definitely more comfortable. However, the car's thirsty consumption figure – 17mpg – meant its usage was carefully rationed, mostly to church-going on Sundays and trips to Dorset to see the grandparents.

book he was working on – *The Carpet People* – and he made that very clear to Lyn, who entirely understood. After all, everyone needs a hobby. But sometimes at the weekend the village shows and steam fairs that Terry had to report on for the paper could handily double as dating opportunities and Terry would invite Lyn to come with him. In due course, Terry had the courage to take her home to Upper Riding, where Lyn, to his relief, said she liked the orange in the décor, bravely endured Eileen's narrow-eyed scrutiny, and admired the view across the Chilterns.

There was no big proposal from either of them – nobody dropped to their knee or produced a ring at some unforeseen but minutely planned moment. They just began talking about it one day when they were out walking – and this was really only a handful of weeks after they met, not even a month into the affair. Getting married just seemed the obvious thing to do.

Neither of them ever had a second thought on that subject, either. Indeed, the engagement underwent and overcame arguably its most significant and probably only test in February 1968 when a meeting between the Pratchetts and the Purveses to discuss the wedding plans caused Terry to miss the last episode of *The Prisoner* on ITV. The cult science fiction mystery series, with Patrick McGoohan's special agent, Number 6, incarcerated in Portmeirion and explaining to anyone who would listen, 'I am not a number, I am a free man,' had been running since September 1967, and Terry and Dave couldn't get enough of it, eagerly convening after each episode to discuss developments. How the story would eventually resolve itself in its clinching episode had been a topic of vibrant debate between them for literally weeks on end. So one can only imagine Terry's deflation when he realized that he had an appointment he couldn't get out of and wouldn't be seeing it.* 'He was

. . . .

* Remember that, in the days before catch-up TV or even video recording, if you missed a television show when it was broadcast you actually did miss it. Short of going to America that summer, where the series was shown later, Terry's best bet would probably have been to wait for the video to come out . . . in 1982. Quite a gap, although, on the plus side, Betamax *and* VHS versions appear to have been immediately available.

terribly upset about it,' Dave recalled. 'He interrogated me about it and I had to explain it all to him, which was the worst of all worlds for him, really.'

Still some years away from meeting his own wife-to-be, Gill, Dave was single at this time and Terry was determined to fix his friend up with Lyn's pal Joanna, of Princes Risborough party fame, so that they could go about together as a foursome. In his attempt to bring this about, Terry applied himself assiduously to arranging seemingly casual meetings between Dave and Joanna, and took to conducting conspiratorial phone conversations in the office, where Joanna was present, in which the key parties had to be given code names to avoid exposure of the plot. Dave, under this arrangement, briefly became 'Aristotle'. Despite Terry's sustained and clearly imaginative campaigning, however, the union never quite crystallized.

So, instead, Terry, Lyn and Dave knocked about cheerfully as a three, heading together to London on a special trip to see the film *2001: A Space Odyssey* in Leicester Square, soon after it opened there in May 1968.* That summer the three of them went on holiday together for a few days to Dorset. Lyn stayed at her family's partially rebuilt holiday cottage while Terry and Dave checked into rooms in The Museum Inn along the road in Farnham. There were evenings in the pub, games of table football and a lot of hysterical laughter.† One night, stumbling home down a country lane following the consumption of beer, they decided to form a human orrery. Dave was the Sun, spinning on the

. . . .

* And three years after Terry and Dave had witnessed Arthur C. Clarke so tantalizingly trailing the film at Worldcon 1965 in London.

† By the time I met Terry, his glory days at table football seemed a long way behind him. Yet evidently one shouldn't underestimate the strength of his passion for the game. In 1975, writing for the *Bath and West Evening Chronicle* and reviewing *The Indoor League*, a book by Sid Waddell and John Meade, Terry notes how this compendium of pub games includes 'two of my favourites, billiards and table football, on which I wasted many a shilling before coming to this heathen skittles country'.

spot. Terry was the Earth, spinning and orbiting Dave. Lyn spun and orbited Terry – the Moon to his Earth.[*]

By now the Dunkley, having played its crucial part in bringing Terry and Lyn together, had descended into its farmyard grave and Terry had replaced it with a Mobylette, only marginally more fashionable and bought off an elderly gentleman for ten shillings. It slightly disturbed Terry how happy the elderly gentleman was to part with this vehicle at that price, but he needn't have worried. By comparison with the buried Dunkley, it was a paragon of consistency and Terry was eventually able to describe it as 'a wonderful little thing, almost Edwardian in its elegance'. It may have been not much more than a sit-up-and-beg bicycle with a tiny motor attached, but it came with a wind-shield and fitted leg-shields, 'just like the big boys'. With the wind behind it, those shields would become sails and blow the thing along like a galleon. With the wind against, however, the machine essentially reverted to being a sit-up-and-beg bicycle, leaving Terry pedalling furiously against the current and making a lung-bursting odyssey of, for example, the twenty-mile trip to Wokingham to visit Dave.

In more clement conditions, though, the Mobylette afforded its driver the satisfying potential for one-handed operation. Indeed, Terry maintained it was the only motorbike he ever rode on which it was possible to drive and eat a sandwich at the same time. Moreover, the previous owner had attached a rheostat to the handlebars, controlling the power going to the headlight. Though this distinctly failed in its mission to increase the brightness of the headlight, which continued to glimmer dimly like a child's torch with fading batteries, the device itself glowed constantly hot, meaning that on a cold day you could steer with one hand and conveniently use the custom-fitted rheostat to warm the other.

That autumn, as the wedding day neared, with assistance from their

* To be more precise, an orrery which only features the Sun, the Earth and the Moon, and not the rest of the solar system, is called a tellurion. I feel sure Terry would have wanted me to point this out.

parents the soon-to-be-married couple put down a deposit on 4 Old Farm Road in the Downley district of High Wycombe. They had wanted to buy an older semi-detached place that was on the market but it was far simpler at the time to get a mortgage on a newly built 'starter home', so their first marital house would be in a short terrace in a close on a modern edge-of-town development where they would have the impression they were practically the only couple without small children.

The day before the wedding, Terry was driving back across the hills from a job in Marlow when the Mobylette finally died on him, leg-shields and all. But at least it had the consideration to do so at the crest of the last hill before High Wycombe, meaning that Terry could freewheel down from there into the town, where the man who was getting married in the morning had an essential appointment with the barber. Hearing, as he snipped at Terry's already receding hair, the story of the Moby-lette's sorry end, the barber became thoughtful for a moment and then offered to take the broken machine off Terry's hands in exchange for the haircut. Terry, sniffing a bargain, agreed. He then walked home to Old Farm Road to meet his father who was bringing over some of the wedding presents for installation in the new house. That evening, while Lyn was with her parents in Dukes Wood Drive, Terry and Dave dined like kings on Chinese take-away – 'gorgeously greasy', in Terry's assessment. There was only one bed in the partially furnished new house so Dave slept on the sofa.

The wedding was at the Congregational Church in Gerrards Cross. The bride wore a white dress and veil with a cameo brooch at the neck and carried a small doll of a chimney sweep for luck. The groom and his best man had rebelled very firmly against the idea that they should be in traditional morning dress with top hats and had opted instead for matching made-to-measure suits in fawn with a very fashion-forward shallow lapel, and lilac cravats. Lyn feels sure that Terry and Dave were going for some kind of 'medieval' vibe, but Dave argues that something closer to 'Regency' was the desired effect. 'We looked like a pair of very neat highwaymen,' Dave suggested. Dave also recalls that the afternoon of the fitting, at a leading menswear establishment in High Wycombe, the pair of them were distracted by a discussion of Frank Herbert's *Dune*, which they were both reading at the time.*

We must also solemnly report that one of the two neat highwaymen spent the day looking a little peaky – not the effect of nerves, nor, as some of the more jocular guests suggested, the effect of heavy drink for confidence the night before, and nor, indeed, the effect of the lilac cravat, but in fact the legacy of that greasy Chinese meal. 'It was all down to something nasty in my chow mein,' said Terry.

This was the fourth wedding that Terry and Lyn had attended in quick succession – but the only one on which the sun shone. After the service, during which Lyn almost forgot Terry's names, and during which the presiding clergyman referred, not to 'people here present', but to 'pieces here present', everyone went next door to the village hall where there were many long speeches from various uncles, a much shorter speech from Dave, and a general sense, as so often at weddings, that the young people at the centre of this occasion were a bit of a sideshow in a far greater spectacular being indulged in by the grown-ups. But no matter. In due course, cake was cut and served and the steel band who had provided the music for Lyn's 21st birthday party put in another shift. The news of this new and lifelong alliance would make the local paper under the headline: 'Gerrards Cross Bride For Bucks Press Man'.

It was 5 October 1968. From that day forward until the end of his life, Terry was the most married person you were ever likely to meet.

There was no money for a honeymoon, so Terry and Lyn stayed in their new house, sorting the place out. Terry built a bookcase. They assembled their wedding present from Dave – a hi-fi with a Garrard SP25 turntable, an amplifier and a pair of bookshelf speakers – and to celebrate its setting-up, Lyn successfully creeped Terry out by playing *Carmina Burana*, over and over again.

. . . .

* Dave was to pull the faux-Regency suit out of the wardrobe again for his own wedding in 1975, though Terry declined to match him on that occasion. Lyn thinks the suit enjoyed some further outings during the 1970s on the rare occasions when Terry was persuaded to dress formally. 'I won't put on a suit for anything less than a Lord,' was a mantra of Terry's, in those days and beyond.

'After the wedding, I didn't expect to hear from them for a while,' said Dave. 'In fact, three days after the big day, Terry rang up and said, "Do you want to come over for supper?"'

It was the first time Dave had seen Terry with stubble. He had already started growing the beard that would permanently occupy his face thereafter and to Dave it felt like a statement – one running directly counter to the hoary old gags about men surrendering their freedom and getting 'tied down' in marriage. Dave, on the contrary, had the impression he was looking at a man who had just *found* his freedom. 'He was free of his parents, free of his mother trying to control him all his life,' Dave thought. 'He was going to be his own man now. It was the start of a new Terry.'

★ ★ ★ ★ ★

Work wasn't all steam fairs, drawn-out council meetings and queasy encounters with over-sharing golden anniversary celebrants. And nor was it all children's stories in which the 59A bus went back in time, and Doggins had an awfully big adventure and Humphrey Newt acquired a thunderbolt carriage. Terry had shown where his talents most comfortably lay and he was increasingly being seconded from news and given the paper's longer and more reflective pieces of writing: features and interviews. In that line, one day in the spring of 1968, George Topley put a book on Terry's desk and told him to go and talk to the author about it.

The book was titled *Looking Forward to the Seventies* and subtitled *A blueprint for education in the next decade*. It was a collection of essays by various writers whose general theme was educational reform – a hot topic at the time, and arguably a hot topic at all times – and its editor was called Peter Bander, who also happened to be the co-founder of the book's publisher, Colin Smythe Limited.

Thus did fate bring Terry for the first time to the door of Cornerways in Gerrards Cross, a detached 1920s stockbroker Tudor house down a tree-lined lane, and the home and headquarters, though he didn't yet know it, of his future publisher and agent.

And I wonder if the scene that greeted the man from the *Bucks Free Press* was really all that different from the scene that greeted me when I first walked through that same hallowed portal for an interview with Colin Smythe so many years later in 1997. It was certainly a scene that had its timeless aspects. At Cornerways, one moved among paintings in gilt frames, cabinets of Lalique glass, and display cases containing ornaments and curios. There was, to my astonishment and delight, in Colin's office, practically buried under 12 inches of paperwork, an ormolu desk that had once belonged to the Irish dramatist Lady Gregory. Around it on the walls were a painting by Anne Yeats, W. B. Yeats's daughter, and sketches by Jack B. Yeats, W. B. Yeats's brother. That's in addition to the set of library steps which had once seen action at Lady Gregory's home at Coole Park in County Galway on the west coast of Ireland. An enormous and slobbering Great Dane called Dante was wandering around amiably and occasionally being lobbed dog-friendly chocolates from a five-litre Tupperware tub, and every available surface seemed to carry a stack of books or papers that extended ceilingwards. It was a world in which scholarly chaos and intellectual bohemianism met well-cultivated and highly-prized English manners – one where whisky was measured in 'fingers' and where there was a visitors' book on the table near the front door.

When my meeting with Colin ran on and I was invited to stay for supper, I rang my girlfriend to tell her I would be late home.

'What was that noise in the background?' she asked.

'That was the . . . *dinner gong*?' I replied.

There appeared to be an actual dinner gong.

The Peter Bander that Terry was sent to write about was 'a handsome man', said Terry, a chain-smoker who wore tinted glasses and spoke English with a strong German accent. (He would later adopt his German mother's maiden name and become Peter Bander Van Duren.) Colin Smythe, his publishing partner, was tall, sophisticated and softly spoken, a graduate of Trinity College Dublin, and the epitome even then of the refined gentleman-scholar. These two weren't much older than Terry, but to him, at the time, they certainly appeared so – accomplished and established and intellectually practised to an extent that Terry, at 20, might even have felt slightly intimidated by, had Terry ever been in the business of feeling intimidated. Peter and Colin's combined interests could without fear of contradiction be said to cover the waterfront: early twentieth-century Irish literature (Colin's specialist subject), the Roman Catholic Church (Peter's specialist subject), heraldry, education, science fiction, fantasy, folklore, cooking, trout fishing, the paranormal, UFOs, children's literature . . . to name only those. In a proudly eclectic catalogue, Colin Smythe Limited would publish books of local interest, such as Geoffrey Edmonds' *A History of Chalfont St Peter and Gerrards Cross*; and they would also publish books which investigated the possibility that the voices of the dead can still be heard, and volumes such as *Link: The Extraordinary Gifts of a Teenage Psychic* by Matthew Manning, who claimed to be able to quell poltergeist activity by automatic drawing, sessions of which allegedly found him channelling great artists including Picasso and Aubrey Beardsley. When I flicked back through that guest book in the hall before signing it, I found the signature of a young Terry Pratchett, naturally enough, and, without any explanation whatsoever, that of Gene Roddenberry, the creator of *Star Trek*. At dinner parties at Cornerways, in the green hessian-lined dining room, scholars of Irish mysticism and Roman Catholic dignitaries rubbed shoulders with the likes of Nicholas Parsons, David Frost, Gyles Brandreth and the nation's favourite TV cookery duo, Fanny and Johnnie Cradock. The odd séance had been known to take place.

Terry must have found all this as eye-opening and as riveting as I did. He also seems to have found it easy to write about Peter Bander and his book. The pair of them conversed at length that day about science fiction and books in general before getting down to *Looking Forward to the Seventies*. The idea of schools being made fairer was a notion with which Terry, still carrying those fresh scars from his various scornings by heads and teachers, was only ever going to be thoroughly on board. He filed a highly supportive article, which appeared in May 1968, headlined with a quote from Bander: 'Education Should Not Be A Political Toy'.

It was the beginning of a flourishing relationship between Terry, the *Bucks Free Press* man, and Colin Smythe Limited – a mutually convenient one, it must be said. For Colin and Peter, with books to publicize, there was no harm in having a local journalist onside. For Terry, Colin and Peter, and their business at Cornerways, looked like being a good source of copy. And so it proved. Geoffrey Edmonds' aforementioned *A History of Chalfont St Peter and Gerrards Cross* made an article for Terry. Terry also wrote about Peter Bander's 1969 book *The Prophecies of St Malachy and St Columbkille*, in a piece headlined 'Three Popes to Go Before We Know If Malachy was Right'. And when Maurice Collis, the former British administrator of Burma, wrote a novel for Colin called *The Three Gods*, Terry wrote about that, too.

More importantly for our story, though, at some point during their various meetings, Terry dropped into conversation with Bander that he had been writing a novel. Whether or not Terry was fishing for this response, Bander urged him to send his book to Colin – to do so even if it were unfinished in fact, which it still was. The novel in question was – or eventually would be – *The Carpet People*.

This, clearly, is the moment in the movie when the unknown author who will eventually sell 100 million books actually *walks up the agent's drive* with a typescript in a manila folder under his arm and knocks on the door. Cut to Colin Smythe opening that door, and cut again to a montage of a thousand golden cash registers pinging open.* Except, of course, it never really works that way, and this is also the fundamentally inauspicious moment a young hack from the local paper leans his bike against the side of the house in the middle of some ordinary midweek afternoon, and drops off a wodge of typescript on the off-chance. Even so, from the second he opened that folder, Colin Smythe knew the promise in this moment, and the promise in Terry.

. . . .

* Parallel moment from almost exactly the same time in the culture: Ray O'Sullivan walks up the drive of the Wentworth mansion of the pop impresario Gordon Mills, manager of Tom Jones and Engelbert Humperdinck, rings the doorbell and says, in effect, 'Can I come in and play you a couple of my songs?' Mills counter-intuitively invites this stranger in, listens as he bashes out 'Alone Again, Naturally' on Mills's piano, changes Ray O'Sullivan's name to Gilbert O'Sullivan and the pair of them spend the next decade printing money. Terry, of course, didn't even need a name-change.

'In the beginning,' said Pismire, 'there was nothing but endless flatness. Then came the Carpet, which covered the flatness . . . Then came the Dust which fell upon the Carpet, drifting among the hairs, taking root in the deep shadows. More came, tumbling slowly and with silence among the waiting hairs, until the dust was thick in the Carpet.

'From the dust, the Carpet wove us all . . .'

'I wasn't going to let it out of my hands,' said Colin. 'I knew immediately that he was going to go somewhere. How far? I didn't know. But this was a very young man. Writing like that already, what would he be like in five years?'

The contract between Colin Smythe Publishing Limited and Terence David John Pratchett for 'The Carpet People', with an option on two further books depending how things panned out, is dated 9 January 1969. As with his original paperwork with the *Bucks Free Press*, Terry's father had to sign it because Terry, despite being three months married by now and a homeowner, was still almost four months shy of attaining the age of majority.

With a deal for his first novel freshly inked, Terry then made a slightly unusual request: he asked if he could completely rewrite the book. Cold feet? Perhaps. But what's more likely is that he simply knew he could make it better. Colin agreed and made a request of his own. Terry had started illustrating his Uncle Jim stories in the paper: in June 1968, a drawing by him had accompanied part four of the eight-part epic 'Bason & the Hugonauts' and many others had followed. Maybe Terry would like to illustrate *The Carpet People*, too. The rewriting, the illustrating – all this would end up taking a while. It would be more than two years before Terry's first book actually made it into a shop. But nobody seemed to be especially in a hurry. Why would they have been? Time was on their side.

* * * * *

In 1969, as Terry reached his 21st birthday and finally became a legal entity, life was falling rather wonderfully into place. He was very happily married. He had his own house. He had a weekly column in the news-paper and a contract for a book. And, on top of all that, he was the proud owner of a Heinkel Trojan bubble car.

That said, the bubble car nearly killed him. Twice. But we'll come on to that.

The newspaper column came Terry's way when the *Bucks Free Press* went bi-weekly, launching a Tuesday edition – the *Midweek Free Press* – which was designed to be more feature- and picture-led than the chiefly news-oriented Friday edition. Within that new publication, Terry was given a fixed, half-page slot which appeared under the byline 'Marcus'. It was an 'off-the-beaten-track' kind of column – a place for slices of local life and 'wry takes'. Importantly for Terry, it was a chance, as formulaic local news reporting was not, to develop a distinctive voice in print, and also to do so under the pleasing cover of anonymity. His first piece, headlined 'Gunsmoke on the Green Green Grass of Bucks', was about a cowboy re-enactment group. Another week he mused about the trial of 'standee buses' in Slough – no seats, standing only – and the implications if they ever arrived in the Wycombe area, with Terry looking ahead to a future of floorless 'runnee' buses. Other times he would turn his attention to a recently published book – sometimes from the Colin Smythe Limited catalogue. And as with the Uncle Jim stories, the Marcus columns in the midweek edition became another outlet for Terry's drawings, which were frequently their main illustration.

Some weeks Marcus would do an interview. He went, for example, to Marlow to the home of Sir Basil Liddell Hart, the retired soldier and mili-tary historian, and the man who claimed to be behind the idea of 'blitzkrieg' – battle by concentrated, rapid and overwhelming attack – and who additionally maintained that his idea had been snaffled by the Ger-mans before the British could put it to use.* Terry's interview appeared under the excellent headline 'Sir Basil – A Man of Peace Despite the Blitzkrieg'.

. . . .

* Some subsequent historians have argued that Liddell Hart, who died in January 1970, overestimated his own influence in this area.

And then there was the time Marcus took himself off to interview local author Roald Dahl. By then, Dahl had published *Charlie and the Chocolate Factory* and *James and the Giant Peach*, but he was still some way from becoming a household name, to the point that Terry found it necessary to introduce him as follows: 'For 15 years Roald Dahl has lived and written in Great Missenden. But to the British public he is probably better known as the husband of actress Patricia Neal, or as the writer of the screenplays for the James Bond film *You Only Live Twice* – "hard work, but great fun," he said – and the spectacular *Chitty Chitty Bang Bang* – "twee".'

A simple exchange of letters had clinched the assignment. On 25 April 1969, using the *Bucks Free Press*'s boldly self-advertising headed notepaper – 'Net Sale Exceeds 42,000 copies weekly' – Terry wrote as follows:

Dear Sir,
As an admirer of your work – both the short stories and the
children's books – I would like, if possible, to visit you at some time
in the near future to write a feature for my paper. I wonder if you
care to contact me at the above address so that we could arrange a
meeting to suit you?

Yours faithfully,
Terence Pratchett

Dahl's equally straightforward reply came less than a week later – one sentence suggesting that if Terry 'would phone me any day here around 12.30 I will see if we can arrange a meeting.' So, Terry found himself invited to the soon-to-be-famous-and-not-just-as-the-home-of-an-actress Gipsy House, where he was pleased to note that a) Dahl had a greenhouse and b) the greenhouse contained orchids. We shall shortly see Terry converting his own first substantial earnings as an author into greenhouses. Yet it seems it took Terry and Dahl a little while to click. 'He seemed very nervous in my presence,' Terry recalled in the notes towards his autobiography, 'making it rather difficult to keep the interview on the road. Then, at last, he said, "Your family come from Wales?" I said that they didn't, to my knowledge. With this, he relaxed, and it was only later when I read his autobiography that I discovered that, as a boy in Wales, he was terrified of a sweetshop keeper called Mrs Pratchett.'*

Indeed, 'mean and loathsome' was Dahl's verdict on that sweetshop keeper. Then again, by his own admission, Dahl and his eight-year-old mates had tormented Mrs Pratchett by putting a dead mouse in her jar of gobstoppers, so maybe it wasn't all one-way traffic.

Terry's piece appeared under the less than arresting headline 'The Success Story of a Man Without A Message'. However, many of the quotes that Dahl gave to Terry during the interview struck a chord with him that quite clearly continued to resonate. For instance, Dahl told Terry: 'The purpose of a writer like me is to entertain, purely and simply. There's no message behind it, except the usual underlying one that any writer tries to get through, which is that some people are very nasty and some are very nice. Most people are very nasty, really, when you get down to it. But basically one is an entertainer, which is what a lot of fiction writers forget – and they become moralists.'

And also: 'It's not easy to write books for children, it might be harder to get a good one. But it is much more rewarding – not financially, but otherwise.'

And also: 'Art is highly overrated in importance, by artists in particular, who walk around thinking that this is the most important thing in the world and that they are, therefore, the most important people. The most important things in the world are things like childcare, and families, and medicine. Artists have a real nerve! They think there's nothing else in the world but them.'

Each of those three statements could be reproduced as part of what would much later become Terry's own philosophy on writing and on conducting himself in public, so in that sense it wouldn't be too hard to

. . . .

* The autobiography Terry refers to was *Boy: Tales of Childhood* by Roald Dahl, published fifteen years after their encounter, in 1984.

consider this coming-together of two multi-million-selling authors before they were multi-million-selling authors formative, at least from Terry's point of view. Something definitely sank in that day at Great Missenden and not just in the greenhouse.

Did Terry drive over to Roald Dahl's that day in his turquoise Heinkel Trojan bubble car? One likes to think so, though the records neither confirm nor deny it. But Terry would certainly have had the car at that time; it replaced the Mobylette which he fobbed off on his barber. The Heinkel Trojan was quite a statement – 'the Smart car of its day', Terry contended, which would be more or less true if Smart cars had three wheels, made a distinctive whirr like a loud hairdryer, and required entry through the side-hinged front panel, the driver heaving himself around the steering wheel in order to take his seat.*

Still, as a piece of late-sixties, faintly hippy chic, a twin-seat bubble car in turquoise had a lot going for it and Terry and Lyn clearly got a large amount of era-appropriate pleasure from flitting about Buckinghamshire under its glass dome. It was just a shame that it nearly poisoned them. That was the day they paused to pick up some clothes from the dry cleaners in High Wycombe, taking them inside the car with them, the Heinkel Trojan not being famous for its generous boot space. They hadn't been driving for long when they both began to feel faint. Trapped in the glass bubble, the chemical waft coming off the newly cleaned clothes had begun to permeate their systems, and both of them were on the verge of passing out when Terry realized what was happening, pulled over, pushed the front panel open and saved them. Just as well. 'Gerrards Cross Bride and Bucks Press Man Asphyxiated in Bubble Car by Own Dry Cleaning' was a headline nobody wanted to read.

There was to be a second near-death incident involving that car when Terry had a collision in it with a much larger and better-constructed vehicle which had pulled out in front of him, thereby definitively

. . . .

* It must say something about the general character of the Heinkel Trojan that its two most prominent appearances in British cinema were both in comedies – *I'm All Right, Jack* (1959) and *Blue Murder at St Trinian's* (1957). In this sense, the Mini Cooper it was not.

answering the question, 'What happens if you crash a Heinkel Trojan bubble car into the side of a Land Rover?' What happens is, the bubble car essentially pops. 'I was left,' Terry wrote, 'sitting on the seat with the car scattered all around me like a fairy ring.' The Land Rover, unsurprisingly, was pretty much unscathed.

The Heinkel was replaced by a fourth-hand Morris Traveller with acute radiator problems which meant that Terry and Lyn had to cart tubs of water around with them wherever they went. They soon tired of that and got rid of it. From then on, the ex-GPO Morris Minor van in olive green would be the couple's motor of choice – 'an excellent car,' Terry continued to maintain, 'in spite of its tendency to go round corners in a series of straight lines'. And in spite of the rust, too. 'Rust was an important component of motor cars in those days,' Terry wrote. 'I think it was sprayed on under the paint.'

Their first Morris Minor van – there would be a series – did Terry and Lyn good service in and around the High Wycombe area. As Lyn recalled, on one memorable wintry night, in conditions which had caused a gritting lorry to overturn, the mighty Morris clung tenaciously to the road and sailed on through. It was also the sort of robust piece of transport in which you might reasonably think about packing up your belongings and heading west. Which was convenient, because Terry and Lyn were about to do just that.

7

THROWN TEAPOTS, FROZEN BEARDS AND SUGAR CRYSTAL CAKE BY THE CARPETS

It's late one Friday afternoon in the Chapel, and I am about to knock off and go home for the weekend when Terry calls me over to his desk.

'Rob, could I have a word about something?'

This is quite early in my tenure as Terry's assistant – early enough that I am still tentatively feeling my way into the job and taking nothing for granted. Early enough that Terry, too, is still feeling his way into the concept of having someone else around over whom he has authority.

I stand there expectantly for a little while. Terry appears to be very absorbed in whatever is in front of him on his desk. The wait seems to last a number of minutes. Terry eventually sits back and now stares very thoughtfully into the distance.

Still silence.

'Everything OK, Terry?' I say.

Terry's pensive expression doesn't change, nor does the direction of his gaze. More time passes. Finally Terry shakes his head a little and looks directly at me.

'No, no, no – I don't want to ruin your weekend. Let's deal with it on Monday.'

'But if there's something . . .' I say.

'No, no,' says Terry. 'Let's do it Monday.'

I go out to my car, extremely puzzled, and also quite worried. Have I done something wrong? Have I messed up somewhere? Have I misfiled something, or accidentally thrown something away? What's my offence here? Have I been less than suitably subordinate to Patch, the office cat, also known as 'the HR Department'? Have I run over one of the tortoises without realizing, driving in that morning? What the hell is it?

Over the ensuing weekend, my worry-level by no means diminishes. It's very hard to get my mind off the matter. I'm thinking back over everything that I've done in the week and trying to see where the problem might have occurred. And whatever it is, what does it all mean for the future of my job – which, incidentally, I'm really enjoying and would be more than sad to lose? It nags at me all Saturday and Sunday. By Monday, I'm pretty much coming apart with the suspense.

Terry is already at his desk when I arrive at the Chapel.

'Morning,' he says casually, and perfectly normally.

I go into the kitchen and put on the kettle. Nothing from Terry, who carries on working. I put a mug of tea down on Terry's desk. He thanks me without looking up from his work. I take my own tea back to my desk and sit there with it anxiously. Still nothing.

Eventually I can't handle it any longer.

'Terry, you said you wanted to talk to me about something.'

Terry looks up, confused.

'Did I?' says Terry. 'Did I really?'

'On Friday,' I say. 'It seemed quite specific.'

Terry picks up his mug and sits back in his chair with it. He continues to rack his brains, shaking his head slowly. Nothing is coming.

'No . . . no . . . Nothing I can remember.'

Then, abruptly, it all comes back to him.

'Oh, yes! Eric Price!'

Eric Price? Now I'm really confused.

'Eric Price!' Terry says again. 'Of course! I'd forgotten! *We'll talk about it on Monday*. Eric Price pulled that one on me in my first week at the *Western Daily Press* in Bristol. I spent the whole weekend worrying about it and then there was nothing, the bastard!'

It appears I have been pranked. It also appears that Terry has forgotten having set the prank up. So maybe I've been pranked twice, then. Does that work? Or maybe half-pranked? I'm not sure.

Terry, though, seems happy enough.

'I've waited about a hundred years to be in a position to try that on someone!' he says, beaming at me warmly.

Terry then goes back to his work. He seems to wear a glow of intense satisfaction for the rest of the day.

★ ★ ★ ★ ★

So who was this Eric Price? And how deeply had he embedded himself in Terry's psyche that Terry could still be interested in performing some kind of cathartic battle re-enactment at the expense of his newly appointed personal assistant some thirty years later?

And even before we get to all that, what was Terry doing with Eric Price at the *Western Daily Press* in Bristol in the first place?

By the autumn of 1970, Terry was 22 and had been working for the *Bucks Free Press* for five years. They had been good years, by and large, and exciting at first, and he had certainly learned a lot, and fast. But he had also settled quite quickly into a rhythm, the rhythm of the paper and its calendar, and the challenges of the job didn't seem to be getting any more demanding. The Marcus column in the new midweek edition had made life more interesting, but he had done nearly a hundred of those now and . . . well, did Buckinghamshire get small, or did Terry get bigger? As Jane Austen, once again, would have agreed, it is a truth universally acknowledged that a young man in possession of his wits, Pitman shorthand and five years on a local paper should be in want of a better job. Otherwise he could be writing about steam fairs, council meetings and golden anniversaries for the rest of his life. Terry had the distinct feeling that it was time to be getting on.

Or was it actually time to be getting *out*? This, too, seems to have occurred to Terry, a mark, perhaps, of a lack of clarity about his ambitions for himself at this point in his life. In a letter to Colin Smythe during 1969, written on *Bucks Free Press* notepaper and clearly composed while at a very low ebb, Terry seems to have been contemplating jumping ship and embarking on a different kind of career altogether.

> I was wondering if you knew anyone in the other publishing houses whom I could approach re. a job? To be frank I am getting thoroughly fed up with life on this paper, and it seems that one cannot get onto a national evening or daily without a long spell on a provincial evening. I have had quite a lot of experience of the production and subbing side – of newspapers – and have probably absorbed enough general experience to be of use . . . I was once sure that I wanted to stay on the writing side of the profession – but now I am having serious doubts.

Colin, who certainly himself had no job in publishing to offer Terry and who, moreover, had an outstanding contract for Terry's first novel and potentially two more novels after that, placated him and urged him to keep on with the writing, and Terry appears to have pursued the idea no further. Instead he reverted to thinking about a change of newspaper, scanning the ads in *Press Gazette*. How solidly his heart was in this, we can't really be sure, but it was certainly, in accordance with established notions about career paths, *the right thing to do*. And, in due course, a vacancy for a news reporter emerged at the *Western Daily Press* in Bristol, a six-day operation in a major metropolis which would surely qualify as an upgrade on the *Bucks Free Press* and a stepping stone towards the nationals, assuming that was what Terry wanted, which he quite possibly didn't, in fact, but . . . you know . . . again, it was *the right thing to do*.

And maybe a move out west would work. After all, Lyn's parents had now completed the renovation of their home out that way. And David and Eileen, courtesy, it would seem, of Eileen's smart work with some savings, had recently secured access to a weekend cottage near Tiverton.* And, of

. . . .

* Terry maintained that he once asked his father how Beaconsfield Urban District Council felt about one of their tenants owning a property elsewhere, and David assured course, the money Terry and Lyn would get from selling their starter home in Downley, considered to be within striking distance of London, would buy them somewhere quite a bit bigger than that, and possibly even detached, in the right, remote part of the west country. So Terry took the job and he and Lyn sold 4 Old Farm Road and began house-hunting. Then, just before Terry was due to start in his new role, they moved in with Terry's godfather, 'Uncle' Reg Dicks, at 3 Tyrone Walk, a cul-de-sac in the Bristol suburb of Knowle West. Lyn got herself a job at Boots in Bristol, and Terry went off to have a horrible time with Eric Price.

Within the newspaper industry, Price was revered and feared in equal measure as a force of nature, said by one colleague to 'hit like a tornado'. He had spent the Second World War driving petrol tankers around France and his experiences in the line of fire included escaping a confrontation with the Germans at St-Nazaire by clambering on board a cattle boat. Those kinds of things can be character-forming, and so can working at the *Daily Express*, which is where Price had been before he arrived in Bristol. The *Express* was a mighty national institution at the time, mighty enough to be described by the Duke of Edinburgh, in an unguarded moment in 1962, as 'a bloody awful newspaper . . . full of lies, scandal and imagination'. Having left the *Express* that very year, in all its bloody awfulness, Price looked around his new domain at the *Western Daily Press* and promptly announced that his mission was to remove what he unhesitatingly called 'the stench of death' about the place.

His main tactic for doing so was the application of a bullish, sleeves-rolled-up, Fleet Street approach to business, meaning the *Western Daily Press* would, as a local organ, have its expected share of flower shows and golden anniversary couples, but it would also now carry national news stories on its front page and become a vehicle for the daily confrontation of authority, going after bureaucrats, quisling politicians and town

. . . .

him that the person in the rents office had merely responded to this news with an encouraging smile and the words, 'Glad to hear that you're moving up in the world.' From which I think we can infer that either David heavily gilded this tale, or it was an exceptionally cheerful day in Beaconsfield Urban District Council's housing department.

planners, stirring things up, making a splash and, in the process, earning its spurs as – Price's tagline – 'the paper that fights for the west'.*

Price's other tactic – and this was properly cunning – was to make the *Western Daily Press look* like the *Daily Express*, on the newsstand, to the point where, according to the legend, an *Express* reporter visiting Bristol once bought it in mistake for his own paper. Maybe a few other people did, too. Either way, Price had raised the circulation of the *Western Daily Press* from a dangerously dwindling 12,000 in 1962 to a burgeoning 80,000 at the point of Terry's arrival.

Perhaps Terry and Eric were never going to get along. Terry, attesting to a long-standing divide within the industry, once described a newspaper sub-editor as 'the person who messes up what the reporter has written before it goes into the paper'.† This would not have been a prudent view to air around Eric Price, who believed that subbing – the trimming and punching-up of copy, the creation of catchy headlines – was a sacred art, and that subs were 'the uncrowned kings of journalism'. Many subs schooled by Price went on to bigger roles and, indeed, during Terry's time at the paper one employee wearily accused Price of running 'a boot camp for Fleet Street'. The master of the boot camp himself, meanwhile, was a workaholic who routinely put in six-day weeks and rarely took breaks, and certainly not for cultural recreation: after his death in 2013, at the age of 95, his obituary in the *Daily Telegraph* told the story of Price declining the offer of tickets to see a

....

* In the area of confronting authority, it's only fair to note, Price was very much an equal opportunities confronter, and stood, according to one assessment of him, against both 'pretentious Tory pomp and interfering socialism'.

† In later years, Terry's antipathy to newspaper subbing would find a particular focus in an episode in which a sub at a newspaper which shall remain nameless, but which was in fact the *Sunday Times*, changed the word 'numinous' in an article by Terry to the word 'luminous'. But here, it wasn't the relatively minor scale of the change that bothered Terry so much as the implication, from which he could not be dissuaded, that the sub had assumed Terry, as a writer of fantasy fiction, would not be someone who used the word 'numinous' but someone who simply *must* have meant 'luminous'. In other words, in that case it was the snobbery that got to Terry rather than the sub-editing.

Shakespeare production at the Bristol Old Vic and saying, 'Nothing wrong with Shakespeare a good sub couldn't put right.'

Clearly Terry's new boss didn't lack a sense of fun – but it was a certain kind of fun. Price's love of pranks extended to putting drawing pins on sub-editors' chairs and starting small fires underneath them as they worked. More typical of his office management style was the regular enraged flinging across the room of the office teapot and, on one occasion, of an entire typewriter, which missed its intended target – a young news reporter – smashed through a fourth-floor window and dropped into the street below.* It was also alleged that Price had slammed his hand down onto the subbing desk in fury one day, only to stab himself quite badly with the dreaded spike.†

This scrappy, punchy, hard-nosed and even self-injuring news-gathering environment was, it's safe to say, like nothing that Terry had come across at the *Bucks Free Press* under the benign Arthur Church, where the idea of becoming 'the paper that fights for Bucks' never seems to have gathered much steam. And such a boilingly uncompromising atmosphere was arguably never likely to dovetail with Terry's temperament, nor with his instant and practically allergic aversion to anything that smacked of tyranny or bullying.

And yet all began well enough for Terry when his first shift in Bristol coincided with breaking news of the death of the Egyptian President, Gamal Abdel Nasser, who marked this opening of a new door in Terry's career by suffering a fatal heart attack at the age of 52. Unlikely to have had Arthur Church clearing the front page of the *Bucks Free Press*, this story was most certainly a hot item for Eric Price and Terry, who had barely finished hanging up his coat for the first time in the *Western Daily Press*'s central Bristol office, found himself assigned to the writing of it.

'It wasn't a bad job, if I say so myself,' Terry wrote in the notes for his

. . . .

* Clearly I got off lightly with the solitary weekend of psych-warfare.

† TGTC (too good to check). That said, Martin Wainwright, Terry's future colleague in much happier times at the *Bath Evening Chronicle*, who relayed this story to me, indicated that it might have owed its origins to 'wishful thinking'.

autobiography. 'It is amazing what a writer can do in half an hour when they have access to press cuttings, one eye on the television next door, one telephone call behind them and a sensible amount of reasonable analysis.' And when, Terry might have added, they have Eric Price breathing down their neck. Either way, that first piece earned Terry a coveted thumbs-up from his new boss and enabled him to head home to Lyn in Knowle West in 'an enthusiastic frame of mind' about his new role and his ability to deal with it.

It was mostly downhill from there.

'I could not cope with the working hours on a daily newspaper,' Terry wrote. 'There was a fractured shift system, not helped by the fact that you could be required to do split shifts, a real bugger. It messed up my sleeping patterns and played merry hell with the social life. It might have been good for someone bent on a job with a national newspaper in a year or so's time, but it left me on the back foot most days.'

Worst of all for Terry was night duty, known as 'the graveyard shift'. One night, when Terry was alone in the reporters' room, the call came in that there was a man on the Clifton Suspension Bridge – a potential jumper. Terry was obliged to head out to the scene and what he saw there would never leave him. It was by no means the only time, either. 'It sometimes wasn't so bad if they landed in the water,' Terry wrote, 'but some hit the rocks.'

One night, driving back to the office from another soul-sapping act of witness at the Suspension Bridge, Terry was stopped by the police and breathalysed. When the reading came up entirely clear, Terry mournfully told his detaining officer, 'I've been with some of your colleagues and everything that could drop out of me tonight has already dropped out.'

We need to stress that there were easier interludes during this period – that life in Bristol for Terry wasn't all gruesome suicides and having the office teapot thrown at him while a small bonfire flickered under his chair. For instance, it was quickly discovered that Terry was the only member of the *Western Daily Press* staff who fitted the office black tie dinner outfit, so he and Lyn had a good run of free three-course meals at official functions in the Bristol area, mayoral and otherwise, with Terry as the paper's rep. Terry managed to write some fiction, too. Like the *Bucks Free Press*, the *Western Daily Press* had a children's page, 'The Sunshine Club', and Terry seems to have made a beeline for it. By as early as November 1970, just two months after arriving, he was supplying that space with short stories. What Eric Price made of 'Mr Trapcheese and his Ark' is now, alas, lost to the tides of history, but a smattering of other tales for that section were to follow, including the six-part 'The Time Travelling Caveman' and the three-part 'Prod Ye A-Diddle Oh!'.*

And that Christmas, equally far from the hard news beat, and with a lot more scope to be himself, tonally and in attitude, Terry found himself dispatched to Bristol's Broadmead shopping centre on a feature-page quest for those Christmas essentials – gold, frankincense and myrrh. All this while dressed in costume as an oriental king, courtesy of the wardrobe department at Bristol Arts Centre. 'Cool lot, Bristol shoppers,' wrote Terry. 'No one took a blind bit of notice of an oriental prince hopping along trying to keep his cloak out of puddles.'†

However, the overwhelming majority of the stories that appeared in the paper under the byline 'Terence Pratchett' were gritty news stories of the kind commissioned by or aimed to please Eric Price: 'Mother Gives a Kidney To Her Son', 'Another Solicitor Fights The Planners', 'Carbon Copy Gun Raid On Bank', 'Road Angle Could Kill, Say Drivers', 'County Crime Hits a Record Peak' . . . And quite apart from Price's anxiety-inducing presence in his life, Terry appears during this phase to have undergone something of an existential crisis regarding the very point of this kind of writing.

'I realized what troubled me about traditional news journalism,' Terry wrote. 'There was hardly any time to get to the truth that lay

. . . .

* Terry also seems to have provided the paper with stories under the pseudonym Patrick Kearns. Certainly drawings by Terry illustrate a Patrick Kearns festive item, 'A Partridge in a Post Box', published on Christmas Eve in 1970. Kearns was Terry's mother's name, and Patrick sits close to Pratchett.

† Broad findings of this quest: gold pretty easy to come by; frankincense and myrrh, forget it. Not even Boots stocks frankincense. Terry's conclusion: 'Next year I'll just buy a hamper.'

behind the facts.' Terry would find himself in the press seats at court, looking across at some hapless youth, in the dock for a wretched and ultimately pointless crime, and wondering 'why him and not me?', before realizing that nothing he was in a position to write about the case would ever produce anything like a satisfactory answer to that question. Another time, he interviewed a mother whose son had just been killed in a street fight and whose trauma was still fresh, and Terry was so appalled by the bluntness and the crassness of the questions he was obliged to ask her that the words began to dry in his mouth.

Yet another time, more comically, he had interviewed a witness at the scene of a domestic dispute and, with notebook poised, dutifully asked her for the standard personal details for attribution. The woman gave him her name and then, proprietorially watching Terry's pen, went on, 'aged twenty-nine comma blonde comma mother of three'. The woman's fluency in newspaper vernacular and her willingness to help a reporter out with the punctuation only brought home to Terry the rampant ubiquity of media-speak, and its hollowness. 'It was language as slices,' he wrote. 'It was box-ticking – shorthand for a longhand world, deflating the currency of communication to the point where journalists could do little more than stack the boxes neatly. It was a language that didn't allow for fine detail and didn't need much thought. Clichés are useful hammers and nails in communication's toolbox, but what happens when they become the whole thing?'

One can perhaps infer the intended answer to Terry's rhetorical question here: what happens is news journalism.

At the end of April 1971, after just eight months in the job, Terry wrote his last piece as a staffer for the *Western Daily Press* – an item about the trains from London getting faster which appeared under the headline 'The New "Bristolian" Speeds Up By Five Minutes'. And then he was gone.

What exactly went on? Terry frequently claimed that Price sacked him. But he also pointed out on many occasions that Price sacked people all the time, fairly indiscriminately, and frequently for the drama of the moment and without entirely meaning it. Sometimes you could be sacked simply because it was your turn to be made an example of. Indeed, so numerous were Price's firings that he could lose track of whom he had fired and whom he had not and, accordingly, staff quickly cottoned on to the fact that if, once fired, you simply turned up for work again the next day, there was a good chance you could just carry on with your job as if nothing had happened.* According to Lyn, Price sacked Terry not once, not twice, but three times in total. So on two of those occasions Terry must have gone back and carried on, as he was perhaps intended to. But the third time he didn't.

'My health was bad,' Terry admitted. He had begun suffering from an upset stomach and then apparently had a couple of blackouts. On one especially fraught and confrontational occasion he allegedly fainted clean away on the office carpet in front of Price, who unsentimentally responded, 'Someone get that body out of here.'† According to Lyn, Terry went to hospital at this time for scans to ensure that he hadn't had a stroke or a heart attack. The verdict was that he was suffering from stress, and the source of the stress wasn't hard to put a finger on.

So Terry, in a bad way, left the *Western Daily Press*. It would be the best part of a year before he wrote anything for a newspaper again.

★ ★ ★ ★ ★

In some respects, a period of downtime for Terry, a spell in which to be at home and nurse his bruises, couldn't have come at a better moment. There was a lot of work to be done on the new house.

Terry and Lyn did not need to rely for very long on the kindness and the spare bedroom of Uncle Reg in Knowle West. Their property searches, conducted on weekend sorties to the countryside in the olive green Morris van, soon turned up a place that they wanted to buy and could afford – a little, low-lying eighteenth-century cottage that had belonged to a retired priest and his wife, in the small Somerset village

....

* As I mentioned near the beginning of this book, Terry's firings of me, although they took place in a much smaller office and were therefore easier to keep track of, were subject to a similar law of forgetfulness, which might be something else he owed to Eric Price.

† TGTC.

of Rowberrow in the Mendip Hills, about fifteen miles south-west of Bristol. The place was called Gaze Cottage. It had once been thatched, but was now tiled, and it had also once been a sweet shop, which explained the outsized downstairs window, and the view from its main bedroom swept across the valley to the Dolebury Warren hill fort. Terry would say it reminded him strongly of his original home in Forty Green.

Adding to the texture of those memories, perhaps, would have been the dilapidated nature, at first, of the house, which didn't run to life-endangering tiles, as Terry's first house had, but did run to a few other shortcomings. Lyn and Terry had moved in during the bleak midwinter of 1970 and just how cold their new cottage could get, especially overnight, was fully discovered by Terry one morning when he woke up to find his beard slightly crunchy with ice. If they hadn't realized it already, they now did: this house was going to be 'a project'. The good news was, they were able to get a grant from the council to assist with the renovation. The bad news was, the amount of renovation that the place needed would very quickly consume the grant and leave them scraping for more.

Every door but one had to be replaced, for one thing. So did the ceilings. In fact there weren't many features of the house that didn't require some kind of attention or upgrade – with the strong exception, that is, of the iron rings on the front wall. Long before it was the priest's in his retirement, Gaze Cottage had been a carter's home and, fixed into its external brickwork on the side-wall to the right of the house, were two rings, the 'carter's links', about three inches in diameter, which the carter had used to tether his horses. The instruction passed down through the ages – or, at any rate, communicated by the Toveys who lived in the valley – was never to cover those rings, or else . . . well, perhaps best not to find out what dark historic retribution might be visited on the household if the rings got covered. The Pratchetts certainly considered it prudent to go along with the tradition, and never under their ownership were those rings anything less than accessible to anyone who needed them, from whatever period in time. Lyn says that, while she and Terry lay in bed at night, they could sometimes seem to hear the sound outside of what they called 'the ghost horses'.

This, incidentally, was not the only spectral noise that Gaze Cottage offered up to its new owners. Terry and Lyn also had the strong impression that the formerly resident priest was still around in some form or other. One morning around 8.00 a.m., after Terry had left for work, Lyn heard a ticking noise enter the room, cross to the fireplace and then go to the window. When she mentioned this to the neighbours, they argued that what she had heard was probably the pocket watch of the house's former owner, and suggested, matter-of-factly, that he might be wondering what she was doing in there. Terry and Lyn called him Preb, short for 'prebendary', and through the ensuing years both of them would hear the ticking of Preb's pocket watch from time to time.

Something else in the house which seemed to have a life of its own: the damp. The cottage seemed to have damp the way that other houses had bricks. Its walls were of ashlar construction – one course of stone thick – and they somehow seemed to draw into themselves rain, mist, dew, steam from the kettle and anything else of a wet nature that was in the atmosphere. Retrospectively, Terry was to realize that the best approach would have been to reach an accommodation with the damp – 'to accept it,' as Terry wrote, 'as an integral part of the property and figure out ways to let the moisture evaporate harmlessly.' Instead, he and Lyn took advice and embarked upon a costly project to install a modern damp course – a tactic which was extremely disruptive and which also, when finished, seemed to have the unlooked for effect of actually increasing the presence of damp. They would get the upper hand over the moisture eventually, but it was a battle they never entirely won.

No matter. They loved where they were – loved the cottage, loved its garden, loved the surroundings. They would stomp together all over the Mendip Hills – above and below, exploring the caves, pot-holes and old mineshafts, relishing the slightly mysterious flavour of the area's medieval forts. From the top of Dolebury Warren, a vista of fields opened up which, on a clear day, rolled all the way to the Bristol Channel. They loved the pubs, too. The advantage of The Swan at the top of the road was that you could draw a straight line from there to the cottage, making navigation home at the end of a night of cider-drinking less perilous than it might have been. But a more deeply traditional Somerset experience was to be found at The Star on the A38, a true cider house with a low-lit parlour, largely peopled by the older kind of citizen whose teeth, or rather their absence, bore witness to lifetimes of enthusiastic scrumpy drinking. Here, of an evening, while your glass was being filled with due mystery in a back room, you might fall into illuminating conversation with a man called Lightning, so named because he had defied the old saying and been struck by it twice. Terry noted, with enthusiasm, among the clientele 'the ancestral hats, dogs and slightly dodgy shotguns', passed down, he felt sure, through the generations. 'The Mendips reminded me in some ways of where I was born,' Terry wrote, 'but there was something anarchic about the area, too – a certain sense of "'tis my delight on a shiny night" – and, of course, a foggy night as well.'*

This was Terry's loose-end period, and it ended up lasting the best part of a year. Lyn continued to work in Bristol. Terry looked for jobs. He read a lot of books, returning to the kind of properly absorbed reading that he hadn't been able to do much of since he left school and started work. He wrote down some ideas for books of his own. He fixed up the house and he supervised others fixing up the house, and he walked and drank scrumpy. And he began slowly to recover his equilibrium after those punishing few months at the *Western Daily Press*.

★ ★ ★ ★ ★

And, of course, this was also the period in which he began to be a published novelist. With the rewrites done and the illustrations completed, the time was finally approaching, fully two years after the signing of the original contract, for the release onto the bookshop shelves of Terry's first proper book.

In October, Colin Smythe took a dummy copy of *The Carpet People* to the 1971 Frankfurt Book Fair, where he forced his way in

---

* Alluding here, of course, with a certain amount of geographic licence, to the traditional English folk song 'The Lincolnshire Poacher'.

among – by the calculation of the *New York Times*'s reporter at the event – 3,522 exhibits from 58 countries touting something in the region of 78,000 new titles. And despite the competition, Colin secured interest in his first-time author from a German publisher – Terry's first foreign sale.[*] Less auspiciously, back in the UK, the printers then produced a run of the book in which the illustrations were upside down. Those had to be sent back where they came from and redone. Come November, however, the book was ready on the pad for launch.

As a small, independent publishing house, Colin Smythe Limited weren't especially in the business of staging splashy, themed parties in order to attract attention to the publication of their books; and nor, in all honesty, were they really in the business of publishing books that suited splashy, themed launch parties. But for Terry and *The Carpet People* they saw the value in pushing out the boat. Accordingly, an early-evening drinks party took place in the carpet department of Heal's, the high-end home furnishings store in Tottenham Court Road in central London. Colin also cunningly secured some sponsorship for the event from the British Wool Marketing Board – a once in a lifetime synergy between the Pratchett brand and one of the UK's leading agricultural commodity organizations.

Terry and Lyn arrived early. A special cocktail, appetizingly labelled Essence of Underlay, was mixed for the occasion, featuring cherry brandy and miscellaneous other ingredients now, perhaps fortunately, forgotten. Guests were also served from trays of Carpet People-appropriate canapés: Smoked Weft-borer and Purple Groad, Fried Tromp and Green Glebe Salad, Stewed Snarg with Master Mushrooms, Chrystobella Cheese, and Sugar Crystal Cake. Publishing types, booksellers and a sprinkling of literary journalists drank, munched and mingled amid the shop's rolls of carpet. Heal's publicity department had rustled up some children from somewhere and Terry staged an impromptu cartoon workshop for them on the floor of the

....

[*] The *New York Times* also noted a shifting cultural current at Frankfurt that year: 'Pornography, which took up an entire hall last year, is down . . . having now to share space with all sorts of socialist texts of the dogmatic and undogmatic varieties.'

store, teaching them to draw Snargs. Later, a speech introducing Terry and hymning his book was made by the then chairman of Colin Smythe Limited, Sir Robert Mayer.* With the kids on the floor doing drawings at one end of the room, and 92-year-old Sir Robert waxing lyrical at the other, Terry's book launch, whatever else could be said about it, almost certainly had the widest age range among its guests of any literary party in London that night. It was Terry's first experience of being the centre of attention at a convivial occasion designed specifically to celebrate his creative achievement and he seemed to adapt pretty well to the concept – indeed to rise to it and expand slightly under the warmth of the public gaze, which is just as well, because there would be one or two other such occasions down the years.

It was his first experience, too, of signing copies of his work, which he also appeared to relish. Dave Busby couldn't make the launch, but Terry gave his friend a copy of the book with the illustrations hand-coloured, in fond acknowledgement of that formative Axminster in Dave's mother's house. The inscription read: 'To Dave Busby, Owner of the Carpet'.

So, that was the crack of the starting pistol, and Terry, now out of the blocks as a published novelist, capitalized on the wind at his back and shot up the track, gathering speed, sales and readers and locking directly into the fast-twitch rhythm of the dizzyingly prolific output for which the world has since come to know and revere him.

Not exactly. There wouldn't be another book for four and a half years. But there would be chickens. And bees. Not to mention goats.

. . . .

* Sir Robert Mayer was a German philanthropist who moved to England in 1896, made his fortune in banking and then founded the London Philharmonic Orchestra and set up the famous Robert Mayer Concerts for Children. He made his appearance on *Desert Island Discs* at the age of 100, and died in 1985 at the age of 105. We should all live as long and as well as Sir Robert Mayer.

8

SPUR-THIGHED REPTILES, CHICKENS
IN BARRELS AND EVERYTHING
BUT THE SOLAR STOVE

It's fair to say that the publication of *The Carpet People* did not instantly change Terry's life. Once the glasses had been cleared away and the crumbs of Sugar Crystal Cake swept up, Heal's went back to being a furniture store and Terry went back to being unemployed in Somerset. The reviews for the book were almost entirely positive. True, the *Sunday Times*, in a brief mention of the novel, seemed to find it a little over-peopled: 'Mr Pratchett's lively invention and neat characterization will please readers if they have the staying power to grasp the identities of so many races and folk.' But for the *Daily Express*, the tale was 'strangely gripping' and the *Irish Times* described the work as 'a new dimension in imagination' and added, glowingly, 'the prose is beautiful.' *Smith's Trade News*, a periodical of the publishing industry, lauded *The Carpet People* as 'one of the most original tots' tomes to hit the bookshops for many a decade' – and though Terry would have reacted quite allergically to the journalese expression 'tots' tomes', he would no doubt have appreciated the hymn in general. And *Teachers' World*, the magazine of the teaching profession, declared Terry's work to be 'of quite extraordinary quality'.*

. . . .

* No sneering at *Teachers' World*. It may not exist any more but it could count on Enid Blyton as a major contributor during the 1920s and 1930s.

For a first children's book by an unknown author to attract any kind of attention in print at all was going some, and a glowing testament both to the magnetism of Terry's writing and to the skill of Colin Smythe in plying the right people at the right time with cherry brandy and novelty nibbles. Nevertheless, of the 3,000 copies of *The Carpet People* that were printed, around 1,000 eventually sold – a significant portion to libraries – while 500 went off to Australia as remainders, and neither Terry nor Colin would be retiring any time soon on those numbers.* Terry was officially and indisputably a fully fledged author of fiction now, which was, of course, hugely satisfying and the fulfilment of a childhood ambition. But being a fully fledged author of fiction still left him in the state he had always assumed fiction-writing would: as a man in need of a job.

Fortunately, a job was about to turn up. In the spring of 1972, Terry, who had been casting around, took a call from a former colleague at the *Bucks Free Press* asking him if he would be interested in returning to his old paper, but this time as a sub-editor rather than as a news reporter. In some ways, such a move could have been interpreted as a climb-down, or even a slightly humiliating retreat. Had not Terry boldly left the nurturing arms of the *Bucks Free Press* in order to step onto the escalator bearing him inexorably towards national newspaper glory? And was he now going to come slinking back, battered by the experience, his confidence dented, to catch his breath in a desk job? For as Terry well knew, 'on the whole, sub-editors are chair-jockeys. They don't go out much, or even talk much, unless it's to call across the office, "'Ere! Who's this bugger Aristophanes?"' Still, this was undeniably where he was, and why hide from it? The *Western Daily Press* hadn't worked out, and the *Bucks Free Press*, under the benign leadership of Arthur Church – the man, let's remember, who had originally spotted something he liked about Terry's 'jib' – must

. . . .

* A good first edition of *The Carpet People* in 2021 can fetch about £450. A hand-coloured one, of which Terry is believed to have produced about a dozen, would easily fetch four figures. None of this would have seemed an especially likely outcome back when Colin was bundling up those remainders for Australia.

have risen into Terry's line of vision at this point as a warm and tempting refuge.

Of course, Lyn and Terry regarded themselves as Somerset-dwellers now – or certainly as Gaze Cottage-dwellers. They had found a home they loved, garden and ghosts included, and they had no desire to sell up and return wholesale to Buckinghamshire. So initially, in the spring of 1972, Terry, aged 24, became a weekly commuter. While Lyn remained in Rowberrow, Terry drove east on a Sunday night, stayed in Beaconsfield with his parents for the week and then drove back down to Somerset for the weekend. But that degree of separation didn't seem to make either Lyn or him particularly happy, so in due course they found a flat to rent cheaply on the ground floor of an Edwardian house on Amersham Hill in High Wycombe, moving in along with a growing collection of tortoises, who also commuted.

The tortoises were Terry's fault: he had discovered that he could not see a tortoise without forming the urge to 'rescue' it. This first happened in a pet shop in the Frogmore district of High Wycombe, and would happen in several other pet shops thereafter until the collection of rescued tortoises stood at around ten – some of the Mediterranean breed, some spur-thighed. Years later, Terry would still be prone to this rescuing urge. On tour in Glasgow in the 1990s, he released a tortoise soon to be known as Big Spotty from its captivity in a city centre pet shop – and was then appalled when someone at the airport told him he couldn't board his plane with it.* 'You can't stop me,' Terry said, rather grandly. 'This is Great Britain.' Big Spotty flew with Terry to Southampton.

Under this new commuting arrangement, Lyn found clerical work in High Wycombe. The pair of them would do their jobs all week and then on Friday, which was the slow day, post-publication, at the *Bucks Free Press*, Terry would try to get away early, and they would box up the tortoises, load them into the Morris van and head for the

. . . .

* These were the days, clearly, before the invention of the 'emotional support tortoise'. Carrying land-dwelling reptiles onto aircraft is presumably a far simpler project now.

west country, mostly by the back roads and with a stop for fish and chips in Marlborough where, according to Terry, 'the chippy was particularly good.' They would split their life in this way for eighteen months.

Terry appears to have slid back into life at the *Bucks Free Press* very smoothly, and most likely with much relief. As well as sub-editing the paper, he resumed his Uncle Jim duties, and 'Children's Circle' once again became the low-key platform for superior storytelling in the form of such tales as 'Johnno the Talking Horse', 'The Time-Travelling Television' and 'Rincemangle, the Gnome of Even Moor' in which readers will have found Terry playing with ideas about gnomes dwelling secretly in a department store that eventually, in 1989, became *Truckers*, the first book of the children's trilogy *The Bromeliad*. Terry also found time to produce some general, ruminative Marcus columns, the first of which appeared on 1 March 1972, and he turned in a couple of short notices relating to the business of Colin Smythe Limited – one on the elevation of the company's chairman Sir Robert Mayer to the Order of the Companions of Honour in the New Year Honours List of 1973, and another on the death that same month of Terry's fellow Colin Smythe Limited author Maurice Collis. What there wasn't under the Terry Pratchett byline this time around was anything on luckless farmers drowned in wells or the victims of domestic abuse. That kind of frontline news-gathering was for somebody else now. Terry was firmly a chair-jockey.

And happier for it, too. For all the inconvenience of dividing their life between two places, this seems to have been a period of much contentment for Terry and Lyn, certainly by contrast with Terry's months in Bristol. From Amersham Hill, they could walk to everywhere they wanted to get to, including work and also the Chinese restaurant, Chinese food having spread from Beaconsfield to High Wycombe by this point. Dave Busby, now working as a screen printer in Reading, introduced Terry to Steeleye Span's 1971 folk rock album *Please to See the King*, and though music had never been especially prominent among Terry's interests, he loved that record and locked on to it, and he and Lyn, with Dave, started spending evenings at the High Wycombe folk club and at nearby pubs where folk bands were playing.* Back at the flat, Terry and Lyn began to make their own wine – plum wine and fig wine, the latter made with the cheap dried figs available at the local International grocery store. Wine bottles stood fermenting around the gas fire in the sitting room, just behind the tortoises in the priority queue for warmth and with Terry and Lyn forming a third, outer ring beyond that.

Also in that room was a table at which Terry would sit and draw cartoons. Colin Smythe Limited had begun publishing, under the editorship of Peter Bander, *The Psychic Researcher & Spiritualist Gazette*, the monthly journal of the Spiritualist Association of Great Britain. Terry was commissioned to supply the publication with a comic strip, and he promptly came up with the concept of Warlock Hall, a craggy English country pile and the headquarters of the government's 'Psychic Research & Development Institute', where, to quote the strip's first panel, 'a crack team of scientists, led by young, dynamic Dr Tom Bowler, replace the old ignorant superstitions with . . . er . . . well, SCIENTIFIC superstitions'. Thus was it clear from frame one that the publication's new cartoonist had no particular brief to take the claims of psychic research entirely seriously, and so it proved. In one cartoon, a sign on the door of the 'Mediums Lab' advises visitors: 'Please Ring, As Knocking Causes Confusion'. Whether the more earnest members of the Spiritualist Association appreciated this kind of ribbing in their monthly journal is not clear, but Terry supplied Warlock Hall strips for seventeen issues.

Also, thrillingly, Terry's association with that journal resulted in a once-in-a-lifetime collaboration between the future author of the Discworld novels and Fanny Cradock – not two people one would necessarily have imagined sharing a page, or anything much else, with the possible exception, I suppose, of a Black Forest gateau. Cradock at the time was probably the UK's most prominent TV chef. Her low and growly voice

. . . .

* An artist called Paul Simon played at High Wycombe Folk Club in the mid-1960s. I wonder what became of him.

was once definitively described as sounding like 'a circular saw going through a sheet of gin-soaked cardboard', and her bullying around the kitchen counters of her husband and assistant, Johnnie, was a bold step for sexual politics and female primacy in an era that was not famous for such things. But what was perhaps less well known about Fanny Cradock was that she considered herself to be psychic, had done so since an early age, and was once suspended from school for staging a séance. Fanny and Johnnie were therefore well placed to co-author a column for *The Psychic Researcher*, which they supplied under the byline 'Red Herring', and in July 1973 that column appeared accompanied by an illustration by Terry, a cartoon of a rather perky-looking fish – the titular Red Herring, we are to assume – wearing a robe.* Alas, the collaboration began and ended there, and Terry's and Fanny's paths were never to entwine again, either in this world or, so far as we know, in any other.

Meanwhile, in between working and drawing and going to the folk club, Terry was putting together his next book. He wondered for a while whether he should write a sequel to *The Carpet People* and he talked about the idea quite a lot, both with Colin and with Dave Busby. But Terry then decided that – as he put it in a letter to Colin – even though he felt a follow-up could be 'as intrinsically good as the first', it might seem to the reader as though 'the convenient background was being exploited' and would also 'take away the mystery of the carpet'. Terry's reservations about exploiting the setup slightly puzzled Colin – and given that he was eventually the author of 41 Discworld books, a reluctance to return to the same fictional space and find new corners of it to poke into would hardly characterize Terry's later approach as a novelist. Perhaps the thoughts he voiced were merely an attempt to rationalize his desire not to make his second outing another children's book, but to try to produce something for adults this time. Either way, his mind was obviously made up, and instead of 'Carpet People II: Return to the

. . . .

* Though the column appeared under a pseudonym, the authors were happy to out themselves in a copyright line at the foot of the piece, reserving its rights to 'John & Fanny Cradock'.

Axminster', Terry began work on a science fiction story which would become *The Dark Side of the Sun*, mostly chipping away at the book in evening sessions where he would set himself the target of writing 400 words, but occasionally applying himself to it more strenuously. In August 1973, for example, during what was ostensibly a week off work in Rowberrow, Terry reported to Colin that he was racing along with the novel – with a 'heavily rewritten' third draft of it, in fact – at the rate of 3,000 words per day.

Writing, and life in general, seemed to be in a steady flow at this point for Terry and Lyn. They were earning some money, they were happy in the flat in Amersham Hill, and they were even more happy when they were back in Rowberrow. The commuting back and forth was the only wrinkle, the excellence of those fish and chips in Marlborough notwithstanding. If only there was a job Terry could find in which he felt as comfortable as he did at the *Bucks Free Press*, but which was within reach of Rowberrow and which didn't force him, Lyn and the tortoises to take their chances each weekend with the Friday night traffic on Marlow Hill. If he could find the right job in the west country, then surely everything would be perfect.

★ ★ ★ ★ ★

The offices of the *Bath and Wilts Evening Chronicle* were in the centre of Bath on Westgate Street. Every afternoon at 3.30, from Monday through to Saturday, the printing presses would rumble into life and the whole building would shake as the day's edition clattered into existence in the basement. Then at 5.00 p.m., everything would fall quiet again.

Two other key things about those offices: they were only 25 miles from Rowberrow and in September 1973 they had a vacancy inside them for a sub-editor.

Terry saw the ad for the job in a staff circular from Westminster Press, the local newspaper group, and he jumped at it. And so it was that he came to leave the *Bucks Free Press* for a second time, yet apparently with Arthur Church's blessing and a very good reference. He would be in Bath for the best part of seven years, until 1979, just after his 31st birthday, and of the three newspapers that Terry worked at, this was certainly where he was happiest. Like the *Bucks Free Press*, it was a thriving yet largely benign workplace. There was a Lancastrian news editor, Maurice Boardman, who would dish it out noisily when people fell short of his expected standards, but even he was agreed to be essentially kind and encouraging. And Terry's immediate boss, Gerald Walker, the chief sub, was clearly an absolute gent, courteous and warm, and from a family with a long association with the *Chronicle*, indeed who may even at one time have owned it. Meanwhile, everyone was hopelessly in love with Rita Hancock, the editorial secretary, and, in some cases, also with her teenage daughter, Christine. Staff amused themselves by trying to sneak the Word of the Week into stories, or by pranking Bob Foulkes, the senior reporter, who once, in the course of following a tip-off about a fire at Windsor Castle, had ended up getting the Royal PR team on the phone and berating them loudly for their lack of helpfulness. The fire was actually at the Windsor Castle pub in Upper Bristol Road.

And if pranking Bob Foulkes wasn't an option, you could always try to find an unobtrusive way to say the word 'golly' in the presence of Mrs Robertson from the local Robertson's jam dynasty, who was a big player on the Bath cultural scene and quite frequently visited the paper's office.* Indeed, visitors in general, and local people who fancied they had a story to tell, would frequently drift through the doors at Westgate Street in search of a receptive ear, and if you happened to write a piece that was critical of, say, Bath's Theatre Organ Society, you would quite likely find members of that society crowding up the back stairs to have a word with you about it. The paper rather prided itself on that openness. 'We were accountable,' said Martin Wainwright, later of the *Guardian*, the author of a piece that was critical of Bath's Theatre Organ Society, and a good friend of Terry's during this period.

'We were also very lucky in our time and place,' Martin said. 'Bath's exceptional beauty was at its height with plenty of melancholy decay and

* Until retired in 2002, Golly was Robertson's increasingly time-worn trademark.

Left: With Florence 'Granny' Pratchett at Forty Green, a few years before she introduced him to G. K. Chesterton and smoking.

Below: Terence David John Pratchett, aged two, in 1950, defiantly refusing to watch the birdie.

Below right: A kid among the pigeons in Trafalgar Square, c.1954, at the feet of his mother, Eileen, and with a family friend.

Below: One of Terry's school exercise books, visibly struggling to contain his imagination.

Science Fantasy

Vol. 20 No. 60

1963

CONTENTS

Editor : JOHN CARNELL
Cover Illustration by GERARD QUINN from "Same Time, Same Place"

...INGS AND SIXPENCE
.. (Australia) Ltd. ... N.Z.

Above: On holiday in Cornwall, 1958, aged ten. A new school term starting shortly, but who cares?

Above left: In print for the first time, aged fifteen.

Left, below: Courting in Buckinghamshire, mid-sixties. Terry, photographed by Lyn; Terry and Lyn together, photographed by Lyn's mum. White polo neck, model's own.

WINSCOMBE (GALES) VIDEO CLUB

Name MR T.D.J. PRATCHETT.

Address GAYES COTTAGE SCHOOL LANE ROWBERROW WINSCOMBE

Membership No. 38

Signature T.D.J.Pratchett

Top: Terry becomes the most married man on the planet, 5 October 1968.

Above: The bride and groom process between a hedge and some shops, Gerrards Cross.

Right: Terry's first video rental card, for Pratchett Family Movie purposes.

Right: Old tech is the best tech. Terry's customized ZX81.

Below: Patent Rowberrow beekeeping/biker-wear.

Above: Terry and Lyn in Rowberrow, enjoying some quality time with Meg and Honey, their Devonshire-bred Toggenburg goats.

Below: The author moves swiftly to contain an unwanted swarming incident.

Above: Terry with Colin Smythe at the launch of *The Carpet People* at Heal's in London, 1971. Sticky cocktails and sugar crystal cake not shown.

Right: Terry on his last day at the CEGB, October 1987. Full-time writing beckons.

Below: Pratchett cats: in this case, Hobbes and the first of three given the name 'Little My'.

Left: With Rhianna, aged sixteen.

Right: Father and daughter at the *Honey, I Shrunk the Kids* exhibit at Walt Disney World Resort, Florida, 1990.

Below: The sketch of Rincewind that Terry drew for Bernard Pearson. Figurines followed.

Below right: On holiday at EPCOT.

general worried expression

Poor, shaggly beard

'ill-fitting' robe

Rincewind

Above: PC blazing, and in full 'nauthor' mode, Rowberrow, late eighties.

Right: On a rock in Australia.

Below: With his mum and dad, Eileen and David, taken by Rhianna in 1998.

Top: Rhianna, Terry and Lyn in full regalia in 1995 for Stephen Briggs's am-dram adaptation of *Maskerade*.

Above: With Jack Cohen and Ian Stewart, taking *The Science of Discworld* on the road, 1999.

Left: A locust cast in silver by Terry, c.1975.

a wistful air of past glories. It was small enough for a reporter to master completely in three years, but much more varied than its genteel image suggested.' All in all, the contrast with Terry's Bristol experience could not have been sharper, as evidenced by the fact that Lyn would bake cakes for Terry to take in to the other subs on the desk, who seemed to become addicted to them, not least the lemon drizzle. 'Think of their little faces,' Terry would say to her, beseechingly, when the requests came back from the office for another one. At no point, to the best of my knowledge, had Terry considered putting a lemon drizzle cake under the nose of Eric Price. As Martin put it, 'I'm sure Terry found the warm, friendly and communal life of the *Chronicle* a pleasure after the tyranny of the *Western Daily Press*.'

And then there was the fact that the *Chronicle* offered Terry a shed to work in, up on the roof of the building, among the chimneys, where he was free to come and go and take thoughtful breaks to feed the pigeons. Or so Terry said down the years, and repeatedly. But there is no record of a shed on the roof of the *Bath Evening Chronicle* offices at Westgate Street, no clear reason why the paper would have had a shed up there, and very little indication that a sub-editor would have been allowed to work on his own in it even if there had been one. Quite apart from anything else, to whom would he have been able to shout, ''Ere, who's this bugger Aristophanes?' when he needed to? Apart from the pigeons, obviously. Put it down to hallucination, perhaps.

Martin remembers Terry at that time as 'quite a shy man with a slightly unconvincing chortle of the "hurr hurr hurr" variety and what I have to admit I thought was a rather contrived sense of humour which later served him so well in the books'. He also recalls Terry's predilection for 'bright, hooped sweaters'. In a photograph taken to mark the *Chronicle*'s centenary in 1977, Terry, bald and with a thick black beard, alone favours the ragged, stripy wool look, in a team otherwise given to shirts and jackets. Though Martin was a news reporter and Terry a sub, they collaborated from time to time on features that were slightly off-beam and which made material for the paper's 'Day by Day' slot – subtitled, somewhat self-consciously, 'and now for something completely different'. Typical of those was a piece headlined 'Yo heave ho, and mind the bananas adrift in the bilges', featuring the strap-line: 'Being the unexpurgated (i.e. incredibly long) account of an 11-hour journey by double canoe from Chippenham to Bath by Martin Wainwright, who did most of the drawings, and Terry Pratchett, who did most of the paddling'.

When Martin, to Terry's disappointment, left Bath in the mid-seventies for a new job at the *Bradford Telegraph & Argus*, he decided to make the journey on foot and insured Terry to drive his Morris Minor so that he could bring it north stuffed with everything Martin owned. They stayed in touch for a while after that, Martin and his wife Penny visiting Terry and Lyn in Rowberrow, and Terry going north to join Martin on the Lyke Wake Walk, a tough 40-mile yomp across rough country in the North York Moors which is intended to be completed in 24 hours. At 2.00 a.m., as the pair of them topped the Cleveland Escarpment after hours in the pitch darkness, a blaze of light was suddenly visible along the Tees below.

'What is that?' exclaimed Terry in wonder.

'Middlesbrough,' replied Martin.

Some time after this, Martin received a letter from Lyn, requesting the recipe for his mum's honey-spiced chicken dish which had featured memorably at Martin's leaving do in Bath, and bringing him up to date with life as it was unfolding in Rowberrow. Lyn reported that Terry was 'glued either to a spade or a typewriter', knocking out 1,000 words a night on a new book which was 'very exciting, full of action involving the Vikings, Saxons, flying carpets, dragons and demons, to mention a few'.* 'Terry gets too tired to worry,' Lyn added. 'If he's not digging, he's writing. Life is hectic but rewarding.'

Indeed. The phase that was well underway at this point would eventually roll on to become two golden decades of growing-your-own at Rowberrow. The notion of self-sufficiency and the anti-corporate lifestyle had penetrated British culture deeply enough that, by 1975, there would be a BBC sitcom on the theme – *The Good Life* – and to the

----

* That would be *Strata*, by the sound of things, which became Terry's third published novel.

casual observer there might have appeared to be a hint of Tom and Bar-
bara about Terry and Lyn during this period of their lives, albeit without
the piping-hot middle-classness. In their cottage garden they cultivated
apple trees, rhubarb plants, redcurrant bushes and blackcurrant bushes,
raspberries and strawberries. The couple of hundred pounds that Terry
received as an advance for his second book were converted directly into a
greenhouse, and the money he received for his third book was converted into a bigger greenhouse. There were tomatoes and potatoes and
beans of several types. There were cats and there were tortoises, of
course – and sometimes, when slippers were left to warm by the open
fire, the tortoises would spot an opportunity and crawl into them. More
dangerously, the tortoises might even creep at night into the fire's still-
warm embers, so you had to be careful, when you re-lit the fire in the
morning, that you weren't accidentally using a tortoise for kindling.
According to Lyn, there was at least one occasion when a tortoise had to
be urgently run under the cold tap in the kitchen. There were also chickens, who initially slept and laid their eggs in a cider barrel and who later
enjoyed conditions of some luxury when Terry adapted and expanded
the outdoor privy for their use. And there were doves – first in a box on
the lawn, and then in a dove house. Later, when Terry and Lyn could
afford to have a garage put up, they made sure to design it with a dove
house built in.

Then there were goats, two half-Toggenburgs and a half-Nubian
with long ears called Henny who one day panicked while Lyn was
walking the three of them down the hill on leads and shot off, dragging
her practically the length of the valley. In due course, Terry and Lyn
expanded their estate by buying an allotment opposite the house that,
according to Terry, had once been owned and tilled by members of a
'non-conformist congregation, all of whom had long since lined up for
the pearly gates'. The allotment was turned over to the growing of vegetables. After that, with a bit of help from Lyn's dad, they acquired a
two-acre field a little way down the hill from the cottage and then up
the hill on the other side, and commenced the monumental labour of
purging it of couch grass roots. They built a shelter on it for the goats,
who could live out there and be walked back to the house for milking.

There were badger sets at the top of that field, and adders in its grass, and Terry one day found the flattened corpse of an adder which had been stamped to death by one of the goats. Goats knew how to look after themselves.

So did bees. A local master of the craft, an elderly man called Mr Brooks, the county beekeeper for Somerset no less, taught Terry the art of beekeeping and was apparently 'happy enough to educate a young man who drank cider and didn't mind getting bees down his trousers'. Terry and Lyn kept three beehives, at first in the garden. However, on more than one occasion, the bees swarmed, billowing out of the hives in a state of some anger, and had to be retrieved, variously, from the honeysuckle hedge, from up a tree and from next door's garden. More generally, some of the bees seemed to resent Lyn putting the washing out and were prepared to make their position on this matter clear by getting in her hair while she did so. In due course, the hives were moved up to the field.

Terry had acquired an MZ motorbike, another in the extending line of bracingly unfashionable machines with which he allowed himself to be associated. Just as Terry's Dunkley Whippet had fallen tragically short in its attempt to ape the stylish Italian cool of the Lambretta, so his MZ would now fall tragically short in its attempt to ape the glossy German engineering prowess of the BMW. Chiefly this machine served the purpose of delivering Terry in no style whatsoever to and from the *Chronicle* at Westgate Street, where he was free to park directly under the office. But the bike could also be pressed into service as agricultural machinery, ferrying Terry up the road to the field and back, along with whatever bits and pieces needed to be taken that way. And thus it was that Lyn would look out of the window from time to time and catch sight of her husband, in full white beekeeping regalia, aboard his motorbike, knees spread wide, precariously balancing hive frames across the MZ's petrol tank, and wending his way gently and not a little surreally between the cottage and the field. In honour of this rare intersection between apiarist activities and motorcycling, Terry decorated the back of his beekeeping overall in thick black marker pen with the legend 'HELL'S BEEKEEPERS', the words arranged around a cartoon skull and crossbones, with the skull depicted, naturally, wearing a beekeeping hat and veil.*

Beekeeping was one of those aspects of Terry's life in Rowberrow in which an interest in the political merits of self-sufficiency could be said to have met a perhaps still larger and more urgent curiosity he and Lyn shared regarding the ancient ways. Spinning would have classed as another. Lyn's mother kept Jacob sheep, the unusual piebald variety that come with horns and whose wool is so thick that it would practically stand up on its own even when the sheep is no longer inside it. Lyn learned how to spin the wool from those sheep on a spindle, and then taught Terry to do the same. Going a step further, Terry acquired a New Zealand-made spinning wheel with a foot-operated treadle, and learned to work it. He and Lyn used to return the spun wool to Lyn's mother who, with Lyn's grandmother, would knit socks and jumpers from it. People at the *Bath Chronicle* thought Terry was joking when he told them his signature stripy pullovers were made from clumps of found material, but he wasn't.

The bees produced honey. The chickens produced eggs. Jars of excellent chutney multiplied, and so did pails of goat's milk, and the manufacture of goat's cheese became industrial enough to spill over into the bathroom. Dave Busby recalls how, during these cheese-intensive periods, the smell of it 'permeated every pore of the house' – and also how Lyn and Terry were cheerfully oblivious to that smell. Dave also remembers Terry at one point deciding to grow and cure tobacco, not because he was a smoker but 'simply because he liked the idea of doing it'. The same went for his sudden desire to produce his own mead.† 'Terry wasn't really a drinker or a bon viveur,' Dave said. 'He didn't like losing control. But he made his own mead because it was a weird and interesting thing to do.' It was another

. . . .

*   For all that one would have loved to witness, of a Bank Holiday weekend, an entire swarm of bike-riding beekeepers in their veils heading down the M23 for the Brighton seafront, Hell's Beekeepers was sadly destined to remain a chapter of one.

†   Mead: an ancient beverage formed by fermenting honey with water, though some mythologies preferred the blood of wise men as their main ingredient. Terry, to the best of my knowledge, stuck to honey.

facet of the highly flexible curiosity which, during these years, also drove Terry to night classes and turned him into, by his own estimation, 'a minor expert in transforming insects into gold'.

Models of insects appear always to have appealed to Terry. Dave Busby recalls Terry in the late 1960s giving him 'a very beautiful gold bee he had made out of nothing more than intricately rolled paper'. He was inspired to take his modelling to another level by the artist and sculptor Michael Ayrton's 1967 novel *The Maze Maker*, a reimagining of the life of Daedalus, the legendary Greek artificer, whose big number was the manufacture of a pair of functioning wings for Icarus, but who was also revered for having made a gold honeycomb so convincing that bees flew to it and filled it with honey.[*] Terry often went back to that novel and he and Dave were intrigued enough by Ayrton to go to the 1969 exhibition of his paintings, drawings and sculpture at Reading Museum Art Gallery. The paintings and drawings passed Terry by, Dave felt, but the crafting techniques involved in the sculpture utterly fascinated him. *The Maze Maker* contains a description of the 'lost wax' method for gold honeycomb casting – wherein the honeycomb becomes its own wax model, which is then burned out, leaving the metal replica – and also implies that the method works, too, with the corpses of bees. The idea of being able to cast his own golden bees seems to have intrigued Terry, and off he eventually went to night school to learn the art of casting in gold and silver, taking with him a little quantity of gold gifted to him for the project by Peter Bander. He almost squandered that gift when, during his first attempt at casting with the precious hot liquid, he failed to batten down the centrifuge correctly and, as he brought the hammer down to set the clockwork chamber spinning, abruptly sprayed a portion of the classroom and an area of the ceiling – though thankfully not himself or anyone else present – with a fine mist of molten gold. But things improved and the student emerged at the end of

....

[*] Daedalus also constructed a hollow statue of a cow so lifelike that the Queen of Crete was able to crouch inside it as part of a cunning plan to become impregnated by Poseidon's bull and thereby eventually give birth to the Minotaur. If you preferred your art to look like what it was supposed to be, Daedalus was clearly your kind of artist.

the course with a perfect gold bee, a gold grasshopper and a handful of silver locusts.

Terry told me much later that he had contacted Michael Ayrton about the 'lost wax' method, and that they had exchanged letters on the subject. Ayrton, in collaboration with a jeweller called John Donald and sponsored by a rich patron, had successfully cast a honeycomb in gold, albeit after sixteen attempts – and yes, when it was placed on the grass, bees had actually flown to it. But he told Terry that he had always struggled with casting bees and could never get the delicate wings right. Terry, as he proudly told me, had devised a secret solution to this problem during his night classes. The wings on his gold bee were, indeed, beautifully veined. According to Terry, Ayrton was bursting to see his successful casts and Terry visited him in Oxford, taking his model insects, carefully wrapped in a Tupperware tub.

'How did you do it?' Ayrton asked him, wonderingly.

'Not telling you,' said Terry, snapping the lid shut on the tub.*

What with the goats and the chickens and the ducks and the bees and the vegetable allotment and the two-acre field and the intricate craft projects based on Michael Ayrton novels and involving insects and precious metals, was any writing taking place in this period at Rowberrow? Yes – but it was taking place slowly. Four and a half years intervened between *The Carpet People* in 1971 and *The Dark Side of the Sun* and another five years would separate the latter from novel number three, *Strata*, in 1981. Somehow the writer who had rushed into print at the age of fifteen and crafted a draft of his first novel by the age of seventeen didn't seem to be in quite such a hurry any more. There were just so many other things to be doing, especially in the summer months when the evenings were light. For a while here, Terry pretty much wrote novels in the way that other people went skiing – in the winter only.

'We were hippies,' Terry wrote, about him and Lyn during this period, 'but hippies with jobs.' And, seeing as he mentioned it: among these many and various anti-corporate, off-grid, stick-it-to-the-Man

. . . .

* And I'm not telling you here, either.

horticultural projects, was cannabis cultivated down there among those Mendip slopes, in the spirit of curiosity, just to see if it could be done, and then, in a similar experimental spirit, dried, ignited and consumed? And if it were, would it have been the case that Terry inhaled any of it?

Let us choose, in the name of discretion, to draw no firm conclusion either way, but instead merely to repeat Terry's allegation that, for him, the seventies was the decade in which he most thoroughly enjoyed the sixties.

* * * * *

In May 1976, Colin Smythe Limited published *The Dark Side of the Sun*. This time there was no fancy launch in a London store with bespoke cocktails and themed canapés. 'Our finances weren't too good in 1976,' said Colin. 'I think Terry and Lyn came to supper.' And thus was 28-year-old Terry's second foray into full-length fiction marked, not with fanfare and hullaballoo in central London, but with the low-key chinking of wine glasses in Gerrards Cross.

Like *Strata*, the novel that followed it, *The Dark Side of the Sun* was a piece of science fiction, not without its moments of pastiche and ironic withdrawal from the form in the pursuit of a laugh, but respectfully and diligently constructed nonetheless, nodding in equal measure to Isaac Asimov and to the US author Larry Niven, for whose book *Ringworld*, published in 1970, Terry had fallen quite hard.* The engine of Terry's novel is a familiar sci-fi trope – the quest to solve the mystery of the disappearance, seemingly an extinction, of a clearly advanced race of forerunners. Within this setup, Terry found space to create a feast day called Hogswatch, which readers of Discworld books would come to hear a lot more about in due course, and also to try out a joke

---

* Ringworld, a torus, a million miles wide, surrounding a star rather than orbiting it, clearly feeds into Discworld, albeit without the supporting elephants and turtle. Terry and Larry Niven met some years later and got along well. Niven seemed to regard *Strata* as a homage to his work, and Terry afterwards described Niven to Dave Busby as resembling 'a small, stuffed owl', which was by no means necessarily a pejorative description in Terry's hands.

about how million-to-one chances are calculated by experts to crop up nine times out of ten – a gag he liked enough to use again more than a decade later in the Discworld novel *Mort* and which he extensively refashioned for further consideration two years after that, in passages towards the end of *Guards! Guards!*.* The *Oxford Times* reacted warmly to *Dark Side* ('unexpected . . . original . . . deft, knowledgeable and good humoured') but it got a slightly tart appraisal from Terry's former home at the *Western Daily Press*, which, in an unsigned review, labelled the novel 'a good-ish mainstream sci-fi yarn, into which the author has crammed everything but the solar stove'. However, even the *Western Daily Press* predicted 'an excellent future for the author' – just as long as he could 'curb ever so slightly the riotous imagination which enables him to write sci-fi in the first place', a compliment with more than a little trace of the backhand in it. Terry would need to get used to those.

Certainly ' "Good-ish" – *Western Daily Press*' was unlikely to make it onto the cover of the paperback version of the novel – but at least there would actually *be* one of those this time, which had not been the case with *The Carpet People*. Colin did a deal with New English Library, who would publish a soft-cover edition of *Dark Side* in 1978, thereby fulfilling another long-held dream of Terry's – seeing a full-length novel with his name on in the plastic carousels. Meanwhile Colin had also once again been hard at work in the frantic souk of the Frankfurt Book Fair, staging an event at which he, Colin, read aloud from *Dark Side* to an invited audience of foreign publishers and emerging with a deal with St Martin's Press in the US – Terry's second foreign sale. Terry and Colin were in the process of conquering the world, clearly. But they were doing it one country at a time – and also, it seemed, just a few hundred book sales at a time. The combined total first print run, in the US and the UK, for *The Dark Side of the Sun* was around 2,400. Despite the

. . . .

* Terry liked to say that he belonged to 'the recyclable school of literature'. Nothing that could be used went to waste and if something you had used looked as though it still had some life in it, there was no reason why you wouldn't use it again rather than bin it. Indeed, you were practically morally bound to do so.

very best wishes of the *Oxford Times*, those copies did not fly off the shelves.*

No matter. Far bigger things were happening. Lyn was pregnant – which was perfect timing in almost every respect, but imperfect timing in the sense that it meant Lyn had to spend the famously sweltering English summer of 1976 wearing what she described as 'hideous thick tights'. She also spent more of that summer than she might otherwise have done eating prunes and custard, her pregnancy fixation, although that at least suggested names for two of the Khaki Campbell ducklings which had arrived – reared in the Gaze Cottage kitchen by one of the bantams, apparently, who continued to try and sit on Prunes, Custard and the others in a motherly way even after the ducklings had become bigger than she herself was.

It was, clearly, a highly fecund time to be in Rowberrow. Nearing full term, Lyn walked into her final appointment with the doctor and announced, 'I can't hang around, I've got a goat in season.' The goat in question was Meg, a half-Pygmy, who had chosen this busy time in the Pratchetts' life to open her own brief window of opportunity for fertilization and was hastily brought together with a male Pygmy from across the valley who, being that much smaller than Meg, was, somewhat humiliatingly, required to stand on a wooden box in order to accomplish the necessary congress.

With Meg's call of nature answered, the Pratchetts' own baby eventually arrived on 30 December when it was almost 1977. During the morning, when Lyn realized the contractions were quickening, she rang Terry in the office and he drove back to fetch her. 'Have you walked the goats?' he asked as he came through the door, causing Lyn to burst into overwhelmed tears. There was even more to think about when the phone rang and Eileen informed Terry that his maternal grandfather had died. Life and death – the full cycle, compressed into the one day. Eileen's

. . . .

* Terry made sure to give Martin Wainwright, his colleague at the *Bath Chronicle*, a copy, though as Martin admitted 45 years later, in 2021, 'I am ashamed to say I have yet to finish it.'

verdict from then on was that Grandfather Kearns had moved aside because Rhianna was on the way.

It was an eighteen-mile drive to Southmead Hospital in Bristol by ex-GPO van, and the winter weather was worsening. But those vans had never let them down before, and they weren't about to start now. The baby was lying awkwardly in the womb and the birth was protracted and complicated, yet Lyn, in the middle of it all, rendered high by gas and air, remembers finding the sight of Terry in scrubs and with 'what looked like a J-cloth on his head' deeply amusing. In the end, their daughter had to be encouraged to make the very last stretch of her journey into the world, just as her father had been, with forceps, and she then spent a few hours in Intensive Care until she stabilized. Terry called her 'the Dome' until her hair arrived, at which point she became 'the baby Grumpling', after the toddler in the *Daily Mirror* cartoon strip 'The Perishers', and then 'Grumpo', and after that 'Grump', but on her birth certificate she would be Rhianna.

Mother and daughter were transferred from Southmead to the general hospital in Wells, where they spent a week receiving antibiotics and where Terry, in a thick Harris tweed suit against the cold, and, thanks to his bald head and beard, looking older than the other new fathers, kept getting mistaken on the ward for the consultant. The ward was under the command of a rather terrifyingly authoritarian nurse who insisted, among other draconian rulings, that all the mothers should feed their newborns for 20 minutes precisely – not a second more or less. Terry promptly nicknamed her Iron Girder.* That stay in Wells was also remarkable for featuring – somewhat controversially within a healthcare setting – an infestation of black beetles, numbers of whom would periodically scuttle across the ward floor. Or, at least, Lyn thought they were beetles. In Terry's recollection they were 'the first cockroaches of the season'. Either way, they were, in tandem with Iron Girder, a reason to stay in the hospital not

. . . .

* Terry would pay a touching tribute in print to that ward sister in 2013 when Iron Girder became the name Dick Simnel gives to his prototype steam engine in the Discworld novel *Raising Steam*.

one moment longer than necessary. Terry collected Lyn and Rhianna in the Morris van and drove them home to begin their new life as a family.

Yet amid all these indelible memories, nothing would top for Terry the recollection of driving back to Rowberrow on the night of the birth, with the baby safely delivered and all well, and with, inside him, the deep satisfaction known to new fathers of a job well done, albeit completely by someone else. And all those years later, after his diagnosis, confronting the bewildering thought that the disease which had decided to lodge itself in his brain might one day empty his mind of its contents, this, very specifically, was the memory that Terry said he lived in fear of losing – the memory whose possible erasure he could not bear to contemplate. Because the way he saw it, who, really, would Terry Pratchett even *be* if he could no longer recall heading home in the dark and the snow that December night, with the Morris van sliding as it pulled up the hills but pushing on? Who would he really *be* if he didn't remember parking by the house and walking gingerly up the slippery path and yet still going down flat on his face in the ice, and finding it only hilarious in the circumstances because all of a sudden he was a father and at that point what else mattered?

A father, and also hungry. 'In the kitchen, I found a lump of stewing steak,' Terry wrote, 'hammered it into submission with a mallet, applied mushrooms, fat and a chopped onion, and cooked it hard, washing it down with quite a lot of a bottle of whisky. No meal, before or since, has ever tasted so good.'

Then he went upstairs in the freezing cold cottage and, with every blanket he could find on the bed, and with two hot water bottles and the cat Oedipuss for added insulation, Terry fell asleep.

9

SURPRISE VIKINGS, VOICES
FROM PLANTS AND EVERY
MAN HIS OWN TREVOR

Because they were so frequently mentioned in the same breath, certainly in the early part of Terry's career, it can often surprise people that Terry Pratchett and Douglas Adams met each other only once.

It was not for the want of trying. 'We dynamically failed to meet on numerous occasions,' Terry wrote, 'the strangest being a college dinner in Oxford which took place in some of the filthiest weather I can remember, with dirty freezing fog turning driving into an exercise in braille. I made it only because I had 20 miles to cover. He would have been coming from London and didn't turn up. We had been seated opposite one another.'

In the end it took much better weather and a film premiere to bring them together. In the summer of 1995, Terry and Rhianna attended the launch in Leicester Square of the movie *Congo*, from the Michael Crichton book — tag-line on the posters: 'When *you* are the endangered species'. Because known instances of Terry Pratchett duetting with the stars of musical theatre are vanishingly rare, this night probably ought to go down in history as the occasion that Terry met Richard O'Brien, the creator of *The Rocky Horror Show*, and joined him in a few impromptu bars of 'Name Your Poison' from *The Return of Captain Invincible*.* But it must also take its place in the record books as the single time that the author of the Discworld series crossed paths with the author of *The Hitchhiker's Guide to the Galaxy*.

At six foot five, Adams somewhat towered over Terry, who was still, despite his success, only five foot eight,† and their long-awaited exchange, amid the boom and bustle of a red-carpet film night, unfolded as follows.

Terry: 'Hello!'

Adams: 'Pardon?'

Terry: 'I said, hello!'

Adams: 'Yes! Hello! Nice evening!'

Terry: 'Pardon?'

Adams: 'Nice evening!'

Terry: 'Indeed.'

And that was it. The crowd swallowed them and the evening moved on.

Six years later, in 2001, I was accompanying Terry on a US signing tour for *Thief of Time*. We were having breakfast at the InterContinental Hotel on North Michigan Avenue in Chicago, and I was glancing through *USA Today*.

'Oh my god,' I said. 'Douglas Adams has died.'

The paper said that Adams had suffered a heart attack shortly after working out at a gym in Montecito in California. He was only 49.

'Well,' said Terry eventually, 'at least it wasn't me.'

This, I should straight away point out, was Terry's standard riposte to the news of someone's death, be they known to him or otherwise, a line

. . . .

* With three songs by O'Brien and Richard Harley, the 1983 film *The Return of Captain Invincible* was a Pratchett Family Movie – stored on DVD, watched on repeat. Other major PFMs: *Time Bandits, Trading Places, The Princess Bride, The Blues Brothers, Ladyhawke, Jurassic Park, Conan the Barbarian*, and *O Brother, Where Art Thou?*.

† On stage at Warwick University in November 1994, Terry set his height in the context of his past as a seeker after sci-fi periodicals: 'Most SF writers are small blokes: they spent a lot of time grubbing on the floor for old SF mags, not stretching up to the top shelf for pornography. As an aside, Douglas Adams is quite tall.'

that he wielded mostly, one felt, for the black comedy and the sheer, dumbfounding inappropriateness of it. Terry was unquestionably fond of deploying tactics like those to, shall we say, change the mood in the room around death. This was the man who broke news to me of the passing of Eileen Pratchett by walking into the Chapel one morning in 2011 and barking, 'Remain seated, all those who still have a mother.'

So, 'at least it wasn't me' is not a useful gauge of the extent to which the death of Douglas Adams affected Terry Pratchett. He would later tell people that the room had gone cold when he heard about it, and that he had sung to himself the Betelgeusian Death Anthem,* and the news affected him to the point where he was thoughtful about it for days afterwards. *The Hitchhiker's Guide to the Galaxy* had been a formative thing in Terry's life – had, in many ways, blazed a trail for him. In 1983, when a reviewer in *Asimov's Science Fiction* magazine declared *The Colour of Magic* the funniest thing he had ever read, Terry's response was, 'He couldn't have read *The Hitchhiker's Guide to the Galaxy*, then.'

He heard it first, in 1978, as a comedy show on BBC Radio 4, and again, with the second series, in 1980. And he read the book, of course, which fell between those two radio runs in 1979 and eventually grew, painfully slowly, through the eighties and into the nineties to become, famously, 'a trilogy in five parts'. The book's set-up, in which Earth is to be cleared by a Vogon construction fleet to make room for a hyperspace bypass, was exactly the kind of collision of the galactically fantastical with the utterly mundane at which Terry's ears would have pricked up and his heart rejoiced. Arthur Dent and Ford Prefect were clear precursors for Rincewind and Twoflower, and they, along with Zaphod Beeblebrox, Marvin the Paranoid Android and Trillian roamed around in Terry's imagination for a long time, as they did in the imaginations of so many of us. But in Terry's case, they were a crystallizing and emboldening force. Adams's creation was out there in the cultural

....

* In *The Hitchhiker's Guide to the Galaxy* the Betelgeusian Death Anthem is said to translate as 'After this, things can only get better', which was also, coincidentally, the theme of a major pop-dance hit for the group D:Ream in 1993, though for some reason people rarely associate the two.

ether while Terry was mulling the ideas and, perhaps more particularly, the approach that would lead him to write *The Colour of Magic* and to set the course for the rest of his career. And, on top of that, it was the reason why Terry finally introduced a television set into Gaze Cottage.

It's safe to say that, during Lyn and Terry's first decade in Rowberrow, activities such as wool-spinning, cheese-making, beekeeping and tortoise-raising took precedence over watching the television. Gerald Walker, Terry's senior on the sub-editing desk at the *Bath Evening Chronicle*, tells a story of having Terry over to dinner one evening and watching a quiz show with him. So excitedly did his guest bounce up out of his seat, and so loudly did he shout the answers at the screen, that Walker formed the impression Terry had never before seen a television programme. Not the case, of course: there was a set at Terry's parental home in Beaconsfield – the one on which Terry watched *The Prisoner*, at least until those wedding planning commitments prevented him from doing so. But there was no television at Gaze Cottage for more than ten years – until 1981, in fact, when the BBC began broadcasting its six-part adaptation of *The Hitch-hiker's Guide*. The show went out on Monday nights and at first Lyn and Terry religiously went round to a neighbour's to watch it there. But clearly that arrangement wasn't optimal – was precarious, even. Terry decreed that there would be no repeat of the debacle surrounding the last episode of *The Prisoner*. He came back from work with a small television set.

So Terry and Lyn got to see *The Hitchhiker's Guide* in the comfort of their own home, and the young Rhianna, a little while later, got to see *The Muppets*. Or at least, she got to see it until S4C, the Welsh channel which, apart from BBC1 and a slightly snowy BBC2, was the only signal the Pratchetts' tiny set-top aerial could pick up with any clarity, decided to replace it with football. By way of vengeful protest, Rhianna drew a picture of 'the scariest thing I could think of – a Cyclops', addressed it to 'the Welsh', and posted it in the red box in the wall near the Swan pub.

What with one thing and another, writing seems to have taken a bit of a back seat for Terry in this phase of his life. As the seventies turned into the eighties, Terry moved briefly in and out of other distractions.

For example, somewhere in the five-year interval between *The Dark Side of the Sun* and 1981's *Strata*, he developed a relatively short-lived but nevertheless time-consuming interest in Citizens Band radio. The CB movement was in full flow, enjoying a cultural moment thanks to movies like *Smokey and the Bandit* (1977) and *Convoy* (1978), which took its cue from a country and western song of that name and familiarized UK residents with US trucker slang: '10–4', '10–9', 'breaker, breaker', 'c'mon', 'bear in the air' . . . In some ways, CB radio was the social media of its day, but with a heavy slant towards traffic updates and with, arguably, an historically unprecedented layer of naffness. And Terry bought in. He acquired a two-way radio with a black handset on a curly lead and set it up in the spare bedroom. He acquired another set for the car.* His call-sign, or rather 'handle': Quill.

One weekend, Dave Busby, who had come over from Reading, spent an evening watching Terry upstairs on his CB set, 'talking over crackly radio transmission with a decidedly miscellaneous collection of people, mostly middle-aged guys and women called Bob or Doreen, using that weird jargon that CB-ers liked'. Some of these Bobs and Doreens were clearly interested in making arrangements over the air to 'eyeball' in lay-bys – 'IRL', as we would later say. But Dave is sure Terry never did that and the conversations he witnessed seemed to be mostly about the traffic in Bristol or the relative merits of various fish and chip shops. 'I really could not see why Terry was in that space,' Dave said. 'I think he was drifting at this stage, his interest in self-sufficiency fading, his writing goals unfocused, not sure where his life would take him. Our friendship nearly lapsed in this period.'

But Terry did find a focus in one area in those years: raising his daughter. Being Terry, he built his own baby alarm to monitor Rhianna as she slept. It was designed to be two-way, but when Terry and Lyn made go-to-sleep-style noises down it, their sourceless voices seemed

---

* Given Terry's reluctance, which I have mentioned, to part with electronic hardware, it was no surprise to me to find both these CB units and their handsets, dusty but intact, in Terry's barn.

to spook Rhianna rather than comfort her, so Terry converted it back to one-way. It also didn't help that the speakers began to pick up Russian radio stations, their signals drifting across the Mendips and then, as Lyn related, bouncing in off certain plants out in the garden which seemed to act as aerials.

There were numerous other construction projects. Just as David, Rhianna's grandfather, came good with a home-made doll's house fully fitted with lights, so Terry set to and built her things: a Moomin house with painted clay figures, a toy beehive with rubber bees, a Wendy house, a market stall with a sign – Grumpo Stores. On the wall on the stairs, opposite her bedroom door, was a mural which had come with the cottage and which Terry and Lyn left intact – a lion-hunting scene with Aubrey Beardsley-style knights on horseback and a pack of dogs.

When she got a little older, they walked the goats to the field, which, when the snow fell, had a good slope for sledging. They walked up onto the Mendips to gather moss for the plants and, as they walked, Terry told her stories about children lost in woods and about children found in woods and about the chalk under their feet. And he taught her about foraging – 'about what was edible, and what was edible only once,' as Rhianna remembered it. They named places in the forest – Old Man's Cave, Old Man's Pool – and they sang very loudly, mostly the song 'Whose Pigs Are These?'. One day out walking, they bumped into Vikings – a whole gang of them, with horned helmets, sheepskin cloaks and thick swords. They were taking part in a battle re-enactment in the valley. Terry and Rhianna offered them a drink from her Asterix-themed Thermos flask. On Monday, Terry sent a note to Rhianna's teacher: 'If she talks about meeting Vikings this weekend, it did actually happen.' When he sat down on the big swivel-chair in front of his computer, she would tuck herself in behind him like a bolster cushion.

Rhianna talks about the Terry of her childhood being 'big-brotherly more than fatherly. Mother was the disciplinarian. He got away with being the good guy.'

What with foraging with his daughter, and tending to his goats and bees, and chatting about fish and chip shops with Bob and Doreen, life for Terry, as he turned 30, seems to have fallen into a nice, easy rhythm. Yet across this rural idyll a dark shadow would pass in early 1979, succinctly summarized by a headline in the *Bristol Evening Post*: 'POISON VILLAGE ALERT'.

The village referred to was Shipham, and the poison referred to was cadmium, a metal which a national survey had found to be present in greater than average quantities in Shipham's soil. Cadmium accumulates in the kidneys and liver, and Shipham residents with access to the *Journal of the Royal Society of Medicine* would have been able to terrify themselves by establishing that 'the effects of chronic exposure are emphysema, proteinuria, and chronic renal failure' as well as 'slight haemolysis'. Later studies would aggressively dispute the metal's association with carcinomas of the prostate and lung, but at the time those consequences seemed to be in play, too.

Oh, and by the way, Shipham was the next village along from Rowberrow, no more than half a mile up the road from where Terry and Lyn, and now Rhianna, were growing and consuming their own fruit and vegetables.

Terry recalled the day that people from the local authority came tramping through the village in the blizzarding snow, 'delivering dry little letters for residents telling us that cadmium levels in the area were potentially dangerous, but not to panic, of course . . .'

'Many of us knew about what local people called "the mineral",' Terry wrote. 'You would find it here and there and it was easy enough to spot. A walker could kick up small lumps of lead left over from when there were mines at Priddy and a neighbour exploring some of the rocky places found a small seam of arsenic – never to be sneezed at.'

Fortunately, this latest panic did not last long. Although the Central Directorate on Environmental Pollution found that people in Shipham had 'twice the UK's average dietary intake of cadmium', that level was quickly declared to be 'well below the threshold for renal damage'. Another comforting conclusion from the environmental people: 'If cadmium contamination has any effect on the mortality pattern in Shipham, it is slight and does not present a serious health hazard to residents.' It turned out the 'Poison Village' was not as poisonous as the *Bristol Evening Post* had suggested.*

'Things quickly settled down,' wrote Terry. 'People began to realize that they were still alive, and a survey of graves appeared to show that people lived so long around there that they probably had to hit someone on the head with a shovel just to get the graveyard started.'

Still, it had been an alarming episode – and also, oddly enough, something of a dry run. Public health hazards were about to become Terry's business.

★ ★ ★ ★ ★

At his interview in Bristol with the South Western Region of the Central Electricity Generating Board in the spring of 1979, Terry, wearing a suit in a working environment for the first time in more than a decade, gave the panel the benefits of his thoughts on the latest generation of Magnox reactors. A lovely little reactor, the Magnox, as Terry would no doubt have insisted, and a trusty supplier of many of the nation's power needs since the 1950s. But, let's be frank, those reactors weren't getting any younger. Indeed, they were nearing the end of their design-life and, while they were doing so, questions were only going to proliferate about their safety and fitness for purpose as time went on. So, seeing as you asked, that was your next big public relations challenge, right there.

To what did Terry owe this expert grasp of trends within the UK's electricity generating systems? To a lifetime's curiosity regarding the national power grid and matters nuclear? Not so much. To a strong moral opinion either way? Definitely not. To a couple of hours with the cuttings files at the *Bath Evening Chronicle*? Much more like it. The great journalistic spirit of 'two phone calls and a generalization' had triumphed again. Except this time, substitute for the 'phone calls' a chat with someone who lived in the village who worked for the CEGB in

. . . .

* One Shipham-related study concluded that, even though all was well, 'children should be deterred from eating soil'. But that's not such a bad idea wherever you live.

Bristol and thought Terry might enjoy life there. In any case, Terry didn't think that it was his suave familiarity with the lifespan of the hardware that impressed the CEGB interview panel, so much as his even demeanour and general lack of fluster under the pressure of their questioning. Or as Terry put it: 'I seemed to have identified myself as the kind of bloke to have around when the nuclear sewage hit the windmill.' He got the job.

Contemplating Terry's decision in the thirty-second year of his life to swap sub-editing at the *Bath Evening Chronicle* for a position in the regional press office of a nationalized industry, perhaps it is helpful to adapt Mrs Merton's famous question to Debbie McGee regarding her marriage to the millionaire magician Paul Daniels: 'So, Terry, what first attracted you to a job at the CEGB with a generous annual remuneration, a private healthcare plan and a company car?' Terry's career had again become bogged down. Sub-editing on a local paper was not making him rich, or even especially comfortably-off, and there was a child to consider now, too. And there was still clearly a part of Terry that felt, or was made to feel, that he ought to be *getting on*. Whatever else you wanted to say about this CEGB role, it had what Terry referred to as 'the appurtenances of a real job'. Terry's pay grade, PAG3, entitled him straight away to three years of expenses-paid motoring in a red Ford Escort 1.6 GL Estate. Not that Terry cared very much about cars, or ever really talked about them, but he wouldn't object to having a free one.* Martin Wainwright greeted with dismay news of his former colleague's departure for 'what seemed to me at the time the living death of PR work'. But that was an unfair analogy, surely. Did living death come with a company pension scheme?

Also, how could someone like Terry *not* have responded at some level to a world in which the direct gamma and neutron radiation from nuclear reactors was known, with supremely poetic licence, as 'shine'?

He took down the sign that he had hung up beside his desk in the

---

* When, after three years, it was Terry's right to upgrade that company car, he promptly chose . . . another red Ford Escort 1.6 GL Estate. That's how little Terry cared about cars.

office on Westgate Street – 'All the news that fits we print', an adaptation of the *New York Times*'s old motto from the point of view of a sub-editor – and reported for work at the CEGB's South Western Region headquarters at Bedminster Down in Bristol.

Just a few months earlier, the CEGB had moved a large chunk of its western operations into new premises called The Pavilions – a specially commissioned tessellation of white buildings for which Arup Associates won architectural awards. The Pavilions was so posh that not only were the buildings immediately listed, but so was the landscaping around them. That said, if in the early days of occupancy the people who worked there got a little tired of seeing parties of visitors being shown around and briefed on the architecture's prize-worthy brilliance, it was because they knew something. They knew that the next time it rained hard enough, they would once again be putting down the waste paper bins to catch the drips from the ceiling.* That early drawback aside, though, 'Bedminster Down', as it was familiarly known, was an uncommonly well-appointed workplace – and not just in the sense that it had purpose-built laboratories and a thick-walled room in the basement for dabbling with things of a radioactive persuasion. Before the move, questionnaires had gone round asking staff what, in an ideal world, they would like in their new office home. Some people had replied, possibly half in jest, 'a swimming pool'. The Pavilions had a swimming pool. It also had a bar, a Sports & Social Club and what was bravely dubbed a 'staff restaurant', although most staff continued doggedly to refer to it as the canteen.

And as for the lavatories . . . well, those were mirrored palaces in which reflections reflected reflections, and on into infinity. True, as Harry Ellam from Scientific Services observed, the reflections tended to swoop off to one side, suggesting that the walls hadn't been put up squarely. But they were still something to behold. And was Terry, beholding them, inspired

----

* An early fault with the design-led 'internal guttering' system, apparently, and eventually resolved. I think we now call it 'snagging'.

to compose some of the passages on 'mirror magic' and receding reflections in the novel *Witches Abroad*? It's hard not to conclude so.*

As he never tired of telling people later in his life, Terry's job in this government-backed Shangri-La – in Pavilion 2 of five, to be specific – was to handle the calls from local journalists who wanted to know 'whether nuclear reactors in the vicinity of their readers had recently blown up or were about to blow up and had any plans to blow up in the near future'. But it was also Terry's more prosaic duty – and, in truth, a more substantial part of it – to pour oil on considerably less exciting, non-nuclear controversies regarding CEGB business as they arose, such as when local objections were raised to the radio mast which the CEGB erected to ease communication between its outpost at Keynsham and the Bedminster Down HQ. 'I wouldn't say the mast was too high,' Terry calmly explained to any journalist who rang in for a quote.

Terry talked about his tactics that day with colleagues over lunch. 'The unspoken bit was: I wouldn't say the mast was too high . . . unless the people paying me were paying me to say it was too high.' Consummate professionalism, right there.

Terry was also present at the launch of the CEGB's prototype electricity generating turbines at Burry Port, the first of which was switched on in November 1982 – a big moment in the history of wind energy in the UK, and marked with a press event at which, allegedly, caviar was served. The story of Terry's, that certain members of the press didn't know quite what to do with the fabled Russian delicacy, and ended up loading it into sandwiches in large spoonfuls, may or may not be a delightful exaggeration.

Entirely true, however – and Terry swore it was so – was the tale which had to be carefully damped down of the worker at Hinkley Point on the Bristol Channel who borrowed a paintbrush from the site and used it to decorate his house, thereby making his entire home lightly radioactive – a gloss finish with a twist. His error might never

. . . .

* 'And your image extends forever, in reflections of reflections of reflections, and every image is the same, all the way around the curve of light.'

have been discovered had he not been responsible enough to return the paintbrush to the site when he'd finished with it, whereupon a scanner appears to have picked up the traces and the worker briefly became a rare instance of someone guilty of taking radioactive material *into* a nuclear station. After that, allegedly, a SWAT team in hazmat suits was dispatched to tear the plaster off those freshly painted walls and safely dispose of it.

And equally hush-hush, apparently, was the story of the power station that accidentally irradiated a local sewage plant by flushing something in error down one of its lavatories. That day the SWAT team clearly earned their money, too, combing fresh sewage for something radioactive.

Before he could start heading off potentially disruptive stories like these, though, Terry had a personal battle to win. Inducted into the administrative system at Bedminster Down, the new PR officer was dismayed to realize that any press releases he wrote would have to be sent to the typing pool, known as the 'local services area', where a member of a team of some forty electric typewriter operatives would be delegated to type the release 'properly'. Quite apart from the questions it raised about time-efficiency, Terry took this proposition as a naked insult to his own well-honed skills at the keyboard, and decided to go to war.

As Terry put it, in the notes for his autobiography, 'My boss was a man called Trevor Jones, and the people running the place asked him to get me to have my typing done by real typists. I told him I wouldn't, so he told them I wouldn't, and eventually a small group of worried clerks and overseers began asking me to get in line. In the end I had to spell it out for them: I said that if I had to write a press release about a nuclear emergency, I didn't want to have to wait a day and a half before sending it out, that being the average length of time you waited for your typing to come back from the famous local services area. Besides, I explained, I was a journalist and couldn't really think without a keyboard in front of me, and therefore perhaps they would consider my use of it as a therapeutic instrument.' Terry was granted the right to do his own typing.

For all the scepticism of former colleagues in journalism, this was undeniably a hot time to be going into the nuclear-related PR business. Terry arrived at Bedminster Down in April 1979, less than a month after the Three Mile Island disaster in the US, and although the South Western Region of the CEGB hadn't been implicated directly in the partial meltdown of a nuclear reactor in Pennsylvania, the incident had nevertheless prompted reviews to the CEGB's existing emergency procedures – as one would naturally expect following a disaster which ended up scoring five out of seven on the International Nuclear Event Scale. Amid a freshened-up set of protocols, the CEGB put in place procedures for the creation of emergency 'Press Briefing Centres' to get the public message out, and where the demands of the media for temporary phone facilities and desks could be met. Members of the emergency response teams, including Terry, were issued with pagers so that they could be called out instantly at any dire moment – 'like the RNLI', said Bill Butcher, one of Terry's colleagues who worked in the Management Services division and was also on call, 'although it never happened.' 'All I remember about my pager,' said Margaret Needles, another colleague, who was an administrator in Operational Planning, 'is receiving odd messages that I didn't understand and being asked to work at Christmas because I didn't drink.'

Still, Bedminster Down was officially braced for the worst at all times, and the worst was frequently practised for in detailed exercises – the fire drill and then some. At such moments, the permanent 'Information Room' between Pavilions 1 and 2, with its array of fax machines and its secure messaging systems, would be fully activated. Meanwhile a 30-minute, slightly Bond-flavoured transformation of the adjacent conference rooms would take place, with the furniture rearranged according to a strict plan, and with the panelling on the walls sliding aside to reveal whiteboards on which the status of the 'emergency' could be swiftly updated. If the phone system went down, there was radio for back-up. Bill Butcher, who was part of the team charged with channelling the details to the whiteboards, remembers Terry, during exercises, 'getting quite short-tempered with me over the timeliness and accuracy of the information'.

An image emerges from this period of Terry in black jeans, black turtle neck and Cuban-heeled boots, running noisily along the hollow trunking that made up The Pavilions' corridors.* For outdoor engagements, he would sling on his standard-issue donkey jacket, with 'CEGB' emblazoned in white capitals across the back, and a vaguely Russian-looking leather cap which was the model's own. The combination of the cap with the beard earned him the nickname 'Lenin' among his co-workers in the PR department – though they chose not to call him this to his face. Margaret Needles remembers him as 'a man in black who was always on the move and couldn't do anything slowly or quietly. He was more of a sensation to me than a reality.' The PR office was part of a large, open-plan space, and André Coutanche, who worked in the adjacent Planning Co-Ordination department, claims that he was familiar with Terry's voice long before he was familiar with Terry. 'When Terry was, shall we say, making himself clear,' André said, 'ten yards away, behind a flimsy partition, you heard it.' He grew famous around the office, and perhaps a little notorious, for opening discussions by saying, 'How can I put this in a way which won't offend?' His colleagues came to recognize this as the conversational equivalent of a four-minute warning. Terry was regarded as very helpful when he had time to be, but people who wandered into his range looking for a chat when Terry was busy would very soon and very straightforwardly be told to bugger off. 'He never started anything that he wasn't going to finish,' said Julian Curtis, who joined the PR department in 1983, had Terry as his boss and was under instruction, when he returned from trips to the Lake District, to bring back sphagnum moss for the carnivorous plants that Terry was now cultivating on a window sill at Gaze Cottage.

. . . .

* There was no strict dress code at the CEGB, but an unspoken agreement seemed to bring the men to work in suits and ties. Terry, continuing the habit of a working lifetime, seems to have chosen to ignore that. He would run to a tie at the CEGB if the occasion was serious enough to merit it, but it would normally be either a leather one or a richly coloured one, which was the equivalent of wearing a tie and being entirely contemptuous of ties at the same time.

When he wasn't fielding phone-calls from journalists, a sizeable part of Terry's brief was editing and contributing to *South West Power*, which was the in-house journal at Bedminster Down, and supplying copy for the CEGB's national publication, *Power News*. As a black-rimmed box in the latter stated, 'If you have any news, sport or diary items for your edition of *Power News*, contact Terry Pratchett on Bristol 648107.' Under the Terry Pratchett byline at this time came stories such as 'Pembroke values its thick black gold': a piece on the virtues of using oil waste as combustion material, which was accompanied by a picture of David Bailey, assistant station chemist at Pembroke power station, gamely holding an upturned beaker of oil sludge above his head in order to demonstrate its highly combustible, sticky thickness.

Then there was 'Cornering hard . . . for five days' which told the story of the transporting of a 140-tonne transformer 80 miles across Devon by road. 'In terms of length and depth of planning, it was like a space shuttle flight, but slower,' wrote Terry. In an accompanying side-panel, Terry also spoke to some of the Devon residents who lined the streets in places to see the lorry and its prodigious load come past. 'For a lot of Devonians, it seemed,' Terry reported, 'a good evening out was a hot Thermos and a big transformer.' 'I've been looking forward to this,' one of those Devonians told him. 'It's nice to have something to look at.'

But perhaps best of all, and certainly closest to Terry's heart, was the story headlined 'Washday stains start buzz of speculation', and strap-lined 'Chemist is puzzled', that told the tale of how mysterious splotches had appeared one day on overalls hung out to dry at Pembroke power station – a worrying sign for an institution permanently on the alert for unplanned emissions. But it seems the chemist's puzzlement was quickly banished. The source of those splotches proved to be nothing more harmful than bees, going about their entirely natural and non-radioactive business. Attributing the insight to 'a local beekeeper' – and who could he possibly have meant? – Terry was able to report that, after long spells cooped up in their hives, bees often choose the first sunny day to head out on 'what is technically known as a "cleansing flight"'. 'Beekeepers' wives,' Terry was also somehow in a position to inform the *Power News* readership, 'believe that they make a beeline for the nearest clean washing.'*

'There was always a pinch of salt,' said Harry Wallace, who was in Management Services (Computing), speaking about Terry's writing for those CEGB journals. 'I don't think he was entirely convinced by his own job.'

Even with the swimming pool and the landscaped gardens and the staff restaurant and the magnificently mirrored lavatories, the most significant asset at The Pavilions from Terry's point of view, and the facility which most profoundly shaped his time there, and indeed beyond, was a metal box which stood in the Sports Club bar adjacent to the canteen: the Space Invaders machine. This was not just because Terry loved Space Invaders; the repercussions of that love in this instance were more profound – indeed, life-altering. Come lunchtime, the games machine would draw Terry like a magnet and it would draw others, too, from other departments: André Coutanche, Bill Butcher, Harry Ellam, Harry Wallace, Martin Hamilton from Clerical Work Measurement, Trevor Storm from Operation Research, Pete Weston from Finance. They would play and they would watch each other play. And then they would have lunch together. And from this incidental chemistry, the Table of Eight was born.

The games moved on, but the Table of Eight remained the Table of Eight and continued to play. Trevor would stand to one side of the machine and observe in silence. After two or three days, he would suddenly say, 'Have you noticed that exactly three seconds after the spaceship appears at the top of the screen, a fuel tank becomes available in the opposite corner?' This kind of in-depth analysis became known to all as 'Trevoring'. One day Trevor was not present beside the screen. 'Every man must be his own Trevor,' Terry announced solemnly. It was not uncommon for members of the Table of Eight to go

....

* Some 'everyday sexism' here, of course, but, if it's any defence, it was 1983. There was nothing from Terry in this article on whether the bees are at all inclined to attack the hair of the person hanging out the washing, but this is information which readers of this book have already gleaned.

to lunch at twelve and still be playing the video machine at ten to two.

If the game in the Sports Club bar hadn't been changed in a while, the Table of Eight would pop over to the King's Head opposite the Pavilions to see what was new in the games line there. One day, rumour reached someone's ears that there was a new game in town – and, moreover, a new game in town *in colour*. That lunchtime, five of the Eight, including Terry, left the building, took a car over to East Street in Bedminster, and entered a little arcade where, true to the rumour, a recently unwrapped Galaxians cabinet was at that point being hammered by a selection of the local youth. The CEGB party, mostly in suits, mostly in their late thirties and early forties, lingered slightly self-consciously behind the game's current players, occasionally craning a little to get a look. Eventually one of the youths cast an appraising eye over the waiting group and dryly announced, in a thick Bristolian accent: 'Play up, lads – the England selectors are in.'

The group's friendship expanded over conversations at lunch. They seemed to have the same kind of mind, and the same sense of humour – educated, interested in science and engineering, immersed in pop culture, unashamedly nerdy. One day they were discussing why toast falls jam side down. Terry mentioned that his cats, by contrast, always landed on their feet. So what, they began to wonder, would happen if you glued a piece of toast, spread with jam, to the back of a cat and dropped it? And the conclusion was that the cat would remain in mid-air, spinning, and the situation wouldn't be able to resolve itself. Ergo, the Table of Eight had discovered anti-gravity, right there over lunch. QED, and pass the salt.

Branching out from the lunches, Terry became a sometime participant, alongside other Table of Eight members, in the CEGB's regular 'Brain of Bedminster' quiz nights: teams of three, no consulting, pride at stake. On one such occasion, Martin Hamilton recalls being asked to spell 'fictitious' and making a hash of it. Terry stepped in for the bonus point.

'L-I-E,' said Terry.

'Nice,' said the quizmaster, 'but *nul points*.'

So secure did Terry feel among these new friends that he was inspired to host a Dungeons & Dragons night for them. When the appeal of CB radio had died down, the fantasy role-playing game had become a new interest of Terry's – and perhaps initially a slightly furtive one. It certainly wasn't anything that he ever felt bold enough to tell Dave Busby about. 'I'm surprised he never mentioned it,' Dave said. 'He was very aware of my poor attention span for computer games, though my aversion never used to prevent him from talking about them in great detail and wondering fretfully why I wasn't an enthusiastic fan of *Doom* and *Quake*.'

Among the Table of Eight, however, Terry for some reason felt more comfortable about sharing this latest enthusiasm and, one winter's evening after work, he organized a D&D evening in the Sports & Social Club. Gathering the other seven round a large table on the dance floor, Terry acted as Dungeon Master, a role for which he claimed to be 'officially qualified' and which seemed to involve the wearing of some kind of hat. It also put him in charge of the twenty-sided dice and the map of the dungeon, as well as the general narrative direction of the game. Apart from Terry, everyone present was new to Dungeons & Dragons and perhaps a little less invested in it than their Dungeon Master might have wished. 'He was expecting things of us and I think we rather disappointed him in terms of involvement,' said Pete Weston, who could recall only one moment where his participation had earned Terry's manifest approval. 'We were about to cross a bridge, and I asked if there was something *under* the bridge, and Terry said that was *a good question*.'

Otherwise most of the participants remember a lot of going around in fictional circles, a lot of endless, committee-style discussions, and a lot of being grateful that the Sports Club bar remained open throughout. That said, there was, perhaps, a certain degree of classiness about the Dungeon Master's storytelling. Harry Ellam recalled Terry directing everyone into a cavern and instructing them to observe a set of hooks in the ceiling, apparently for the use of resting dragons. Some while later, Harry would read *The Colour of Magic* and reach the Wyrmberg, the upside-down mountain with its Roosting Hall where dragons could hang from the metal rings after their flights, and he would think to himself, 'I recognize this.'*

During a pause for refreshment, Terry confided to Martin Hamilton that he was being generous with the decisions given by the dice – 'i.e. he was ignoring them,' said Martin, 'and making it up as he went along.' At the resumption of the game, Martin, who was very bored, went rogue, abruptly announcing, 'The elf runs across the river and into the tunnel opposite,' and then going to sit on the other side of the dance floor, from where he began a covert campaign to assassinate other members of the group with crossbow bolts. Fantasy ones, obviously. At the end of what was agreed by all to have been a very long evening, Terry displayed the map of the dungeon and suggested that the group had completed about ten per cent of what would normally be expected from a set of novices. 'We did not have another Dungeons & Dragons evening,' said Martin, 'much to my, and I think Terry's, relief.'

Far more successful was the CEGB's Computer Club. Terry, as the owner in 1981 of a Sinclair ZX81 in kit form and as a man who – I've mentioned it already – had taught it to speak, was an engaged and informed participant in the monthly meetings, also held among tables on the dance floor in the Sports & Social Club. Twenty or so members of staff would come back into work in the evening, some of them bringing their children with them.† The meetings were, according to Bill Butcher, 'a chance to exchange ripped off software and show off expertise on the various games. We once upset security by opening a security door to pass out an aerial lead and compounded the wrong-doing by driving a car

. . . .

* It is hard to be entirely sure at which points Dungeons & Dragons bled into the fiction and at which points the fiction bled into Dungeons & Dragons. But certainly the Luggage was invented by Terry for role-playing games – not at the CEGB night, but on another occasion. He wanted something in which his character could carry *a lot* of equipment around without being encumbered – hence a chest with feet. The idea would, literally, run and run.

† One of those children, Bill Butcher's daughter Louise, who was then in secondary school, remembers those nights and 'how supportive and inclusive everyone was, including Terry'. She went on to write code for a living.

onto the grass to act as a "backplane" for the aerial.' But there were guest speakers and presentations, too. One evening, a guest brought in his 'digital clarinet', hooked it up and gave an extended demonstration of its musical charms. Another speaker enlightened the assembled group on using some new-fangled device called a modem to connect a computer to the outside world, deploying a thick plastic cradle onto which a telephone handset had to be lowered. Terry himself gave a presentation, on early moves in home automation, befitting someone who had recently pro-grammed a door in his cottage in Rowberrow to say 'Glad to be of service – please enjoy your trip through this door,' in honour of the Heart of Gold, the spaceship in *The Hitchhiker's Guide to the Galaxy*.

One lunchtime, André and Terry made a trek to the Comet store on Barton Hill and returned each clutching an Amstrad CPC 464 computer.* Terry – being 'a flash git', as André put it – promptly added a disk drive to his. They were pioneers at the dawn of home word-processing, frontiers-men at the bleeding edge of unutterably complicated floppy disk management – what was where and what was backed up to what – and definitely prototype victims of woefully inadequate memory space. The development of microcomputing through the first half of the 1980s would form the backdrop for practically all the Table of Eight's conversa-tions in that period, with special weight given, of course, to computer games, which were, at this stage, primitive in the extreme, bizarrely content-free, and yet utterly enthralling. On the ZX80 there had been *Mazogs*, which came with crude black and white graphics, offered almost nothing to see on the screen at any point, and yet, as Terry would fondly point out, was constructed in such a way as to be irresistible. And then there was *Manic Miner*, which, joy of joys and breakthrough of break-throughs, had in-game music, but which also had no 'save' feature,

....

* A relatively expensive piece of kit at the time, but in Terry's case tax-deductible. It appears among the freelance business expenses he filed with his accountant for the tax year 1984–85: 'Purchase of Amstrad CPC464 computer, monitor, disk drive, daisy wheel printer, and associated cabling: £789.46'. Terry also claimed for '25 x 3" floppy disks – £104.25'. For the record, Terry's total freelance earnings that year, only two years before he decided to go full time as a writer, amounted to just £3646.88.

meaning you had to work your way dutifully through all the easy, early levels every time you played it. Terry told André that, in a generational twist on Eileen Pratchett's 'penny for a page well-read', he had started paying Rhianna to play through those tiresome early levels on his behalf, easing her out of the seat and retaking the controls when it finally got interesting.* The games would only get better, and Terry's attraction to them would only get firmer.

In due course, Terry got the CEGB to agree to him having an Amstrad CPC machine in the office – though not for gaming. Or not explicitly. Terry's approach to negotiations with Trevor Jones over the necessity of this item was to say: 'Look, let's just pretend we've had the stand-up row, I've won, and let's get on with it.' Somehow this tactic worked, and a CPC 464 was soon being unboxed in the PR department. Naturally – and no doubt this was Terry's priority all along – this piece of equipment would lead to major gains in efficiency across the office. But – an afterthought, surely – it would also enable Terry to bring disks from home containing pieces of writing that he was working on and snatch half an hour in his lunch break to get another 200 words down.

Which was handy because Terry's somewhat neglected writing sideline was once again beginning to gather pace.

---

* Rhianna does not recall this act of parental bribery but says it sounds like something her father would have done. She does remember tucking in behind him in his office chair to play *Knight Lore*, *Head Over Heels* and *Alien Highway*, as well as sitting beside him and drawing maps for him on graph paper. Rhianna would end up writing about, and then for, games, eventually winning a 2016 Writers Guild of America award for her work as lead writer on *Rise of the Tomb Raider*. The finger of blame for this disreputable career choice would appear to point fairly irrefutably at Terry. Rhianna dedicated her award to her father and only wished that he had lived to see it.

10

SICKENING SMASHES,
THE RIGHT WORD FOR YELLOW
AND AIMING FOR 400

One day over lunch in the CEGB canteen, Terry mentioned to André Coutanche that he wrote novels.

'Oh, really?' said André. 'Under what name?'

There was a slightly awkward pause.

'Terry Pratchett,' said Terry.

'He wasn't boastful about his writing,' André told me. 'He didn't exactly go round announcing it to everyone.' Nor, at this stage, was the writing announcing *itself* especially loudly. Terry had been at the CEGB for just over two years when Colin Smythe Limited published *Strata* in June 1981. For all its merits as a piece of adult science fiction – a 'relentlessly inventive story' according to the reviewer in *British Fantasy Newsletter*, a certain Neil Gaiman, aged 20¾ – Terry's third novel was very far from exploding into the national consciousness and becoming the topic of water-cooler conversations. Not even, clearly, at the water-cooler in Terry's own office.

Around this time, something clicked, though. Dave Busby remembers going for a long walk with Terry in Somerset one weekend, early in the eighties: Terry striding out, galvanized by plans he had for a new book, and a new direction for his writing. 'He told me about this idea he'd had for a little imp inside a pre-industrial camera, responsible for quickly painting the pictures that came out,' Dave said. 'A few ideas went back and forth between us.' It was clear to Dave that *The Hitchhiker's Guide* had flicked a switch in Terry. 'He decided he was a humorous writer, and that was what he was going to be.' There had been humour in Terry's writing already, not least in the bits of Larry Niven that shaded into *The Dark Side of the Sun* and, particularly, *Strata*. But this felt like a complete makeover and a fresh start. Dave, who hadn't really gone along with his friend's shift of allegiance from science fiction to fantasy, admits that he was now sceptical, too, about this graduation to comedy, and that he said as much to Terry as he stumped after him on the Mendips. 'I can remember being dubious about the whole thing,' said Dave. 'I thought it was a bit naff, somehow. But Terry wasn't a delicate flower. He could shrug it off. He knew the kinds of things I would say.'

The book that Terry had in mind was going to be called *The Colour of Magic*.

Three novels into Terry's career, Colin Smythe now found himself drawing up a contract for what the paperwork would define as 'a collection of short stories'. That was how Terry had pitched it to him – probably four separate tales 'with no discernible plot', as Terry openly put it, loosely interwoven and set in a fantasy world of some kind. Collections of short stories, plotted or otherwise, are notoriously harder to sell than novels, but Colin – the definition in this regard of the gentleman publisher – seems to have bitten his lip about that. His approach with Terry from the beginning had been to let him find his own way as a writer, and he couldn't see any reason to alter course now.

One thing Colin did want to change, though, was Terry's paperback publisher. New English Library, who came on board for *The Dark Side of the Sun*, had not over-achieved. Certainly, what they had done in the sixties for Harold Robbins they had thus far significantly failed to do for Terry Pratchett. *Strata*, which they put out in May 1982 with an ominous, lightning-riven cover image painted by Tim White, did not sell well. NEL printed around 5,000 copies, Colin thinks, couldn't shift them, and remaindered their edition in 1985. 'They had been in the middle of a takeover by Hodder & Stoughton,' Colin said. 'I think their eyes perhaps came off the ball.'

NEL still retained the option on Terry's next book, however. Which was a shame, because Colin knew there was interest in Terry from Diane Pearson, a senior editor at Transworld who was in the market for some new authors for Corgi, the company's paperback arm. Corgi would have the clout to print and distribute Terry's work in far greater quantities than NEL had managed.

It was at moments like this that it was good to have a gentleman publisher on your side. Colin now spotted an opportunity to turn *Strata*'s under-performance into leverage. He picked up the phone to NEL and, in a reversal of the usual direction of traffic on such occasions, began to talk them out of doing business with his client. 'I said something like, "As *Strata* sold so badly, you probably won't want to publish Terry's next book, will you? Oh, dear. Well, never mind. We'll just have to cast around and see if we can find something else for him."' Terry's next paperback would be published by Corgi – and so would practically every paperback with Terry's name on after that.*

Colin Smythe Limited brought out the hardback of *The Colour of Magic* in November 1983. 'In a distant and second-hand set of dimensions, in an astral plane that was never meant to fly, the curling star-mists waver and part . . .' And here in public for the first time was Terry Pratchett's Discworld, a flat planet borne through space on the backs of four elephants – Berilia, Tubul, Great T'Phon and Jerakeen – who are themselves positioned on the back of the giant star turtle Great A'Tuin, an arrangement quietly borrowed by Terry from Indian mythology† and which was somehow fundamental to what went on in the book and, at the same time, almost completely beside the point. *The Colour of*

. . . .

* Even though Terry was very often the beneficiary of Colin's ability to find a middle ground that seemingly didn't exist at the point at which he went looking for it, his diplomacy could still irritate Terry from time to time. 'People think the way to keep Terry happy is to keep Colin happy,' Terry mused one day. 'Actually, the way to keep Terry happy is to keep Terry happy.'

† 'I filched it,' as Terry wrote, 'and ran away before the alarms went off.' Indian mythology may merely have been the place where the world-on-a-turtle image was most prominent. Terry's further explorations indicated that practically every mythology you could find had a soft spot at some time in its life for turtles flying through space. And why not?

Magic introduced the inept wizard Rincewind, and Twoflower the tourist, and the Luggage, and the concept of Octarine, the eighth colour of
the Discworld spectrum, visible only to wizards and cats. It also introduced the concept of being spectacularly funny in a fantasy novel. And it
was spectacularly funny because its real subject, in the end, wasn't elephants or astronomically huge turtles or wizards, nor even cats, but
human foibles, which its author clearly, even though he was still honing
his craft, had found a unique way to expose and articulate. This book was
intended, Terry always said, 'to do for fantasy fiction what *Blazing Saddles*
had done for the western' – and, of course, what *The Hitchhiker's Guide to
the Galaxy* had done for sci-fi – and if you read it and loved it, and if it
gathered you up and carried you along, that's pretty much exactly what
you felt it had done by the time you finished it.

It got some good reviews – more reviews, and better reviews, certainly,
than anything Terry had written before. 'Verbally witty', 'imaginatively
resourceful', 'frothy', 'inventive', 'so much fun' – these were among the
garlands laid at its door, albeit mostly in low-circulation, specialist journals. 'Heroic barbarians, chthonic monsters, beautiful princesses and fiery
dragons; they're all here, but none of them is doing business as usual,'
observed *Publisher's Weekly*. And then, because this was many years before
the invention of the 'spoiler alert', the reviewer felt free to add: 'Nor
would you expect them to, in a book that ends with the heroes falling
over the edge of the world.' Meanwhile, in the sci-fi magazine *White
Dwarf*, David Langford described it as 'one of those horrible, anti-social
books which impel the reader to buttonhole friends and quote bits at
them. My ceiling is covered with brown spots from when I tried to read
Pratchett's jokes and drink beer at the same time. Only native sadism
makes me recommend this disgraceful work.'

Terry himself would outgrow it, of course. He would write far better books, books with 'discernible plots' in them, and come to regard
this first try-out for the series almost as if it were juvenilia – albeit the
juvenilia of a 33-year-old writer who had been a published author for
eighteen years. As Terry said in the speech he gave as Guest of Honour
at the 2004 World Science Fiction Convention in Boston: 'I find it now
rather embarrassing that people beginning the Discworld series start

with *The Colour of Magic* and *The Light Fantastic*, which I don't think are some of the best books to start with. This is the author saying this, folks. Do not start at the beginning with Discworld.'

In 1983, however, it was all people had to go on. And for the handful of readers who latched on to the book straight away, it was plenty. Those readers really did only amount to a handful, though. The notion that *The Colour of Magic* instantly sold in thousands, thereby blasting Terry into the publishing stratosphere in a shower of hot sparks and leaving him to dwell there for ever more, is a myth. And, as so often in this story, it's a myth greatly magnified down the years in public utterances by Terry himself, who was apt to insert his success into the 'overnight' category for purposes of convenience and greater drama. At the time of writing, editions of *The Colour of Magic* exist in at least 35 languages, including Catalan, Chinese, Macedonian and Hebrew. We should remember, though, that in 1983, with Colin Smythe Limited in a position to print only a little over 500 hardbacks, it was barely even available in its native English. The truth is, an awful lot of people missed 'the book that started it all' the first time out, and had to go back for it later.

Once again, there was no attention-grabbing launch party. 'A party would have eaten the possible profits pretty much whole,' explained Colin, who thinks he probably gave Terry and Lyn dinner at Cornerways again. Beyond sending out some review copies, there was no budget for marketing, either.

There was, however, a radio serialization – and this was important. It didn't happen for another six months, but it was still important. Thanks to a smart piece of work by Diane Pearson at Corgi – straight away repaying Colin's faith in her – *The Colour of Magic* was accepted by *Woman's Hour*, BBC Radio 4's female-leaning current affairs magazine show which was then broadcasting every weekday at 2.00 in the afternoon and liked to have a book on the go.* *Woman's Hour* proposed serializing the novel in ten

. . . .

* The paperwork for this deal referred to the book in at least one place as 'The Colour of Money'. There is no suggestion, however, that *Woman's Hour* didn't know what they were getting.

parts, abridged. Later on, when he was established, Terry's contempt for abridgements of his work tended to border on the acidic. This was much to the confusion of the actor Tony Robinson, who loaned his voice to many of those abridgements for the audiobook versions, and who, for a long time, laboured under the impression that Terry really disliked him. Terry didn't dislike him at all; he disliked the abridgements. His feeling was that the people in charge of the editing always took out the wrong bits and, in fact, shouldn't have been taking out bits in the first place. At its saltiest, Terry's position was: if he had intended the book to be any shorter, he would have written a shorter book.

At this early stage of the journey, though, he was in no position to demur, especially as the abridgement was going to be read by Nigel Hawthorne. That in itself was quite a coup: Hawthorne was at that point widely familiar to the nation as the smoothly manipulative civil servant Sir Humphrey Appleby in the BBC sitcom *Yes Minister*. So, in ten consecutive weekday episodes of the show, starting on Wednesday, 27 June 1984, and in Hawthorne's impeccable tones, Terry's loosely linked and now considerably compressed tales were heard alongside a feature on the commencement of Dr Billy Graham's 'Mission England' crusade, a piece by Liz Armitage on 'the pecking order in her exotic poultry breeding business' and, ahead of the final episode, a feature on cystitis. Given the stereotypical image that later emerged of readers of Terry Pratchett's books – overwhelmingly male, underwhelmingly adolescent – it's worth pointing out that the first major public exposure of Terry's writing was to an audience of well-read women. It's worth pointing out, also, that the audience of well-read women loved what they heard. 'The producers said they could not remember a reaction like it to a book they had featured,' Colin said. *Woman's Hour* would be back for another helping of Pratchett soon after this, and with even greater effect.

After *The Colour of Magic* was broadcast, Colin received a call from NEL, wondering if by any chance those paperback rights were still available. 'Sadly not . . .' said Colin.

Was the summer of 1984, then, the point at which the engine truly fired into life and the accelerator went down and the momentum finally started to gather under Terry's career as word-of-mouth began to do its thing?

Yes, it probably was. But there was no time to consider all that. Terry had a train to crash.

★ ★ ★ ★ ★

Exactly one week after *Woman's Hour* and its listeners got to the end of *The Colour of Magic*, Terry drove to Leicestershire on behalf of the CEGB, and the rest of the country, to take his place on the front line. His object: to do his bit for the nation and to serve in the mission known as Operation Smash Hit.

Make no mistake, the British people were worried in those days. They were worried about the trains. Not just the regular passenger services: the British people had always been worried about those and perhaps always would be. But they were *really* worried about the trains with nuclear waste on them. You would see those trains, in broad daylight, travelling through built-up areas of Bristol, among other places, loaded up with nuclear flasks, bearing irradiated fuel rods away from nuclear power stations to the reprocessing plant at Sellafield on the Cumbrian coast. It made people nervous. Was that . . . safe?

Of course it was safe, said the CEGB. And had they not proved it by dropping those nuclear flasks from a rig in a disused quarry in Cheddar to show how indestructible they were, and how unlikely they were to split while passing the bottom of your garden on a train?

Yet somehow the British people were still worried. They needed something more reassuring, something more . . . demonstrative.

They needed Operation Smash Hit.

So, on the overcast and slightly muggy day of 17 July 1984, the CEGB and its nationally coordinated press departments arranged for a 22-year-old Type 46 diesel locomotive, travelling at 100mph with three carriages attached to the back of it, to collide with a stationary nuclear flask at Dalby Test Track near Melton Mowbray. Twinning earnest science with the high-gloss values of a 24-carat publicity stunt, this literal train crash was conducted in front of 1,500 accredited witnesses, including, in his capacity as press officer for CEGB South Western Region, Terry Pratchett, and was designed to vouch for the absolute security of Britain's nuclear-waste transportation by rail. The speed of the train, as Terry was forever fond of pointing out, had to be 100mph – not for any good scientific reason, but simply because 100mph was a story and a guaranteed newspaper headline in a way that, say, 97mph, or even 102mph, simply wasn't.

On the day, the press and spectators were positioned on temporary bleachers in an adjacent field. Terry ensured that his guests were where they needed to be and then sat back to watch the show. One observer likened the atmosphere to Cape Canaveral on launch day and, within the general picnic mood, if you'd had a pound for every time someone punningly asked someone else whether they had brought a flask, you would have been able to fill the press refreshment table with caviar. There was a small delay to proceedings while the police dealt with a posse of anti-nuclear protestors, who had broken through the fence to chant and raise banners. But then, monitored throughout by a helicopter and no fewer than 40 strategically placed cameras, the driverless train was unleashed eight miles away, down a section of the former Melton Mowbray-to-Nottingham Midland line, whereupon it accelerated to 100mph (not a mile per hour more, not a mile per hour less) and smashed, actually quite sickeningly, into the stranded flask. There was a deafening crack on impact, followed by what one spectator described as 'a surprisingly muted rolling rumble' as the doomed loco, forced upwards by 30 degrees, ploughed onwards in a gale of metal splinters and an eventually all-enveloping cloud of smoke and flames before coming to rest in a deep pit of ballast.

The result? Not good news for the train. Its front end was practically vaporized and the stubby remainder came to rest on its side, although those three carriages remained stoically upright and in line behind it. But the flask? Barely a scratch on it. Once the engineers had made their measurements, the public was invited onto the ballast to inspect the damage. The 6.9 bar pressure in the flask had dropped by an entirely negligible 0.02 bar, meaning the lid had hardly moved in the smash, let alone opened. Mission accomplished. The stunt made an item for the

BBC's *Six O'Clock News* and a nine-minute promotional film for Magnox which you can still find on YouTube, and anxiety about the transport of nuclear waste across Britain abated, at least for a while. Any lingering tension could be dispersed by the stock joke in the wake of this event, which was: let's see them try that with a British Rail sandwich.

Terry headed back west, glad to have been of service.

★ ★ ★ ★ ★

Corgi's paperback edition of *The Colour of Magic* came out on 15 January 1985, with a cover blurb that was hedging a few bets: 'Jerome K. Jerome meets *Lord of the Rings* (with a touch of *Peter Pan*).' The illustration on the cover, however, was less compromising: it was commissioned from Josh Kirby, then in his fifties, the artist who designed the jacket for Ian Fleming's *Moonraker* and whose work had appeared on sci-fi books by Ray Bradbury, Robert Heinlein and Brian Aldiss, among many others.* Oddly, given the degree of control that would later be exercised in this area, neither Terry nor Colin saw the cover before it was printed. Had they done so, one of them might have spotted the fact that, taking literally a joke about his bespectacled-ness in the pages of the book, Kirby had drawn Twoflower with four eyes. Either Terry or Colin might also have suggested a trim for Rincewind's beard, which in the picture flows, grey and Merlin-like, but is actually, as described by Terry, red and patchy – the beard of someone who is struggling to grow a beard.† However, even with those discrepancies, Terry seems to have loved the image, in all its rolling, colourful, outlandish chaos, and to have loved, also, the association of his work with Kirby.

....

* Who wasn't a Josh at all, but was actually a Ronald. Josh was an art school nickname that stuck, pinned to him in honour of the resemblance between his work at the time and that of Sir Joshua Reynolds.

† When it came to offering guidance for the visualization of Rincewind, Terry often at the time raised the image of Nicholas Lyndhurst as Rodney Trotter in *Only Fools and Horses*.

Kirby would be commissioned to provide the jackets for every Discworld novel, hardback and paperback, until his death in 2001.

In the week after the paperback publication, Terry embarked on a whirlwind publicity tour, confined, in fact, to a solitary appointment for lunch in a Chinese restaurant in London with the correspondent from *Space Voyager* magazine. The correspondent in question was a tall 25-year-old with tousled black hair and a general demeanour which bore witness to long hours at gigs in small clubs and possibly even longer hours in front of the comic racks in Forbidden Planet. His name was Neil Gaiman and he would turn out in due course to be quite good at this story-writing business himself, but at this stage he was grubbing a living as a freelance journalist, reviewing books – such as *Strata* – and trying to make his way. He could also, as of 1984, legitimately describe himself as the author of the world's first full-length biography of Duran Duran, titled, imaginatively, *Duran Duran*, though he might not have mentioned this piece of work at the time to Terry and would almost certainly have drawn a complete blank had he done so.[*]

Neil arrived for the interview in a grey homburg hat – 'sort of like the ones Humphrey Bogart wears in movies,' he later wrote, before conceding that he didn't look like Bogart, in fact, but 'like someone wearing a grown-up's hat'. He was slowly learning, he explained, that, no matter how hard he tried, he could not 'become a hat person'. Terry at this point already *was* a hat person – although not *that* hat. That hat would come later. On this occasion, he was in his CEGB-era, Lenin-style leather cap which here, in combination with a harlequin-patterned pullover, arguably made him look less like a Russian revolutionary and more like a weekending bank manager who had stopped off on his way home after a light round of golf.

The interview appeared under the headline 'The Colour of Pratchett'.

. . . .

[*] In 2015, Neil told the *Daily Telegraph* that *Duran Duran* was 'the worst thing' he'd ever written and that he wished he'd never done it. Consequently copies now change hands on eBay for three-figure sums.

Neil was pleasantly laudatory, and Terry was Terry. Asked to unpack Corgi's Jerome K. Jerome/Tolkien/Barrie cover blurb, Terry replied, tartly, 'Don't ask me to explain what publishers say.' Setting the template for so many future interviews, he also offered Neil, apparently un-prompted, the benefit of his long years in journalism: 'An interview needn't last more than 15 minutes. A good quote for the beginning, a good quote for the end, and the rest you make up back at the office.'

But there was chemistry between them. Neil concluded that the author of *The Colour of Magic* was 'ferociously intelligent', and also that he was 'having fun'. He would also later claim that the two of them realized they had 'the same sorts of brains'. Terry very quickly found in Neil someone to whom he could send disks of work in progress and to whom he could pick up the phone sometimes when he hit a brick in the road of his writing, and ask, ''Ere, what's funnier – a dwarf who thinks he's a giant, or a giant who thinks he's a dwarf?' 'What if you had both?' was Neil's well-gauged reply. As early as *Equal Rites*, the third Discworld novel, Terry was thanking Neil in the dedication for his loan of 'the last surviving copy of the *Liber Paginarum Fulvarum*',* and a lifelong friendship was underway. Even so, did it occur to either of them at this juncture that a fruitful collaboration was on the cards? Clearly not. After all, how frequently did a successful novel get written by committee?

Terry told Colin Smythe that he thought his next novel, too, might be set on Discworld. 'I don't think I've exhausted all the possibilities in one book,' Terry said, thereby inadvertently producing one of the greatest understatements in publishing history. But he could sense that he was finally getting somewhere, and it inspired him to push on hard. And exactly how hard we can see from a diary that Terry started to keep in a file on his Amstrad CPC 464.

He started the diary in February 1985, when he was just finishing his

---

* Latin for Yellow Pages – a shared Gaiman/Pratchett gag. See also *Good Omens*. Neil would later suggest that they used the wrong Latin word for yellow, and that there was another one, closer to the yellow of the fabled business phone directory. Indeed, *fulva* does seem to translate more as 'strawberry blonde'. Neil may have been thinking of *flava*, or possibly *lutea*. Not to labour the point or spoil the joke.

follow-up to *The Colour of Magic* – which he had decided to call *The Light Fantastic* – before heading straight on into another book, which began life as a file named, simply, 'girl'. Do the entries which Terry typed into this document – presumably in the small hours at the end of the working day on many occasions – tear back the curtain to yield a searing insight into his innermost thoughts and feelings and the state of his heart at this critical phase in his personal and professional life? No, they don't. But they do tirelessly track, calculate and recalculate his nightly word-rate.

On 10 April, for example, regarding *The Light Fantastic*, Terry notes: '11.5 files done since Feb 1, equals 11.5 x 1700, equals 19550, equals nightly speed of 280 words. Est. 43,000 words done, at current rate first draft should be completed by April 10 plus 60 days, or June 9.' In fact, by 29 April, the 'overall average [is] 328 words per day', and on 30 May, Terry is writing 'Book finished, now on draft 2.'

A gap in the diary follows, lasting a month and a half, but on 14 July Terry returns and reports that he is already 7,000 words into the file called 'girl' and whipping himself along: 'Target is 250 words a night,' he writes. 'A 60,000 target, that means 212 days. No, let's say by Christmas which means 370 words a night. Aim for 400!'

Such entries seem to bear witness to the re-emergence, after a decade in relative abeyance, of the obsessive Terry. The Terry who went from being a reluctant reader at eleven to being the reader of everything at twelve, is now the Terry who goes from lightly tinkering with the occasional sci-fi novel between beekeeping duties to writing in every free second of the day that is available to him.

Inevitably at these rates of progress, the file titled 'girl' soon became a novel. It was called *Equal Rites* – a title arrived at following a brainstorming session over lunch in the staff restaurant at Bedminster Down. Now that he was officially 'out' among them as a novelist, Terry was free to consult the Table of Eight's hive-mind on work in progress, and frequently did so. They might not have gone with him very far down the Dungeons & Dragons path, but they were happy to turn their thoughts, in idle moments, to the workings of Discworld. What if, Terry said one day, the Watch – Colon, Nobby, Carrot – had sort of semi-accidentally saved the city of Ankh-Morpork from certain destruction and were summoned before the Patrician and invited to choose their reward? And what if the only things they requested were comically humble and mundane in the context? What might a bunch of returning heroes ask for that would be funny? Someone at the table suggested a kettle, someone else a dartboard. Flash forward to the concluding stages of the 1989 novel *Guards! Guards!*: 'We could do with a new kettle, if it's all the same, your Lordship . . . I suppose a dartboard would be out of the question—?'

In February 1986, Terry, now approaching his 38th birthday, sat down at his Amstrad and looked back. 'Review of year since began diary: well, not bad; two books written and accepted for publication (probably). More to the point, a decent nightly word average.' Larry Finlay, the managing director of Transworld, recalls Terry updating the entire company on that word average in a short speech he was invited to give at the Transworld Sales Conference, held in early 1986 at the Gatwick Wena Hotel which also, at the time, seemed to be hosting a number of mice. In that same speech, Terry issued the plaintive line: 'If you carry on selling my books at this rate, maybe I'll be able to give up the day job.'

And then on he went again. The next few months would find him 'doodling a play' while getting around 40,000 words into a new science fiction novel, notionally called 'The High Meggas' and potentially the first in a new series. When Terry told Neil Gaiman about it, Neil said he thought it sounded interesting, but that what he really wanted to read was a book centred on his favourite Discworld character so far, Death. Neil remembers the phone ringing soon after this conversation and Terry's voice saying, 'You bastard. It's called *Mort*,' before the line went dead. Terry abandoned 'The High Meggas' on 21 July 1986 and on 31 August could report that 'Mort is shaping up well – 483 a night.'*

The doodled play, incidentally, came to nothing, but it did permit

. . . .

* Twenty years later, the 40,000 words of 'The High Meggas' would supply the foundation for the *Long Earth* series, written in collaboration with Stephen Baxter.

Terry a brief and almost entirely unheralded association with the great British actors Bernard Miles and his wife Josephine Wilson. Bernard Miles was part of Terry's childhood, not just for his appearances in war films and in David Lean's *Great Expectations*, but also for his recorded comic monologues, one of which was among Terry's Desert Island Discs in 1997.* Now Lord Miles, he had founded the Mermaid Theatre in London, where Josephine Wilson, now Lady Miles, had started The Molecule Club, an educational project in which science met children's theatre. Terry's brief seems to have been to come up with some sort of science-rich children's entertainment for the stage.

In late February 1986, Terry sent Lady Miles what his accompanying letter described as 'some early pages of the proposed play . . . a sort of evolutionary pantomime in which every stage of the chain – plants, fish, amphibians, reptiles, birds, mammals and man – all declare that they are the best but end up learning the gentle ecological message that they all have a role to play'. Scenery, Terry suggested, would be 'minimal, although I'd like the time machine to be fairly impressive'.

We don't know how the proposal for an impressive time machine went down, but the pages seem to have gone over well. At any rate, three weeks later, Terry's diary states: 'Bernard Miles rang yesterday, would like me to continue with play, is talking about retainer plus £10 per performance.' Was Terry about to take Theatreland by storm?

Sadly not. On 19 May, Terry writes again to Lady Miles:

> I am sorry, although not surprised, that we cannot go further with Evolution, but if you really think we may be able to do business next year then let us, perhaps, give some thought to Time.
>
> I think I can have some fun with the subject while, at the same time, it lends itself to demonstration: candle clocks, water clocks, hour

....

* 'The Race for the Rhinegold Stakes', which was Wagner's 'The Ride of the Valkyries' with a horse-racing commentary – 'probably in a sense one of the ancestors of Discworld,' Terry told Sue Lawley. 'It is just a beautifully drawn-out joke which initially appears to be going on for too long and then, merely because it is going on for so long, becomes even funnier.'

glasses, sundials. There's the 'time we found' – the year, month and day – and the 'time we invented' – the week, hour and minute. If I had to pull a plot out of the air, I'd start the play with time running down, and follow the progress of our 'heroes' as they tried to get it started again. As you may gather, I have been turning this one over in my mind for a week or two.

If you'd prefer to gently extricate yourself from my amateurish efforts in an unfamiliar genre I'll certainly understand!

It seems Lady Miles did prefer to extricate herself, as Terry so delicately put it. But at least he tried. And perhaps, even at this stage, he already knew where his real talent lay. As Terry always said, later on: 'As a play-wright, I make a pretty good novelist.'

How good, he would now find out.

11

LEMON-POWERED MELTDOWNS, FLY-FISHING FOR FRIARS AND LA RUE'S MOTHER GOOSE

It wasn't something he thought to tell his diary about, but while Terry was doing his best to drive up his word-count every evening in Rowberrow, work at the CEGB was challenging him in unprecedented ways. For instance, this was a period in which Terry was obliged to sacrifice a precious weekend in order to drive to Wales and stumble through three feet of freshly fallen snow outside the town of Brynmawr, where ageing overhead electrical cables were in danger of falling onto a small cluster of houses. The CEGB had arranged for the residents in the affected properties to be relocated to a nearby luxury hotel for two nights, all expenses paid, while the cabling was replaced, an invitation gleefully accepted by all of them with the exception of an elderly brother and sister, who were refusing to leave their modestly appointed cottage for even one night with a turn-down service and a chocolate on their pillow, let alone two nights. It fell to Terry to apply the necessary diplomacy – not always his best subject, as he himself would have admitted. Sadly, history does not record the exact details of the ensuing negotiations. We do know, however, that the pair eventually consented to leave.

Even more demandingly, this period saw the single, authentic, 100 per cent this-is-not-a-test alarm-bell on Terry's eight-and-a-half-year watch at the CEGB – the Hinkley Point Incident. On 25 October 1985, during maintenance work at the Hinkley B reactor by the Bristol Channel, a pressurized steel bolt shot out and pierced a boiler tube, causing gas to leak. Because the escaped gas was potentially radioactive, a 'station muster' was performed and the workforce on site were issued with potassium iodide anti-radiation tablets – never a great sign and, in fact, only the second time this emergency measure had been taken in Britain.

As it turned out, radioactivity discharge was eventually declared to have been 'well within the authorized limits' and there was no evidence of contamination beyond the perimeters of the site, which was the general marker for when the public needed to start packing up its cars and heading for the hills. In a four-page report which included the wonderfully breezy line that there was 'very little to worry about', the CEGB insisted that it was guilty of nothing more than an excess of caution.*

Nevertheless, as the story broke and briefly threatened Armageddon, it was an understandably frantic day in the press office at Bedminster Down, where the phones rang off the hook with journalists from every conceivable news outlet demanding to know what was going on at Hinkley Point and how bad this so-called leak actually was and what the CEGB was intending to do about it. And for Terry, finally confronted with the kind of real-time catastrophe for which the organization had been carefully rehearsing all these years, it did not go well.

Julian Curtis, who was sent across to Hinkley Point for the day to handle the press at the site, remembers eventually returning to the Bristol office at 7.00 p.m., looking around and asking where Terry was. 'He's had a heart attack,' somebody replied. 'He's been taken to hospital.'

At some point, with the crisis raging and the calls piling up, an overwhelmed Terry had collapsed and passed out on the office floor. The

. . . .

* Some scepticism about this internal verdict was still being voiced in the Houses of Parliament as late as April the following year, when the Member for Yeovil, one Mr Paddy Ashdown, argued for a wider investigation in the interests of 'openness in relation to nuclear matters'. Had he been asked, Terry would no doubt have been prepared to be as open with Mr Ashdown as the CEGB was paying him to be. But he wasn't asked.

CEGB's on-site medical staff attended to him and decided to call an ambulance. With the phones still ringing, Terry was stretchered away.

At the hospital, where Terry was by now fully conscious, they ran some tests. Not a heart attack, in fact: a panic attack – much like, it seems, that time Terry collapsed onto the carpet in front of Eric Price at the *Western Daily Press*.

Lyn drove to Bristol Royal Infirmary to be with her husband and then, when he was discharged, drove with him to Bedminster Down to pick up his things. Julian met her at the Security Lodge with Terry's cap, bag and donkey jacket. Terry, possibly a little sheepish at this point, stayed in the car.

* * * * *

It had become clear that Colin Smythe Limited had, as a publishing house, reached the limit of what it could achieve for the career of Terry Pratchett. In fact, from here on in, being attached to a tiny, home-run, independent business specializing mainly in academic books about Irish literature could probably only hold him back. 'Terry wanted publicity,' said Colin, 'and I couldn't get him that.' When they talked about where he might go, Terry had only one idea. 'He wanted to be with Gollancz because he thought they had the best science fiction list,' said Colin.

Further advantages of having a gentleman publisher on your side: Colin had published a book on fly-fishing.* In the course of that project one of his academic authors, Jo Rippier, had suggested Colin seek advice from a friend of Jo's and a fellow fly-fisherman, David Burnett. Colin duly did so, and a friendship was formed. David Burnett, when he wasn't fly-fishing, happened to be the publishing director of Gollancz. Colin was easily able to mention to Burnett this writer he happened to know who would surely make a Gollancz author.

. . . .

* For the avoidance of confusion, the book in question was *A Man May Fish* by T. C. Kingsmill Moore. It was not the one that J. R. Hartley spent a lot of time trying to track down a copy of in the famous advertisement for Yellow Pages, or, as we should possibly know it here, the *Liber Paginarum Fulvarum*.

Malcolm Edwards, who was in charge of Gollancz's sci-fi list, remembers, soon after this, 'David Burnett sidling up to me and asking what I thought of "this fellow Pratchett"'. At this point, although aware of Terry's growing reputation, Edwards had not read *The Colour of Magic*. He was also snowed under, editing the entire sci-fi list single-handed, 'without so much as a part-time assistant'. The manuscript of Terry's next book, *Equal Rites*, which Colin had helpfully forwarded, thus ended up getting passed to David Burnett's desk editor, Elfreda Powell, whose most prominent skill lay in translating, among other things, the work of the French playwright Françoise Sagan. It wasn't, perhaps, the obvious fit. 'I'm not quite sure she realized it was meant to be funny,' suggested Edwards.

Realizing that an outside opinion might be a good idea, Edwards commissioned a reader's report on *Equal Rites* from David Langford, who had so positively reviewed *The Colour of Magic* for *White Dwarf* magazine. Langford, who was 33, had a reputation himself as a humorous writer for sci-fi publications, so presumably *would* recognize that *Equal Rites* was supposed to be funny.* And so it proved. Langford sent over his verdict on 5 February 1986, reaching the following conclusions: 'Terry Pratchett is a genuine humourist and this book provokes many smiles, if fewer belly laughs than "The Colour of Magic" . . . Routine bridging passages are usually enlivened by a swift one-liner . . . I feel, though, that humour needs the support of a certain plot tension: unless the humorous invention is continuous, jokes alone won't carry the story through slack periods . . . The book is well-written and quite publishable as it stands. I hope it will be published – but would first prefer some tightening-up throughout the first two hundred pages.'

It was the start of a significant editorial relationship for Terry. Practically encyclopaedic in his knowledge of British comedy writing, Langford was in a position to both deeply impress and deeply irritate

. . . .

* Langford's 1984 novel *The Leaky Establishment* was a comedy set in a nuclear research centre. When it was republished in 2001, Terry supplied an introduction which began: 'I hate Dave Langford for writing this book. This was the book I was meant to write. God wanted me to write this book.' Terry regarded that novel as 'a neglected classic', and ranked it with Michael Frayn's *The Tin Men*.

Terry by knowing that the name Rincewind came from a recurring red-bearded dwarf character, Churm Rincewind, in J. B. Morton's 'By the Way' columns for the *Daily Express* in the 1950s and 1960s.* Langford was to provide Gollancz with similar early reports on drafts of *Mort* (an initial critique which ran to ten pages), *Sourcery* and *Wyrd Sisters*. At that point Terry began to communicate with him about the books directly, initially in exchanges of letters, and from 1994 via email, all the way through to *Thud!*, the 34th Discworld novel. Terry came to know this as submitting the work for 'Langfordization', and its impact in the shaping and tidying of Terry's writing was substantial.†

If Gollancz were encouraged by Langford's *Equal Rites* report, they were possibly even more encouraged by the fact that Diane Pearson had again come up trumps publicity-wise by securing a serialization for the book on *Woman's Hour*. And they were perhaps yet more encouraged by the fact that Corgi had already commissioned a full-colour Josh Kirby illustration for the paperback cover, which would save Gollancz the trouble and expense of doing so. Either way, they proposed a deal for *Equal Rites* and two further Terry Pratchett books, all three of which would appear under the Gollancz imprint 'in association with Colin Smythe Limited'.

On 14 March 1986, Terry wrote in his diary: 'It now seems that the Gollanz [sic] deal will go through with a £3,000 advance per book.' The contract was signed on 2 May 1986, whereupon Terry received £4,500 immediately and the guarantee of a further £1,500 on publication for each of those three books. That would be the equivalent, in 2021, of

....

* Terry had suppressed this memory of J. B. Morton, and thought the name 'Rincewind' was his own invention, and he didn't enjoy being reminded that it wasn't. Incidentally, G. K. Chesterton, no less, reckoned that J. B. Morton, who wrote 'By the Way' under the pseudonym Beachcomber, had 'the greatest comic fertility of any Englishman'. Morton certainly knew a decent prank when he conceived one, once leaving a stack of empty brown ale bottles on the Bloomsbury doorstep of Virginia Woolf.

† The exceptions, David pointed out to me, were the Tiffany Aching novels which 'needed no Langford commentary because Terry's vision of these narratives was so clear and intense that, to quote from memory, all he had to do was type out the words he could see on the insides of his eyelids.'

receiving £11,200 up front, with three further payments of around £3,700 to follow.* It was by no means life-changing money, then. But it was certainly money. And, of course, if the books sold, there would be royalties on top. *If* the books sold.

With that deal in place, *The Light Fantastic* was published in June 1986, the last book of Terry's to appear as a Colin Smythe Limited hardback. 'What makes you laugh?' asked the reviewer in the top-shelf men's magazine *Knave*, before expressing his instinctive aversion to any book declared by its own blurb to be funny. 'It almost never is.' But here, this reviewer felt, was an exception. 'Go out and buy this book. Right now. I mean, it's *funny*.' The author of this urgent acclaim? That distinguished man of letters W. C. Gull, also known as Neil Gaiman.†

Dave Busby suggested to Terry the previous year that this might be a good moment for him to get back on the sci-fi convention circuit, if only for publicity purposes. 'He shuddered at the thought,' Dave said. Yet, in September 1985, Terry went to Fantasycon in Birmingham where he appeared on a panel and where one account has him sitting at the bar, with a bag full of his own books, introducing himself as an author to anyone who would listen. Terry's Amstrad diary merely notes, dryly, 'Rather an in-group.'

A month later he was in Coventry at Novacon 15, the Midlands sci-fi convention, where he had dinner with John Brunner. And the following Easter he was at Eastercon in Glasgow. 'Nothing special. Driving took 7+ hours,' Terry notes, although he straight away adds, 'Have booked for Eastercon in Brum next year.' September 1986 would then find him back in Birmingham at Fantasycon – 'clique-y again, and leaning too heavily towards horror' – but just before that he had been obliged to decline a request to attend a computer games fair, a moment at which we see Terry's

....

* Figures arrived at using inflationtool.com and based on an inflation rate in the UK between 1986 and 2021 of 151.07%.

† Neil, who is a man of impeccable principle, stopped writing for *Knave* shortly after this when the magazine took a turn down-market and became substantially about the pictures of naked women, as opposed to only partly about the pictures of naked women.

day job and his night job starkly rubbing up against each other. 'I shall be at a signing session at Andromeda* on Saturday,' Terry wrote, in a letter of apology to Mandy Keyho at Macmillan Software, 'and I've got to be down at one of our power stations on Sunday.' *That* old excuse. Were there any other British authors at this point dividing their weekends between book signings in Birmingham and CEGB-run open days at Berkeley? These competing obligations – to his book sales and to the public image of Britain's national electricity supplier – would only grow more unwieldy.

Corgi published the paperback of *The Light Fantastic* hard on the heels of the Colin Smythe Limited hardback, on 5 September 1986. And now things really did begin to pick up. Just two months later, at the beginning of November, Terry wrote to Mark Smith, his editor at Corgi, in a state, clearly, of some surprise: 'The royalty returns for "The Colour of Magic" record something over 19,000 sold during the whole of 1985, so from what you tell me "The Light Fantastic" has ALREADY sold considerably more in its first three months. And TCOM . . . has now hit an average of over 1,000 a month – presumably dragged up by TLF. Have I got this right?'

He had. Corgi had printed 34,100 copies of *The Light Fantastic* and they were selling quickly. On top of that, the people who were buying them were promptly going back to pick up the first book. A snowball effect was underway and, in the light of this phenomenon, and confronted with the hard sales figures, some of those tensions that Terry felt a decade earlier around the issue of sequels clearly began to relax in a warm bath of pragmatism. His letter to Mark Smith went on:

'As far as the future is concerned, then, received opinion is that the publication of a book in a series stimulates sales of earlier volumes. Disc-world books are easy – well, fairly easy† – and the temptation is to stick

. . . .

* Roger Peyton's specialist sci-fi bookstore in Birmingham.

† Important note: fairly easy *for Terry*. Don't try this at home. Or rather, by all means *do* try this at home, but don't be disappointed if what you end up with doesn't turn out looking exactly like the picture on the packet.

with them until I've mined the vein (I hardly dare to tell you, as MORT is within a few weeks of completion, that the plot of a fifth Discworld book – with Rincewind and the Luggage to the fore – is fermenting at the back of my mind). In a nutshell, if you as a publisher will say to me, "We can sell the Disc if you can write it, no worries," then a lifetime of writing for money inclines me to respond positively.'

It was beginning to occur to Terry that there might, after all, be something like a living to be scratched from the writing of fiction. The only question now was whether he could afford to give up his day job in order to find out.

* * * * *

Equal Rites was published in hardback on 15 January 1987, again with no evening of white wine and nibbles for Terry, even though he now had a brand new publisher. 'Gollancz rarely threw launch parties,' said Malcolm Edwards, 'Livia [Gollancz, the chairman] being militantly teetotal.' No matter. With exquisite timing, in the run-up to publication, the book was broadcast on *Woman's Hour*, as arranged by Diane Pearson. Naturally, the novel was again condensed, with no surviving objections from Terry, and it was read this time by the English actor Sarah Badel and summarized in that week's edition of *Radio Times* very efficiently, as follows: 'When the wizard Drum Billet dies, and bestows his magic staff on a new-born child, centuries of hallowed custom are sent tumbling. For the baby isn't, as supposed, the eighth son of an eighth son, but a daughter. And everyone knows "Women can't be Wizards"!'

It was the book in which Terry introduced Granny Weatherwax, who would be back very shortly in *Wyrd Sisters* (1988), and Eskarina Smith, who wouldn't be back for 23 years, until *I Shall Wear Midnight* (2010). And it was the book in which Terry made clear that if he was going to pick apart the conventions of fantasy fiction, then that would include picking apart its chauvinism and misogyny. To this extent, *Woman's Hour* was the perfect platform for it. The story again unfolded across ten consecutive programmes, but this time in and around features on the legal implications of divorce, the woman in charge of commercial business at Dunfermline Football Club and an interview with the drag act Danny La Rue, who, that festive season, was giving the people of Bath his Mother Goose. And the reaction from the audience was, again, pure delight.

At home in Rowberrow, ten-year-old Rhianna heard the phrase 'written by Terry Pratchett' spoken on the radio and had her first intimation that this hobby of her father's that seemed to be incessantly drawing him away to his computer in the evenings had some kind of currency in the world beyond their walls. She placed her bright yellow cassette player close to the radio, and pressed Record.

So now *Equal Rites* was out there – a credit to 'the rompingly comic Mr Pratchett', according to *The Times*, and, after Gollancz's cagey initial print run of just 2,750 copies, destined to be reprinted six times in hardback. And *Equal Rites* was sending people back to *The Light Fantastic* which was in turn sending people back to *The Colour of Magic* and the snowball was now growing and growing.

Terry watched all this happen. He was 39, on the way to 40. He had a deal for two more books with a major publishing company which, if it wasn't paying life-altering money, was at least paying *something*. And he had a whole wodge of material waiting to go. If he didn't take the plunge now, when would he?

On 15 July 1987, Terry wrote to Martin Kay, the Public Relations Field Manager at CEGB South Western:

Dear Martin,
Further to my more informal letter last week, I think it best to give you notice of my intention to leave the CEGB by the end of October. This amounts to a notice period of some three months.

While I will obviously do my best to assist with any difficulties my departure may cause, I do not think I can formally agree to any longer notice period which, I think, would almost certainly then become self-extending.

Yours sincerely,
Terry Pratchett

And then he wrote to his accountant, with whom he had been duti-fully filing the annual details of his not especially substantial freelance earnings. Had Terry been blessed with foresight he would have been able to tell him: 'You're going to need a bigger calculator because it's about to start raining money.' What he actually wrote was more circumspect:

> Various contracts in which I'm now involved will make it probably more profitable and certainly more pleasant to become self-employed. I would like to meet you at some suitable time in the near future to discuss certain aspects of this. The main source of income will be creative writing, with freelance journalism as a back-up.

And then he rang Colin Smythe. 'He said to me, "I'm giving up my job,"' Colin said. 'He didn't tell me until it was a fait accompli, but he had clearly thought about it very hard and had been doing the sums. His con-clusion was that he thought he would see a dip in income in the short term, but then he would quite possibly be all right.'

In fact a strong indication that he might indeed survive this reckless transition came far sooner than Terry expected. With *Mort*, the fourth Discworld novel, on the schedules for publication in November, and with *Sourcery*, the fifth, ready to go the following May, Colin was now con-templating Terry's next publishing deal and considered this a good moment to look to the longer term. Deciding not to mess about, he began to solicit offers for Terry's next six books. Gollancz, naturally enough, as the incumbent publisher, were first port of call. Malcolm Edwards took Colin and Terry to lunch at Two Brydges Place, a members-only water-ing hole favoured by literary types, down a back-alley on the edge of Covent Garden in London. There, over sausage and mash with onion gravy, Edwards told Terry, unreservedly, 'I can make you a bestselling author.'

The negotiations went back and forth for a while. According to Terry, Colin phoned him in the office at Bedminster Down during September, when he had only a few more weeks left of his notice period, and mentioned the sum of money that Gollancz was prepared to pay to secure his services for the foreseeable future.

'Colleagues say I put the phone down very carefully,' Terry wrote, 'went and got a cup of coffee, stared out of the window for a while, then rang him back and said, "What?"'

The figure was £306,000 – roughly the equivalent in 2021 of £740,000.* Gollancz had bid £51,000 per book for Terry's next six novels. It didn't look as though there would be a 'dip in income' after all, then. That possibility had just been entirely blown off the landscape.

The deal was not completed until 8 December 1987, when Terry finally put his signature and initials on a contract for 'WYRD SISTERS and five further adult novels of a broadly comparable nature', thereby triggering a £72,000 initial payment for himself and the security of knowing that he would receive another £13,000 every time he delivered a book, every time the hardback came out and every time the paperback followed it, each of which three pay-out points would be reached, at Terry's current rate of industry, twice a year. Meanwhile, Colin stepped out of his dual role as Terry's agent and associate publisher and became solely Terry's agent, doing so with the solid gold reassurance of a typically Pratchettian personal endorsement ringing in his ears: 'He told me, "You are the person I distrust least."'

Leaving the CEGB now seemed notably less risky than it had when Terry first handed in his notice, back in July. It was still going to be emotional, though, breaking up the Table of Eight. His parting gift from Julian Curtis and his other colleagues in the PR department was a packet of Hamlet cigars and a cassette of Bach's 'Air on a G String' mounted in a frame, and with a notice across the bottom saying, 'In case

. . . .

* Calculated as before, using inflationtool.com, which estimates the rate of inflation at 141.99%. The £51,000 for each book would be the equivalent of £123,000 per book, and Terry's initial payment of £72,000 would have felt like £174,000 in today's money, where today = the summer of 2021.

of nuclear emergency, break glass.'* At the ceremony, Julian plucked up the courage to ask Terry the question he'd been meaning to ask him for a while. 'Am I a character in any of your books?' Terry said that he would just have to buy them all in order to find out.

His leaving present from the Table of Eight was a fully operational 'pressurized lemon reactor', set on a plinth and featuring two lemons under matching glass domes, rigged up to power an LED meter. They also gave him a cuddly orang-utan holding a banana in one hand and a book in the other – a homage to the Librarian at Unseen University. The joke among them all was that Terry was the only known example of someone leaving a nationalized industry because they felt it got in the way of making money.

Terry wrote later from Rowberrow to thank them for his parting gifts, constructing his letter in the form of a 'Lemon Reactor Safety Review', addressed to the attention of 'The Nuclear Safety Committee, Citrus Division'.

'The PLR is still operating successfully,' Terry wrote, 'despite severe corrosion problems on one half of the fuel, which has turned a nice blue-white colour. On-load refuelling has been critically examined and appears possible; we are confident that by the time it becomes imperative to dispose of the lemon we will have found some publicly acceptable method of so doing.' He also mentioned that he was thinking of substituting apples for the lemons: 'I will feel more at home with reactors that have a core in them.'

He sent news, too, of the Librarian: 'The new deputy manager has not yet finished his banana. However, his good listening manner and deep understanding of human problems is such that I am thinking of making him Personnel Manager.'

He clearly missed his old colleagues. On 9 November, still adjusting to a daily commute that took him no further than the desk in his home office, and to a workplace where the staff restaurant was now his own kitchen and where

....

* 'Happiness is a cigar called Hamlet,' as a ragingly popular series of advertisements insisted at the time, stressing the product's properties as a relaxant in moments of crisis.

the lavatory only had one mirror, Terry composed a slightly mournful-sounding letter to the Table of Eight at Bedminster Down.

Dear All,

As I sit here struggling with the cold waters of self-employment, wondering where all this money has actually got to, I think of you and the quiet, even pace of life we used to know at Bedminster Down. Talking to a bunch of science fiction fans in Manchester last night about nuclear power, I still found myself using the word 'we', so I have now made an appointment at the Bristol Royal Infirmary to have the CEGB surgically removed from my head.

This is what I have found out so far about working from home: daytime television still has a long way to go.

It was an interesting seven years* and you were a great bunch to work with. Gulp. I've just realised: I may never see another AE17 again.†

See you soon, though, I suspect.

Terry

He did see them soon. He met the Table of Eight for the CEGB Christmas dinner the following month and went out of his way to re-unite with them in Bristol almost every Christmas thereafter until he died.

He knew, though, that he had made the right move. At the weekend, Terry did some work in the garden. Lyn took out a cup of tea and found him sitting under a tree in a ruminative mood.

'Are you all right, Terry?' Lyn said.

'Yes. I think I am,' he said. 'If I play my cards right, I may never need to do another day's work in my life.'

. . . .

* Almost eight and a half, in fact.

† The standard CEGB out-of-pocket expenses claim. Never abused, it goes without saying.

PART TWO

12

LORD NELSON'S TITFER, A SCREAMING APE AND THE SECRET OF THE SHERRY

And now here's Terry Pratchett one night in 2006, wearing a purple velvet dinner jacket with black silk lapels and sitting in a chauffeur-driven silver Mercedes as it crosses the Chiswick flyover on its way into London and passes below a bright electric hoarding reading: 'TERRY PRATCHETT'S HOGFATHER'.

Here's the former press officer of the Central Electricity Generating Board, South Western Region, with his name in lights – Terry Pratchett at the peak of his powers.

And here he is, as the car pulls up outside the Curzon Cinema in Mayfair, putting on his signature black fedora and gathering up his purely decorative ebony cane with its silver Death's Head handle, and stepping out of the limo into a blizzard of flashbulbs and a gale of shouting photographers and hollering fans who are jammed along the pavement.

And here he is with David Jason and Michelle Dockery and Nigel Planer, smiling for premiere-night photographs on the red carpet which is actually a white carpet because, after all, this is *Hogfather*, and who isn't dreaming of a white Hogswatch?

And here he is, following the screening, at the after-party in the Zeta bar in the basement of the Park Lane Hilton, where trays of vanilla

Martinis circulate and where the bar bill – footed by Sky – will come out just short of £15,000. But no matter, because David Jason is about to do Sky's promotions team the inadvertent favour of getting snapped looking somewhat unsteady between the hotel door and the back of his car, thereby triggering a slew of 'Luvvly Jubbly Bubbly' headlines in the next morning's tabloids, which is publicity like you just can't buy.

And then here's Terry Pratchett the morning after, back at his desk in the Chapel, where there is no fondly going back over these glitzy events, and where the previous night is, in fact, of no interest, because it happened yesterday, and because, for all these major outward ripples in the world – the over-subscribed book tours, the packed-out fan conventions, the premieres of television adaptations – the focus must always come back eventually to a man in his gardening clothes, sitting at a screen, getting on with the next book.

'Your reward for doing something good,' Terry has taken to saying, 'is to do something else good.'

★ ★ ★ ★ ★

He left it a bit late, of course, and he would think about that ruefully near the end, when time was running out and we were losing him at 100 miles per hour.

In September 2010, *I Shall Wear Midnight*, the penultimate Tiffany Aching-centred Discworld novel, was launched with a special after-hours event at Waterstones' London megastore on Piccadilly. After a count-down to midnight, Terry, in a red, Wee Willie Winkie-style nightshirt and matching nightcap with a fluffy bobble hanging from it, signed copies of the book until 1.00 a.m.* I sat beside him and applied the rubber stamp to the signed pages, which was the tactic we had started using to combat the deterioration in Terry's handwriting. Initially the

---

* As midnight struck, Philippa Dickinson, Terry's editor, made the point that a 'midnight signing' should be completed within the midnight hour. This was certainly true from a literal point of view, but it meant the queue of waiting book-buyers got hurtled through at unprecedentedly breakneck speed.

stamps went on first, providing a box for Terry to aim at, the black lines guiding him in through his spatial confusion. Later they were a way of adding a little piece of official decoration to the limited mark that he could make. For *Dodger* in 2012, by which time operating a pen was almost completely beyond him, the stamp was a frame in which he could press his inked thumb. But once again, that night in Waterstones, I found myself in wonder at Terry's continuing ability to throw himself into an event like that, without appearing to be remotely drained by it. And then I realized that events like these were, at this stage, actually the nuclear power plant from which he was drawing his energy.

That was the night he publicly voiced the regret that I just mentioned. Before the midnight signing, Terry stood on a platform on the Waterstones shop-floor and did an hour-long Q&A interview with the actor Tony Robinson – by now amply reassured that it was the abridgements Terry objected to, and not himself. Tony, his wife Louise, Terry, Rhianna and myself had spent the earlier part of the evening preparing for this aspect of the event by working our way through the cocktail menu at Veeraswamy, the Indian restaurant on Regent Street. Terry and Tony were then given further preparatory time together in the Green Room at Waterstones, though by then it was clear that they were going to be ad libbing it. The cocktails had already decreed this.*

At one point in the ensuing interview, Tony asked Terry what advice he would give his younger self.

'Get more sex while you can,' Terry straight away replied.

But then he thought about it more seriously. 'I wish I had started writing for a living earlier,' he said eventually. 'I could probably have started to write full time about ten years before I did.'

What would those ten extra years have amounted to, in Pratchett terms? Another 20 books? Whatever, it would explain why, in 1987, having finally taken the plunge and left the CEGB for Gaze Cottage and 'the cold waters of self-employment', as he put it in that letter to

. . . .

* I say 'working our way through' the cocktail menu, but we did hover for quite a while over the bright green, sticky, melon-flavoured one.

his former colleagues, Terry tore into his new occupation like someone already determined to make up for lost time.

Being relieved of the daily commute into Bristol did at least allow him a more relaxed start to the day. He no longer had to be up and out. He came to like the sound of the kettle in the morning, Lyn told me, and would sit in bed for a while, drinking tea, downloading the ideas that had been working their way through his brain during the night, talking them through with her. She, for her part, would read him bits from the newspaper.

But after that he needed structure – the structure of an office day, only stricter. He sequestered himself in his room, with only the carnivorous plants on the window sill and perhaps the occasional cat for company. There were to be no interruptions. Those daily word-targets became, if possible, even more important to him, 3,000 becoming the expanded target he now set himself. Disconnecting himself at last from a formal workplace seemed only to make him more driven. 'He was totally focused on making a success of this new life,' Dave Busby said. 'He told me that on a Friday afternoon, for relaxation, he would go through what he had written and do the spell-checking. That was his idea of a lighter work-load.' In a profession famous for prevarication and self-indulgence under the general heading of 'creativity', and with a stereotypical image which allowed, in extreme forms, for the possibility of days spent in silk nightgowns and glasses of champagne by 11.00 a.m., Terry seems to have decided that his approach to the business of being a novelist would be utterly blue-collar – industrial, even. Furthermore, he would be adamant about prioritizing that industry in the face of all other claims on his time.

Aged nine or ten, Rhianna drew a picture of a hat and wrote underneath it: 'I love my father but he is very busy.'

He was busy writing and, increasingly, he was busy promoting that writing, too, which took him away from home, to book signings, sci-fi and fantasy conventions, games fairs, publishing sales conferences. He promoted as avidly as he wrote. At the sci-fi conventions he was hooking up again with those writers he admired whom he had first run into when he was a teenager with a single published story behind him – Brian

Aldiss, Michael Moorcock, John Brunner. They had called him 'The Boy' back then, but now that he had broken through and was beginning to sell books and gain a profile . . . well, they still called him 'The Boy', in fact, which grated on him enormously. 'The thing about fandom,' Terry said, 'is that you never elevate from the position at which you enter it.' Still, this was the job now. He put in the miles.

He was building a following – growing his brand, we would now say. The hat helped. The hat had been bought, in early 1988, at Lock & Company in St James's Street, in a rare moment of extravagance on a trip to London to see his publishers. Lock & Company's eighteenth-century shop, with its dark green paintwork, was itself a lasting fascination for Terry, not to mention a location to adapt eventually for the book *Dodger*. He liked Bates, opposite Piccadilly Arcade, too, with its stuffed cat – Binks, a denizen of the shop in the twenties and eternally memorialized in his top hat, smoothly smoking a Turkish cigarette. But it was Lock & Company who had put homburgs on the head of Churchill and bowlers on the head of Charlie Chaplin, and Lock & Company who had supplied Admiral Lord Nelson with the bicorne he was wearing when he died on HMS *Victory*. In the early 2000s, when Lock & Co. pitched for a hipper, trendier demographic with a promotion entitled 'Lock'n'Roll', Terry was highly disapproving. 'You need some age under you before you can shop in Lock & Co.,' he said.

The hat which the 40-year-old Terry Pratchett bought was, as he emphatically clarified for anyone who made the error, *not* a fedora but a Louisiana. Later, on a future visit to Lock & Company, the staff would explain to him that, no, it actually *was* a fedora, and had been so all along (their 'Louisiana' model). But never mind. This single item gave him, with almost absurd ease, an image. It placed him – even for people who didn't read his books or especially care to. In those early days, he accessorized the fedora with a black leather satchel and a black Levi's jacket, from back in the day when Levi's still made such a thing, and those items, too, would come to encapsulate Terry for early Pratchett fans. But it was the hat that possessed the truly transformative magic, in the sense that, simply by putting it on, he could become the public Terry Pratchett that he was increasingly being asked to be. And of course, inversely, by the equally simple act of removing it when he walked back through the door of Gaze Cottage, he could become himself again. It was, as he used to say, 'an anti-disguise'.*

For all his expanding profile, however, not everyone was as yet fully updated on Terry's change in status. Once when he was away on a book-signing tour, Lyn found herself woken by the house phone at 1.00 a.m. It was a journalist with an urgent enquiry for Terry Pratchett.

'But he's not here,' said Lyn. 'And it's the middle of the night . . .'

'Is this not the number for the CEGB press officer?' said the voice.

Such calls would continue to come at various times of the day for more than a year after Terry resigned his duties, overlapping with the increasing calls for Terry Pratchett the author.

When he returned from those early trips, Lyn would collect him from Bristol Temple Meads train station in her putty-coloured Austin 1100, a car that did not especially stand out from the crowd. One evening, arriving home with the other commuters during rush hour, Terry walked out of the station to the line of waiting cars, pulled open the passenger door, climbed in and began to put on his seatbelt. A woman he had never seen before looked across at him from the driver's seat and said, 'I suppose you think I'm your wife.' Terry made his apologies and climbed out again.

This was a period of practically incessant work, but it was apparent very quickly, and very gratifyingly, that it was paying off. One Sunday,

....

* Further down the line, following trips to Australia, the fedora became the Akubra. Those were normally khaki in flavour but one of the Australian fan conventions had one made for Terry in black, which he was utterly thrilled with.[1] 'I can't deny that any day with a new hat in it is a very good day indeed,' Terry once wrote. His willingness to shop for hats was in stark contrast to his policy with other items of clothing which tended to be worn until extinction. I once walked into the London Book Fair with Terry to find a giant promotional photograph of him on the wall in which he was wearing a shirt with 'Australia' written across its pocket. The photo had been taken a number of years earlier. Looking across at the real Terry, I noticed he was still wearing that same shirt.

[1] The convention was 2011's Nullus Anxietus III,[a] held at Panther's World of Entertainment in Penrith, outside Sydney.

[a] Which is Latin, approximately, for 'no worries'.

with Terry on a rare day off, Lyn opened the newspaper at the page with the bestseller lists on it and immediately went out into the garden to find him.

'Terry, you're number two!' she said.

Terry let it sink in for a second, before typically putting a dent in the glory of his own moment.

'Who is number one?' he said.

'Stephen King,' said Lyn.

'Yes,' said Terry, 'and I bet he's not in his back garden fixing a puncture on his daughter's bike.'

★ ★ ★ ★ ★

It all got very big, very quickly. These were the years when Terry's career caught fire and properly blazed and when all the crucial numbers began to escalate vertiginously. Coinciding with Terry's first days at home as a full-time writer, the Corgi paperback of *Equal Rites* was published in November 1987 with a print run of 61,000 copies. Demand for it was so great that it had to be reprinted that year, then twice the following year. A year later, in November 1988, the Corgi print run for the paperback of *Mort* was 111,500 copies, and, again, they sold so fast that a first reprint had to be commissioned almost instantly. The paperback print run for *Sourcery* was 154,500 copies, for *Reaper Man* 175,000 copies, for *Lords and Ladies*, 242,000 ... Where the Colin Smythe Limited print run for the hardback of *The Colour of Magic* in 1983 had been a little over 500, the first print-run for *Carpe Jugulum* in 1998 was 160,000 hardbacks, with 322,000 paperbacks following it a year later. And all of these books sold. Heading for Christmas 1998 *Carpe Jugulum* was the number one hardback at the same time as *Jingo* was the number one paperback. Earlier that year, *The Last Continent*, in which Terry had travelled to the furthest regions of Discworld to discover somewhere that felt suspiciously like Australia, had spent twelve weeks at number one on the hardback bestseller list. Through the 1990s, Terry sold an average of three million books each year. Nobody in Britain sold more and, as the newspaper profiles liked to express it, if you set end-to-end every Terry Pratchett book ever bought, they would reach . . . well, from wherever you are to a very long way away.*

Inevitably, Terry's advances grew, too. They went from £51,000 per book to £200,000 per book, and then to £400,000 per book. And they would have carried on growing if they hadn't met resistance from a perhaps unlikely source: Terry himself. After the six-book Gollancz deal which had floated him away from the safe harbour of full-time employment and which ended with *Witches Abroad* in 1991, he decided he no longer wanted the pressures of such a long-term arrangement, the responsibility of which seemed in practice to worry him more than make him feel secure. He instructed Colin to strike deals for no more than two books at a time, waiting until they were both well underway – and in some cases until one of them was finished. At that point, Terry would phone Colin and say, 'I think we have a book.' And then Colin would phone the publisher and the negotiations would begin.

Except in the sense that they took place over extended and wine-fuelled lunches, those negotiations would not always run to type. Terry had strong and, some might even say, puritanical ideas about how much money he should accept in advance of a book's publication. If he couldn't be confident that the advance would earn itself out inside three years and that the book would go into profit and yield royalties, he refused to accept it. As Terry's qualms in this area were not widely shared among authors, his attitude made for some atypical dealings. At one point, for example, Transworld offered Terry £125,000 for a book he had proposed for younger readers. This was in the mid-1990s, when a generous offer for a children's book of its nature would have

----

* The line would stretch from London to Morocco, according to one 1990s estimate. By now, in 2021, we can probably imagine that Terry's books are well on their way to the Cape, perhaps having gone slightly out of their way to check out Malawi. In the same way that he knew 100mph was the only real speed at which to crash a train, Terry also understood that the only properly newsworthy measure of sold books was if they stretched to the moon. We did once devote an idle afternoon to calculating how far Terry's books had got on that particular journey, but when it became clear that Terry wasn't even getting out of near-earth orbit, his interest in the analogy rather waned.

been in the region of £25,000, so that six-figure offer was an emphatic demonstration of confidence in Terry's writing. Colin, naturally, was excited to tell Terry about it. The conversation they had was short and pointed. Colin then found himself ringing Transworld and saying, 'I have conveyed your offer to Terry, and I'm afraid he is not at all happy with it.'

Colin says he left a small pause at this point so that he could at least enjoy delivering the pay-off.

'No, he says it's far too much and he would like me to agree a deal with you for less.'

Similar qualms on Terry's part affected the price paid up front for *Good Omens*, his 1990 collaboration with Neil Gaiman. During 1985, Neil had shown Terry a file containing 5,282 words which he had written, exploring a scenario in which Richmal Crompton's William Brown had somehow become the Antichrist. Terry loved it, and the concept stayed in his mind. A couple of years later, he rang Neil to ask him if he had done any more work on it. Neil, who had been spending that time thinking about his 'The Sandman' series for DC Comics, said he hadn't really given it another thought. Terry said, 'Well, I know what happens next, so either you can sell me the idea or we can write it together.' Neil knew straight away which of those options he preferred. As he said, 'it was like Michelangelo ringing up and saying, "Do you fancy doing a ceiling?" '*

So, mostly in the spirit of experiment, the two of them started building a book together. It was a lark, really – a side-project with nothing hingeing on it except their own diversion. According to Terry they were 'two guys who didn't have anything to lose by having fun'. They were also two guys who operated at different ends of the day. Neil, at this point in his life, was largely allergic to the morning and would wake around lunchtime to flurries of crisp answerphone messages from his

....

* History – and book sales – amply vindicate Neil's decision on this occasion, but, of course, his response means that the world will never know how much, exactly, Terry would have been prepared to pay him to take that idea off his hands.

collaborator, which were generally variations on the theme of 'Get up, you lazy bastard.'

One weekend, Neil stayed over in Rowberrow to work on the book. On the Sunday morning, waiting for their guest to rise and greet what remained of the day, Terry and Lyn heard the noise of a commotion in the upstairs spare room. They went and stood on the landing outside the door and listened. From within came repeated soft thuds and what sounded like the flapping of wings.

What was he *doing* in there?

Terry gently opened the door to find Neil in bed, staring up in freshly awoken bewilderment at two of the Pratchetts' doves who had flown in through the open window and were now frantically trying to get out again.

Yet somehow, despite all the unsynchronized to-ing and fro-ing and the interruptions by confused birds, a book emerged, in which the angel Aziraphale and the demon Crowley got together to head off the end times, and in which lastingly important thoughts were set down about witches, prophecies, the Four Horsemen of the Apocalypse and pets.[*] Pausing only to change the title from 'William the Anti-Christ' to *Good Omens: The Nice and Accurate Prophecies of Agnes Nutter, Witch*, the pair of them handed it over to their respective agents to see if it could be sold. Whereupon, this being a genuinely funny book with a manifest commercial appeal, the bidding rose rapidly into six figures and, according to Colin, would have happily continued rising if Terry hadn't panicked and called a stop to it.

There it was again – that anxiety about being paid too much, getting caught out and thereby destroying his good name for ever. And it never left him. In 2006, I was in the Chapel with Terry when the offer came in for a collection of his non-fiction writing – the book which eventually became *A Slip of the Keyboard*. The sum was £750,000. Terry was

. . . .

[*] 'Despite thousands of years of man-made evolution, every dog is only two meals away from being a wolf.'

appalled. These publishers were all mad, flinging money around. 'It's just testosterone,' he exclaimed, in high dudgeon. 'I withdraw the book.' The book remained withdrawn for eight years.

Everything that Terry feared in this aspect of the business seemed to have a physical manifestation in an apparently innocent bookshop on Sidney Street in Cambridge called Galloway & Porter. Now no longer in business, Galloway & Porter specialized for many years in the sale of remaindered books, volumes rescued from the jaws of the pulper and offered to the city's student-flushed population at dirt-cheap prices. Terry was familiar with the shop from his trips to Cambridge to do signings around the corner at Heffers, and then later at Borders, and this book-vending equivalent of the Last Chance Saloon utterly haunted him. He had had a vision of walking past Galloway & Porter and seeing books with his name on piled high in its window, and it stuck in his mind.

It was the same fear that drove him to put up on the wall of his pre-Chapel office in the house he eventually bought in Salisbury a large picture of WH Smith's book-pulping machine. Essentially the publishing world's Grim Reaper, that device for a while seems to have functioned as Terry's inverse muse, the voice whispering threateningly at his shoulder. The picture was there, he said, to remind him to write a better book.

It wasn't that Terry was squeamish about having large sums of money connected with his name. On the contrary. 'Thank you for all the words,' fans would say at the signings. 'Thank *you* for all the money,' Terry would reply. He was never inclined to draw a polite veil over the fact that writing paid him well and certainly, once the label applied, he never shied away from describing himself as a rich man. To that extent he was, perhaps, eternally a working-class boy made good. Why go to the trouble of being rich if you aren't going to be proud of it? But he had an equally entrenched working-class belief that money had to be *earned*. Otherwise, what was there to be proud of? Jeffrey Archer was a writer with whom, through the nineties in particular, Terry repeatedly found himself going head-to-head for the number one bestseller

slot – a battle Terry routinely won, and by some margin in terms of sales.*
And Terry railed against the stories of Archer allegedly receiving advances that ran into millions, because he could see no way in which those
books would ever earn out and start to pay their own way. Terry could not
have lived with himself under those terms. He would say: 'It's not about
the money, but it's *all about the money*.' And what he meant was, in a world
which did not seem overly inclined, certainly in that first decade, to
reward him with critical praise or mainstream prizes, the money was – to
use another Terry expression – 'a way of keeping score'. But, precisely
because of that, he needed the score to be accurate – not distorted by
news-grabbing and ultimately unworkable advances, but genuinely and
calculatedly reflecting his status as a seller of books.

Alas, though, the one thing money didn't buy Terry, which it might
easily have done, was the freedom from worrying about money. 'Terry
was truly the most financially insecure person I have ever known,' said
Dave Busby. 'Even as a multi-millionaire he fretted about the possibility
of financial disaster. He never felt safe.'

Which would explain one of his earliest financial decisions, taken in
the late 1980s, when money had just begun to arrive in the larger
denominations. As mentioned before, it was always Eileen Pratchett's
desire that her son should find good, *pensionable* employment, as his
younger cousin Richard had done, getting a job with Royal Mail
Engineering, a fact Eileen would often mention. It therefore discom-
forted her to see Terry, at 39, turn his back on precisely that kind of
solidly bankable arrangement inside a nationalized industry and take his
chances instead in the uncertain and, above all, pension-free world of
freelance writing. Now, Terry, as we have seen, was capable of resisting
Eileen's larger plans for him and going his own way. Yet he remained,

. . . .

* It was in Cambridge in 1998 that Terry's signing at Heffers coincided with a Jeffrey Archer
event round the corner at Waterstones. At the time, *The Last Continent* was number one, and
Archer's *The Eleventh Commandment* was at number two. I was sent out to report on the
relative queue-lengths. Terry was gratified to learn that Archer's line was considerably
shorter. He was also gratified to learn that I had overheard Archer ask his publicist, 'Who *is*
this Pratchett fellow anyhow?'

clearly, for the whole of his life, the kind of son who hoped for the approval of his mother. Accordingly, where some writers might have spent their first big cheque on a fast car or a new house, Terry did not. 'One of his first acts, once he had a large advance, so he told me,' said Dave, 'was to purchase a pension in one instalment.'

Some while after Terry died, Coutts, who managed his finances, rang me in the Chapel. By this stage the value of Terry's estate had been calculated and the probate process was to all intents and purposes completed. But Coutts had just unearthed an historic investment in Terry's name which none of us had known anything about and which had slipped down the back of the sofa, as it were, during the passing years. Untouched and quietly accruing for around a quarter of a century, Terry's rainy day, mother-appeasing pension fund from the 1980s was worth an eye-watering seven-figure sum.

Whether or not she ever knew about the pension, there is no doubt that Eileen reconciled herself eventually to her son's choice of work and its relative long-term security, and came to be proud of him. She lived to see him knighted in 2009, attending the ceremony in her wheelchair. She was slightly disappointed that the proceedings did not allow for a personal meeting with the Queen for herself, but she was still thrilled. And she was possibly even more thrilled when Terry was made an adjunct professor at Trinity College Dublin in 2010. My son, the professor! Whether she regarded what he did as work by the ordinary definition, though, remained an open question. One day, I rang to let Eileen know that Terry would be adding a couple of weeks to the end of his Australian tour and taking a holiday, which was actually going to be his first break in many years.

'Holiday from what?' asked Eileen.*

----

* Eileen remained heroically immune to the charms of Terry's writing, and she and David owned a large collection of Discworld novels in immaculate condition with uncracked spines. After the stroke which deprived her of the power of speech, I helped her move from Wales, boxing those books to go into storage and taking her in a rental van to the care home that Terry and Lyn found for her in Salisbury. It was quite a long drive, with just the two of us, but I had a CD of the audiobook of *Mort* and I thought it might provide an amusing soundtrack for our journey. We had gone very few yards when Eileen slammed her hand with surprising force across the buttons on the dashboard to silence it.

Definitions of 'work' aside, though, the truth is that very few novelists have interpreted the term 'full-time' in the expression 'full-time writer' as literally as Terry Pratchett did when he quit the day job. Sometimes, in that first decade, there was so much work going on, and so little time in his week for anything else, that it would even enrage him. At such moments, he would lash out at the forces that were relentlessly cracking the whip – forgetting, of course, that chief among those forces was himself.

'He once phoned me up in exasperation that he was being totally taken for granted by his publishers,' Dave Busby told me. 'He was fuming. He had had enough. He was going to take a sabbatical. No more writing for at least six months. I felt very pleased for him. He needed that break. I think he planned to do a lot of travelling. I did not hear from him for about six months and when we made contact again, I asked him what he had done in his sabbatical. He replied, irritably, "I wrote two books."'

★ ★ ★ ★ ★

In 1988, Terry attended his second Transworld sales conference, this time as a bona fide full-time writer, rather than as someone moon-lighting from his day job. Since his 1986 appearance, the company had upgraded from rodent-afflicted accommodation near Gatwick Airport to what Larry Finlay, then working in the marketing department, recalls as a rather superior hotel in the Mallorca beach resort of Cala Vinyes. Here, over five days, staff were encouraged to take part in what were not quite yet known as 'team-bonding' exercises, including canoe racing, fancy dress designing and – that timeless conference-goer's favourite – alcohol consumption. Meanwhile, Transworld authors were flown in to read, mingle and generally present themselves in as attract-ive a light as they could muster to the sales reps. At some point during these proceedings, either before or after his no doubt eagerly awaited report to the company on his daily word-rate, Terry found himself in conversation with Philippa Dickinson, who was Corgi's children's edi-tor. They talked about great children's books – *Stig of the Dump* and

The Secret Garden, which both of them greatly admired, and *The Wind in the Willows*, which Philippa liked less than Terry did. Philippa, who had read Terry's Discworld books but knew nothing of *The Carpet People*, asked Terry if he would ever consider writing something for children.

Those first years of Terry's full-time writing life were, of course, the years of establishment for Discworld on Roundworld. This was when he wrote the ornately plotted *Pyramids*, digging down into the Disc to unearth the ancient riverland of Djelibeybi, a feat of literary archaeology exposing a panoply of myths and misguided building projects, and containing at least one zinger which both P. G. Wodehouse and Raymond Chandler would arguably have fought to buy off its author – namely, 'the old lady was as tough as a hippo's instep'. This was when he wrote *Moving Pictures*, which somehow compressed the entire history of cinema into a handful of months, except in this possibly better-adjusted version of the story, it's a 50-foot woman who carries a screaming ape to the top of a wobbling skyscraper in the big climax. This was when he turned people into fans of Terry Pratchett, and, more particularly, into fans of Terry Pratchett's characters: of Rincewind, of Granny Weatherwax, of Vimes, of Lord Vetinari. This was when he wrote *Reaper Man* and *Small Gods*, *Men At Arms* and *Soul Music*, producing these teeming volumes at the rate of two per year, constructing and refining a fictional world that seemed capable of containing all the stories about our own world that he would ever need to tell.

Yet these were also the years in which Terry wrote six novels for children – and wrote them with an equally powerful sense of a mission, and possibly even a stronger one. As much fun as he was having, and would always have, with Discworld, there was always a central part of Terry that longed to be able to bring about for others the miracle of release that *The Wind in the Willows* had performed for him at the age of ten. Becoming the writer of *that kind of book* was the culmination that Terry seemed to have been seeking since the earliest days – since volunteering so swiftly for Children's Circle duties in the *Bucks Free Press* and since deciding that his first novel would be *The Carpet People* – and he turned himself to the project again as soon as the opportunity was there. The difference was, he could now bring something extra to the task. These days he was someone who had walked all over the Mendips inventing stories for his daughter. He was someone who had read *The Hobbit* aloud to Rhianna, sitting together in the big green velvet armchair in front of the fire at Gaze Cottage. He was someone watching a little girl grow and explore and start to find her own way in the world, an experience which would shape his writing for ever more. Children's writing had always felt like a personal mission. Now it was even more so.

Soon after that sales conference, Terry sent Philippa a draft of *Truckers*. It was an expansion of an idea that Terry had tried out in the story 'Rincemangle, The Gnome of Even Moor' in the *Bucks Free Press* fifteen years previously, which was in turn based on Terry's childhood memory of drifting in wonder through Gamages department store at Christmas. In some senses, the book was built on a standard sci-fi 'awakening' scenario: here were the Haberdashari, a tribe of 'Nomes', convinced that the store in which they were living – Arnold Bros, motto: 'All things under one roof' – was the full extent of the world, but forced by visitors to consider the possibility that there was an 'outside', a greater universe beyond their knowledge. But the additional gift here, and the thing that set the tale apart, was the layering. It could be taken at a clip, as a romping adventure story with noisy jokes in it; or, if the reader had a will to, it could be allowed to percolate and prompt thought and the mulling of ideas – religion, politics, the limits of scientific understanding, education. It was, in other words, the perfect younger readers' book.

Philippa told Terry she thought it was fantastic, but that there was a problem with it. He had written it, as he wrote his Discworld novels, straight through, without chapters and with simple line breaks separating narrative segments. 'Of course, you're going to have to divide it up,' Philippa said.

She sensed Terry bridling.

'The thing is,' Philippa said, pressing on, 'that's how these books work. You need chapters for children reading to themselves. And you need them for parents reading to children: "OK, one more chapter and it's lights out . . ."'

Terry grudgingly conceded that she had a point. He divided the book into chapters and did the same with all his children's books thereafter.

Philippa was, in many ways, the perfect editor for Terry. She was the daughter of a journalist-turned-novelist – Peter Dickinson, who wrote children's books and detective stories – so she understood very naturally where Terry was coming from. Her father had frequently test-read his books to the family and Philippa well recalled the time she had raised an objection to something in one of them, only to be met with the reaction: 'You are quite wrong.' She was, then, armed in advance for those sentences of Terry's, during editorial conversations, which opened, 'I'm beginning to wonder . . .'

As in: 'I'm beginning to wonder whether you've read the book.'

And as in: 'I'm beginning to wonder whether you're really rather thick.'

Philippa also quickly recognized that editing was the least interesting aspect of the process for Terry. The book was finished and he was already on to the next one, which he was now more excited about, and very often the one after that was beginning to take shape, too. The journalist's mentality still operated for him: new day, new piece of writing. He had to be pulled back over old work entirely against his will.

Yet, as crotchety as he could be about it, Terry knew the value of editorial shaping. And, from the people he trusted, he sought it very early in the process, when the stories were still malleable, and when there were still gaps to be filled and as yet undefined directions to be taken. The drafts sent to Philippa were often labelled 'Draft Zero' and she got used to coming across a gap on the page, bridged by the note: 'FUNNY BIT HERE.' The first draft of *Johnny and the Bomb* that she saw contained the audacious instruction: 'BRILLIANT BIT TO GO HERE.'

With all of its bits intact and in the right order, *Truckers* was published in September 1989, and Terry rapidly followed it with two more tales of the Nomes: *Diggers*, just seven months later, in April 1990, and *Wings*, just five months after that, in September – the 'Bromeliad trilogy', as the sequence came to be known. There were lucrative offers from some big players to convert these books into film and television, but Terry, in what would become something of a signature move, plumped for the relatively small-scale operation on the table, Cosgrove Hall Films. Based in Chorlton-cum-Hardy near Manchester, Cosgrove Hall were the team behind the popular kids' cartoons *Dangermouse* and *Count Duckula*. But of far more relevance to Terry was the fact that, in 1983, they had made a stop-motion animated version of *The Wind in the Willows*. *Truckers*, similarly using stop-motion puppetry, went out on ITV in 1992, the first small-screen adaptation of Terry's work, and the happiest of outcomes for him.*

Much to the relief of his publishers, Terry wasn't taking a break from Discworld to write these books; he was simply adding them into his schedule. With equal alacrity, he then produced the Johnny Maxwell trilogy: *Only You Can Save Mankind*, in which the twelve-year-old boy-hero gets sucked into a video game, *Johnny and the Dead*, in which Johnny interacts with spirits in a soon-to-be-redeveloped cemetery, and *Johnny and the Bomb*, a time-travel adventure set in the Blitz, and complete with added 'brilliant bit' – in fact with several of them.

'They were all good,' said Philippa, 'but in *Johnny and the Dead* you could feel an extra depth opening up. These books were giving him the opportunity to explore things that he couldn't shoehorn into Discworld. They were a different platform, and one he obviously relished.' In 1994, Philippa had the pleasure of ringing Terry to let him know that *Johnny and the Dead* had been shortlisted for the Carnegie Medal, the most prestigious prize in British children's writing. However, even given her familiarity by now with her author's temperament, Terry's response to this sought-after endorsement took her by surprise. 'He said he didn't want anything to do with it,' Philippa said. 'He told me to get his name removed from the list.'

Philippa can't remember exactly what reason Terry gave for this piece of self-sabotage, and it's perfectly possible that he never offered her one.

. . . .

* By contrast, a film version of *Truckers* would be ten years on the slate at Dreamworks before eventually coming to nothing. But we shall cover this agony later in the book, when we come to consider what I think of as 'Terry's voyages through Development Hell'.

What she *can* remember is gently pointing out to Terry that the Carnegie was the closest thing to a Nobel prize that children's literature in the UK knew, that it was a promotional device like no other, and that, accordingly, the reaction within her office to Terry's withdrawal would be so violent that she would certainly end up having to hide under her desk while nuclear war raged overhead. Terry duly relented, but the prize ended up going to Melvin Burgess for *Junk* and Terry simmered darkly about the whole episode for a long time afterwards.

The problem was, the idea of getting shortlisted for prizes and not winning them was worse to Terry than the idea of not getting shortlisted for them in the first place. This had been his mindset since at least 1989, when *Truckers* was nominated for a Smarties Book prize, only to be ruled out on the contentious grounds that the story seemed to be inviting – as indeed it was – a sequel.* And it most definitely remained Terry's mindset, as I found out with great clarity in 2007, when *Wintersmith* was shortlisted for Children's Book of the Year at the National Book Awards. In a strong field, Terry's fellow nominees included John Boyne for *The Boy in the Striped Pyjamas* and Francesca Simon for a volume in her eternally popular Horrid Henry series. Nevertheless, Transworld had done as much subtle sounding-out in advance as they possibly could, and the rumours that came back were all positive: nobody was saying exactly who was going to get the prize, but the implication was very strongly conveyed to the Chapel that Terry would not, let us say, nudge nudge, regret turning up. On that premise, Terry and I got changed and drove into London for the night.

When the winner was announced, the picture on the big screen cut to a satellite shot of a theatre somewhere, possibly Ipswich, where Ricky Gervais apologized for his absence and gratefully accepted the prize for *Flanimals of the Deep*. His acceptance speech was barely over when Terry

----

* This qualm, as Philippa subsequently pointed out in an unamused letter to *The Bookseller*, would have written off the claims of *The Lion, the Witch and the Wardrobe* to a Smarties Book prize, had such a thing been around in 1950. You would be stripping a few 1973 Oscars off *The Godfather* under these criteria, too. Terry would wait until 1996 to win a Smarties prize – a silver award in the 9–11 age category for *Johnny and the Bomb*.

leaned across to me at the table and growled, 'Get the car.' We left under a low cloud and in an absence of graciousness.

If things went more smoothly in 2002, when Terry actually won the Carnegie Medal, that was because he had been told he was the winner a month in advance and sworn by Philippa to the strictest secrecy – terms of engagement with which he happily complied.* On the night of the ceremony, I found it extraordinary to reflect that, no more than a year and a half before this, I had been sitting with Terry, in the evening after an event, drinking beer in the Pied Piper bar at the Palace Hotel in San Francisco.† A basketball game was playing on the television screen, but Terry's attention was entirely occupied by the painting that hung behind the bar above the shelves of bottles. It was a giant canvas by the American artist Maxfield Parrish – *The Pied Piper of Hamelin*.‡

It was always the skies you needed to look at with Parrish, Terry told me, and I joined him in staring at the translucent blue that seemed to start out behind the painting's distant mountains and end up in the room we were sitting in. Then Terry suddenly said, 'You know the whole thing was a scam, don't you?'

'What do you mean?' I said.

And with that, he was off, telling me a story which had perhaps been percolating through his mind for some time, but only now emerged in a rush – the tale of a cat who lived on Discworld and was a battle-hardened con artist who had devised a nice little rat-catching hustle but then ran into grave difficulties. It was the Pied Piper story, but with a new, dark twist, and Terry told me the whole thing, beginning, middle and end, there and then, seemingly as it fell into his head beneath that

. . . .

* Peter Dickinson, Philippa's father, was also shortlisted that year, for *The Ropemaker*. If Philippa had mixed emotions about Terry's triumph, she kept them very well concealed.

† A local beer, obviously. Terry joined me in insisting on local beers wherever in the world we ordered them, made with the local water and therefore connecting you wholesomely with the region. Or so we enjoyed believing.

‡ Maxfield Parrish, painter and illustrator, 1870–1966. A neo-classical Norman Rockwell, you could say. He had an enormous hit with *Daybreak* (1922), a print of which at one time was believed to hang in one in every four American homes.

glowing Parrish painting. And then we went up to his room, opened the laptop and he began to dictate it to me, with me clattering away at the keyboard in an effort to keep up with him.

'Rats!

They chased the dogs and bit the cats...'

And now here he was, not even eighteen months later accepting the medal for *The Amazing Maurice and His Educated Rodents* – accepting the medal, I should say, and then promptly peeling off its gold casing and biting a lump out of it, to the confusion of the assembled worthies.

A little sleight of hand there, ladies and gentlemen. That tip-off had given him a month in which to plot. I was sent into Salisbury the weekend before the ceremony to source a chocolate coin of the right size and heft, finding one eventually in Woolworths. David Blaine, eat your heart out.

It was Terry's first mainstream literary award. Mary Norton's *The Borrowers*, Arthur Ransome's *Pigeon Post*, Richard Adams's *Watership Down*, Philippa Pearce's *Tom's Midnight Garden* . . . these were the stuff of Carnegie Medal winners, and now so was Terry Pratchett's *The Amazing Maurice*. And maybe that, too, was a part of his initial desire to turn his back on the whole deal, back in 1996. He had complained for so long of exclusion by the literary world – '16 years of disdain by the literary establishment', as the *Guardian* put it in its report on the Carnegie award – that in many ways its consistent snobbery had become a kind of motor for him, driving him out to a position on the edges, where he could feel righteous in his exclusion. So what would become of Terry if the institutional literary world, as he saw it, now started to acknowledge him and beckon him into their fold? True, the Carnegie was judged and bestowed by librarians, making it practically unimpeachable in Terry's view. Nevertheless, Karen Usher, the chair of the judges, declared *The Amazing Maurice*, without equivocation, to be 'an outstanding work of literary excellence'. It was hard to avoid the conclusion that, in a potentially troubling development, Terry had just been found guilty of literature.

'Writing for children is harder than writing for adults, if you're doing it right.' So Terry said in his Carnegie acceptance speech, and that was a sincere belief for him. But both those kinds of writing get easier with a good editor, and though he would not have admitted it publicly, and possibly not even under conditions of torture, Terry was amply blessed along the way in that respect.* When Diane Pearson retired from Transworld in the early 2000s, Philippa was the natural person to start taking care of Terry's adult books, too. One of the first of those novels for which she was in the hot seat was 2005's *Thud!*, the 34th Discworld novel, in which Commander Vimes is required to solve the mystery surrounding the death of the dwarf demagogue Grag Hamcrusher. Philippa read the first draft quickly and got straight back to Terry with her initial thoughts. They knew each other so well by now that she felt she could cut straight to the point.

'I said to him, "This is supposed to be a whodunnit, Terry – but my problem is that I've finished the book and I still don't know who did it."'

The line went very quiet and the phone call ended shortly afterwards.

That night Philippa lay awake wondering whether she had presumed too much and whether she had just entirely blown out a fifteen-year relationship which was of some importance to her company.

The next day her phone rang. 'I have decided that you are not a cantankerous bat after all,' said Terry. The storm had passed, as it invariably did. He was already reconfiguring the book to sharpen the plot and its resolution, dutifully collaborating with his editor to make a better novel which, after all, was the whole point.

* * * * *

In December 1993, Terry and Lyn sold Gaze Cottage and moved to the Chalke Valley outside Salisbury in Wiltshire, to Terry's 'Domesday Manorette', a characterful, gently rambling mansion in weathered stone, and exactly the kind of place you might expect to find a 45-year-old

----

* 'Does Terry *ever* say thank you?' Anne Hoppe's assistant once asked her. And Anne, who was Terry's children's editor in the US, had to say that, well, actually . . . no.

bestselling author. The move was, after all those years, a wrench, especially for Lyn, who felt deeply attached to Rowberrow and could have stayed there happily for the rest of their lives. On the other hand, Terry had all this money now, and what else were you supposed to do with money? So they became residents of the Chalke Valley, which had passed Terry's key criterion by being remote enough to be completely unoverlooked, and yet within striking distance of a stationery outlet. As Terry said, 'I could have bought a Scottish island. But where do you go when your printer runs out of toner?'*

He and Lyn looked at a couple of other houses. They were very close to making an offer on a place near Milton on Stour in north Dorset, which had 30 acres and a spring, a huge walled garden that had been maintained by the same gardener for 40 years, and a stable yard and a coach house. The vendors gave them tea and cake in the garden and they saw a kingfisher while they sat there, which seemed like a good omen. Yet it felt a bit close to the town, somehow.

And then there was the former rectory near Axminster in Devon that seemed to share a floor-plan with the Cluedo board and had a secret passage running diagonally through its basement. Terry and Lyn briefly considered the possibility of getting statues made of each of the Cluedo murder weapons – the lead pipe, the candlestick, the dagger, the rope, the spanner – and putting one in each of the downstairs rooms. But that house seemed to have a housing development nearby and creeping ever closer to it, and that might have spoiled the fun.

So they went back to the house they had seen first, which had the additional advantage of being not far from where Lyn's mother was living. It was in a hollow, encased by hills. It had 67 acres of rolling grounds, strewn with meadow flowers. The River Ebble ran through it, which had water voles and would in due course reveal its own kingfishers and, on

. . . .

* Another measure of how remote the house was: it once took a German fan an entire fortnight to find it. Lydia had been staying in the area but her daily explorations and enquiries among the locals failed to bring her to the door until the final evening of her trip. Terry consoled her by taking her up to the pub for bubble and squeak.

one memorable occasion, an otter.* There would be plenty of scope for chickens and vegetables and fruit and tortoises and owl boxes, and also sheep. History abounded, too. Through the trees, in winter, you could glimpse the former home of Sir Anthony Eden, and the man in the village shop could remember the time that Winston Churchill had visited. Not far away was Reddish House, where Cecil Beaton entertained Greta Garbo and converted the upper floor for cockfighting – heady days – though Toyah Wilcox lived there now and cockfighting was illegal. William Golding had lived nearby, too, and was buried in the local churchyard.

On top of all that, considerably adding to its appeal for Terry, the place had a tennis court. Not that playing tennis was of any more interest to Terry than signing up for the local golf club, but he knew on sight that that large flat surface would make the perfect foundation for a really terrific greenhouse, the largest he would likely ever own, set inside a walled garden, with raised beds, pergolas, ponds and water features. And he was right; it did.

'What are you going to do with all that land?' asked Terry's friend Bernard 'the Cunning Artificer' Pearson.

'Walk on each bit of it and say, "I own you, I own you, I own you . . ."' replied Terry.

They moved into the house in time for Christmas. It snowed that year and Rhianna, then aged seventeen and home from school, recalls walking across the village with her father to her grandmother's house, singing the old favourite 'Whose Pigs Are These?' (traditional, arr. Pratchett). She also remembers locking herself out one night and having to fling snowballs at her parents' bedroom window to wake them to let her in. The house was, of course, much grander than Gaze Cottage, which hadn't had, in its parlour, as the manor did, a massive stone

. . . .

* And on another memorable occasion, an emu. Or so Terry thought, when he came crashing into the Chapel. 'There's a f——— emu!' As we hurried down to the river bank, he adjusted his estimate: 'It might have been an ostrich.' It was, in fact, a rhea and, alas, very dead. And in that state – fair play to Terry – it did look very like an emu, albeit Rod Hull's emu.

fireplace, nor, next to that fireplace, a walk-in butler pantry, which in due course became the holding pen for the various bottles of oddly coloured liqueurs and startlingly alcoholic spirits with which Terry would be presented on foreign tours.* There was much more room for overnight guests, too: upstairs was what would eventually become the Craig Charles Memorial Suite, after a weekend when the *Red Dwarf* actor came to dinner and ended up staying over. And in due course the place would have its own observatory, as we shall discover. But ultimately the atmosphere was the same: the cosy furnishings, the books on every flat surface, the ready supplies of home-made chutneys and jams and cakes, and, of course, the cats, who, in the case of Garfield, soon learned to leap the river in one astonishingly athletic bound.

Aside from checking that all the cats were with them, Terry's approach to packing up Rowberrow was not particularly sentimental or even especially careful. A large selection of his papers and some of his schoolbooks would later be found by the new owner in a case in the attic. But Terry had recently chopped down a tree and created a stack of excellent firewood, and there was no way he was going to leave *that* behind. He made a special trip back to Somerset to load the logs into the back of Lyn's car. Somewhere during this crucial operation, Terry slipped on the cottage path, just as he had done in the snow on the night of Rhianna's birth. But this time he hit his head on the slate threshold stone and was mildly concussed for a short while.

There were no lasting effects from this minor scrape, but one thing Terry now found he couldn't locate was a rather important piece of paper. It had arrived at Rowberrow, sent by Colin Smythe, just before they started packing up to move, and Terry knew he had put it somewhere safe, with a view to dealing with it later. What he no longer

---

* Here, indeed, were the finest wines known to Slovakia. Plus a bottle of Harvey's Bristol Milk for when Eileen came. It had to be Harvey's Bristol Milk – Terry's mother would accept no substitute. Except that Harvey's Bristol Milk grew increasingly difficult to source, eclipsed by the more readily available Harvey's Bristol Cream. Which meant that Terry frequently had to pour his mother's 'Bristol Milk' furtively, out of her sight. Another reason why a walk-in butler pantry is a useful facility to have.

knew was where that 'somewhere safe' was. Was that the effects of the bump on the head, or was that just Terry being Terry? No matter. He would have to ring Colin at some point and see if he could do anything about it.

The piece of paper was a royalty cheque for £248,000.

Clearly, if this kind of thing continued happening, Terry was going to need a personal assistant.

13

CURRIED SULTANAS, MARMALADE AND CORRUGATED IRON

In the summer of 1995, a Terry Pratchett fan was in a craft shop called Curiosity Corner in Lavenham in Suffolk, browsing its selection of officially licensed Discworld figurines. After careful deliberation, he chose the Dried Frog Pill Box* and took it to the counter.

'You read Terry Pratchett?' the man at the till asked.

The fan replied that he did – that he had read the lot, in fact, and been to a couple of book signings, too.

'Well, you might be interested in this,' the shopkeeper said.

He handed the fan a leaflet from a pile on the counter, advertising something called the 'Clarecraft Discworld Event'.

Which is how, on 12 August 1995, I ended up in a tin-roofed warehouse on a business estate in a mined-out sandpit on the edge of the Suffolk village of Woolpit. Because, reader, I *was* that Terry Pratchett fan. To be frank, in my naivety, I thought I would be the only person there. I was out by several hundred.

The hosts of this slightly thrown-together, rough-at-the-edges but

. . . .

* Dried frog pills: medication used by the Bursar of Unseen University to control his insanity. Dried frog pill pot: pot in which to keep dried frog pills, obviously. With a nicely modelled frog on its lid. A complimentary plastic pot of dried frog pills was issued to guests at Terry's memorial event at the Barbican. They were, in fact, breath mints, and contained no frog whatsoever, dried or otherwise – as we hope guests realized.

well-attended and above all extremely cheerful Discworld gathering – the first of its kind – were Bob and Trish Baker. They owned both the tin-roofed warehouse and Clarecraft Ltd, the company upon which Terry had bestowed the licence for the creation of Discworld-related collectables. Such as, for example, the Dried Frog Pill Box (catalogue number, DW63), but also, as my shelves at the time would have attested, the model of Rincewind (DW01), Death on Binky (DW24)*, and the limited edition 'skinny' variant of the Nanny Ogg figure (DW07), of which, I can confidently inform you, there were only a dozen made.†

Clarecraft's founders were Bernard and Isobel Pearson. Since 1980, they had been creating, in their Suffolk studio, individually made models and sculptures, mostly in ceramic or pewter, and including some pieces commissioned by the Tolkien Foundation. Isobel had heard *The Colour of Magic* on *Woman's Hour* and began reading the books; Bernard was initially put off by the Josh Kirby covers, which weren't to his taste, but he overcame his reservations when he saw how much Isobel enjoyed the novels, and he tore through them, too. In 1990, they decided to look into the possibility of exploiting an obvious gap in the market by re-imagining some of Terry Pratchett's fictional world as highly desirable, hand-crafted and hand-painted figurines. All this was entirely in accordance, of course, with the immutable law linking fantasy writing and collectable ornaments since time immemorial: where there is fantasy, collectable ornaments will not be far behind. That much is simply understood.

Terry longed to see his literary creation brought to life in this way – but only, it probably doesn't need saying, on his own, very precise

. . . .

* Paul Kidby, who succeeded Josh Kirby as the chosen Discworld illustrator, brought a fine artist's eye for anatomy to bear on this model: Binky the horse's ears lie flat against the head, whereas the ears of a horse actively rearing in this manner would be alert. 'Yeah, but you try casting them upright,' was Bernard's pragmatic response.

† Terry's eye for anatomy spotted that the first Nanny Oggs were insufficiently rotund, and they were immediately withdrawn and redone. I only ever knew of two other owners of the 'skinny' Nanny Ogg: Colin Smythe and the late Sir Terry Pratchett. Somewhere there are nine others. Check your shelves.

terms. Selling the licence for Discworld merchandise to some kind of giant, plastic toy empire appealed to Terry not one bit; selling it, on the other hand, to a garrulous, pipe-smoking policeman-turned-potter who was part of a bohemian husband-and-wife sculpting team that had named their business after their home village in Suffolk . . . well, that would be an appropriate way forward – a more Terry way of doing things.

Bernard and Isobel had an initial meeting with Terry and Colin Smythe at the Stafford Hotel in St James's in London, at which Terry did some drawings. 'No warts!' he wrote, emphatically, beside his sketch of the witch Granny Weatherwax. Also, 'beaky nose' and 'tight bun'. Beside his sketch of Rincewind he wrote, 'general worried expression', 'poor, straggly beard' and 'ill-fitting robe'. Colin kept the originals of those drawings and faxed Bernard a copy. From these instructions Bernard sculpted a 14cm-tall Rincewind in soft jeweller's wax. He then carefully took his model to a second meeting, inconveniently arranged to take place outdoors in Covent Garden on a blazing hot June day. While some kind of oompah band played in close proximity, Bernard gingerly unboxed his Rincewind and then felt his heart lurch as Terry instantly reached out to grab it. Fortunately, Terry only touched the wooden base, the model survived the heat, and the ensuing discussion somehow got through the gaps in the noise of the oompah band. After Terry had requested some minor alterations to Rincewind's eight-sided pendant, a deal was struck. Clarecraft launched their first Discworld figures at a trade fair at the NEC in Birmingham in 1991. Terry, who was in his turbocharged phase of going to everything that could be regarded as promotional, went along for the day, taking a bag of his own books to sign.

And now here they were – Bernard, Isobel, Terry – together, four years later, under that tin roof on what had to be the hottest day of the year in one of the hottest summers ever.* And there was I, too, not knowing any of them, sweating gently, and eventually not so gently, as the building grew gradually more oven-like, and as about three

----

* 1995 was the driest UK summer on record, out-parching even the famously parched 1976.

hundred Discworld fans joined in communion, eager to be in the presence of Terry Pratchett, and of Pratchett-related things, and of each other.

But, boy, the heat . . . 'It was like Klatch*, with slightly fewer flies and no camels,' remembered Bernard, who also noted how sand from the former pit gradually crept into the building throughout the day. Terry eventually abandoned the fawn-coloured fedora he had been wearing when he arrived – the more lightweight Terry Pratchett summer look – and replaced it with a tea-towel soaked in cold water. Thus bandana'd, he sat at a table for a considerable portion of the day and signed anything that anybody asked him to.

Somehow in this climate, some of the attending Discworld fans still found the energy to go outside and take part in a re-enactment of the Unseen University Boat Race.† That's when they weren't milling among the Discworld stalls and the Discworld art exhibition and pondering the purchase, for £10, of a limited edition, made-for-the-occasion, framed City Watch badge.‡ And because someone had suggested that dressing-up was what happened at fantasy conventions, there was a masquerade. As Terry watched from the audience, people climbed onto the makeshift stage to parade in costume as Rincewind and the Luggage and – especially daring on a hot day – as the Librarian, in an all-body orang-utan outfit. One fan made a dramatic entrance in a perfect Granny Weatherwax costume, complete with face-blanching makeup, and froze there for what seemed like ten minutes, chilling the room – no small achievement, in the context – before slowly extending a long arm and finger and pointing directly at Terry. Then she turned and left. Terry's voice was audible across the room: 'I don't know who you are, but don't ever do that again.' Her name was Pam Gower, in fact,

---

* An arid, rimward nation on the Disc. Home to some very strong coffee.

† The absence of a river was, of course, no drawback for this one. The Unseen University Boat Race takes place on the notably turgid waters of the River Ankh and features two teams of students in flat-soled shoes who carry their skiffs and run on its crust.

‡ Yes, I bought one. And the dwarf bread, as sculpted by Bernard.

and as well as being a Discworld fan, she was an actor, which probably gave her an unfair advantage, masquerade-wise, but nobody seemed to mind. On the contrary, everyone seemed lastingly impressed. Terry referred admiringly to Pam for ever after as the embodiment of Granny Weatherwax.

Soon after the appearance of that formidable Granny-alike, someone else arrived on stage dressed as the Opera House Ghost. Terry was again audible: 'Bloody hell! She's from a book that hasn't even been published yet!' I remember being utterly boggled by that, although, of course, there was no real mystery to it. In the nascent days of this new-fangled thing called the internet, many of the day's attendees were regular frequenters of the newsgroup alt.fan.pratchett, where the author himself would often sign in, of an evening, and chat directly to readers about his work in progress. All of this was revelatory to me. Here was a whole layer of fan engagement, at once exciting and intimidating, that I had known practically nothing of until now.

Terry closed out the event by reading an extract from *Maskerade*, which would be published the following autumn, complete with the Opera House Ghost in its pages. That was a highlight, but if I'm being perfectly honest, the day's real triumph for me was discovering that the Clarecraft stall was exclusively selling 'whites' – the figures from their Discworld collection, but in unfinished form, so you could take them home and paint them with your own Winsor & Newtons.* If you had told this Terry Pratchett fan, as he left Woolpit and headed home that sultry August evening with a bagful of this bounty, that one day he would have two photographs taken of him by Trish Baker's daughter Sally – head-on and in profile – and become the model for the

. . . .

* 'I bet you were the kind of person who painted your model kits before you assembled them,' Terry once said to me, accusingly. He was absolutely right: otherwise, whither civilization? Terry, by contrast, was an 'assemble first, then paint' modeller. I could never get the red right for Rincewind's cloak. Eventually someone from Clarecraft gave me some paint from their pre-mixed tub. The tub was labelled, I was gratified to notice, 'Rincewind Red'.

Clarecraft Discworld Collection figure of Shawn Ogg (DW 136)*. . . well, I would have assumed that the August heat of 1995 had got to you in some really quite worrying way, and perhaps to me, too. But a lot was about to happen.

From those modest and sandy stirrings on that business estate in Wool-pit, a Discworld Convention grew. The Clarecraft event had shown that there was obviously scope for this kind of thing, but done even bigger, and, with Clarecraft again present, it happened in Manchester the follow-ing summer. Terry, who, at not quite sixteen, had taken himself off to Peterborough in the hope of a glimpse of Arthur C. Clarke, now, at the age of 48, had a convention of his own.

When I applied for a ticket for Manchester – jumping on it early, I thought – they had already sold out, much to my horror. I made up my mind to go anyway, and work something out when I got there, but as it happened I managed to find someone online who would sell me one. Thus, on 28 June 1996, I checked into Sachas Hotel, where my room had a very nice mural of the Manhattan skyline but no external win-dows. The first event on the programme was a panel on the theme, 'So you want to be a published author'. The panel was supposed to consist of Colin Smythe and two others, but come the big curtain-up only Colin seemed to have made it into a chair. Nevertheless, the leader of the panel soldiered on, set out the discussion's theme – how, exactly, does a wannabe author with a freshly written manuscript in their hand make that big leap and get into print? – then introduced Colin, to a round of applause.

'Well, I don't know why you're asking *me* . . .' said Colin.

It set the tone for a weekend which was a huge amount of fun, even while being a touch shambolic and, in places, very clearly held together by sticky tape and string. There was a quiz – *Unseen University Challenge* – and a gala dinner on the Saturday night, at which Terry appeared in a white dinner jacket and black bow tie. Terry had recently made his first

. . . .

* The youngest of Nanny Ogg's children and the inventor of the multi-purpose Lancrastian Army Knife. I suppose I was right to feel flattered. It could certainly have been a lot worse.

appearance on the *Sunday Times* Rich List, with a quoted net worth of
£21 million. During his event the next night, the accuracy or otherwise
of this figure, and how rich, by implication, one could conclude Colin
Smythe was, was the subject of much banter between Terry and Colin.
Terry then read from his work-in-progress before declaring, as impressively accessible as ever: 'Right! I will stay here and sign everything you've
got.' By way of a curtain-down moment, and with Terry presiding, Paul
Rood*, the chairman of the organizing committee, was ceremonially
dunked in a paddling pool filled with custard.

I really wanted to be involved. I wasn't as immersed in the Pratchett
fan-world as some others were: I didn't spend time on alt.fan.pratchett,
not even lingering in the background as a 'lurker', and I had no interest
in costuming. But I loved the books and I loved the vibe at the Convention and I knew, with my technical background, that I had organ-
izational and other skills that would be useful in taking the event forward,
if I ever got the chance to apply them. So I went and introduced myself
to Paul Rood.

Paul was a building surveyor from Essex and, like me, in his mid-20s.
When he'd originally had the idea of a get-together for Discworld readers,
he was thinking along the lines of a small gathering in a room above a pub
somewhere. It had rapidly become apparent that he would need to upscale.
In due course, I attended a Convention committee meeting at Paul's house
in Romford, thereby becoming one of a group of about ten people who
worked on the programme of events for the second Discworld Convention,
scheduled for 1998 and set to take place in Liverpool. Paul put me in charge
of 'guest liaison' – arranging the speakers, organizing their transport, ensur-
ing they were OK on the day, etc. This was unpaid labour, of course, but,
at the same time, it was a job which would mean going around with a radio
and an ear-piece during the convention itself, and how would you ever put
a value on a perk like that?

I also decided to interview Colin Smythe about his collection of

. . . .

* Paul later adopted his wife's surname, becoming Paul Kruzycki. Terry's response to this
 news was, 'But he'll always be Rood to me.'

Pratchett first editions and write it up for the convention programme book. That was my first visit, mentioned earlier on, to Cornerways in Gerrards Cross, with its papers and books, its dogs and Lalique glass, its Anne Yeats painting and its dinner gong. Upstairs on the landing, and apparently extending way beyond in all directions, there were shelves of Terry Pratchett editions from around the world that seemed to go on for miles. Colin and I talked about those, but we also talked about his business more generally. In Colin's mesmerizingly untidy, book-lined office, a stack of paper rose up which was, at a rough estimate, six feet tall – Terry Pratchett's royalty statements, I realized. A leaning tower of royalty statements. Occasionally Colin's Great Dane would brush past it, causing it to teeter. For a significant portion of the lower half of the tower, the edges of the paper seemed slightly thick and congealed. Was that . . . *dog slobber*? It seemed it was.*

So this was the operation behind Terry Pratchett. It surprised me that it wasn't a bit more . . . slick?

'My feeling is that there's no order here,' I said.

'What do you mean?' said Colin. 'Of course there's order.' He picked up a piece of paper from his desk, took it to the leaning tower and, with great panache, placed it on top. 'There's the order,' he said. 'Newest on the top, oldest on the bottom.'

I told Colin that I could digitize his business and help to streamline it, if he ever wanted that done. By the time I got back home to Cheltenham, Colin had already rung to ask me to come and work for him.

★ ★ ★ ★ ★

The friendship with Bernard and Isobel Pearson that grew out of Terry's connection with Clarecraft was among the closest and most

---

* Working through those royalty statements in the process of digitizing them, I employed a scalpel to separate the affected pages. They had set like concrete. Stephen Briggs, Terry's friend and collaborator, once made the astute point that Terry's agent had the kind of office you would expect a writer to have, while Terry himself had the kind of office you would expect an agent to have.

important relationships of the later part of his life. The three of them hit it off very quickly. Bernard, who was normally to be found in dungarees and a cloud of pipe smoke, had an ornate way with words, a rich, growly voice emanating from a full-face beard, and a large personality, suitable for filling a room. He was ex-army and a former beat copper, and he entertained Terry with stories of frontline soldiering and of trying to arrest people on their wedding day in Halstead in Essex. He was also a walking encyclopaedia of some of the more arcane policing arts, culled from walking the streets, such as knowing when to let things happen, knowing when a judicious amount of violence might help out in the longer term, and, perhaps most important of all, keeping out of the rain. Terry, when he was in the mood for it, couldn't get enough of this stuff. Deeply respecting Bernard's sculpting skills, he dubbed him 'the Cunning Artificer', and the nickname stuck. Isobel, meanwhile, who was calm and wise, was regarded by Terry as 'the Oracle' and also referred to as 'the Responsible Adult'. Terry and Lyn would see the Pearsons at Christmas, heading over to their house on Boxing Day, taking with them mounds of what Terry referred to with relish as 'tracklements' – swathes of hot mustard and horseradish for which Terry insisted the roast beef was 'merely the medium'.* And Terry and Lyn would have Bernard and Isobel to dinner at the weekend in the chalk valley, where Terry would delve into the butler pantry to break out the 'wines of interest' from Slovakia and beyond. Bernard and Isobel enjoyed his attention – and sometimes they even enjoyed his inattention.

'He listened forensically,' Bernard said. 'Terry's ears would be cocked to conversations going on elsewhere in the room and you wouldn't realize. One night, in the pub, I was obliviously in the middle of an anecdote and Terry's hand suddenly went up. "Shhhh, Bernard!" he said, nodding slightly in the direction of a table to our right. "We're just getting to an interesting bit." ' In 1996, Terry dedicated the novel *Johnny*

---

* Similarly, oysters Kilpatrick, another Terry favourite, were, he would insist, just a convenient means for getting Worcestershire sauce into the mouth.

and the Bomb to 'The Royal Meteorological Society, the Royal Mint, and Bernard Pearson, who, if he doesn't know something, always knows a man who does'.

At the same time, the friendship between Terry and the Pearsons was forged in business, and laced through with business, and throughout history, business combined with friendship has been regarded as a potentially combustible mixture. When Terry was involved, it's fair to say it was no less so.

Over the years, Bernard and Isobel would encounter Terry at his most generous, and Terry at his most capricious and, just occasionally, Terry at the absolute end of his tether. Chiefly he would be at the end of his tether over the failure of his merchandising operation to meet the dreams he had for it, and not least the dreams he had for the speed at which it should be doing things. In 2004, when the Discworld stamp collection, inspired by the novel *Going Postal*, was slower to get off the ground than Terry would have wished, Bernard was on the receiving end of a lengthy and classically lacerating Pratchett email:

> There's some good work been done here, and I do, still, have faith in your ability to pull this one off and stop us <u>both</u> looking like twits. But please – this one has got to work. Disc can't make musicals and can't manage movies, but if we can't manage paper with holes in I might as well give up.*

On the other hand, there was the time Bernard and Ian Mitchell, a young craftsman Bernard had taken on to help him, had to go to a meeting about a Discworld project at the offices of Transworld in London – the Black Lubyanka, as Terry always called the building. 'It was real "country bumpkin" territory,' remembered Ian. 'There we were, the two of us, up in the big city. I was in a dinner jacket, which was the only thing I had that was smart, Bernard had pipe burns on his

. . . .

* Terry was spared early retirement. The stamps did happen, and very quickly became an enormous success.

shirt, and we were in this corporate world, meeting these six Transworld honchos, feeling very nervous and out of place.' Terry knew how uncomfortable they were going to be. Not long into the meeting, a phone rang in the room.

'Phone call for you, Bernard,' one of the Transworld team said. 'It's Terry Pratchett.'

Bernard took the receiver. 'At the other end of the line, Terry asked me to give him chapter and verse on some aspect of military history which I happened to know about,' said Bernard. 'I duly did so. When I'd finished, Terry said, "I don't care. But I bet you look important now, don't you?"'

Bernard and Isobel had left Clarecraft in the late 1990s, in search of a fresh start, and set up B&I Waxworks, for which Bernard turned his skilful hand to a line of ornate candles, or, as Terry promptly dubbed them: 'Pre-dribbled candles for the young wizard in a hurry'. It was, to be ruthlessly honest, an inherently flawed business plan – candles that were just too lovely to set fire to – and it did not thrive. But Terry encouraged Bernard to start sculpting miniature models of Ankh-Morpork's buildings, the 'Unreal Estate' series. Bernard began with the whole of Unseen University, offered piece by piece, by subscription, and those *did* sell. In 2000, Bernard and Isobel moved to Wincanton in south Somerset, a little over 20 miles from Terry's manor, and, with a bridging loan from Terry against an inheritance that would imminently fall to Isobel on the death of her father, opened a Discworld-themed shop called The Cunning Artificer in the centre of the town. During the period of the bridging loan, Terry would tease Isobel by asking her questions such as, 'How's your father? Is he well? Oh. Pity.' 'I genuinely found it funny,' Isobel said, 'although other people seemed to take offence on my behalf.' The loan was duly repaid – with interest, at Terry's insistence – and the shop quickly established itself. In 2011, when the aforementioned Ian Mitchell and his partner, Reb Voyce, formally joined the business, it changed its name to The Discworld Emporium. Until Bernard and Isobel's retirement from behind the counter in the summer of 2021 and the decision to take the merchandise catalogue entirely online, the Emporium was the sole bricks-and-mortar destination for Discworld fans and tourists. It was something of a destination for Terry, too. Every now and again, in the later years, the Emporium would get a call from the author, clearly looking for distraction. 'Is there anyone in the shop? Do they look *clean*? Right, I shall come over and spend some time among my people.'

Terry liked having a sculptor in his phone book, not just for his merchandising operation but also for personal commissions. It was Bernard who cast Terry's Death's Head rings, in various metals, and several of the handles for his ornate canes. And in 2004, when Transworld celebrated 21 years of Discworld with a party at the Royal Society of Arts in London, it was Bernard who built the thick oak lectern with, chained to it, a mock-up of the Octavo – the book of spells held in a sealed room in Unseen University's cellars – that was Terry's surprise gift that night, albeit that, given Terry's well-known abhorrence of surprises, the lectern had been constructed in collaboration with Terry and to his precise specifications. Indeed, Terry had impatiently wrested the lectern from Bernard and taken it back to the Chapel, a week before the presentation, so that he could add some finishing touches to it. Terry and I spent that weekend cutting a cavity in the Octavo and tricking it out with sparkling lighting effects using fibre optic cable. At the official unveiling, Terry's reaction of stunned amazement and startled delight was one for the ages. The lectern resided thereafter in the Chapel library.

It was also Bernard who tried to respond to Terry's desire to have Discworld cast as a fountain for the grounds of the manor. This was an unusually grand scheme for Terry, who wasn't ordinarily given to the celebration of his creation in large, outdoor private monuments. At the same time, Great A'Tuin, the elephants, the Disc, the oceans flowing off the rim . . . you could see how it might work. 'But there couldn't be any glass fibre,' Bernard said. 'Terry was very insistent about that. "I don't like glass fibre," he said. "They make boats and Lotus cars out of it." ' Detailed plans were drawn up, complex fluid dynamics were calculated, but in the end the major parts of the fountain were beyond the space Bernard had available to cast them. The plan came to nothing. By way of bespoke garden ornaments, Terry settled for a modest set of statues symbolizing the elements – fire, water, earth and air.

But the thing about capriciousness, of course, is that you never know when it's going to strike next. In 2001 Bernard brought to the Chapel for Terry's perusal a wax model of the next addition to the 'Unreal Estate'. It was wrapped, as they always were on these occasions, in newspaper and laid in a plastic mushroom crate. Bernard unpacked the model and set it on the table, and then he and Terry fell to discussing it. This was a scene I always wished fans could see – to witness the extent of the collaboration between the two of them, the attention to detail and the sense that the tiniest touches in this area really did matter. The model in this case was of the Watch House. Terry was in the middle of writing *Night Watch* and he showed Bernard a couple of passages in which Vimes, stalked by an assassin, needed to break into the Watch House after hours. The two of them talked about where to add a drainpipe to the building that would make this possible.

At the end of this perfectly positive and productive conversation, Bernard rewrapped his model and returned it to the crate. 'Thank you, boys,' he said cheerfully. 'I won't take up any more of your time.'

He was almost out of the door, when Terry, who had now returned to his desk and seemed to be giving his screen most of his attention, casually said, without looking up: 'Bernard, after this one, I don't think there's room for any more buildings.'

Bernard looked across the room at me. He was utterly crushed. This was a devastating blow. Without Discworld buildings, he didn't really have a business. He left with his spirits in his boots.

However, the conversation was never mentioned again, and it turned out that the buildings weren't cancelled at all. They continued to come for several more years, until Bernard's fingers were no longer agile enough to sculpt them.

★ ★ ★ ★ ★

Throughout the 1990s, Terry did two three-week book tours in the UK per year – one in May, another in November. On each day he would attend two or (very occasionally) three bookshops and write his name in anything up to a thousand books. This brought him enormous satisfaction, except when it didn't, which was an awful lot of the time. 'On tour, I'm fairly spiky,' Terry conceded, admitting that signing books for seven or eight hours per day 'tends to be a bit corrosive of the social graces'.

I would always try to get to one of the signings in those years before I worked for him, in the same way that I would try to go and see a favourite band when they came near my town. Those of us, like me, who queued up, set our newly purchased books down in front of him to be personalized, and had our few moments in the presence of the author, tended to leave content enough. But how much these tours were costing Terry personally in terms of persistent low-level irritation – and sometimes persistent high-level irritation – can be gauged very accurately from the tour reports that Terry wrote and submitted after-wards to his publishers. Designed to assess the performance of bookstores and to assist the selection of locations for future tours, these entirely unsolicited end-of-term reviews were both eagerly and nervously awaited at the publishers. To make things crystal clear, Terry used a bespoke star system, mostly to grade the shops and/or the event but, just occasionally, to grade the hotels which the publishers had put him in as well. He explained the system each time in a key at the top of his reports.

No stars: Might as well not have bothered.
★:   A signing was held, no frills.
★★:   A few things out of whack.
★★★:   A good basic signing, with the shop up to speed on things like tables, layout and organisation.
★★★★:   A three star with extras – welcoming staff, friendly atmosphere, a general feel-good factor.
★★★★★: Only Allah is perfect.

Praise would be heard, where it was applicable, but stores whose stock-rooms Terry wished never to be darkened by again would be placed without ceremony on what the author unequivocally dubbed 'the Shit List'.

Reading through these reports now, it's hard to avoid the conclusion that Terry was a one-man Tripadvisor before Tripadvisor had been invented. Sometimes he knew immediately what he didn't like – the 'smell of fish in the lift' in his Folkestone hotel, for instance, and the underwhelming fast food he ate after a signing at a branch of Ottakars on the Isle of Wight: 'Had a McDonald's Filet-o-Fish for lunch, and the taste of stale fat stayed with me for days.' Other times, in order to work out what he didn't like, he had to think about it quite hard. 'I'm trying to work out why I hated it so much,' Terry wrote, of a signing session on his *Soul Music* paperback tour. 'I think the word is probably "insolence", or possibly "condescension" . . . Staff stood behind me and chatted on to one another about how tired and rushed off their feet they were . . . I felt like some sort of exhibit . . . The shop's on the Shit List.'

But mostly, in these reports, he straightforwardly railed. He railed against inadequate tables, shops who made their customers queue outside in the cold when there was plenty of room in the warm, and hotels where the cord of the vacuum cleaner apparently didn't stretch as far as the corners of his room. He railed against shops continuing to take dedication requests for pre-orders despite Terry having insisted for years on end that this simply wasn't practical in terms of his time. He railed against bookshop managers in general, and against the staff of one chain-store in particular: 'languid Media Studies graduates who find it all mildly amusing but a little tiresome to have these popular authors in their shops'.

He railed against curly sandwiches and, worse still, the complete absence of curly sandwiches, and also against the smell which came from his hotel room's kettle when he boiled water in it. He railed against cheap hotels – 'I will kill someone rather than stay in a hotel like this again' – and he railed against expensive hotels – 'a bit too full of its own poshness'. And sometimes he just railed against the whole concept of hotels. 'A typical British hotel. Yes, that bad.' And as for hotel staff . . . 'This was a comprehensive example of the inherent sullen unpleasantness of British hotels, staffed by people whose spiritual home is Mrs Jones's Bide-A-Wee Guest House, 5p extra for cruet.' At another hotel: 'Staff ought to go on a body language course.' At another: 'A dump . . . staff gormless, even by hotel standards.'

He railed against bookshop managers who didn't say anything to him, and against bookshop managers who said too much. 'The manageress was nice and chatty and within three minutes she had told me she couldn't get on with my books. Why did she feel this was necessary? Who knows?' At another shop, 'the manager bobbed around the place like a lost soul.' At another, 'the manager acted as if I'd been ordered and paid for.' And as a general point of order: 'The next manager who tells me what a great day it was when Miss Glitz was there and signed one fifth of the books I signed will be found stapled to his desk.'

He railed against interviews dropped into the schedule without warning, and he railed against interviews booked into the schedule in advance. 'Had dinner and lounged in the Langham Hilton until the Richard Allinson show at 11pm. As soon as he said, "So . . . tell listeners what the Discworld is all about, then," I knew we'd wasted the evening.' Encountering Sheridan Morley for a slot on BBC Radio 2's *The Arts Programme*, Terry concluded: 'He probably wouldn't read the book if it was printed on fivers, but we filled 10 minutes.'*

On the May 1997 tour for *Feet of Clay*, he railed about being fed a 'pie made out of wax', and he railed about being hurried along by someone at Jarrold's, the department store in my home town of Norwich, where the queue wound through the shop, way beyond the precinct of the book department. 'Halfways through my cup of not very nice tea, I was requested to start signing "in case they wander off – they're up to Menswear already".' Terry noted that he 'hurried out with bad grace before they could get into Lingerie'.†

. . . .

* On the plus side, when tours brought Terry to BBC radio, and, by extension, the Langham, opposite Broadcasting House, Rhianna, living and working as a writer in London, could join him for breakfast – 'quality time', as Terry called it, over the hotel's unusually sumptuous breakfast buffet.

† Too late! My father was in that queue, buying me a gift, and he did, indeed, find himself stationed for a while in the lingerie department. Ahead of him in the queue was a headmistress, and behind him was a matron from the Norfolk & Norwich Hospital, and, as they waited,

Sometimes he felt ill, and sometimes he felt cross, and sometimes he felt ill *and* cross, and he railed about all of that, too. 'Unfortunately, something – the heat, the salad for lunch, the smell of burnt carpet that always seems to pervade Waterstones – hit me like a sort of whole-body migraine. Got through it without throwing up, which surprised me.'

And here was the thing: it wasn't like he was asking for much. Joan Collins, Terry was agog to learn from the gossip in one bookstore, needed freshly squeezed orange juice in a glass, served on a silver platter, and preferred her books to be passed across to her, pre-arranged in stacks of no more than four.* Oh, and she had signed for 60 minutes and 60 minutes only, before rising grandly from her seat and leaving them wanting more.†
In that context, Terry's requests for a cup of tea, a decent chair and a table that he could settle down at for however long it took, looked almost unimaginative.

But in a way, that was the crux of it. It was precisely this contrast – between how little he was asking for, and how infrequently he was nevertheless getting it – that grated on Terry so remorselessly and ended up driving him to greater and greater heights of Pratchettian exasperation as the tours and the years went by.

'There was no signing table!' he wrote, in abject disbelief, in a shop in 1995. 'What there *was* was a fixed low bookshelf with no place for the knees until I insisted that a shelf be taken out . . . Then the chair provided was so low I looked like a toddler having dinner with the grown-ups.' The indignity of his seating position became a constant theme in the reports, reaching perhaps its apogee on the *Jingo* tour of 1997, where Terry wrote: 'In order to be half-way comfortable at the signing, I had to sit at the table with my legs open wide like an old lady at the seaside giving her gussets an airing.'

. . . .

they talked to him about their love for Terry's books. My father was not a Pratchett reader, but those encounters changed his mind for ever about what he had assumed to be the typical Pratchett demographic – i.e. his son.

* TGTC.

† Also TGTC.

When he came out swinging at the bookshops, then, it wasn't as a rock star whose demand for colour-themed bowls of M&Ms had not been met; it was very simply as a bloke who had been driving for a number of hours and was looking for somewhere to sit.

> I don't expect freebies. I don't even expect pens. But I do demand that they know how to organise a sodding signing! This means a <u>table</u>! And a <u>chair</u>! And the table and chair should be such that someone can sit and sign at speed for three hours or so in moderate comfort so that the shop makes lots of <u>money</u>! Ye gods, why should we have to point out something so fundamental as this? Before the November tour we <u>must</u> circulate the chosen shops with a tactful little letter – because from now on, if I'm shown a low bookcase and a tatty chair, the fit will hit the shan, queue or no queue.

Throughout this period, Terry came to know the thousand small indignities that an author's publicity tour is naturally heir to – and, it has to be said, greeted many of them with good humour. He knew what it was like to sit prominently on display in a branch of WH Smith and overhear a passer-by mistake him for Terry Waite.[*] He had a name for a certain kind of onlooker at signings – 'the Uzis', as in 'Uzithen?' and also as in 'Izzeeonnatelly?' and also as in 'Nevrerdovim'. Terry knew what it was like to sign books against the backdrop of, as he put it, 'a susurration' of such remarks.[†] Once, in Milton Keynes, arriving late at a signing and pushing through the crowd towards the table, Terry was halted by a security guard. 'Sorry, mate – the queue's back there.' Terry simply turned and headed to the end of the line. 'It's your lucky day,' he

· ·

[*] The Anglican hostage negotiator had been freed from captivity in Lebanon a few years before this. Waite had in common with Terry a first name and a beard, but was considerably taller and way more Anglican.

[†] 'Susurration' was officially Terry's favourite word in the English language, even though, like the teachers in *The Wee Free Men*, he knew plenty of other long words such as 'marmalade' and 'corrugated iron'. Tiffany Aching thinks very hard in that book about the word 'susurrus' – 'a low soft sound, as of a whispering or muttering'.

told the people waiting there, and started signing their books. On another occasion, as he signed pre-orders in the backroom of a shop in Chester, somebody put their head round the door with a report on the state of the queue outside: 'You've already got more than the giant vegetable man,' they said, and Terry didn't know what to be more proud of – outnumbering Jeffrey Archer, or outnumbering the giant vegetable man.

However, it was also the case that in Basingstoke, at the end of a very long day and not in an especially jolly mood, Terry walked into the store and said directly to the manager, 'Get me a gin and tonic or I will kill you.' Mind you, it worked. 'Right away!' the manager said cheerfully, and the gin and tonic was in Terry's hands in under 90 seconds. 'First impressions are so important,' Terry would later note.*

Let's be under no illusion: much about those nineties tours was stacked in Terry's favour. For his publishing chaperone, he would frequently have Sally Wray from Transworld – the publicist by whom, as far as Terry was concerned, all other publicists were to be judged. Sally would write ahead to stores to suggest that they might like to have a bag of frozen peas available with which to cool Terry's wrist – a tactic which he had to employ many times, and increasingly felt the need for.† Oh, and could they possibly ensure that people couldn't pass *behind* him while he signed, because that unnerved him and made him worry that he was about to get attacked by a mad axeman.

Moreover, Terry liked the driver Transworld hired for him, and the car he drove – a slick silver Jaguar. Around Salisbury, Terry's personal

. . . .

* When Rhianna went for her first job, at the gaming magazine *PC Zone* – the 'scaly hands of journalism', as Terry put it, having reached out for his daughter just as they had reached out for him – there was an awkward moment when she realized she was being interviewed by someone who, in a former life at WH Smith, had encountered a particularly aggrieved book-touring Terry Pratchett and still bore the scars. Somehow Rhianna manoeuvred the conversation around this unhelpful sticky patch and secured the job.

† In 1997, Bernard Pearson found Terry a wrist-support with twin built-in ice packs. He tried it out on a tour of Australia, but it proved too cumbersome. That year Terry was already considering the possibility of 'cumulative damage' to his wrist by over-signing.

driver was Chris Whitmarsh, a former HGV man who wore a cardigan with football buttons, drove a slightly battered Mercedes in which at least one of the emergency check-lights always seemed to be on, although you couldn't be sure because he stuck a shifting screen of black electrical tape over them so as not to alarm Terry, and who entertained him royally with tales of long-distance hauls and dark nights on the road. But for tours, Transworld would supply him with Graham Hamilton, who had driven for Freddie Mercury, although Terry was more impressed by the fact that Graham had worked for politicians and, accordingly, had done a course on 'evasive driving techniques'. It seemed to reassure Terry to know that he had exactly the right kind of man behind the wheel if things ever got *really* nasty at Watford Waterstones.*

And, of course, there were many triumphs to record and enjoy in this period. In Colchester, in November 1997, for example: 'Just over three and a quarter hours of queue, beating Manchester. How does this medium-sized town beat a major city?' And at Forbidden Planet in London, in 1996: 'The unofficial time of this event was four hours and 42 minutes, making it the longest uninterrupted signing I've ever done, by more than half an hour.' That record would eventually be overtaken when Terry spent a massive five hours and 38 minutes signing copies of *Jingo*, among other things, at that same venue in 1998. There were even – praise be – culinary triumphs. 'Jacket spud for lunch came with salad and coleslaw,' Terry noted, approvingly, at the end of a long morning of stock signing. 'Decent sarnies,' he observed on another occasion. 'Another two-hour queue. Nice displays in the shop, cold drinks, happy fans. The kind of signing you feel good about doing.'

But somehow those high points – these times when it clicked, and the shop, the fans and the baked potato all came together in one glorious bookstore-event fusion – were never quite enough. 'Right now,' said Terry in 1998, 'when I realise that I've spent at least a year out of the last ten on signing tours, I just feel depressed.' Even the uncomplicatedly

* Graham, with Terry on board, once beat me on a trip from Manchester to Glasgow. Which wouldn't necessarily be worth recording, except for the small detail that I went by plane.

wholesome experiences didn't seem to be bringing him pleasure. In May that year, he gave a talk at the *Sunday Times* Hay Literary Festival in a giant and full marquee. Eileen and David, his parents, who were now living in Hay-on-Wye in the cottage that Terry had bought them and which they had named 'Daveen', sat proudly in the front row. The interview went well and afterwards Terry signed books in the bookshop tent for two hours. 'But . . . let's just say I'm not going again,' he wrote. 'It was pretty much as condescending as I'd feared – the usual "Attila the Hun visiting the Roman Senate" treatment.'

In truth, though, there were signs of strain as early as November 1996, at the conclusion of the tour promoting *Hogfather*. 'Every day sees me signing (queues and orders) for at least six hours, invariably seven, sometimes more,' Terry wrote then. 'The queues are longer and more like production lines, there are more orders, more and more frequently I arrive at shops minutes before I'm due to sign. I can't keep this up indefinitely. It's doing in my head as well as my wrist. Adrenaline can help a lot, but sooner or later the bucket's going to hit the bottom of the well.'

Yet somehow it never did. On the tour for *The Amazing Maurice and his Educated Rodents* in 2001, Terry went through a particularly bad patch. In Stockport, on the very first engagement, the table was too near the door: 'Even my feet were frozen and the books were unpleasantly cold to sign.' Straight after that, in Manchester, a room-service sandwich order failed to materialize, meaning that 'dinner was the bottle of cashews from the mini bar.'* And then a bookshop in Lancaster was still in the distressed aftermath of a refit: 'You would not have believed it. A sensible manager would have cancelled. A sane author would have fled. Break my legs if I suggest this again.'

A little further down the road there was an unsatisfactory encounter with a shopkeeper. 'I met the manager, I think. Not much was said. He

. . . .

* I can't over-stress how much this would have grated on Terry, who was immensely averse to paying the ramped-up prices of the hotel mini-bar, wherever it was in the world and however hungry he was.

may have been annoyed. With booksellers, who can tell? After all, people had been filling his shop and buying vast numbers of his books and that always upsets the smooth running of things.' This slight was followed by some under-par snack provision in Ipswich: 'There was a plate on a shelf of the dullest sushi it is possible to buy (fish paste rolls) and some dry sausages. I think they were an offering to some local spirit, because they weren't mentioned at any point.' And then, the final straw: 'In Reading, I found I'd been signing under a H*rry P*tt*r display. Nice one.'

Afterwards, Terry wrote up his conclusions. He was clear that he'd had enough of big tours. 'It has stopped being fun. It's just punishing.' He was fed up with being treated as part of some kind of author/publicist package. 'It arrives, you put it in a room, it signs orders, it signs books, it goes away.' The schedule was too tight, the demands too many. He was eating erratically and not getting enough sleep. It was playing havoc with his health. 'For most of the middle week I had a persistent headache that needed a regular intake of soluble aspirin all day even to hold it at bay.'

And was it even worth it, he wondered? 'It's anyone's guess how many sales are *created* by a signing.' The idea that it bred brand loyalty in the shops seemed unlikely to him: 'like fairy gold, it evaporates overnight.' And even the fans now had come to think of a signing in their town as to some extent an entitlement, and were annoyed with him when they didn't get one.

'I've been doing these things for thirteen years,' Terry wrote, in a moment of self-examination, 'and I think I've become one of those "difficult" authors I despised when I started out. My only defence is that it's been forced on me. I don't demand smoked salmon and walk out at the end of an hour, but the good shops don't lift me up as much as the bad shops knock me back. I don't know if there's something new we could try, but I'd like to try it.'

He really sounded resolute this time. He was drawing the line. 'I think, please, that it's time to call a halt to these big tours,' Terry wrote to his publishers. 'I think these big tours ought to go the way of the dinosaurs before I do.'

The following year, in 2002, Transworld published *Night Watch*, the 29th Discworld novel, and Terry picked up his hat and his bag and went back on the road to promote it.

★ ★ ★ ★ ★

There was one genuinely significant repercussion from Terry's experiences on the road in the nineties, and in the end it had nothing to do with dodgy baked potatoes or hotels with 'floorboards you could orchestrate'. Midway through the nineties, Terry set off on a signing tour, only to find the shops where he was supposed to be signing had no copies of his new book for him to sign. This mistake by the distributors used by Victor Gollancz at the time would have mattered wherever it had occurred, but the fact that it had occurred in Australia only deepened Terry's sense of grievance. Australia is a long way for an author to go to not sign books, as Terry very quickly made clear. However, Colin, and eventually Terry, decided to take the lenient view: mistakes acknowledged, lessons learned, wouldn't happen again, etc. Therefore when it *did* happen again, the very next time that Terry flew all the way to Australia, Colin felt he had no option but to move his client on. Malcolm Edwards had long since left; it was a pity to lose the input of Jo Fletcher, who had been Terry's Gollancz editor. But needs must. In 1998, Transworld became Terry's hardback publisher through their Doubleday imprint as well as his paperback publisher, through Corgi.

That same year, the second Discworld Convention took place in Liverpool, at the Adelphi Hotel, whose staff – not least the formidable manager, Eileen Downey – were still bathing in a certain amount of fame's glow following the previous year's BBC television series *Hotel*.* Nearly 1,000 attendees were offered the chance to enjoy Luggage Wars – a low-watt version of *Robot Wars* – readings by Terry of as yet unpublished passages from *Carpe Jugulum* and *The Fifth Elephant*, and a

----

* *Hotel* was a tentative venture by the BBC into a format called 'reality television', which would surely never catch on.

charity auction, which seemed to go on for ever, particularly for Bernard Pearson, who was conducting it, dressed as Mustrum Ridcully in a steaming hot outfit made predominantly from bits of old carpet. The available food included what was widely agreed to have been one of the last ever servings of that dying culinary phenomenon, the Great British Curry, complete with obligatory sultanas, and there was something jelly-based for pudding.* Just to ring the changes, the ritual convention-closing dunking of the organizer, Paul Rood, was in a paddling pool filled, not with custard, but with tapioca. Yet, again, as it had in Manchester, the event brimmed with fun and friendship. It's no exaggeration to say that, when it was over, some attendees wept to leave.

Someone who had agreed to attend that weekend – a little hesitantly, it would appear – was Patrick Janson-Smith, the deputy managing director of Transworld, who afterwards sent an internal note about his experiences to key Pratchett-related staff at the company. 'I'm almost ashamed to say it, but . . .' Patrick began, '. . . I had a very good time at the Discworld Convention.' The originator of the highly successful Black Swan imprint, which published Joanna Trollope and Mary Wesley, and often to be seen in a blue blazer with gold buttons, Patrick was perhaps an unlikely fantasy convention-goer. Or was he? He had once put on a dress to play Princess Diana in the annual Publishers' Panto, so he might at the very least have related at some deeper level to the masquerade aspects of the event. And in any case, who *was* the typical Discworld fan? That was one of the questions Patrick went to Liverpool to try and answer. 'I found the mix of people attending the convention quite riveting,' Patrick reported back to his staff. 'Plenty of the beard'n'anorak brigade, but also middle-class husband and wife types, sometimes with children in tow, and some delightfully oddball characters, such as Tony Lewis, ex-education officer, now retired and

---

* The Convention committee visited Liverpool in advance for a food-tasting and selection session, but I excused myself from that trip, figuring that convention food would always be convention food, and the fewer opportunities you give yourself to taste it, the better.

living on a canal boat; a gravedigger from Thurrock; and Rocky Frisco, ex-pianist with the J. J. Cale band, a man who'd once driven a motorbike halfway across America to meet Elvis Presley and got him to autograph the engine.'* Perhaps there really was no mileage in trying to squeeze a one-size-fits-all jumper over the heads of the Discworld Convention crowd. The only time Terry ever generalized about them was when he said, 'They drink like the rugby club, but they fight like the chess club.'

Of his author's performance in Liverpool, Patrick wrote, 'Terry, needless to say, was in his element. He really does lap up all the attention, but I'm bound to say he's extremely good at dealing with the fans. He was up every night until the wee small hours, mingling, having his photograph taken, signing books, T-shirts, models, scraps of paper . . .'

Patrick concluded that it had been 'a very warm-hearted occasion' and said, 'I'd even consider going again!' Before he left, he parted with £70 at Bernard's charity auction for one of the AA's large yellow road signs, directing traffic to the Convention. The deputy MD carried it home on the train to London and hung it in his office at Transworld.

'I hear you're working for my agent,' Terry said to me at the end of that convention, as, in my role as 'Guest Liaison', and with my ear-piece proudly in place, I walked him out to his blue Ford Mondeo in the Adelphi Hotel car park. I was, indeed, working for Colin Smythe Limited – going to Cornerways every day, gradually digitizing the leaning tower of royalty statements, creating a website for the company and generally imposing some computerized order on things. Not long after that, I started getting sent down to Salisbury to do jobs for Terry – electrical jobs, administrative jobs. And Terry seemed to approve of the work I was doing. Certainly, the number of days I was spending out of the office on secondment gradually grew until it began to rival the number of days I was spending at Cornerways. Indeed, at the maximum point of demand, it got to a point where I felt like I was in some kind

. . . .

* A massive Pratchett fan, a regular poster on alt.fan.pratchett, and also a car restorer, the late Rocky Frisco had a Mini Cooper that he named The Luggage.

of Beatles song, and working four days of the week for Colin, and the other four days of the week for Terry. Essentially, I got poached – but surreptitiously and over a period of several months. And finally the balance tipped and Terry asked me if I wanted to play the part of Amanda to his Jilly Cooper.

My first day in the job was a Friday at the beginning of December. It was lashing with rain when I drove through the gates, parked in the yard and walked quickly down the slope to the house. Anxious, and not really knowing at all what to expect, I sat in the kitchen and talked slightly nervously to Lyn, who made me a cup of Earl Grey tea, milky, just how I like it. It wasn't exactly clear where Terry was. Perhaps he was rising late, in a leisurely manner. I wondered if he would eventually descend in a velvet smoking jacket and a silk cravat. It seemed unlikely, from what I already knew of him, but maybe this was how it was, with authors at home.

After about 20 minutes, the back door crashed open in a blast of cold, damp air. In came Terry in a full-length brown leather duster coat and a battered hat, entirely soaked and very bedraggled. He had been feeding the tortoises.

'What are you doing?' said Terry, by way of greeting.

'Er . . . nothing, Terry,' I said.

'Well, you'd better do *something*,' Terry shouted. 'Anything! I'm paying you now.'

14

RUBBER GLOVES, TV SNOBS AND
AN OLIVETTI ON THE LINE
AT WATERLOO

When I started working for Terry, he made something clear to me right away. He told me he had a bugbear about people trying to look busy when they weren't. The specific examples he mentioned were assistants in largely deserted boutique clothes shops, straightening piles of already immaculately folded jumpers on perfectly tidy shelves; and workers on underwhelmed building sites leaning industriously on shovels. 'Honestly, Rob,' Terry said, 'don't ever do that. If you find yourself with nothing to do, then read a paper or go up to the Studio and switch the news on. Don't feel you have to try and look busy.'

It was good of him, as my employer, to put that out in the open, I thought. It suggested an admirably enlightened attitude to conduct in the workplace. And I would have happily gone along with him, and spared Terry any amount of irritation by going off to watch the telly when I wasn't busy, but for one little detail: I never wasn't busy.

Now, this is not the same as saying that I was always busy *working*. As I have already mentioned, there were certain portions of certain days when what kept Terry and me engaged was, if not the opposite of work, then definitely *not quite* work – those activities which we categorized under 'A' for 'Arsing About'. However, I can honestly say that there wasn't a single moment during my many years in this job when I wasn't occupied with *something*. Putting my feet up and reading the paper? It didn't happen. Ever.

On that first rainy Friday, we went up to the Chapel together. 'Have you ever done a VAT return?' Terry asked. I confessed that I hadn't. He tossed a thick manila folder of paperwork across to me. 'Familiarize yourself with that,' he said. So that was my first few hours – acquainting myself with the ins and outs of a quarterly HMRC report, VAT-able expenses and non-VAT-able expenses, values of sales and values of purchases, while Terry sat at his desk and carried on writing the book he was in the middle of, which was *Thief of Time*.

And at some point during the morning I made tea, of course, which was something I *had* done before.* There was something slightly surreal about it all, at that stage. I remember standing in the Chapel's galley kitchen, putting teabags in mugs while the kettle boiled, and thinking: 'That's actually *Terry Pratchett* in there. Writing *the next Terry Pratchett book*,' while feeling a certain sense of disbelief and a general oddness about the situation.

Later on, Terry suddenly stood up and announced: 'Right! Let's answer the mail.' He took a yellow cardboard folder from his desk and up-ended it on the floor. There were quite a few letters, but by no means an overwhelming amount. It surprised me, in fact. I thought there would be more.

Then Terry reached down to the floor beside him and picked up a large fabric tote bag, and tipped that out on top of the pile. That was more like it: that was more how I imagined a week's worth of Terry Pratchett's fan mail might look.

Then Terry reached down to the floor again, and picked up another fabric bag, even bigger than the first, and emptied that one onto the floor as well. At that point, we were looking at a mound of envelopes that came up as high as my knees. Terry wasn't remotely fazed.

. . . .

* The teabag of choice in the Chapel was Earl Grey until one day when a disastrous supply issue necessitated a shift to Lady Grey. There was no going back. When it came to feeding our crazy bergamot addiction, it was Lady Grey all the way after that.

So now I had a better picture of the mail issue.

Terry at the time had one of those allegedly posture-improving 'kneeling' chairs, and he positioned himself on that, with a mug of tea, while I sat at the keyboard, reaching down for letters, opening them and reading them aloud. Then Terry dictated his response. And thus, over the next four hours or so, did we work our way as far as we could into the foothills of the mail mountain. During this journey, I began to get a view of the range of Terry's correspondence. Quite a lot of people, it seemed, just wanted to say thank you for the books, prompting Terry's standard response: 'Thank *you* for the money.' Other correspondents were keen to know where Terry got his ideas from: Terry's answer to this was typically along the lines of 'a warehouse in Croydon', or 'a bloke who runs a kiosk round the back of Basingstoke Station'. Other correspondents, less specifically, were keen to know *how he did it*. 'What was the shortcut?' often seemed to be the question between the lines here. 'I think they want me to find a button you can press,' Terry would say, 'or a website you can go to, or a correspondence course you can sign up for.' Somehow you felt that the honest answer which he provided them with – that what it took in his own case was hours and hours of writing, including at unsociable times of the day, plus the inevitable stroke of inexplicable good fortune – would not have been quite what they were in the market to hear. Still, he gave it to them straight.

Related to these letters, there was a smattering of queries along the lines of, 'I've written a novel – what do I do now?' (Terry: 'Get yourself a decent agent.' There was an unspoken emphasis on 'decent'.) Then – another rich vein in the correspondence – there were the specific enquiries relating to characters from the books: what, for example, happened to Sam Vimes between *Jingo* and *The Fifth Elephant*? What had he been up to in the time between those novels? (Terry: 'Nothing. I made him up.') There were numerous requests for signed photographs. 'Why on earth do people want signed photos of *authors*?' Terry asked, rhetorically, before adding, after a short pause, 'Especially *me*.' And there were the letters written in green on purple paper, which often had a drawing of a bat, or similar, in the top corner of the page, and which we would often set aside to the end of the session, when we were properly in the flow.

There were many requests for interviews from contributors to school magazines and pupils on school-related projects and from student journalists – just the once, as we saw earlier, inspiring Terry to get straight on the phone, but normally giving rise to an apology for general busyness and best wishes for the future. Sometimes a thick A4 envelope would turn out to contain individual letters from an entire class of 35 – clearly the product of some kind of 'write to an author' project. In those cases, Terry would never reply solely to the teacher, which would have been my instinct: he would reply to each member of the class. And there was a particular type of letter from parents – normally mothers – thanking Terry for inspiring their children – commonly their sons – to read books. Sometimes those parents additionally informed Terry that his books were the only things their son would read. This was clearly, taken at face value, an extraordinary compliment – a testament to the special allure of Terry's writing and to the power it had to defuse what was daunting in other books. Yet, from Terry's point of view, it was a compliment that, with repetition over time, had come to assume many of the characteristics of an insult: he won't read proper books, these mothers seemed to him to be saying, but he *will* read yours. Nevertheless, Terry dictated a grateful answer to these letters, too.[*]

It bemused me, at first, that he was ready to devote so much time and energy to this task. Didn't he have a novel that he needed to be getting on with? Well, yes, obviously he did. Nevertheless the letters remained high on the agenda. This was, I realized, partly because there was a piece of Terry which was forever the science fiction fan who had written to Tolkien and got a letter back – and by return of post. He knew what it meant to reach out in that way and be heard and be rewarded with contact. But I came to believe there was something protective in the mix, too. It was undoubtedly the case that, for a certain kind of literary critic, reservations about Terry Pratchett's writing – to

....

[*] After Terry died, Lyn and I eventually summoned the will to go through some of the fan mail that had built up. The very first letter she pulled out of the pile was in the 'mother thanking Terry for getting her sons reading' category. It was from Cilla Black.

which anyone was entitled – often somehow became the excuse for an impromptu attack on Terry Pratchett's readers, which seemed a much more niche and far more puzzling reaction to the books. A notable example of this ricochet tendency was a panel discussion in 1994 on BBC2's now long since cancelled arts show *Late Review*, in which the poet Tom Paulin did not limit himself to despairing remarks about Terry's prose – 'a complete amateur! He doesn't even write in chapters!' – but also maintained, of Pratchett readers, that it was 'like lifting up a *stone*: you see all these *insects* scurrying around and you think, what on *earth* are they up to? And you put the stone back and go away.' Next to Paulin on the panel, the columnist Allison Pearson gave a little moue of contented amusement at this point and added that she would be 'surprised if any women wanted to read these books' – a critical hunch which would have been onto something if you had been prepared to ignore just over half of Terry Pratchett's actual readers. Such knee-jerk hostility and generally unpleasant ignorance masquerading as informed reaction made Terry not only more dismissive of the reflexive snobbery of BBC2 arts review programmes, but more than averagely protective of his fans and inclined to honour his ties to them when he could. Why should *they* get stick? The world out there was full of snipers with peculiar agendas; it was important to band together and man the barricades.

But the letter-writing went deeper than that, too. Terry had clearly formed the notion that his success derived in some vital way from his accessibility: the book signings, the conventions, the letters, not to mention his postings on alt.fan.pratchett. When he connected with readers, it wasn't just through words on the page, it was through these other means, too. And, at least in Terry's view, all those readers who didn't even go to the book signings or the conventions or send him letters, nevertheless somehow knew him to be *that sort of writer*, and thought of him accordingly. Therefore answering the mail was practically a superstition with him: if he didn't at least attempt to keep on top of it, he assumed a fundamental link in the chain would break, and his entire relationship with his readers would come undone.

That afternoon, we printed the letters Terry had dictated, using

Terry's gigantic laser printer – practically a museum piece, and the size, more or less, of a tumble drier, which sat, boiling and snorting away, in the corner of the room. Soon enough, under the strain of the task, it ran out of toner. Terry snapped on a pair of rubber gloves, and showed me how to refill its mighty toner reservoir from plastic bottles, a laborious and messy process which was archaic, even then. I couldn't have been more impressed. Here was the geek mentality, which the pair of us shared, of keeping electronic items going well beyond their intended life-cycle. We both loved tech, and looking out for the very latest development. But retro tech – tech sustained in full working order, against the odds and the relentless march of time – that was surely the best tech of all.

That was why Terry had a fax machine for several years after faxes stopped being a thing. The last fax ever to enter the Chapel on official business came from Colin Smythe, sometime around 2002. It was the first time the machine had clattered into life in many months and the ink was so hard in its cartridge that what emerged appeared to be a few scattered lines of Morse Code on an otherwise blank sheet of paper – not so much a document, more a cry for help. I had to ring Colin and ask him what he had sent us, which sort of defeated the object. Still, it was the principle of the thing: yes, the world had moved on and everybody was doing email now, but that fax machine had survived and remained operational, give or take its ink supply, so it was not to be cast out.

Alas, the poor beleaguered laser printer was not so durable. One day, quite soon after I arrived, it snorted and spat its last. At that point, Terry sent me to Gloucester to meet a guy he had found somewhere on a newsgroup who was flogging refurbished HP printers at knock-down prices – all entirely legitimate and above board, I'm sure. I parted with £100 in Terry's used notes and came back from that Gloucester lock-up with three of them filling my car. Why three? So that two of them could be cannibalized for spare parts to keep the first one alive when it inevitably broke down, which, equally inevitably, would happen just after that model of the machine had been withdrawn from sale. As a fully paid up retro-tech geek, you had to stockpile against that moment.

That little piece of business in Gloucester kept the office in functioning printers for a while. Then, in 2003, Terry won a WH Smith award for *The Wee Free Men* in the 'Teen Choice' category, and, rather sweetly, chose to spend his £500 prize money on a printer which – get this – printed things *in colour*. This was a huge addition to the armoury of the office. From that moment on, the randomly multi-hued Pratchett drafts could, when necessary, be rendered in all their glory.

So, my first day with Terry was VAT and letters. My second week was trench-digging. The trench was two feet deep and a foot wide, and ran for 150 feet in a curving arc between the Studio and the Chapel, and I dug it, old-school, with a spade. This was December, I would ask you to remember. Did Amanda ever dig a 150-foot trench for Jilly Cooper? In December? Someone should ask her.

Incidentally, this wasn't some military-style exercise that Terry had decided would be good for my discipline. I had suggested that it would be useful to create an electronic link between the Chapel and the Studio, which had been Terry's office before the Chapel was built and which was now used as workshop, secondary office and storage space. It was the place Terry's old computers went to die – or rather, to live on. Through the modern miracle which was Cat 5 cabling, the two places could be made to communicate with each other, using intranet messaging and an intercom. Moreover, Terry's writing could be automatically saving and backing up on the Studio computers, guarding absolutely against any further mishaps involving floppy disks, shirt pockets and the washing machine. Of course, these were the times before domestic wi-fi generally, and certainly before domestic wi-fi in rural areas deep in the Chalke Valley. In those days, if you wanted computers to talk to one another, you needed wires running between them. And if you wanted those wires to run through 150 feet of garden and four-foot stone walls, you had to dig them a hole. Terry was keen at first to string the wires on miniature telegraph poles – for the look of it, as much as anything. We had a short tussle over that. I pointed out that a lightning strike would have the potential to fry the computers at both ends. Terry backed down and we went for the hole.

For someone not exactly used to manual labour, it was hard work.

But I got it done, and on the Friday, Terry came down to the Studio where, like Alexander Graham Bell testing his experiment in telephony on Mr Watson in the room next door, I proudly showed him, on the screen there, the message I had sent: 'Hello from the Chapel.' Terry was highly sceptical. 'You could have done that from down here,' he said. So I got him to key in his own message – 'Hello Chapel from the Studio, love Terry' and we set off back up to the other building – where, abracadabra, there on the screen was Terry's greeting. Chapel and Studio were now officially talking to each other.*

'That was a really good week's work. Thank you,' Terry said, as I knocked off for the weekend. I was chuffed. This was the first time an expression of unalloyed gratitude had come my way from the boss. Terry being Terry, I believe it may also have been the last time, too.

Synching the Chapel and the Studio was just the first of a number of electronic projects that Terry and I carried out over the ensuing months with a view to automating the life of the office. Some of these projects we did because they were genuinely useful, others we did simply because we *could* do them and for the sheer joy of it. We rigged it so that Terry's key in the door of the Chapel in the morning would deactivate the alarm, start up his computer and open the file he was last working on, so that by the time he had hung up his coat and sat down in his chair, he was ready to go. We arranged it so that we could not only monitor the temperature in the greenhouse from Terry's desk – something Terry had been doing since he lived at Gaze Cottage – but also remotely open and close the greenhouse vents without leaving the Chapel. We installed a remote system for the sprinklers, for no good reason, really, except that any way to use tech to unnecessarily complicate watering the carnivorous plants was of interest to us. The greenhouse also housed Terry's wormeries, so we set up a system whereby the temperature in the wormeries could be regulated remotely. We also installed

. . . .

* The trench also carried wiring for a conventional intercom. One of Terry's first uses of it was to buzz me in the Studio and say, '10-17 for a coffee.' It was the first glimpse I ever got of Terry's past as a CB radio jock, which he otherwise kept extremely well hidden.

meters in the Chapel which would monitor the observatory, a short walk away across the grass – the temperature of the telescope, and the temperature of the air inside and outside the building. And we rigged the observatory itself with a lightning detector which would automatically cause the roof to close when it picked up electrical activity in the atmosphere. We were extremely keen to see this piece of tech in action – and enormously frustrated when no storm would oblige by coming close enough to trigger it. So we kept tweaking its parameters, pushing them further and further out – storm chasing, I guess you could call it. Finally, lightning struck somewhere on the Isle of Wight, a highly unthreatening 50 miles away, and, to our intense satisfaction, the observatory roof solemnly closed over our heads. Job done.

Each of these projects was conducted by the pair of us, working together with, in the time-honoured ethos of hobby electronics, cheap passive components soldered onto prototype Veroboard. Professionals might have turned their noses up at that, but this was how we rolled, and if you are raised in the church of home electronics, some traditions are immutable.

My other early tasks included going down to the house to install a multi-region decoding chip in Terry and Lyn's thunderous DVD player so that it would play American discs as well as domestic ones, and replacing the flimsy hinges on Terry's Olivetti Quaderno. That was the primeval machine that Terry had bought in 1992, at the misty dawn of portable computing, and which he still took on the road with him in order to be in a position to write in spare moments as they arose, such as in cars and airport lounges and studio green rooms and bookshop stockrooms and on flights, including in those otherwise empty minutes between boarding the plane and taxiing out to the runway.* He was

---

* Terry took a resoundingly broad view of what constituted a 'spare moment' in which to write. Anne Hoppe, Terry's US children's editor, nurtures a fond memory of a small lunch given for Terry by publishers and representatives of the Barnes & Noble bookstore in a private room at the Gramercy Tavern in New York during Terry's promotional trip for *The Wee Free Men*. As genial conversations flowed between the dozen or so attendees around the long dining table, Terry, the guest of honour, sat with his laptop, hard at work.

very strongly attached to that computer. And I was pleased with the job I did on its hinges, spending a weekend casting entirely new ones using Araldite and matchsticks. They were better than the originals, I would humbly claim, which appeared to have been made from an amalgam of dust and cheese. They were certainly better than the piece of duct tape that Terry had been using to hold the machine together.

But disaster struck. At Waterloo Station, hurrying back to Salisbury with my handiwork, I heard the ominous sound of my bag splitting, followed by the sickening crack of an Olivetti Quaderno bouncing once on the concrete before slithering into the gap between the train and the platform. I was beside myself – as anyone would be, I guess, who had just thrown their new boss's computer under a train. Kindly station workers retrieved the machine from the track, albeit extensively scraping it the length of the platform wall as they hauled it up, but it was now clearly in need of much more than new hinges.

That was a very long journey to Salisbury. I couldn't imagine that Terry was going to look on this accident particularly equably. In fact, I couldn't have been more wrong.

'Never mind, Rob,' said Terry mildly. 'These things happen. Cup of tea?'

OK, not really. He was utterly *incandescent* and took four hours to cool off. Opening up the pock-marked computer and surveying the black and cracked liquid crystal screen, he said, mournfully, 'It looks like amoebas.' I could entirely understand his anger. In Terry's eyes, and indeed my own, I had damaged a precious antique – and a precious antique that was still in use. However, he didn't sack me, and ultimately I believe he even forgave me. Possibly.

One project we didn't manage, despite devoting much thought to it, was a 'black box' system for Terry's hard drive. This was intended to operate in the event of fire breaking out in the Chapel and destroying all Terry's stored writing and more importantly the work in progress. The plan was to attach a rocket to the hard drive, and to assemble a network of rails running up through the building's rafters. A fire in the Chapel would ignite the fuse on the rocket which would be propelled along the rails and fly out through the specially loosened roof tiles, taking the hard drive with it. At a certain height, the rocket would give out and a miniature parachute would deploy, Apollo Mission-style, bringing the hard drive down into the grounds of the manor, away from the Chapel, where it could be traced and recovered after the conflagration. In many ways, of course, the requirement for this emergency procedure was removed by the separate back-up system for Terry's writing which was now running in the Studio. But rather more pressing in both our minds was the realization that, had we ever built this device, we would have been sorely tempted to set fire to the Chapel just to see if it worked.

Completing a task as complex as any electrical upgrade involving rocket science, I set up a small flat-pack desk from IKEA just inside the Chapel's door, and that was the initial base of my operations. Terry was delighted that his new personal assistant's workstation had an in-tray on it. He would come and lay a piece of paper in the in-tray and then return to his seat, and the formal delegation implicit in this act seemed to please him enormously. We were both somewhat self-conscious and playing it by ear in those early weeks. I was working out what my role was, and Terry, for his part, was adjusting to the strangeness, after all those years of insistently preserving his solitude, of having someone in the room where he was writing. That process of acclimatization took a little while and was not without its hiccups. I had been in position at the desk by the door for some time when, completely out of the blue, Terry said, 'Don't take this the wrong way, Rob, but, much as I enjoy your company, I think it would probably be better if you worked up in the Studio.'

There was no explanation and I was left to wonder whether I had put a foot wrong somewhere, or whether, all this time, I had been irritating Terry in some way without realizing. Still, he was the boss. I took my work up to the Studio for the rest of that day, and went there directly when I arrived the following morning.

I hadn't been in the Studio very long on the first full day of my exile when the intercom buzzed. 'Do you fancy coming down and doing a little light work?' said Terry. I went across to the Chapel, Terry and I did some work together, and the question of banishing me to the Studio never came up again.

* * * * *

Between automating the greenhouse vents, protecting the observatory tele-scope from rogue lightning strikes, and developing rocket-based emergency contingencies for the Chapel, some books got written. Three were pub-lished in 2001 alone: *Thief of Time*, *The Last Hero*, which was a novella with extensive illustrations by Paul Kidby, and the Carnegie Medal-winning *The Amazing Maurice and his Educated Rodents*. In the following three years, Terry would write *Night Watch*, *The Wee Free Men*, *Monstrous Regiment*, *A Hat Full of Sky* and *Going Postal* – an extraordinary run of form, in both adult and children's fiction, in which his writing seemed to change course each time, and expand and reach new heights of accomplishment. It can still strike me as somewhat fantastical that I was in the room while all this writing was happening. But I definitely was.

Terry was 52. He was no longer Britain's best-selling living novelist, a position he had surrendered to J. K. Rowling, whose Harry Potter series, commencing in 1997, seemed to be going down quite well with book buyers. OK, so if you categorized J. K. Rowling as a children's author, Terry could still squeeze through as Britain's best-selling living author for adults. But that was a bit of a fudge, and there is no question that the loss of undisputable, no-fudges-necessary top-cat status nee-dled him. On the other hand, Rowling's success was so phenomenal and so utterly record-smashing that she almost seemed to have created an entirely separate category of competition, so from that point of view it was slightly less chafing than it might have been. But it still chafed. Perhaps it was a little like what Bing Crosby said about Frank Sinatra: 'Singers like Frank come along once in a lifetime. So why did he have to come along in mine?' In many ways, from Terry's point of view, the most irksome aspect of J. K. Rowling's coming along in his lifetime was that the press were constantly trying to set him up for a fight for which he had no real appetite. When Terry took exception publicly to a pro-file of Rowling in *Time* magazine for its reductive attitude to fantasy

Top: Twin-screen pleasure in the Chapel, Wiltshire. Further screens were soon on order.

Above: Fortieth wedding anniversary celebrations, featuring Eileen and a large cake at the Castleman restaurant, Chettle, 2008.

Above: Guilty of literature. Terry with Rhianna at his OBE presentation, 1998.

Right: Even more guilty of literature. Knighted by the Queen in 2010.

Below: Directly after, Colin Smythe leads Terry to his first meal as Sir Terry.

Below right: With Lyn at the *Hogfather* premiere, Mayfair, 2006.

Above: Director Vadim Jean and producers Rod Brown and Ian Sharples deliver some furniture to the Chapel after the shooting of *The Colour of Magic* in 2008.

Right: Ready for his close-up. In Hungary on location for *Going Postal*, 2009.

Below: Biggles flies again – in a cap borrowed from me, as it happens.

Above: Authentic blacksmithery with Hector Cole – every knight should have a sword.

Left: Terry and me on board a klotok, seeking orang-utans, Borneo, spring 2013.

Below left: We both knew this trip would be the last of its kind.

Below: Terry finding an orang-utan. Or an orang-utan finding Terry.

Top: Another day in the office. Ian Stewart and Terry – not sleeping, thinking – and I work on *The Science of Discworld IV.*

Above: With Neil Gaiman in 2014, using my car to record a cameo for the BBC radio version of *Good Omens.*

Top left: Back where it really started: Beaconsfield Library, 2013.

Top right: Ceremonial sausage-cutting duties in the village.

Above right: At Hobbiton in New Zealand, a film set like no other.

Above: Still in the cab. At the launch of *Raising Steam* in 2013.

Above: Rhianna and Terry in a portrait taken for the *Sunday Times*'s 'Relative Values' feature, London, 2012.

Right: Terry and me in front of a green screen, amused by something that would probably have been keyed in later.

Terry as we love to remember him.

writing in general, it was reported as if his beef were with Rowling rather than with the article in *Time* magazine. But 'Pratchett Attacks Rowling', as the BBC website reported it, was always going to be a more alluring headline than 'Pratchett Attacks Piece in *Time* Magazine'.

For Terry the greater indignity was now quite regularly being asked whether Hogwarts (founded 1997) was the inspiration for Hogswatch (founded 1976, in *Dark Side of the Sun*) or whether the bespectacled boy wizard Ponder Stibbons (born 1990, in *Moving Pictures*) was any kind of tribute to the bespectacled boy wizard referred to by Terry in his tour report as H*rry P*tt*r.* Equally irritating was seeing Rowling casually credited with 'revolutionizing' the 'hitherto moribund' world of fantasy fiction. On the BBC, Andrew Marr immortally introduced Terry by suggesting that he was 'following in the footsteps of Philip Pullman and J. K. Rowling'. Terry was bound to bristle, during this period of intense and culture-tipping Pottermania, and wonder what had happened to his *own* footprints.

Behind the scenes, though, magnanimity prevailed – albeit that it sometimes appeared to be magnanimity of a quietly smouldering kind. Terry wrote to Rowling to congratulate her on replacing him at the top of the pile, asking her in the letter whether she had 'had the moment yet', before explaining that for Terry 'the moment' had come in the lavatory cubicle of a first-class cabin on a transatlantic flight, when he had looked at his reflection in the mirror and thought to himself, 'Why me?' It wasn't, perhaps, the most gushing of tributes. It was, in fact, a little thorny – a faintly Roman-style reminder for the victor, in this moment of glory, that luck always plays its part. But you would have to say that it was at least honest, and even sympathetic. Terry and J. K. Rowling were later together at an event in Edinburgh during the Festival and

....

* When Paul Kidby presented Terry with an early stab at a drawing of Ponder Stibbons, Terry told him to 'think more Bill Gates'. Paul had gone with a John Lennon feel. Nobody was thinking Harry Potter. However, in an interview with the *Independent* in November 2001, it was pointed out by the writer that Terry Pratchett 'lives in Wiltshire with his wife and five cats and has a personal assistant who looks like a grown-up Harry Potter'.

bowed to each other graciously across the room. They also had a brief but entirely convivial exchange, at the end of which Rowling apologized for needing to leave.

'You've probably got to sign off on a Harry Potter toilet roll holder,' suggested Terry.

Rowling laughed. 'Terry,' she said, 'you have no idea.'

However, for all the discomforts, smaller and larger, around being nudged off the uppermost perch, it's possible that the experience galvanized Terry to some extent – that it was perhaps even liberating. Number one status clearly wasn't coming back any time soon; that was no longer his burden to fret about. He had been there, and had nothing to prove in that regard. So maybe he was a little freer than he had been to please himself. It was certainly the case that he now embarked upon a sequence of books unlike any he had attempted before.

Much about Terry's writing process amazed me, and still does. There were no index cards. There was no whiteboard. There were no Post-it notes slapped on the wall near his desk, ready to be shuffled into order. There weren't even any jottings in a notebook. I assumed there would be some kind of grand plan – some sort of big diagram containing at least the outline of things for these 300- to 400-page stories and the stories still to come. There wasn't. The plots of each novel unfolded as he wrote them, and during the writing he stored, flipped, rotated and scrolled backwards and forwards through the whole thing in his head. What's more, he did so effortlessly. Every aspect of the unfolding story seemed to be at his fingertips.

He would refer to it as 'the Valley of Clouds'. Writing a novel was setting out on a journey from one side of the Valley of Clouds to the other. The valley down below you was full of mist but, with any luck, you could see the other side of it from where you were, and you could also see, quite clearly, just above the valley's mist, the tops of one or two trees or other prominent landmarks. So the job was to set off in the direction of one of those landmarks – to descend into the mist and see what became visible to you along the way, but always with a view to emerging at the point you'd chosen on the other side. To that end, Terry often found it useful to write the final scenes of a proposed book first – or, at least, to write down straight away the scene on the other side of the valley as he saw it at the point of departure. That might not be where the journey actually ended up, but those words could be rearranged or adapted if necessary – or even taken out altogether, having served their purpose, which was just to give the journey a sense of direction at the outset. People frequently speak of having had a great idea for the start of a novel. Terry knew that the art to it, and almost certainly the more difficult bit, was having a great idea for the *end* of a novel. And having got that destination fixed, more or less, he was ready to walk off down into the mist. From that point on, as witnessed from beside him at the keyboard, the entire process could appear to be an act of improvisation, except that many of the things that happened along the way, during the journey to the other side of the valley, and that turned into the novel's key scenes and incidents, would have been gestating in his mind for weeks, months and even years beforehand.

I quickly learned the whereabouts and workings of 'the Pit' – the place on the computer into which were lobbed stray ideas, rogue passages and orphaned sentences. Things could be pulled out of the Pit at any moment and used further down the line. All this was in accordance with, as mentioned previously, Terry's membership of 'the recyclable school of literature' and the principle of letting nothing go to waste that could be used. In *Unseen Academicals*, the 'Hunt the megapode' scene was extracted from the Pit and attached close to the front of the book very late in the process. It was a passage that Terry had found himself writing one day, a chase sequence for the fellows of Unseen University, based on ancient and variously mad Oxbridge traditions featuring ducks and swans. It had no home until eventually it did. 'Take a stroll through the Pit and see if there's anything there,' Terry had said. Then Terry planed the edges and smoothed it into place until you couldn't see the join.*

. . . .

* Colin Smythe observed Terry's brilliance in this area very early, during the editing of *Strata*. Colin noticed an abrupt transition, early in the book, and suggested that Terry add some material to smooth it over. Terry sat down at Colin's typewriter and instantly knocked out some extra words. When the book was printed, Colin was never able to pick out the added passage.

He wrote like that, in separate, self-contained passages, seemingly unrelated, which he then stitched and trimmed to fit, discarding excess matter – or, rather, relocating it in the Pit. And then he would polish the finished object down and polish it down again until, ideally, you could see your face in it. The metaphor he used a lot was 'carpet squares': the writing was separate blocks of fabric, which he then brought together and snapped into place to create the pattern of the whole. But whichever metaphor you chose, it was clear that Terry had a very strong sense of the novel as something *made*. It related to his feeling that writing was 'just another useful thing you could do with your hands'. And it related to his father, the mechanic, whose practicality Terry never stopped admiring, and to Terry's own unending determination to pull things apart and see how they worked before putting them back together again. There was a strong strand of the mechanic in the novelist, and a strong strand of the mechanical in the novels, and it passed down to Terry from David Pratchett.

However, Terry now decided to delegate to his newly appointed personal assistant the most overtly mechanical part of the novel-writing process – the typing of them. That development happened very fast. There was that first, unnerving instruction to 'just tidy that up, would you?' as Terry left the room one day, leaving me to sort the fonts and spacings on some freshly delivered prose. Almost immediately after that, though, I was at the keyboard taking letters by dictation and Terry suddenly told me to open a new file and got me to take down some paragraphs intended for *Thief of Time*. I happily did so, rather agog. This quickly became a regular occurrence. Terry would sit in my chair, with his hands behind his head, and I would sit in *his* chair and clatter away at the keyboard – touch-typing at 60 words per minute, because he didn't hold back. It suited him to talk it out in this way – to hear the sentences spoken aloud before they landed. It seemed to help him with the rhythm of them and the shaping of them.

He could use me to gauge the reaction of the reader, too. He now had a sounding board on hand each working day, and, even though this was not something that I had imagined I was signing up for when I took the job, I was thrilled to be that sounding board. Having Terry

Pratchett dictate a new novel to you in real time was a good deal more exciting than VAT returns, after all, and certainly beat digging a 150-foot trench. Indeed, for someone who had happily queued in bookshops on publication day to buy these novels at the earliest opportunity, it was a privilege bordering on the bizarre, and I relished it. In *Thief of Time*, when the milk cart belonging to Ronnie Soak, the Fifth Horseman of the Apocalypse – the one who left before the group got famous – went past the window of the undertaker's, revealing his name in reflection to be 'Kaos' . . . well, that was an utter revelation. I must have typed the word 'soak' 200 times by that point without seeing it coming. And, frankly, I don't think Terry had seen it coming until it occurred to him at that very moment, either. I was out of my chair, punching the air and shouting, 'Yes!' Terry merely sat with his arms folded across his body, his chin down, nodding slowly in a very pleased-with-himself-but-determined-not-to-show-it kind of way.

After these bouts of dictation, Terry would get me to read back to him what he had just come up with. At that stage, he would go back to the keyboard to mend things and type whole new passages for himself. But it was clear that dictation was working for him, and he chose to write that way more and more until, within a couple of months, it had become his dominant method. Writing, which had for all those years been a solitary activity, suddenly, with the appointment of a personal assistant, had a communal aspect, and something in Terry, perhaps to his own surprise – and certainly to mine – responded to that.

Thus did *Thief of Time* get written and, beyond that, *The Amazing Maurice* and *Monstrous Regiment* and *Wee Free Men*, and onwards to *Unseen Academicals* in 2011, which has the dedication: 'To Rob, who typed most of it and had the good sense to laugh from time to time.' If you are a reader of Terry Pratchett, I will not need to assure you that the laughter was no effort – that it came very easily indeed. Many times at the keyboard over those years, I would reflect on the absurd good fortune of my position – getting paid to laugh.

'Where are we? Where are we?' Terry would ask, and I would read out the word-count. Once we'd got above 100,000 words, nominally the commissioned length for the novel, he would say, 'Right – we're working on our own time now.' And on we went.

I had, by default, become part of the small team facilitating Terry's output. He had always had his consultants. These were the people to whom he could pick up the phone when he had reached a knotty moment and needed to achieve some clarity in order to find his way forward. They included Bernard Pearson, David Langford, Dave Busby and Neil Gaiman. For them, these calls could come at any hour of the day, including nights and weekends, and tended to open with Terry saying, ''Ere, you know how this one goes,' before recounting the plotline that he was currently engaged with. As Rhianna put it, 'He wasn't necessarily talking about the work because he wanted your opinion. He was talking about the work because he wanted to talk about the work.' Accordingly, all who were in receipt of this particular type of call from Terry grew used to the phone suddenly going down without a 'goodbye' or even a warning of any kind, and without them necessarily having said very much, or even anything at all. That was the point at which Terry realized he had talked himself out of the knot and could go hurrying back to the screen to proceed. I now seemed to be one of these often mute, yet some-how encouraging consultants, but with the added advantage of being on hand, in the office.

Beyond that group of consultants, there was the small ring of experts to whom Terry could turn with questions about things. On most mat-ters of science, there were the Professors, Jack Cohen and Ian Stewart. Jack, who died in 2019, was a biologist, and Ian a mathematician. They met Terry in 1999, when Warwick University awarded him an honorary doctorate. Terry, in turn, made Jack and Ian 'Honorary Wizards of Unseen University' and the three of them eventually collaborated on the *Science of Discworld* book series.* Then there was Stephen Briggs, a civil servant who worked for the Department for Environment, Food

....

* One of Terry's carers told me that, very near the end, when Terry was almost non-verbal, he had asked him who was the cleverest person he had ever met. 'Jack Cohen and Ian Stewart,' Terry said, without hesitation.

and Rural Affairs and dabbled in amateur dramatics, and who wrote to Terry early in the 1990s to ask if he could adapt *Wyrd Sisters* for the stage. Terry not only granted permission but went to see the production and took champagne for the cast. Many more adaptations followed. Stephen, in collaboration with Terry, constructed the city map of Ankh-Morpork and then the atlas of Discworld, both of which were published in the 1990s, giving rise to *The Discworld Companion* and several other Discworld-related publications. His recall for what was where on Discworld was, when Terry needed it, arguably more precise than Terry's own. And there was Jacqueline Simpson, a folklorist, who happened to be in the line at a book signing where Terry was asking people how many iterations they knew of the Magpie song – 'one for sorrow, two for joy' etc. 'At the last count, seventeen, Terry,' said Jacqueline, in her soft Germanic accent, thereby blowing the rest of the room out of the water and inserting herself straight into Terry's phone book for all queries on folk lyrics, fairy tales and mythology. Terry and Jacqueline eventually collaborated on *The Folklore of Discworld*.

Why, you might ask, in his line of work, would Terry need significantly qualified academic back-up? Was there really a peer-review protocol for fantasy novelists? He made it all up, didn't he? Well, up to a point, yes. At the same time, being wildly imaginative in the fiction you constructed was all very well, but if you were going to take the readers along with you, that fiction needed to answer scrupulously to its own internal logic. And if your purpose was ultimately satirical, and your satire was about life as it is lived, then in order for that satire to land, your book needed to answer to the logic of the actual world, as well. This, it turned out, was the difficult thing about fantasy: it needed to be real to be believed.

That's why Terry would phone Dr Pat Harkin and ask him how much torque someone would need to be able to generate to twist the head off a human. Pat was a convention-going Pratchett superfan and a collector of Pratchett memorabilia who also happened to be a doctor of medicine and an admissions tutor at Leeds University. Pat, too, was on Terry's top table of expert consultants. Terry enjoyed reminding him that, while Pat had qualified as a doctor just the once, Terry, thanks to the munificence of universities, who began honouring him in 1999 and continued doing so in a fairly steady stream for the rest of his life, was a doctor many times over.

'Dr Harkin?' Terry would say, when Pat answered the phone. 'This is Dr Dr Dr Dr Dr Pratchett.'* And then he would ask him how much earwax the average human generated in a lifetime. Or, indeed, how much torque the average human would need to generate to tear the head off another average human.

Pat's conclusion on the latter was that no average human could do so.

'But it's an orc that's going to be doing it,' said Terry.

Pat thought about this.

'You're inventing an orc, Terry ... so, really, whatever you write is going to be the right answer.'

'But I want it to be the *right* right answer,' said Terry.

And that cut directly to the heart of it: the quest was for the *right* right answer. That's why, during the writing of *Going Postal*, we spent a day on the floor of the Chapel, grabbing whatever was to hand to mock up a clacks communication system, making towers from matchboxes and definitively establishing that you would need two people in each tower for the system to function as it was written.

There was a limit, though. Very infrequently, but just occasionally, Terry would lose patience during these negotiations with the logic of the known world, and the right of the novelist to at least a small helping of poetic licence would kick in. Pat Harkin knew about this moment. At the launch event for the DVD of the television adaptation of *The Colour of Magic*, which took place at the Forbidden Planet store in

. . . .

* Warwick University were first to give Terry an honorary doctorate, then Portsmouth (2001), then Bath (2003), then Bristol (2004), then Buckinghamshire New University (2008), then Trinity College Dublin (2008), then Bradford (2009), then Winchester (2009), then the Open University (2013), then the University of South Australia (2014). So, by the end, it was Dr Dr Dr Dr Dr Dr Dr Dr Dr Dr Pratchett, in fact. And let's not forget the honorary fellowship from University College London (2011) and the adjunct professorship from Trinity College Dublin (2010).

London, Terry was delighted to see Pat Harkin arrive, unexpectedly, at the table where he was signing copies.

'Ah, Pat – excellent,' Terry said. 'I have a question for you: how long would a body have to sit in a cave before it turned to dust and blew away?'

With the queue waiting behind him, Pat thought about this for as long as he felt able to, and quickly concluded that it simply wouldn't happen.

As Pat left the shop, Terry shouted after him, 'I don't care what you say. It's going to happen.'*

And I knew about that moment, too. I knew it after Terry and I had the argument about the plate and the pea. This was quite late on. We were in the pub in the village at lunchtime, having bubble and squeak, which was Terry's invariable order at these moments. Terry had this idea for a Discworld novel with the working title 'The Turtle Stops'. Great A'Tuin, the star turtle bearing the Disc, was going to become unwell. This would lead to an exploratory journey into the turtle, in preparation for which Terry had, needless to say, consulted a zoologist that he knew, John Chitty BVetMed Cert ZooMed CBiol MSB MRCVS, no less, in order to determine what, exactly, you would find if you ever ventured inside a turtle. But the pressing issue now was, how would the wizards of Unseen University come to know that Great A'Tuin was sick? We batted it back and forth between us in the office and then, that lunchtime, in the pub. Would there maybe be magical vibrations of some kind, which the wizards would be able to pick up? No. Too easy. Too close to Dr Who's sonic screwdriver: not a proper solution.

So, what if, Terry suggested, it was possible to observe the slowing of the turtle's interstellar paddling motion, from somewhere very high on the Disc?

This seemed problematic to me.

'Terry, there would be nowhere on the Disc from which this phenomenon was visible.'

....

* *Nation* was the book that Terry was thinking about at this juncture.

Terry was insistent. 'Why not? They could sit on top of the Tower of Art, with a telescope.'

'No, even then, they wouldn't be in a position to see Great A'Tuin.'

'Yes, they would,' said Terry. 'It's the tallest building on the Disc!'

'But it still wouldn't be tall enough,' I said. 'It simply doesn't work.'

In order to make my point, I grabbed a plate with the remainder of my lunch on it, balanced it on my fingertips and held it up between us.

'OK, so my hand is the turtle, the plate is the Disc, the pea on the plate is the tower. There is no way that anyone standing on that pea is going to be in a position to see my hand under the plate.'

Terry's arms wrapped tighter and tighter around himself, normally a fairly reliable indication that he was about to blow. Sure enough . . .

'Look,' he shouted. 'It's my f—— world and I'll do what I f—— want with it.'

There was a silence lasting several seconds, which seemed to absorb the entire pub. And then we both burst out laughing – in part at the sheer excellence of that line as an argument-clincher, and in part at the utter absurdity of everything that had gone on in the previous 20 minutes in the lives of two fully grown adults.

Back at the coalface, when the arguments had died down, and the *right* right answers had been found, or the need for them overridden, the book would go off to Terry's editors – to Philippa Dickinson in the UK, to Jennifer Brehl or Anne Hoppe in the US – who knew Terry well enough to call him as quickly as humanly possible, and preferably the very next day, with a response to the 80,000–100,000 words he had just dropped in their in-trays. There would be more detailed editorial conversations to come, so these first calls were really just to acknowledge that the book had been received and read and, with any luck, enjoyed. From across the room, I would watch Terry on the phone during these calls, and see him listening silently and occasionally saying, 'OK'. Eventually he would hang up, look across from his desk at me and announce, 'We got away with it again.'

And then he would return his attention to the new novel in front of him, already several thousand words or more down the line.

★ ★ ★ ★ ★

In September 2001, when I had been in the job for just under a year, Terry and Lyn went on holiday. Excluding Christmas, it was the first time since I had been in Terry's orbit, including my period at Colin Smythe Limited, that I had known Terry to take so much as a day off, let alone whole weeks.* It felt like an emblematic moment. That summer, Terry had also begun talking about 'dialling it back a bit' – even about retirement. This year with three books in it seemed to have brought him to a saturation point. He told me he was going to take time to think about the future very hard when he was in Australia. 'You won't need to worry,' he told me, dryly. 'I'm told everyone's got a novel in them.'†

He and Lyn flew to Sydney and then on to the Sails in the Desert resort, which is within striking distance of the iconic and sacred Aboriginal site of Uluru, formerly referred to as Ayers Rock. Here, finally, after years of solid endeavour, Terry relaxed and got away from it all. And when he had finished relaxing and getting away from it all, which may have taken him as much as a day, he sat in the shade and worked his way through the page proofs of *The Amazing Maurice*, which had arrived at the Chapel in the week before he flew out. And when he had finished correcting the page proofs, he started work on a novel with the notional title 'Forest of the Mind'.

About halfway through the holiday, on 11 September, terrorists flew planes into the towers of the World Trade Center in New York. It was a bad time to be away from home. I took a phone call from Terry and scrambled to find him and Lyn flights back to England at the earliest opportunity.

....

* On more than one occasion, I took calls from Terry in the afternoon on Boxing Day in which he rather hopefully wondered whether I was 'fed up with all this family shit yet' and therefore, by implication, whether I was free to go over for 'a little light work'.

† I once pressed Terry on this familiar line of thought. 'Do you really think everyone's got a novel in them?' I asked. 'Actually, I believe they do,' he replied. 'Whether they've got a *good* novel in them, though . . .'

The world still felt dizzied and unstable a month and a half later, when Colin rang with the sad and sudden news that Josh Kirby had died. He was just shy of his 73rd birthday.

The first time I went to Josh's studio, near Diss in Norfolk, I had a set of expectations based on the limited amount that I knew about him. I knew that he drove a red Porsche and that he lived in a house called The Old Rectory. I also knew that his art was on the jackets of dozens of best-selling novels, many of them by Terry Pratchett. I could only imagine he lived a life of some luxury.

In fact, the Porsche was an ancient and peeling 927 – an S registration, dating back to 1977 – and the Old Rectory was an early seventeenth-century plastered timber house, extremely nice but ramshackle and possibly still in possession of its original kitchen, with its polished and worn-down flagstone floor. The front door had at least a dozen keyholes because its locks had been replaced so many times. Invariably in the same outfit – jeans, a denim shirt and desert boots – Josh painted, by daylight only, in what had been the butler's pantry. His easel was a pile of old newspapers with the canvas propped on it. Leaning against the walls throughout the house were stacks, some of them three feet deep, of original paintings, because he could never bring himself to part with them, even though people would have paid him thousands of pounds for them. There was a handwritten sign laid across these pictures – 'More posters like these – 50p' – which was intended to deter burglars. Each of those jacket images took Josh between a month and six weeks to complete. According to Josh, he was paid £750 for the hardback and £750 for the paperback. At the point at which he died, this lovely man and brilliantly successful commercial artist, whose work was instantly familiar to millions of readers around the world, wasn't earning enough to put him above the threshold for income tax.

Meanwhile, Terry was in receipt of a request to write a short essay for the brochure of a prestigious tech company. It was the sort of commercial work he would normally have declined, but this pitch had got his attention, and the old mentality of the freelance journalist had kicked in.

'They're offering to pay *£8 per word*!' Terry said, in disbelief. 'I think this may be too good to turn down.'

I agreed with him that it was an extremely generous rate of pay, worth setting aside the time for. But then I thought about it.

'Wait, though. How much are you getting per word for writing this novel?'

'I don't know,' said Terry. 'How much *am* I getting per word?'

It wasn't a difficult sum – yet, the mentality of the novelist being somehow separate from the mentality of the freelance journalist, it wasn't a sum that it had ever occurred to Terry to do, up to now. This, then, was the maths: Terry was receiving £1 million for each novel. Each novel was 100,000 words long. Therefore he was being paid as a novelist at the rate of £10 per word.

The offer of the company brochure, at £8 per word, was politely declined on the grounds that it would not have been an economical use of Terry's time.

15

CONVENIENT SOFTWARE, HORIZONTAL WEALTH AND BOWLS OF CHILLI WITH A GUITARIST

The successor to Josh Kirby as 'Discworld's artist of choice', to use Terry's phrase, was Paul Kidby. In 1993, Paul had been given a copy of *The Colour of Magic* as a 29th birthday present by his sister Linda and, like me, had first met Terry at a book signing in the nineties – in Bath, in Paul's case, where, in a classic longshot, he handed Terry an envelope of his drawings in the hope that Terry might see something in them. Terry had liked them so much, he rang Paul up at the end of his tour to talk about them, and that conversation led to Terry asking Paul to do the pictures for *The Pratchett Portfolio*, an illustrated compendium of Discworld characters which came out in 1996.

Terry then asked Paul to work on the illustrated novella *The Last Hero*. A good lump of my first full year in the Chapel, 2001, was spent collaborating with Paul to put that book together, chasing hard against the publisher's tight deadline. Again, the spirit of the cottage industry prevailed. It wouldn't have occurred to us to buy specialist software for this project – regarded as a monumental expense in those days, even for the office of a millionaire novelist. But, with fortuitous timing, some-one from Adobe had met Terry at a book signing in the US in 2000, and had gifted him a CD which turned out to contain a version of Photoshop 6. That was our tool for producing the book, but first we had to get Paul's acrylic-on-board paintings onto the computer we were using – the second-highest-spec laptop that I could afford at the time.* For me, this involved a 100-mile dash to Dunstable, where we had uncovered a specialist with the right hardware to scan the images at the resolution we needed and transfer them to CD for us. Doing our own scanning, with the technology we had available to us, would not have been an option. I would do the Dunstable run several times per week, as Paul's pictures were finished. Then I would drive the 100 miles back to Salisbury, load the images onto the laptop, and Paul and I would go at them with our conveniently acquired software in all its grinding slowness.

Everything seemed to take forever, and whole afternoons went by while we waited for the computer to catch up with the requests we were making of it. I remember one particularly long wait for the screen to reveal our attempt to add a 'motion blur' effect to a picture of Cohen the Barbarian slicing a dice in half with his sword – only for us to take one look at the image, say, 'God, that's awful,' and start again. The ponderousness was compounded by Paul's absolute perfectionism as an artist.† Somehow, though, we got through in time, and produced a book we were all very happy with – never reprinted thereafter without all its original illustrations, in accordance with Terry's strict wishes.

Eleven years previously, in even more primitive circumstances, Terry had published *Eric*, with Josh Kirby doing the illustrating, and, as we put *The Last Hero* together, I seriously thought that this might be the future for Terry, a new rhythm for his work: two full-length novels, maybe, followed by an illustrated novella, and then back to the novels, and so on. So much for that: we never did another one. 'Short stories cost me blood,' Terry always used to say. They ate up ideas and they absorbed

. . . .

* It was a point of principle with me, as it was with Terry, never to buy the highest-spec model of anything, but always the second-highest-spec, which was invariably going to be better value.

† This might be a good moment to mention that the logo for Paul's business was two snails facing each other or, to use the correct armorial term, two snails rampant.

energy. And it seems he felt that way about novellas, too. He preferred to devote himself to the longer run.

The first Discworld novel for which Paul was commissioned to provide the jacket was 'Forest of the Mind'. Paul, by this stage, was one of the recipients of Terry's famous phone calls, in which plots would be discussed, perhaps rather more for Terry's benefit than for the benefit of the person at the other end of the line, and Terry had also sent him some early pages. One day Paul arrived at the Chapel and anxiously unwrapped a painting of Sam Vimes, eyepatch in place, chewing on a cigar, at the head of the members of the City Watch, rendered as a pastiche of Rembrandt's *Militia Company of District II Under the Command of Captain Frans Banninck Cocq*, a painting also known, for short, as *The Night Watch*. In the space where Rembrandt painted himself, peering through from the rear of the group, Paul had painted a portrait of Josh. It was stunning – the perfect tribute. And, on top of that, it automatically yielded a far better title for the novel. Thanks to Paul, 'Forest of the Mind' became *Night Watch*.

Was *Night Watch* Terry's masterpiece? I would say so, and many other readers would, too. There was a strong sense of Terry reaching for something as he wrote that novel – literally. It was in his body language – the way he walked up and down the Chapel as he dictated passages to me, reaching out to make grabbing and squeezing motions with his hands, almost as if he were hunting in the air for the words he needed and pulling them down. Large passages of the story seemed to arrive overnight, with Terry storming into the office in the morning, bursting to download what had come to him while he lay awake. There was a darkness to the book that was new to him. It was a beautiful darkness, and some very sparkly humour still studded it, but it was a darkness none the less. It took the character of Sam Vimes and his mind into far more cynical, reflective and world-weary places than any previous novel in which he had appeared. And perhaps most significantly, there was a daunting anxiety, threading through its pages, about what would happen to a largely jovial scepticism regarding the after-life – the condition of being 'amiably uncertain', as the book puts it – when it was actually confronted by the inevitable end. It was written six years before Terry's diagnosis, but I have often wondered since whether it was the first intimation that Terry knew something, somewhere was up. Whether that's accurate or not, there is no other book, in my opinion, in which Sam Vimes contains quite so much of Terry, and there is no other book quite like it in the Discworld series.

Wherever we ultimately decide *Night Watch* sits in the Pratchett catalogue, it can definitely go down in history as the only Discworld novel to feature a character named after Ken Follett. The Welsh novelist bought himself an appearance in a future Terry Pratchett book for £2,200 at a charity auction, the beneficiaries of his largesse being the Medical Foundation for the Care of the Victims of Torture.* Follett told Terry he wanted to be a giant. Terry simply looked at him and said, 'How do you want to die?' – which was, as Follett conceded, 'a little disconcerting'. 'Pratchett to Kill Off Follett?' asked the headline above the *Guardian*'s diary story. In fact, Terry spared him. The character of Dr Follett, the former Master of the Assassins' Guild, is given the attribute of being an accomplished lute player – Follett is a bass guitarist and a balalaika player – and, in another allusion to reality, is handed a magnificent head of hair. 'Is that his own?' Madam Meserole asks her nephew. The nephew does not reply.†

In 2003, when the BBC published the results of 'The Big Read', a survey of the public to find the nation's Top 200 novels, *Night Watch* made it onto the list at number 73. It was one of five Terry Pratchett novels in the top 100. There was only one other author who had as many titles in the top half of the list: a certain Charles Dickens.‡ Now, one needs to

....

* An instance, this, of the noble literary tradition known as 'Tuckerization', after Wilson Tucker, the American sci-fi writer, who was fond of borrowing the names of his friends for minor characters in his stories.

† This was a teasing joke in the novel and there is no intended implication, either there or here, that Ken Follett's magnificent head of hair is anything other than rooted in his scalp. Incidentally, in *Night Watch*, the characters of Roberta Meserole, Ned Coates, Dr John Lawn and Andy Hancock are also Tuckerizations. We'll have something to say about the butler Willikins and the Nac Mac Feegle known as Rob Anybody later on.

‡ The other four Pratchetts in the Top 100 were: *Mort*, *Guards! Guards!*, *Good Omens* and *The Colour of Magic*. Dickens's big five were *Great Expectations*, *David Copperfield*, *A Christmas Carol*, *A Tale of Two Cities* and *Bleak House*. It was the best of lists, it was the worst of lists . . .

acknowledge the tendency of such polls to skew towards things that are recent and therefore fresh in the memory. *Night Watch* had only been out a few months, and Dickens, let's face it, hadn't published anything for ages. Maybe what Terry once said of J. R. R. Tolkien would also apply here: 'He's more dead than I am.'* A general theory of recentness would also help us explain why *Captain Corelli's Mandolin* (1995) so emphatically beat *War and Peace* (1859).

Whatever, for those of us tuning in from the Salisbury area on the night, the real mystery was: what happened to Terry's *other* two books? In advance of the list's announcement, the BBC had sent a crew down to the Chapel to film an interview with Terry for the programme. And during that interview, it was made clear to us that seven of his books were in the Top 100 – a figure which would have poked him above even the mighty Dickens in the overall popularity rankings.

Yet somewhere between Terry being interviewed and the programme being broadcast, the quota of Pratchetts in the Top 100 had dipped by two titles to five, making it a dead heat with Dickens, and all references to Terry having seven books in the top half of the list were expunged from the filmed interview.

Most odd. The Case of the Missing Pratchetts. What, nearly two decades on, are we to make of this peculiar discrepancy? Was it the product of a genuine miscalculation, later quietly and humbly amended? Or was it – as the conspiracy theorists would no doubt have it – the result of a little nudging and noodling behind the scenes? Was the will of the people seen to prevail, or did the idea of Terry trumping Charles Dickens prove just too strong to stomach for the UK's national broadcaster, when push came to shove?

. . . .

* Terry said this to Alan Titchmarsh during a live appearance in 1995 on the BBC daytime show *Pebble Mill*. 'Comparisons are odious,' Titchmarsh had begun – very often a decent indication that someone is about to make an odious comparison. And sure enough . . . 'Do you get a bit upset when people say, Are you a bit like Tolkien, then?' Terry's 'more dead' response perhaps didn't entirely tally with the overall daytime telly vibe, although Terry's choice of outfit for this occasion – a cream-coloured bomber jacket and matching slacks – certainly rang all the right bells in that respect.

I know how Terry chose to see it, and his interpretation of events can probably be summarized in one word: fix!

But over these potentially awkward considerations, let us draw time's kindly veil. Instead, let us merely observe that, when it came to number of titles in the full Top 200, Terry had a total of fifteen, and nobody was touching him on that score, not even Dickens (seven). And certainly not Tolkien (two). And not Tolstoy, either (also two).*

★ ★ ★ ★ ★

Terry used to describe himself as 'horizontally wealthy'. By this, he meant to suggest that money hadn't really changed him. He was still the same person, and interested in the same things, and all money did was enable him to afford more of those things. So, for example, before he had money, he had always bought books. Now he bought more books – and made a library for them, with beautiful shelves, in what had been the double garage and gardener's equipment store adjacent to his office in the Chapel.†

And before he had money, he had always bought greenhouses. Now he simply bought a bigger greenhouse. True, it was enormous, constructed on the manor's former tennis court, thrumming with plants, because absolutely anything seemed to grow there, and was referred to by Terry as 'Jurassic Park'. But it was still a greenhouse.

And before he had money, he had always travelled on aeroplanes, at least when he needed to. But now he travelled on aeroplanes in the first-class cabin, typically saying, before he turned left at the door, 'Neil Gaiman would be turning right at this point.'

. . . .

* His nearest rival was Jacqueline Wilson with fourteen, followed by Roald Dahl, nine. Thomas Hardy? Jane Austen? George Orwell? Way back on four, three and two, respectively. Maybe write a few more books next time, eh, guys? And write them more recently.

† Bursting to use his new library shelves, Terry had brought up wheelbarrow-loads of books from the house and filled them completely before the carpenter could return to apply the final coat of varnish.

And before he had money – long, *long* before he had money – he had always looked at the stars. But now he looked at them, not through that cheap telescope given to him by his parents that made the moon over Forty Green look wobbly, but through a crisply precise Meade LX 200 with a built-in GPS tracker, located in a purpose-built, lime-rendered brick and flint, copper-domed observatory, positioned across the grass from the Chapel.* Terry wanted to call it the Patrick Moore Memorial Observatory, and Patrick Moore, who was still very much alive at this point, had granted him permission to do so, also providing a signature which we were going to get etched in copper for the name plate. Alas, it was one of those things that was left undone when Terry died.

The reason Terry had been in a position to seek Patrick Moore's permission was that he had become a frequent visitor to Farthings, Moore's house in Selsey, West Sussex, for Saturday night star-gazing sessions. Terry adored Moore – because of his appearances on *The Sky at Night*, obviously, but also because he was a polymath and a vast repository of wisdom, yet at the same time someone who didn't seem to take himself even remotely seriously. Terry didn't really do deference around famous people. I was once in a position, in Dublin, to introduce him to Bono from U2, explaining, as I did so, that Bono owned the hotel we were standing in. 'Ah, good,' Terry said to Bono. 'Can you get me a milkshake?' Which he did. But Patrick Moore was different. The first time we visited him at Farthings, Terry went and knelt beside his wheelchair, utterly in thrall to him.†

. . . .

* Even before the observatory was built, Terry and I had conducted star-gazing sessions from the gardens, taking advantage of the blackness of the rural Wiltshire sky, and we once erected a system of aerials on the grass which enabled us to listen to Jupiter. Why? Because we wanted to. Jupiter, by the way, sounds like waves on a beach, with short bursts of what Terry described as 'popcorn popping'.

† 'Farthings!' I suddenly announced, as we passed the house sign, driving out on our way home that night. 'Far things. Geddit?' I record this here proudly as the only time in our relationship that Terry had cause to be piqued that he hadn't worked out something before I did.

Farthings was a stockbroker Tudor-type house with a narrow gravel drive and a glass lean-to on the front, which visitors were obliged to use as 'an airlock' on the way in to stop Patrick's beloved cats from getting out. Inside was his full-size xylophone and every piece of wall space was wedged with artefacts. Patrick, who was in his 80s, lived alone with carers at this time, but at those star-gazing sessions, Terry and I would find ourselves in the company of a motley and cheerful party of astronomy obsessives, including Dirk Maggs, the extrovert and goatee-sporting audio producer, Jon Culshaw, the impressionist – who happily did Patrick for Patrick, to Patrick's delight – and Brian May, the astrophysicist who was also known in some quarters of the public as the guitarist from Queen. Bowls of 'astronomer's chilli' would be served in the kitchen and then we would stand out in the garden and watch the Perseid meteor showers or whatever other light-show the heavens had to offer us at the time. I remember the surreal sensation of being at Patrick Moore's stove, stirring the chilli pot, while on either side of me, Terry and Brian May discussed their relative states of fandom, eventually concluding that you either do it for nothing, or you do it for all the money in the world. Terry then quoted something he had heard David Jason say about acting: 'You are your own currency, and you must spend it wisely.' 'I think you'll find that was Ronnie Barker,' said Brian May, correcting him. Terry would eventually pay for Patrick Moore to get his coat of arms drawn up and officially confirmed – something which knights of the realm are entitled to do, but at their own expense of £5,000. Terry presented the coat of arms to Patrick on a special edition of *The Sky at Night*.

The spirit of Patrick informed the building of Terry's observatory – although, in fact, what he constructed, while much smaller, was far more swish than Patrick's own observatory, which was essentially a concrete slab with a corrugated metal roof that clanked merrily as it rotated. Terry's copper dome opened quietly and smoothly and – most important – automatically, and the oak stairs and the red leather banister, in combination with the copper, the wood and the flint, lent the place something of a Jules Verne feel. A 100-watt light-bulb was used to warm the scope, and it switched automatically to red as we crossed the dark lawn towards the building, so as not to spoil our night-ready vision on entry. At one stage we wired up a special CCTV system to the telescope's viewfinder so that images from the scope could be viewed from the computer screens in the Chapel without stepping out to the observatory. But that was a step too far. 'That's not the point,' Terry said. 'You need to feel the chill around your breeches.'

So, the well-fitted observatory, the giant greenhouse, the copious books on their custom-made library shelves . . . these things were without question the indulgences of a wealthy man – but only a 'horizontally wealthy' man. They were ways in which Terry merely became more Terry than ever. Meanwhile, the aspirational appetites of the 'vertically wealthy' – those in whom money awoke a wholly new interest in boats, mansions in the south of France and gold-plated helicopters – had no hold on his imagination. Terry was, in many ways, given his circumstances, a startlingly non-acquisitive person. He kept it horizontal.

And that's why he never owned a collector's-item, gull-winged DeLorean DMC-12, like the one in the movie *Back to the Future* – although he almost did. We both loved that film, and talked about it a lot. In one of our discussions, we decided that the gull-wing doors on the car which transports Marty McFly into the past were the most iconic car doors ever produced. Never mind the DeLorean's fancy stainless steel body: without those doors, it would have disappeared into history like it does in the film, but not come back. With them, however . . . well, this was a *proper* car.

'Right,' said Terry. 'I'll have one.'

I was delighted. I thought this was exactly the kind of car that Terry Pratchett ought to have around the place. I thought it would bring him a lot of pleasure and amusement. Dr Emmett Brown's car! I started researching – this was before the internet was the internet – and found the number of a dealer in Belfast. He had a left-hand-drive model on his books, for sale right there and then, and Terry, whose enthusiasm was running high, was keen to jump straight on it. Given how this all panned out, I wish I had gone with him on it. But I suggested to him that we should hold out for a right-hand-drive so that he could more safely use it while attempting to pass tractors on Wiltshire's country roads, and he reluctantly saw the wisdom of that. The Belfast dealer told us to leave it with him.

Some eight weeks passed, with no word, and I began to wonder whether our request had dropped off the radar. Then suddenly one day Terry handed me the phone.

'He's got one!'

It was the perfect specimen – an extremely rare right-hand-drive, registered in Northern Ireland: low mileage, new engine mounts, fully serviced, entirely drivable, and available to us for the snip price, surely, of £12,000. I sent a cheque for the deposit and then began organizing the car's journey from Belfast, across the water and down to Salisbury. The plan was that I would fly up to Scotland, pick up the DeLorean as it came off the ferry at Stranraer, and then drive it south. No hardship for me, this. I was already sourcing a McFly-style gilet and Nike trainers for the job.

A week before D-Day, Terry got cold feet about the whole idea and changed his mind. 'The thing is,' he said, 'the DeLorean of your dreams will never break down, never need servicing, never need garaging. Whereas this one . . .'

In truth, Terry could have afforded to employ someone to look after a Pratchett garage containing a whole fleet of DeLorean DMC-12s, and any number of other collectable cars with histories in the movies, had he so desired.* But no. He preferred to own the DeLorean in his mind. I called the dealer to cancel the delivery, writing off the deposit in the process. Within the hour, the fast-running tide of Terry's thoughts had carried the idea of buying the *Back to the Future* car so far out to sea that it was no longer visible.

But Terry did need *some* kind of car and, in the real world, as a token of his better upholstered status, he eventually traded his old blue Ford Mondeo for a Jaguar – the traditional marque of the self-made

. . . .

* I speak as someone currently in possession of all the vehicles – motorbikes, children's bikes, Reliant Robins, the 1936 Bentley Derby – used in the second season of Amazon Prime's production of *Good Omens*.

working-class man. At the same time, it was a Jaguar S-Type, the least extravagant Jaguar money could buy. Indeed, the S-Type was the closest a person could get to owning a Ford while actually owning a Jaguar. Its 'walnut' trim and its 'chrome' grille were both plastic, to keep its price down. Its colour was officially described by the manufacturer, and also by Terry, as 'gold', but, somehow significantly, whenever I entered the car's details to pay the London Congestion Charge, it came back as 'beige'.

Going to buy that car was nothing that Terry had any inclination to turn into an occasion. He simply went off to the dealership one Sunday morning in his gardening clothes and returned an hour or so later having ordered a new car. He told me on the Monday that he had been enormously impressed by a story the dealer had told him about a recent purchaser of this model – an Irish farmer who had used it to carry a sick sheep to the vet. I thought that tale might have been best filed under 'TGTC', and that the dealer had maybe seen Terry coming, but Terry seemed utterly swung by it. Apart from its potential as an ad hoc animal ambulance, the feature of the Jaguar which most seemed to impress him was the digital compass on the dashboard. He made me get in the car with him outside the Chapel and reversed it around to show me how the compass on the display rotated when the car moved. His mind was blown – and, to be honest, so was mine. Then we went back indoors and, after that, the car was barely ever mentioned. He bought it and drove it while at the same time practically forgetting about it.

He could be enormously cautious with his money, but he could be impulsively generous, too. When he gave money away, which was often, it tended to be for projects that were on his doorstep. He paid for floodlights at the local sports centre – a generous move for a man who had never found any use for a sports centre in his entire life. He put money into relocating the village shop – and took part in the opening ceremony which saw him cheerfully cutting a long chain of sausages with his sword for the benefit of the local press photographers. He helped build the new village school and a few years later bought solar panels for its roof. Further afield, he gave £35,000 to build a hedgehog hospital near Aylesbury and found money for an Owl Parliament at

Birdworld in Farnham. He put £10,000 towards the reward for information leading to the arrest of swan killers near Burnham-on-Sea.* He donated *a lot* of money to the Orangutan Foundation, for whom he had a particular soft spot, and, after diagnosis, he gave $1 million to the Alzheimer's Research Trust and £120,000 to the Dignity in Dying charity to help them push a bill through Parliament. Around the time of the publication of *Going Postal* in 2004, he donated to the Bath Postal Museum and restored their perforating machine. But what Terry preferred to do, in so far as possible, was to keep things local and to give money to 'projects that I can walk to'.

Which is why we found ourselves, one summer's evening, heading down the lane to the next village along from the manor to attend a meeting about a church roof. £75,000 was needed for repairs and Terry was keen to be involved. This was not the first time that he had considered donating money to the restoration of a local church, even though a church, local or otherwise, was somewhere he would never be found on a Sunday, any more than he would be found up at the sports centre. A committed atheist, Terry used to say, 'I have never in my adult life entered a church with religion aforethought.' He nevertheless believed that looking after churches was, as he put it, 'every Englishman's right and duty'. Accordingly, two other churches in the area had benefited from his largesse, and now, evidently, this one, which was tiny and dated from the thirteenth century, would, too. Terry, it was clear, could take care of these repairs on his own. £75,000 was a sum he could easily afford.

There was a lovely summer light as we walked to the church that evening, so I took out the little point-and-shoot digital camera that I carried with me and got Terry to pose against a fence post in his leather jacket and hat, with a green field rising up behind him. Months later, that improvised portrait was used on book jackets as Terry's author

. . . .

* This donation started a relationship between Terry Pratchett and Burnham-on-Sea which culminated magnificently in 2011 with Terry switching on the town's Christmas lights. Such are the giddy heights of fame.

photo, but I can only see in his expression what I know was on his lips at that point, which was: 'Get on with it, take the goddam picture, and let's go.'

The meeting was packed – which in a church this small meant there were at least 20 people there. Watching from the back of the nave, I felt a swell of pride as Terry stood up to play the role of local angel and fix this problem at a stroke.

'Now, I'm a very rich man,' Terry began, 'and I can easily write a cheque for the sum needed.'

A sense of euphoria ballooned in the room.

'But I'm not going to do that,' said Terry.

The balloon of euphoria burst, and my swell of pride along with it.

'This has to be a village effort,' he went on. 'I'm ready to play my part, but I think other people should be involved, too.'*

It seemed that solving problems with one twist of the sonic screwdriver – or, in this case, one wave of the magic chequebook – no more appealed to Terry in real life than it did in fiction. And fair enough. In this case, he knew that he wasn't, by any means, the only rich person in the room. If he gave the impression he would happily pay for everything, where would the requests stop? And there were *a lot* of requests. Terry had the rich man's constant wariness of being taken for a ride: as he used to put it, 'I may be a multi-millionaire, but I know that £10 is too much to pay for a cup of tea.' And, in the case of this church roof donation, wasn't there even something a bit patronizing about grandly taking on the whole burden at a moment like that? Certainly Terry balked at doing so. There was a Pratchett family motto, passed down through the years, and recalled by Rhianna: 'Dad always told me: "Pratchetts help those who help themselves."'†

---

* The village is the smallest in Wiltshire, with two houses – an eighteenth-century manor farm house and a seventeenth-century former rectory – and ten cottages. The adult population is nineteen, just one more than was recorded in the Domesday Book in 1086.

† Terry often referred to this philosophy as 'Brewster's Millions', by which he meant you have to spend to receive. That's a misunderstanding of the plot of *Brewster's Millions*, but never mind.

In the case of that church roof, the policy worked, too. Other funders immediately stood up and a village fete was duly held, with Terry as the guest of honour, that got everybody in the area involved, which was what Terry wanted. The money was raised and Terry gave his share.

I was never sure that he entirely got his head around the quantity of money that he had. Or maybe he enjoyed giving the appearance of not doing so. Certainly the scale of it sometimes seemed to defeat his understanding. One time, it was pointed out to Terry that it would be an expedient use of the capital he had accrued to set a lump sum aside and create a charitable foundation, which could be used to fund worthwhile projects. Terry seemed very taken with this idea. Kevin O'Malley from Coutts Bank, who managed Terry's finances, came down to the Chapel as part of a small delegation for a meeting and, over tea and Lyn's lemon drizzle cake, they thoroughly set out how such an arrangement could be made to work, what the inheritance tax implications were, and so on.

Terry nodded approvingly throughout this presentation, and when they had finished speaking, he said, 'I'm up for this, and I'm thinking – twenty-five grand?'

There was an awkward silence from the bankers and a little bit of shuffling and throat-clearing on their side of the table. It turned out that the sum they had in mind for getting the ball rolling on a scheme such as this was a little bit more than that – to be exact, £1,975,000 more: an initial investment of £2 million.

The meeting broke up shortly afterwards.

Terry did come around eventually, though. After a bit more thought and a few more chats and a slightly longer consideration of the bigger picture, he invested the recommended sum. So, out of those discussions came the Discworld Foundation, which to this day continues to fund projects in children's literacy and wildlife and other areas that Terry cared about.

But complex schemes of tax avoidance from which Terry might have stood to benefit personally were of no interest to him whatsoever. Terry was a scrupulous payer of income tax, and took pride in being so. One day, amid news of an impending rise in the top band of income tax, he rang Mark Boomla, his accountant.

'I've been reading a lot of stuff in the papers about hot-shot account-ants sparing their clients from paying their tax bills,' Terry said. 'As my hot-shot accountant, what's your advice to me in this matter?'

At the other end of the line, Mark Boomla, recognizing a test, said, 'As your hot-shot accountant, Terry, my advice to you is: pay your tax.'

And Terry did.

★ ★ ★ ★ ★

Instead of a DeLorean DMC-12, Terry bought a shepherd's hut. It didn't have gull-wing doors and it probably wouldn't have been of much use to Marty McFly, but it was, in its own way, capable of time travel. It was where Terry had the idea for the character of Tiffany Aching, and it was where he began talking about the story which, in 2003, became *The Wee Free Men*.

As he drove out of the valley where he lived, Terry would see the abandoned chassis of old shepherds' huts out on the hills – bits of wood-and-metal wreckage, nineteenth-century relics, some with wheels still intact, overgrown by grass. He was fascinated by them. He had the idea of bringing one back to life from scrap and putting it on his land.

It was important to Terry that the hut's DNA was from the valley – that it had an original chassis and wheels, and old corrugated iron for its sides. Terry found somebody locally who could put all this together for him. The first time Terry saw the finished object he was as close to hop-ping from one foot to the other with glee as I had ever seen him.

'Look!' he told me. 'It even has gravity-defying paintwork on it!' I had no idea what he meant. Then I looked closer. Some of the re-appropriated corrugated iron panels had been nailed on upside down and the paint-drips on them appeared to be heading upwards.

Terry initially placed the hut in the field beyond the barnyard – a field he called Crots, though I have no idea why. Then he moved it down to the field below, next to the river. One day when he was there with Rhianna, they became aware of a distressed sheep in another field. 'It was like the hut had given us shepherd's sight,' said Rhianna. The pair of them then spent a while dragging a terrified and soaking wet ewe from a bramble patch where it had got stuck. During the lambing season it was out of bounds to us; Pat, the shepherdess who looked after the sheep on Terry's land, would stay in it, returning it to the use for which it was intended. But on other days, when the weather was good, we would take lunch down there: sandwiches, Scotch eggs and the all-important pickles. Terry would sit inside and I would sit on the steps, taking dictation on an old Sony laptop. There was no wi-fi, no phone, no possibility of disturbance. Those hours always felt magnetic, somehow – on top of the chalk, with the hawthorn and the willow nearby, the sound of the river running, the occasional bright blue flash of a kingfisher, flickering into your peripheral vision like a Mac Nac Feegle, whom Terry made blue for this reason. Those times were as close as I came to being on Discworld with him. For Terry, the words would flow like the water of the river Ebble when he was down in that hut. 'The first draft is just you telling yourself the story,' he would often say, and it was in the hut that most of the first draft of *The Wee Free Men* happened, Terry telling himself the story of Tiffany Aching, who finds herself on the Chalk in Granny Aching's 'old wheeled shepherding hut on the hills', where 'green downlands roll under the hot midsummer sun', and where the ground is allegedly 'too soft to grow a witch on'. As Terry wrote:

> Tiffany didn't make noise when she was up at the hut. She just loved being there. She watched the buzzards and listened to the noise of the silence.
> There wasn't enough time for silence. There wasn't enough time for listening.

We had no idea how true that last sentence would turn out to be.

16

GONKS, SMASH HITS AND
POLYSTYRENE TEETH

Through the 1990s and on into the 2000s, there was one thing that Terry Pratchett continuously had in common with the pop group Take That: neither of them had managed to break America.

Take That had attempted it with two different line-ups and an array of radio- and stadium-ready international smash hits; Terry had attempted it with 33 internationally bestselling Discworld novels. But the results had been the same. Top 10-wise, neither Terry nor Gary Barlow seemed to be exactly what the United States felt it wanted during this period.

Did this needle Gary Barlow as much as it needled Terry? I'm not in a position to say. But I can certainly report that it needled Terry – and sharply. The prestige around having a title on the *New York Times* bestseller list, and thereby being able to label yourself a *New York Times* Bestselling Author, inevitably called out to him, as it calls out to nearly all writers – and ever more loudly the more time went by and it didn't happen. The year 2000 was essentially year 29 and counting for this particular ambition. Although Terry's very first foreign rights sale had been American – with St Martin's Press for *The Dark Side of the Sun* – things in the States after that had merely spluttered and fizzled and failed to ignite. Terry seemed to be capable of having hits almost anywhere else in the world but there. To quote a stark headline from

2000 in the *Chicago Tribune*: 'Discworld enchants the globe, but not the US.'

What was the explanation for this protracted failure to enchant the world's biggest marketplace for books? There was the argument, which Terry heard a lot, that the books, and in particular the humour of the books, was, in the end, just too 'British' for American ears. But being 'British' didn't seem to have stopped these same books getting into the ears of Estonians, Spaniards, Australians, Russians, Finns, Bulgarians . . .

Then there was the theory that Terry's books had simply been the repeat victims of bungled publishing – and that was a theory to which Terry seemed much more inclined to subscribe. Not that America was the worst offender, in Terry's view, when it came to the fudged publication of Pratchett books. That prize had long since been awarded in the form of a lifetime honour to Germany, where Heyne Verlag used the same jacket illustration on both *Mort* and *Wyrd Sisters*, touted *The Light Fantastic* as the first book in the Discworld series because they hadn't initially owned the rights to *The Colour of Magic*, and then eventually put out a twin edition of *The Colour of Magic* and *Sourcery* with a cover illustration by Josh Kirby depicting a flying Morris Minor, a cluster of British 'Bobbies' running around waving their truncheons, and a gasometer. Bearing absolutely no relation to events depicted in either *The Colour of Magic* or *Sourcery*, this in many ways quintessentially 'British' image might better have graced the front of Robert Rankin's comic novel *The Sprouts of Wrath* – and there was a good reason for that: it had already done so, having originally been commissioned for exactly that job.

But, as if asking Terry to jacket-share with another author wasn't withering enough, Heyne then utterly outdid themselves by producing an edition of *Pyramids*, in 1991, with an advert for instant soup inserted into the body of the text. This staggeringly brazen act of product placement would have been bad even if the marketing department had had the tact to consult Terry about exactly where, in his work, he would ideally like a soup advert to go, assuming he would like a soup advert to go anywhere at all. But they didn't ask him. Terry was understandably indignant. He hadn't taken up writing because he wanted to be an instant soup salesman. He moved his German publishing elsewhere as soon as he could.*

There was nothing to match these farcical shortcomings in Terry's American publishing history, but the release of Discworld into the US market had still been unhelpfully ragged in places. Up to the time of *Witches Abroad*, the twelfth novel in the series, the only hardback versions appeared via the niche outlet of Nelson Doubleday's Science Fiction Book Club, which was a direct invitation to people not interested in specialist science fiction to ignore them. After that the books were taken on by HarperPrism, the fantasy and science fiction arm of HarperCollins, who merrily released them out of sequence. American readers came upon *Soul Music* before they came upon *Lords and Ladies* or *Men at Arms*, *Feet of Clay* before they came upon *Interesting Times* or *Maskerade*, and *Jingo* before they came upon *Hogfather*. Did it make a big difference? Possibly not, but, understandably, it massively irritated Terry. In 1999, when HarperCollins acquired Avon Books and its sci-fi imprint Eos, and brought the lists together, Terry found himself part of another internal shake-around. None of which would have mattered very much if he had felt he was getting anywhere. On the contrary, he felt as though he was being shunted about aimlessly and making no headway at all.

It was with a view to untangling some of these knots and focusing a few minds that, during the 1990s, Terry decided to get a US agent – someone who could be more forcefully present on Terry's behalf on that side of the Atlantic than Colin Smythe was in a position to be. For a writer like Terry, with Terry's ambitions, there really was only one contender. Ralph Vicinanza had assembled the world's most formidable client-list of bestselling sci-fi, fantasy and horror writers, including Stephen King, Robert Heinlein, Frank Herbert, Peter Straub and George R. R. Martin. Shaven-headed and bright-eyed, Ralph had

* Product placement! In a book! The mind totally reels. The brand of soup was Maggi. When it comes to filling that lunch-shaped hole in your day, there's no finer soup than Maggi – and no easier soup, either. Maggi – for all your instant soup needs.

about him something of the clean-cut presence of a retired Apollo astronaut, although he seemed to live in considerably more style than retired astronauts tended to. Seen in an advertising campaign for Capgemini, the Paris-based information technology company – other subjects included David Bowie's record producer Tony Visconti, and the Australian tennis coach Darren Cahill – Ralph was depicted doing some sketching in the fountained driveway of what appeared to be an enormous, turreted Walt Disney castle but was, in fact, his home on Long Island. That same campaign styled him as 'literary advisor to Stephen King', which is a definite upgrade on 'agent'. Arriving at Claridge's in London, where he always stayed, Ralph would instantly over-tip the concierge in order to guarantee himself the very smoothest service during his visit. But for all this expensive elegance, he was also a terrier-like negotiator who could be explosively forthright when the situation demanded it.

Terry was at once suspicious of Ralph, which was Terry's default position with regard to newcomers in his by now well-established team of associates, and, at the same time, quietly impressed by him. Terry was also, without question, thrilled to contemplate what it said about Terry that he was on Ralph's books. Ralph now began to apply his considerable influence to the shaping of Terry's American future.

Someone who turned out to be even more central to Terry's fortunes arrived in his life soon after this, in 1999. An editor at HarperCollins in New York, Jennifer Brehl had developed a reputation around the office as, by her own definition, 'that girl they gave the weird books to'. In due course, the weird books she was given started including Terry's – except that Jennifer realized very quickly that these books weren't weird, in fact, and that, actually, 'weird' was one of a small cluster of unhelpfully constricting labels that had become attached to Terry's writing that it would be useful to find a way to shake off, others being 'sci-fi' and 'comic'. 'The work was far broader than that,' Jennifer said. 'It went beyond the funny factory. This was social satire. It had things to say about the ways in which people behaved and interrelated. You could get so much more out of it than just "yuks".'

Terry and Jennifer didn't meet for a while. At first, they talked only on the phone, Jennifer gamely weathering, and staying positive in the face of, Terry's ingrained scepticism about the likely extent of her powers to change anything with regard to his US fortunes. Eventually, on a trip to England, Jennifer visited the Chapel – and, just through the door and not even divested of her coat, was instantly unsettled when Terry clicked his fingers loudly, right under my nose, and barked, 'Rob – fetch the tea!'* She soon recovered her poise, though, and over the next couple of hours, she and Terry bonded firmly, to the point where Terry came to feel she had been in his life for ever. He recognized in Jennifer what he had been lucky to find in Philippa Dickinson, his UK editor: not just someone in close sympathy with him, but someone capable of achieving absolute clarity about the work he presented her with – what it contained, what it lacked and what it needed to make it the best it could be. Any foreign author on the list of a major US publisher is going to need a four-star general inside the building, someone to rally the troops across the departments and start creating some momentum. Terry finally had one.

With the US publication of *The Fifth Elephant*, in April 2000, things went up a gear. No longer unhelpfully cloistered in sci-fi corner, Terry was now getting published on the mainstream HarperCollins fiction list. It enabled a kind of reset. Five thousand special editions of that novel went out, with a sixteen-page appendix introducing 'The World of Terry Pratchett' – a beginner's guide to a series then 24 volumes old. It would still take time, but slowly, from there, the momentum built with each book, the reviews increasing, the interest accumulating, the readership growing – on through *The Truth*, *Thief of Time*, *Night Watch*, *Going Postal*, *Monstrous Regiment*, until, finally, the big breakthrough came.

It was the autumn of 2005, and HarperCollins had just published *Thud!*. In those days, the coming weekend's *New York Times* list would

. . . .

* Terry did not normally click his fingers under my nose to demand tea. Indeed, this was the first and only time, in my experience, that he did so. Quite simply, it wasn't his style. But, clearly, if he thought it would get the attention of a new editor, visiting for the first time from New York, he was prepared to give it a go for effect.

be released in advance to publishing houses on a Wednesday evening, any time between 5.00 and 7.00 p.m. This particular Wednesday, Jennifer Brehl had left the office for her two-hour commute home before the list arrived. Therefore the news reached her Blackberry when, inconveniently, she was on board a packed Metro-North train heading out of Grand Central Station. Worse than that, Jennifer realized she was seated in a 'quiet' carriage, where mobile phone use was frowned upon. But what the hell, this really couldn't wait. She called the Chapel.

'Oh, my god – it's hit, it's hit! Terry! Terry! You're a *New York Times* bestseller!'

There were disapproving 'shush' noises from her fellow commuters in the carriage, but Jennifer chose to ignore them.

At his desk in England, a bemused Terry said, 'Jennifer . . . are you *crying*? You're crying! Jennifer – it's just a list.'

'Terry!' Jennifer exclaimed, both to her author and to the rest of her carriage. 'We worked so hard on this and *you are going to allow me to cry*!'

At this point, the shushing took on a more aggressive note.

'I've got to go,' she said, crossly, and hung up.

The only question now was whether Terry could repeat that success in America with a children's book. Very early in their relationship, Terry had told Jennifer, 'Me and children's publishing in the US don't get on.' They were talking about a book that would be coming out in the UK that year, but in which the US had thus far expressed no interest. It was probably too late at this stage, but Jennifer made sure a copy of the manuscript reached the desk of the reader in HarperCollins's children's division, Nancy Geller. One day soon after that, Geller said to her boss, Robert Warren, 'I really liked that Terry Pratchett manuscript.' This turned out to be a highly serendipitous moment, 1) because Nancy Geller had a voice penetrating enough to carry beyond the confines of her office and 2) because the editor to whom her voice happened to carry on this occasion was Anne Hoppe. Anne had read and enjoyed enough Discworld novels to find that her ears were highly attuned to the mention of Terry Pratchett's name. She got up from her desk and went straight into Nancy Geller's office. 'I have an almost – but not quite – shameful memory of literally taking the manuscript out of her hands,' said Anne. 'I have been forever grateful that I didn't give her a paper cut in my enthusiasm. It was a close thing.'

Two US editors had cast the book aside before Anne took it up and ran off with it, and also before she then came back and convinced the rest of her department that they ought to publish it. The book was *The Amazing Maurice and his Educated Rodents*.* By the time a deal was done with Ralph Vicinanza, just two months remained for Anne to turn the book around and get it printed in order to publish simultaneously with the UK. She quickly commissioned a jacket design and sent it over for Terry to look at.

'Terry told me that the only thing he liked about it was the fact that it was rectangular,' said Anne. 'I thanked him for his gracious endorsement of the shape of the book.'

Thus did Anne, who describes herself as 'healthily terrified' of Terry in the early days of their partnership, commence a working relationship with Terry which quickly saw her become the third key editorial figure in his life. That, of course, as Philippa Dickinson and Jennifer Brehl also discovered, meant confrontations, conversations where social nicety disappeared off in the direction of the window, and sustained periods of all-out antler-locking. When Anne sent Terry a detailed set of notes, running to several pages, in response to his first draft of *Dodger*, Terry phoned her up and said, 'What you're really trying to say here, Anne, is, "Write a better book."' Then he put the phone down. But of course, in a calmer moment, he then went over the points she had made, and he *did* write a better book, which, as ever, was what it was about.

Maurice, despite the haste surrounding its publication, made it onto American year-end lists in 2001 and received prize nominations. There was more time to build something for *The Wee Free Men* in 2003 and for *A Hat Full of Sky* a year later, and more time still for building the book beyond that. In 2006, Anne found herself writing Terry an email

. . . .

* It was, of course, retitled for American audiences – at least to the extent that, where it was always 'The Amazing *Morris* and his Educated Rodents' in the UK, in the US it became 'The Amazing *Moreece* and his Educated Rodents'. Such distinctions matter.

which began, 'Dear *New York Times* Bestselling Author of *Wintersmith*'. Five years after that, Terry would be such an established figure in US children's books that the American Library Association would be honouring him with a career award for Contributions to Young Adult Literature.

So now he really had made it. He was a *New York Times* bestselling author in both his chosen categories, and he had two committed and fully switched-on editors – and their teams on both sides of that divide – who would ensure that he stayed there with each book he published for the rest of his working life.

There was only one hurdle left to leap: Hollywood.

Which proved a little more difficult.

★ ★ ★ ★ ★

In 2003, a year after the smash-hit movie of *Harry Potter and the Chamber of Secrets*, and two years after the smash-hit movie of *Harry Potter and the Philosopher's Stone*, and one and two years, respectively, after the first two smash-hit movies in Peter Jackson's *Lord of the Rings* trilogy, Terry recorded a Q&A interview for HarperCollins, his publisher in the US. It contained the following exchange:

> Q: *With fantasy now perceived as being big box office, what is it that keeps Discworld off the screen?*
> TERRY: *Er . . . me, mostly.*

This was unquestionably true. Time and again during the career of Terry Pratchett, Hollywood came calling for Discworld, with big blockbusting plans for big-budget adaptations scripted by high-end writers and directed by premier-league directors and peopled with big-hitting actors. And time and again those plans fizzled away to nothing. The major reason for that?

Er . . . him, mostly.

He found it impossible to let go. And in a creative endeavour built on teamwork and requiring extensive amounts of willing delegation and compromise, that was always going to be a problem. This was the man, remember, who had insisted on supervising every tiny detail on the Discworld figurine line. He had held this business so close to himself for so long – and had been so successful while he did so – that the idea of surrendering it to the workings of a giant industry, where the decision-chain at any one point could contain dozens of people, none of whom were Terry . . . well, this cut against the grain of everything in which he believed.

And the way he expressed it, he had no reason to compromise. 'What exactly would be in it for me?' Terry said, in that 2003 interview. 'Money? I've got money. Fame? I doubt it. Rincewind or Vimes or Granny Weatherwax in bendable plastic? Does the world need this?'

In truth, though, there *would* have been something in it for Terry – and, not far below the surface, he knew this. There would have been the immense satisfaction of seeing his work turned into a successful movie, something he strongly and increasingly yearned for, and a yearning which was only fed by the sight of people thronging the cinemas for the Potter and Tolkien films, in what was clearly a gold-rush period for fantasy on the big screen. Terry was a film fan – and a fan of popular films most of all. When in Phoenix, Arizona, for the 2009 US Discworld Convention, we took time out to visit Tombstone so Terry could indulge his interest in Wyatt Earp and reawaken his youthful memories of Burt Lancaster and Kirk Douglas in *Gunfight at the OK Corral*. When in New Zealand, we made a trip to the Hobbiton Movie Set and did the tour – having recently paused, as we climbed out of the car in fifties-flavoured Matamata, to burst simultaneously into a few bars of 'Mr Sandman', in honour of Marty McFly on his arrival in 1950s Hill Valley.* Terry was by no means a natural tourist. I once puzzled him, during some downtime on a US signing trip, by setting off to see the South Rim of the Grand Canyon. 'Why?' Terry said. 'It's just a hole in

....

* On the Hobbiton set, we were, I don't mind admitting, quite giddy to pass through the cutting, as seen at the beginning of *The Fellowship*. They were readying it to shoot *The Hobbit*. Terry and I agreed that we had been on a lot of film sets, but this was not the same. It had a magic to it. It was *real*.

the ground.' But film-related pilgrimages – as long as it was the right film – would bring him out.

Nevertheless, here he was, in 2003, at the age of 55, with nearly 40 books published and not one solitary movie based on his creation under his belt. The production company Film4 had recently told Terry that Discworld was 'too cerebral and genteel' to make movies from, which had irritated him immensely. Someone else had told him that a movie of *Equal Rites* would 'end up looking like a parody of Harry Potter' – and that had irritated him most immensely of all. 'I tried to come up with an answer to that,' Terry said, 'but the top of my head kept unscrewing.' He was already in the habit of sounding jaundiced by the whole business – no longer even disappointed or infuriated by the myriad ways the movie industry contrived to frustrate him, but simply resigned to its exasperations, and immune to them, even. 'After you've been around for a while,' Terry said, 'you learn that most movie deals mean – what's that lovely term? Oh, yes: diddly squat. Lots of people offer deals, but few of them seem to have the capability to get a movie made. They just want to own the rights – lots of rights. Well, to hell with that.'

Yet every time he boldly cast it off, the whole ghastly business somehow reeled him back in again. Even that 2003 interview for HarperCollins, with its clear declarations of contempt and dismissal, contained the following evidence of a little glimmer of hope in his heart. 'The Dreamworks movie of my *Truckers* trilogy does seem to be moving now,' Terry said.

Suckered again. Terry's encounters with Hollywood and bendable plastic were really only just beginning.

Dreamworks Animation had acquired the rights to the Nome trilogy in 2001 for just under $1 million. Their idea was to make Terry's three children's books, *Truckers*, *Diggers* and *Wings*, into one animated feature, notionally called 'Truckers', under the direction of Andrew Adamson. In order to convince Terry that they were the right home for this work, Dreamworks invited him on a tour around their studios in California. I didn't go with him on that trip, to my lasting regret, but I know that while he was there he was shown a rough cut of Adamson's latest film and left with a stuffed goody bag whose contents included a plush toy of some kind of green ogre holding an onion. Terry hadn't thought much of the film he had seen, but a lot of people would eventually disagree with him. By the time the 'Truckers' deal was struck, *Shrek* had been released and was on its way to grossing $484 million, and 'Pratchett Gets the Shrek Treatment' was the BBC News headline.

'There are few authors whose work lends itself to animation as well as Terry Pratchett's,' said Jeffrey Katzenberg, the CEO, co-founder and 'K' of Dreamworks SKG*, at the announcement of the film. Terry himself was quoted as saying, 'I liked *Chicken Run* and *Galaxy Quest* and you've got to be impressed when someone from Dreamworks phones up from Hollywood one night and turns up for lunch in Wiltshire the very next day.'† Adamson spoke excitingly of his hope that 'every time people walking out of the theatre see something out of the corner of their eye, they will think it is one of the characters from the movie.' Alas, Terry had lasting cause to rue the green ogre with the raw onion in that goody bag. The major, Oscar-winning success of *Shrek* meant Adamson was suddenly busier than he might have been. He went on to make *Shrek 2* and then got drawn down into Narnia for *The Lion, the Witch and the Wardrobe*. 'Truckers' and those characters that were going to haunt you outside the cinema were no longer on his horizon, and Terry took to dryly remarking that maybe the film would get made 'just as soon as they've finished *Shrek 27*'.

Years then passed – getting on for seven of them – in which nothing happened, which turns out to be a regular feature of this process, and is one of the things that drove Terry utterly nuts about it, long passages in which nothing happens being the natural enemy of the fantasy novelist. Eventually, though, in 2008, word reached us that the British director Danny Boyle had been attached to Dreamworks' 'Truckers' – only to

---

* The 'S' is Steven Spielberg and the 'G' is David Geffen.

† TGTC – although, for the record, I don't recall anyone from Dreamworks Animation coming for lunch in Wiltshire, either the morning after a phone call or at any other time during this saga. But it's a good line and would no doubt have caused a moment of subdued reflection for a few of Terry's fellow authors, which was possibly the point of it.

become detached from it again when the global banking crisis struck in the autumn of that year, and the film once again got stashed on a high shelf. A year after that, in 2009, Simon Beaufoy, the writer of *Slumdog Millionaire*, was signed up to work on the script. But we never saw anything from that appointment and, a year after that, in 2010, the job passed on to John Orloff, who had written the children's fantasy animation *Legends of the Guardians*. At the same time, the proposed director of the film now became an Englishman, Anand Tucker. Was this the point at which the project might finally come alive and cameras might finally start rolling? The flames did seem to be under it again – so much so that, in 2011, I accompanied Terry and Colin Smythe to a meeting at the Four Seasons in Piccadilly, London, with Tucker and Jeffrey Katzenberg.

Tea and scones were served on the well-starched linen. I suppose in some ways we were marking a decade of collaboration between Dreamworks Animation Studios and Terry Pratchett, though, given that at this point not a solitary frame had been animated, nobody was quite phrasing it like that. Katzenberg, who was warm and friendly and extremely approachable for a studio head, was in London for the premieres of *Shrek: The Musical* and *Kung Fu Panda 2* and I remember being distracted by the fact that on another table in the restaurant was Jack Black, who had flown in for the second of those events. Nevertheless, I was fully focused when Katzenberg delivered Terry an eye-opening lesson in how far along projects could get and still not be made. Our understanding was that Dreamworks had now spent a gobsmacking sum on their various thus far fruitless attempts to generate a movie from the Nome trilogy. And, although that was slightly terrifying to contemplate, there was also something reassuring about it: Dreamworks were in so deep, surely, that the movie would *have* to be made.

Not necessarily. Katzenberg told Terry that Dreamworks had, in the past, spent $18 million developing a project which they had then thrown away.

'Why would you *do* that?' Terry asked.

'So that we don't lose *another* eighteen million dollars,' Katzenberg replied dryly.

Nevertheless, the message was, 'We're going to see this through.'

Anand Tucker was full of brilliant ideas for the story, and, within the now standard framework of Terry's belief that none of this actually meant anything, Terry very much warmed to him. We left that meeting and drove back to Salisbury feeling sure that the project was, at the very least, moving again. Or, at least, *I* felt that. Terry had already started thinking about something else.

And he was right to do so. Once more, nothing happened. Another two years went by. Eventually, in 2013, Dreamworks acquired the rights to the Troll Dolls toy line – those little plastic elfin figures with a shock of upswept, neon-coloured hair, frequently found dangling from schoolbags and known in the UK as 'gonk trolls'. Plans were then put in place for a synergy in which 'Truckers' was filmed, but with the parts of the Nomes played by Trolls. Bingo! Instant merchandising! Dreamworks drew up some roughs for us to look at of Nomes that were, in fact, Russ Berrie Trolls. Another meeting took place. Terry flicked through these images on the iPad that was passed across the table to him, with a visibly sinking heart. It seemed he would now be putting words in the mouths of a pre-existing plastic toy line and the very worst of his fears about what happened to novelists when they got involved with Hollywood was about to be realized. The deal was off.*

Neil Gaiman has the following wise words to say about proposed film adaptations of his books: that only when he's in the front row of the cinema with his popcorn in his hand and the lights are going down will he allow himself to believe that the film is actually going to be made. By contrast, Neil will confirm that Terry took an even less romantic view: there was only one time to believe that a film of your book was going to be made, and that was never.

As far as Terry was concerned, the end of these discussions, and of all negotiations with the film world, was preordained: it was disappointment. The best way to pre-empt that disappointment was to get right

....

* Dreamworks went on to make *Trolls*, which came out after Terry died, in 2016, and in which the parts of the Trolls were played by Trolls – a happier fit, I guess, though I couldn't bring myself to watch. I would have found it, as we now say, 'triggering'. The film yielded a sequel in 2020. I avoided that, too.

out ahead of it and proceed throughout the negotiations in the full expect-
ation of nothing at all. As Terry said, in words which now have an
unbearably poignant resonance, 'Hollywood is full to the brim with
people who have the ability to say no, and only about one person who can
say yes. You could die waiting for Hollywood.'

The benefit of this attitude from Terry's point of view, of course, was
the mostly relaxed manner that it enabled him to take into meetings
about such projects, and also, less comfortably for the rest of us, the ease
with which he spoke his mind during them. And that in turn would
account for the little falling-out he had with Sam Raimi over Tiffany
Aching.

In January 2006, a deal was announced with Sony Pictures for *The
Wee Free Men*, the first Tiffany Aching adventure. The director was going
to be Sam Raimi, just as soon as he had finished working on the third
film in the Spiderman trilogy. I suspect that even Terry allowed himself
to feel quietly excited about that. Meanwhile, the screenwriter appointed
to the movie was Pamela Pettler, who had worked extensively in US
television and had written the screenplay for Tim Burton's *Corpse Bride*,
a film which Terry liked. In due course, Pamela flew in from America,
apparently by private jet to Bristol Airport, which impressed us enormously. Arriving in the Chapel, she immediately hit it off with Terry,
browsing the bookshelves, pulling volumes down from them which she
had read and talking enthusiastically about them. She also picked up off
the shelf, and enthused about, the figurine of the Pictsie Rob Anybody,
from the Chalk Hill Clan, which Paul Kidby had recently sculpted for
Terry's birthday. All of this chimed with Terry very directly. Pamela
stayed for the day and at one point she and Terry went out for a walk
across the chalk, talking about the local geology, which she was interested in, and discussing the character of Tiffany Aching. Pamela was
clearly entirely sympathetic with the book and understood completely
where Terry was coming from. The meeting couldn't have gone better.
In a sure sign of her acceptance into the fold, that evening Terry took
Pamela, along with Lyn and myself, to the Castleman restaurant in Chettle, probably his favourite restaurant in the world, mostly on account of
its Mediterranean fish stew and honeycomb ice cream. There, wine was

poured and further conversations about books ensued, and eventually, inevitably, honeycomb ice cream was ordered. It was a thoroughly enjoyable evening, and the perfect way to launch a new working relationship. The next day, Pamela flew back to LA to start writing.

Six months later, a draft script for 'The Wee Free Men' was couriered over from Sam Raimi's office in Los Angeles. We couldn't wait to see what had become of Terry's book when all the signs were so promising. Thus far, none of the slated US studio film adaptations had yielded an actual script that you could hit the desk with. Here, at last, was a visible stride forward for Discworld's advance on the world's cinemas: bound paper. The moment seemed to demand that some fuss be made. Lyn had acquired for the Chapel a huge brass lectern that had once belonged to a church, and this had become Terry's and my default podium for major readings of finished passages from the books or drafts of speeches. I dragged this monumental piece of furniture out into the middle of the Chapel floor, straining many important ligaments as I did so, plonked the script down on it with a satisfying 'thwap', and prepared to give Terry, sitting at his desk, the benefit of my one-man read-through.

I need to concede, at this point, that there are definitely better readers-aloud of scripts out there than me. And there are definitely better readers-aloud of scripts featuring nine-year-old witches and fearsome Pictsie warriors with Scottish accents. Likelihood would strongly suggest that my attempt at Glaswegian began somewhere around north Wales, veered wildly across England in the direction of Leeds, stopped for refreshments in Bristol and, pausing only to make a short detour to southern India, came to rest eventually in my home county of Norfolk.

No matter. Terry listened intently and silently as I read. It was only when I had reached page 21 of the 80 or so that he reacted.

'Stop!' he shouted. 'Stop! Just stop!'

I stopped. Terry was boiling with rage. Was it my Scottish accent? No. It was . . . absolutely everything. The feisty, self-determining, intellectually quick Tiffany Aching, had become, in Terry's words, 'a kind of Disney princess', wishing on a star for her dream to come true.

'Get Sam Raimi on the phone,' said Terry.

I pointed out that it was around 4.00 a.m. in Los Angeles and Raimi's office would be closed. We would have to wait a few hours before Terry could say whatever it was he wanted to say. It was clearly agony for Terry to be thwarted in this way by the inconsiderate existence of the time difference. He was straining at the leash. There followed a very long afternoon, with Terry trying to work but finding it next to impossible and constantly lifting his head to ask, 'What time is it now? Is it still too early?'

Finally we were deep enough into the UK day to make a call to LA seem viable.

'I have Terry Pratchett,' I said. 'Could we speak to Sam Raimi?'

I heard the call get rerouted and signalled to Terry to pick up his phone. There was a further, quite long delay while hold music played and while Terry sat and, presumably, made the final adjustments to the oration that had been forming in his head for the last five or so spectacularly frustrating hours.

Eventually, the person who had answered the phone came back on the line.

'I'm so sorry,' they said. 'Sam's not available right now. Is it about the screenplay?'

Here, finally, was the window for Terry's long-gestated response.

'Yes,' said Terry. 'It's shit.'

'O . . . K . . .' said the voice at the other end, hesitantly. 'Well . . . thank you for that.'

Terry put the phone down. I sat, stunned and not a little horrified, on the other side of the room. The idea that this first draft was just Phase One in a process of back-and-forth in which accommodations would be made until a common ground was found from which all parties were happy to operate . . . well, clearly, Terry hadn't really seen it that way. He now went on silently with his work.

No further phone calls ensued – literally, not one – and no Sam Raimi version of *The Wee Free Men* ensued, either.

★ ★ ★ ★ ★

When a properly realized, live-action version of Discworld did eventually make it onto the world's screens, it came not via Hollywood and cinemas, but televisions and Sky TV. Which, incidentally, Terry didn't have.* But a relationship took root in that perhaps unlikely ground which, over the course of six years, grew into three well-received Pratchett adaptations and finally provided Terry with some lastingly satisfying experiences in this vexed area of his working life.

Sometime in 2005, a man wearing white snakeskin shoes turned up at the Discworld Emporium in Wincanton during one of the fan events that Bernard and Isobel Pearson would regularly host there. The place thronged with Discworld aficionados in costumes, but those white snakeskin shoes still stood out. The man standing in them was Rod Brown, from a production company called The Mob, and he had come bearing a proposition for Terry. None of us, at this point, had heard of The Mob, nor knew much about anything they had been involved with. Prominent on Rod's personal CV was his work on *Dream Team*, a long-running Sky TV drama about a fictional football club, and a programme so wild in its plot developments that it made the Roy of the Rovers comic look like a Ken Burns documentary.† Terry, obviously, hadn't seen that show, having neither access to Sky nor any interest whatsoever in football. Rod had also worked on the ITV gameshow *Strike It Lucky*, hosted by Michael Barrymore and, for a while, the fifth most-watched television programme on British television, and that, quite possibly, Terry *had* seen or, at least, more or less knew about. But none of this really mattered. The fact was, Rod had taken the trouble to come to Wincanton, so Terry listened to him. An impromptu meeting was convened round the table in Bernard and Isobel's dining room, to the rear of the shop, and Rod made his pitch: a lavishly costumed,

* Terry was definitely of a generation for whom paying anything for television other than the annual licence fee smacked of utter and outright barbarism.

† The episode of *Dream Team* in which Harchester United's goalkeeper, rendered desperate by gambling debts, took the entire team hostage and was shot dead by a SWAT unit in the ensuing conflagration, was arguably a high point in this regard.

expensively upholstered adaptation of *Hogfather*, presented as a two-part, three-hour festive event, for a channel, Sky, that was eager to launch itself as a major investor in original drama. Rod, in his presentation, was engaging, amusing and convincing. Terry, to coin the phrase he was so fond of, liked the cut of his jib. At the end of the meeting – as much to Rod's surprise, I sensed, as to anyone else's – Terry stood up and said, 'Right. All you've got to do now is make it.'

There was a second meeting, a couple of weeks later, this time at the Chapel. Rod now brought along his production business partner, Ian Sharples, and Vadim Jean, an English director in a black Range Rover and a puffa jacket, who had made the British comedy film *Leon the Pig Farmer*. They talked about *Hogfather* and what they were hoping to achieve with it, how they could envisage turning the tale of Discworld's annual winter festival into one of those family staples that get shown at Christmas on cycle, every year. A few casting ideas were thrown around. David Jason was mentioned for the role of Albert, Death's manservant. Jason was TV royalty as far as Terry was concerned. And what about asking Ian Richardson to supply the voice of Death? Terry had no problem with that, either. Again, all felt good. If these Mob guys weren't especially slick and corporate, then, in Terry's eyes, that only increased their appeal. Terry also undeniably liked the extent to which they seemed ready to involve him. Plus they seemed to have opened all the necessary doors at Sky. Hollywood could go hang for a while. This project felt like it might actually come to something.

Now, did Rod, Vadim and Ian subtly imply to Terry that The Mob were further down the line with Sky than perhaps they were? And were The Mob subtly implying to Sky, at other meetings at which we weren't present, that they were further down the line with Terry Pratchett than perhaps was the case? In other words, was there some playing-off going on here? Let's put it this way: several times in the ensuing weeks and months, Terry would phone Rod and ask for a progress report on this new project, and it would appear that there was, as yet, no progress of any kind that could be reported. Long after the event, it often occurred to Terry and me that we had royally celebrated a three-way deal between Terry Pratchett, The Mob and Sky TV that was, in fact, still some way short of being finally bolted together at the point at which we royally celebrated it.

No matter. All credit to The Mob, however they did it: they pulled it off. Eventually Sky gave the green light to the project, which would be called *Terry Pratchett's Hogfather*, and assigned it a £6 million budget, which probably wouldn't have covered the catering on a Hollywood production, but which made it the biggest filmed drama Sky had ever been involved with. The script, of course, which Vadim Jean wrote, could have proved a major stumbling block for Terry. But, as it happened, even that came together quickly and smoothly. Perhaps not coincidentally, Vadim's screenplay had the enormous virtue, from Terry's point of view, of using large passages of unaltered dialogue from the book.

This, perhaps, is how you soften the case-hardened, sceptical author who suspects that no adaptation will ever find the true spirit of his work. Alternatively, you can try offering them a cameo role. For *Hogfather*, Terry gladly accepted the part – not in the book – of a toymaker, delivering the single line, 'Would you like me to wrap that up for you, sir?' This major moment in film and television history was shot, wasting no time, on the first day of principal photography, on location in Woburn Walk, just north of Tavistock Square in London, when the artificial snow lay thickly on the ground. Immersing himself in the role with an attention to detail that would have shamed Robert de Niro, Terry gave his character the name Joshua Isme, even though he was anonymous in the script, and called his shop, equally unnecessarily, Toys Is Me. He spent an hour getting costumed – including with a pair of shoes which, he gleefully noted, were 'like something Baldrick would have thrown away' – and would gladly have spent several more if there hadn't been a tight shooting schedule to meet.

Terry had an open invitation to visit filming, and he took the producers up on it, spending every minute that he could there, drinking it all in, watching carefully, occasionally chipping in. One day, they were filming a shot in which Banjo Cropper, played by Stephen Marcus, had to blow his nose loudly. After the call of 'cut', Terry said, 'I think it would be much better if someone blew his nose for him.' Vadim tried it that way, and it stayed in the film, one of a handful of ways in which Terry earned his eventual end-credit: 'Mucked About With by Terry Pratchett.'

The whole process made him extremely happy. So *this* was what it could be like. The adaptation of his books for the screen had become a tiresome abstraction, associated with vapid meetings, unhinged schemes, and promises filled with air that burst as soon as you touched them. This, though, was solid; this was happening in front of his eyes. Now he could know the special revelation of seeing his characters brought to life, embodied – a novelty to him even as their creator. As Terry admitted, 'I hear their voices more than I see their faces.' And it wasn't just the actors, it was all aspects of this extraordinary business – a business with which he now realized he could entirely relate, because it was *his* life's work, too: the painstaking pursuit of realism in an entirely fantastical context. Walking onto the set one day, Terry stopped to talk to a scenery painter who was applying a brush to a fake stone wall. 'I'm just snotting it up,' the painter told him. Terry fell on that expression with glee: henceforward 'snotting it up' was used in the Chapel for any act of adding grime or grit, or the weathering that makes things real, to a scene in the prose.*

On Terry's last day on the set, he loaded into the boot of his car a large plastic sack stuffed with polystyrene teeth from the props department – a few little pieces of the film to take away and call his own, and, of course, ideal material for that tricky Discworld Convention prize or charity auction item.

It all came together. Through December 2006, Sky themed up its channel idents to say 'Happy Hogswatch' and pushed the show in trailers and on billboards. That large silver Mercedes bore Terry to the premiere, and the two 90-minute instalments were shown on consecutive nights in the week before Christmas, when it drew an audience of 2.8 million – huge for Sky at the time. It was then repeated on

. . . .

* With regard to that 'snotter-up' and his work, Terry later sighed deeply and said, 'If I'd known jobs like that existed, I'd never have taken up writing.'

Christmas Day and Boxing Day, and, in a fulfilment of The Mob's founding vision, has been shown every Christmas since.

Terry got the chance to repeat this highly gratifying experience in 2007 when The Mob returned to the Chapel with a proposal to shoot *Terry Pratchett's The Colour of Magic* — in fact a conflation of that book with the second in the series, *The Light Fantastic*. Vadim sent over his script and drew a compliment from Terry that was couched in the traditional Pratchettian negative: 'It wasn't the slaughter I'd been anticipating.' But after last time, Terry was more than happy to proceed — although he did strongly object to the casting of Sean Astin as Twoflower the tourist. He knew Astin as Samwise Gamgee in Peter Jackson's *Lord of the Rings* and he couldn't see him as Twoflower at all. Terry told Rod Brown, 'Rod, he's not Twoflower and if you persist in casting him, I will make it clear I disapproved.' But Rod stuck to his guns and cast him anyway. And Terry also stuck to his guns and made it clear he disapproved — and in the most blunt way that he could have done. With the whole cast assembled in the giant boardroom at Pinewood Studios,* ready for the script's first table-read, Terry walked straight up to Sean and, without waiting for the nicety of a formal introduction, said, 'You are not Twoflower.' Less confident actors might have wilted in that moment, but Sean, to his immense credit, laughed it off and got on with the job. As the production came together, and Terry saw how wrong he had been, the two developed an entirely affectionate relationship. By the end of the shoot, Sean was referring to him amiably as 'Uncle Terry'.

David Jason returned, this time to play Rincewind — which, in fact, had been the condition under which he had accepted the role of Albert in *Hogfather*; a Terry Pratchett reader, Jason had always longed to play Rincewind. He and Terry bowed to one another on the first day of shooting at Pinewood, like old familiars reuniting. Terry again made

....

* Our thrill at being present at Pinewood, the home of so much British film comedy, never diminished. History simply surrounded you. Our production office had, in a former life, played the part of the British Consulate in *Carry on Up the Khyber*. We were dizzy with awe.

himself present, and useful, on set, delighting at the actors' various discomforts in the water tank for the ocean scenes, and expanding his own thespian range by appearing as Astrozoologist #2 at the opening and closing of the film.* The two parts went out over Easter weekend in 2008, and although the screening didn't quite attain the 'event' status of the *Hogfather* premiere at Christmas, it was at least felt to have been faithful again to the Discworld spirit.

Then, two years after that, came the third in what we should probably think of as The Mob Trilogy. *Terry Pratchett's Going Postal*, from the 2004 novel, didn't lend itself to large-scale borrowing of the book's original dialogue in the same way that *Hogfather* had. The story needed to be re-crafted and lines changed. That would possibly account to some extent for Terry's blowing hot and cold during this production, to a degree that he hadn't during the other two. Some days it was the best adaptation ever; other days it had nothing going for it at all and he wanted to pull the plug on it in despair. Nevertheless, he once again enjoyed his cameo – this time appearing as a postman, dropping a letter into a deep hole and saying, 'That's a bit of an embuggerance.' He also went home with the bell off the post office desk. It stood in the Chapel from that day forward and was rechristened 'the Ellipsis Bell' – a vital writing tool. Every time we reached an ellipsis in the text ... *Ding!* Whichever of us was nearest would reach out and ring the Ellipsis Bell to remind us that, ideally, unless in extraordinary circumstances, we should permit ourselves the indulgence of an ellipsis a maximum of once per day.

When post-production on *Terry Pratchett's Going Postal* was complete, we got together to watch a rough cut of the finished film at the manor. Much of the shooting had taken place in Hungary, in Terry's

. . . .

* Terry decreed that if he was going to get into costume, I was going to have to do so, too. I make about a dozen fleeting appearances in *The Colour of Magic*, including as 'man who gets thrown out of The Mended Drum with a spear sticking out of his chest'. As a birthday 'treat', I was made to lie in a puddle at the feet of David Jason, again with that spear sticking out of my middle, for an excessively long time. In the finished film, much to my amusement, only the top of the spear is visible.

absence, so it was new to us and we were excited to see how it had come out. Rod Brown turned up with the DVDs in his new jet black Jaguar XJ6, parking it alongside Terry's gold/beige number and immediately making the latter look somewhat wan and understated. He then amused Terry enormously by telling him what the dealer had said to Rod in the showroom: 'There's only two types of people who buy a car like this – High Court judges and getaway drivers. And by the look of you, sir, you're not a High Court judge.' All in good spirits, we then settled down in the living room to watch the first of the two episodes.

I tried to concentrate on the screen but I was too busy watching Terry – watching his arms go across his body and then tighten their hold, and then tighten further. This was not a good sign. He was clearly unhappy with what he was seeing. Extremely unhappy.

At the end of the first half, Terry rocketed up out of his seat and confronted Rod.

'You just don't f—— get it, do you?' he shouted, stiff with anger.

At this point, with impeccable timing, Lyn came through the living room door with a tray of tea and lemon drizzle cake. By doing so, she almost certainly averted a major altercation. It's well known that nobody can seriously exchange blows in the presence of a home-made lemon drizzle cake. It's why you so rarely see fights spilling out of Nan's Pantry on a Sunday afternoon.

During the somewhat stilted tea break that inevitably followed, Rod, who had remained admirably placid throughout, calmly encouraged Terry to stick with it and watch the second episode. Pacified somewhat by lemon drizzle, Terry reluctantly did so. Again, as the film ran, I found my attention was about 20 per cent on the screen, and 80 per cent on Terry. He still didn't look happy. His arms were still wrapped tightly around himself, his chin low.

At the end, after the credits had rolled, the room fell silent. I was worried. Surely only the entry of Lyn and another lemon drizzle cake could save us now, although that seemed unlikely.

Terry got up slowly, walked over to Rod . . . and hugged him.

'If I'd known the ending could be like that,' Terry said, warmly, 'I'd have written a better book.'

To understand in full the remarkable dimensions of this moment, one needs to know that Terry was by no means a hugger. Indeed, at the point at which this unprecedented interaction happened, he may well have been among the least tactile people on the planet. I still wince to recall the moment, at one of the Discworld Conventions, when Terry was sitting with some others around a table and an attendee came up behind his chair and casually began to give him a shoulder massage. 'Awkward' does not begin to describe the ensuing seconds as Terry, rendered seemingly numb from scalp to toenails by this moment of overfamiliarity, sat very still and waited for it to end. When people, not least in the world of film and television, made the mistake of going in for a hug with Terry, and I was nearby, Terry would hold up a hand and say, 'Rob does my hugging for me.' Hugging was simply not in Terry's repertoire.

And yet here he was, initiating warm bodily contact with Rod Brown because the adaptation of *Going Postal* was that good. And he was right: it *was* that good.

★ ★ ★ ★ ★

'Do you think I killed Ralph Vicinanza?' Terry asked me, one day in September 2010.

I didn't think so, as it happened. Ralph died in his sleep at home in New York, from, according to the reports, a cerebral aneurysm. That said, during the previous week he had been dealing with Disney over the possibility of a film production of *Mort*, and those dealings had been nothing if not heated. One of the Disney lawyers involved in the negotiations told me later that he was used to being shouted at – and, indeed, was tempted to consider it a routine feature of his job – but that he had never before been *screamed* at.

On that one, I guess we all felt like screaming eventually – everyone on every side, and certainly Terry. The campaign to get *Mort* onto the screen as a Disney animation proved intractable and exhausting and ultimately depressing. And, as ever, it had all seemed so exciting at first . . .

At the Discworld Convention in Birmingham in August 2010, an American called Karen Tenkhoff had introduced herself to me. She said she was from Walt Disney Animation Studios, and that she had John Musker and Ron Clements with her, and would I be able to arrange a meeting for them all with Terry? Terry was actually taking part in a panel at this point, but I ducked around a corner and used my phone to do some hasty Googling, belatedly educating myself in the process. Musker and Clements were the directors behind *The Little Mermaid*, *Aladdin*, *Hercules* – distinguished Disney filmmakers with 25-year histories at the company. Karen said they were in England to do some location scouting. Did animators scout for locations? Apparently so. They had looked around Stratford-upon-Avon, among other places, and had then come on to Birmingham to scout for Terry. I was, naturally, very excited to set up that meeting. John and Ron were sharp, funny and brilliant company – and they wanted to make a Disney animation of *Mort*.

So that was the start of it – and even that seemingly innocent and ad hoc initial get-together caused its own ripple of unhappiness, as practically everything connected with this project seemed to. Ralph Vicinanza didn't think that any such meeting should have happened without him, and said so, which led to a blazing row with Terry in which Terry told him, 'You're the agent, I'm the principal. You don't tell me who I can and can't talk to.' Meanwhile Transworld, Terry's UK publisher, when they got wind of the negotiations, were instinctively worried about what an arrangement with Disney would portend for Terry's books and his brand. 'I'd been conflicted about this,' said Larry Finlay, Transworld's Managing Director. 'I knew it was a deal that could have made Terry a lot of money, but I was also convinced that he would have hated what Disney would have done to his stories and to his characters. I felt in my bones that it was a Faustian bargain, one that Terry would live to regret massively. When I heard that Terry would be getting a mere two per cent on all merchandising rights, including any spin-off books – of which there would be very many – with no creative control residing with him, I was absolutely determined to persuade Terry NOT to sign *Mort* to Disney.'

Larry and his team invited Terry to a meeting in 'the Black Lubyanka' in Ealing, at which they had prepared a table by covering it with heaps of movie tie-ins and spin-offs, most of it low-grade, shiny-covered tat – cheap kids' story books mounded in a huge, sickeningly sugary pile. It was meant to sound an unignorable warning: do you really want *this* for Discworld? Because this is the way it's going if you're not careful. Terry knew what his reaction was intended to be – and he was also determined not to give Transworld the pleasure of eliciting it. He took a lingering look over the quease-inducing pile and announced, brightly, 'Cool!' Point made, though.

The film deal was still up in the air when Ralph died. Colin, Terry and I flew out to New York for the funeral and checked into our hotel the evening before. Something deeply alarming happened that night. Malcolm Edwards, formerly Terry's editor at Gollancz, arrived after us and found Terry wandering the hotel in a state of confusion, convinced that he had missed the funeral. Malcolm helped him back to his room. Since Terry's diagnosis, three years previously, there had been moments of disorientation and vagueness, but nothing like this. I flushed to think what might have happened if Terry had drifted out on his own into the streets of New York. It was one of those end-point moments. From then on, we were going to have to make some major adjustments to the way we did things.

That morning, we got clogged up in terrible traffic leaving Manhattan for New Jersey and arrived late, slipping in at the back when the service had already begun. And then, after paying our respects to Ralph's family and his partner, Terrance Rooney, we headed back into the city to continue the *Mort* negotiations with Disney, in their offices above the New Amsterdam Theatre on Broadway. Our meeting that day was just about the oddest I have ever attended – a meeting at which you actually saw the deal fall apart in front of your eyes. Normally, deals end in the gaps between meetings. Not this one, which melted like butter in a pan while we all sat round the table watching it disappear.

Present were Terry, Colin and myself, with Vince Gerardis there on behalf of Created By, Ralph Vicinanza's production company, and a handful of people representing Disney. It emerged that if Disney deemed the film a success – the definition of which could apparently even encompass the film making a billion-dollar loss – they would be able to exercise a right to all the other Discworld books involving *Mort*'s characters, which is to say anything with the character of Death in it, or, if you will, every Discworld book apart from *The Wee Free Men* and *Snuff*. They could also exercise the right to any future use of those characters. And they would also own the right to the use of all of *Mort*'s settings, including Unseen University and the entire city of Ankh-Morpork – again, both in the past and in the future. In other words, by making this one film, Disney would come, in effect, to own Discworld, both as it stood and as it was still to come. As Colin said, 'We came close to losing the business in that deal.' By the time we got up to leave, the film of *Mort* wasn't happening any more.

That was the low point. We stood on the street feeling thoroughly deflated. 'Do you want to go for dinner,' said Terry, 'or do you want to go home?' That trip was the first time we had shelled out for fully flexible first-class tickets – causing Terry to ask me, at the time of booking, whether I had just quoted him the price of the flight or the price of the whole aircraft. Still, in the circumstances, it proved a good investment. There we were on Broadway, with a whole evening stretching ahead of us, but so dispirited that we didn't even have the appetite to stick around for dinner, let alone for a show. We went out to the airport and caught the next plane home.

Just to depress us still further, we later heard an allegation that Ralph had been arguing that he should receive a 'finder's fee' from Disney for his part in putting them together with Terry. In other words, he had possibly been trying to cut himself a share on both sides of the deal – and that impressed none of us, especially as Disney seemed to have found Terry perfectly easily on their own, during an animators' location scout.

All in all, it was a wake-up call. In the early summer of 2012, Terry and I took a flight to Dublin for an event at Trinity College. On the plane I was reading the in-flight magazine. There was an article in it about Griff Rhys Jones, who had not long since sold Talkback, the production company he founded with Mel Smith in 1981. Rhys Jones talked about how, during their first years of working at the BBC, they had none of the money and none of the control; and how, by founding Talkback, they brought about a situation where they had *all* of the money and *all* of the control. I read passages from the article to Terry. It was by no means the first conversation we had had in this area, but the wisdom of the idea had never been so clear. 'This is what I've been talking to you about,' I said. 'We could do this ourselves, with good legal representation.'

It made so much sense. Instead of getting, as Terry would have put it, 'blown around like a ping pong ball in a hurricane' between other people's production companies, we could determine our own future, be the originators. It wouldn't save us from production hell, because that was just something that was built into film making. But it might save us from production hell *all the time*. And at least, when production hell occurred, it would be our *own* production hell – a production hell of our own devising and one where we defined our own ways out. Which had to be better, didn't it?

Terry didn't have to think about the idea for very long. 'Go and talk to the accountant, then,' he said. 'Make it so.'*

When we arrived at the Westin Hotel, Terry left for his event and I stayed behind and called Mark Boomla, and, there and then, we began to put the groundwork in place for Terry's own development company, Narrativia.

* In Pratchett World, there is no greater demand than a 'make it so'. You don't mess around with a 'make it so'.

17

A SINGLE RAISED EYEBROW,
A CACTUS HAT AND THE
BICYCLE CLIPS OF FLAME

It's the summer of 2007 and Terry has just finished writing *Making Money*, a second tale featuring the reformed conman Moist von Lipwig, who had initially taken the stage in *Going Postal*, a couple of years earlier – and who, incidentally, for 24 hours, was called Moist von Hedwig, until I suddenly remembered the name of a certain owl in the Harry Potter books and persuaded Terry that calling a character Hedwig might be asking for trouble.*

Examining the precarious mix of mathematics and trust that enables the functioning of the Ankh-Morpork mint, *Making Money* will be published that autumn, directly into the aftermath of the run on the UK bank Northern Rock, and into the face of a looming international banking crisis. This will cause *The Times* to suggest, not entirely jokingly, that the book 'should probably be reviewed on the business pages'. In the meantime, I am fresh from the experience of hammering at the keyboard while those extraordinary pages spilled from Terry's imagination,

. . . .

* For a few delightful minutes at the keyboard that morning, I was on a particularly juicy mission: Search & Replace <Hedwig>. Terry had put up a fight, though. His Hedwig was going to be an allusion to the nineties rock musical *Hedwig and the Angry Inch*. He was pretty miffed that he'd been beaten to it.

struggling to keep up while Terry, in full flow, was bringing an angry mob with pitchforks through the streets to the Royal Bank of Ankh-Morpork, intent on retribution from the troubled Vice Chairman – namely, Moist – who, finally resigning himself to his fate, threw open the bank's door to find . . . well, at that exact moment, nobody in the world, including the author, knew what lay on the other side of that door that could spare Moist a dire end. And nobody *would* know until Terry had paced the floor and thought about it for a short while, and then emphatically dictated the resolution, producing another of those moments when I was actually out of my seat and punching the air. At such times, I was pretty sure that I had the most enjoyable job in the world with the possible exception of Lewis Hamilton's.*

But now *Making Money* has been written and revised and edited and sent on its way, and we are in what Terry always refers to as 'the honeymoon period' – a phase lasting maybe a week, or sometimes, at a stretch, a fortnight, during which, with the latest order packed up and shipped out the door, the pressure is off in the factory and the machinery can be left to cool down for a bit, while preparations for the next consignment proceed quietly. The 'honeymoon period', which does not preclude writing some part of the next novel, is as close as Terry generally gets to taking a holiday.

Except it turns out that *Making Money* isn't quite as finished as we thought it was. A call comes through from Jennifer Brehl in the Harper-Collins office in New York. 'Can we tie up the story of Cosmo Lavish at the end?' she wonders. 'It's flapping in the wind a bit.' Cosmo Lavish, in the company of his exceptionally high-maintenance beard, has spent a lot of the novel trying a) to steal and assume the identity of Lord Vetinari, and b) to pull off the gesture of suavely raising a solitary eyebrow, which seemed to work for Roger Moore in the Bond films but looks more like a nervous derangement when Lavish attempts it. And it's true

. . . .

* Non-spoiler alert. There were very deliberately no spoilers in that paragraph, for the preservation of your future reading pleasure in the event that you have not read *Making Money*. Round about the time that I was typing up the mob scene at the bank, Lewis Hamilton was finishing on the podium in his first race in Formula 1.

that Lavish, his beard and his eyebrow, have been allowed to slip out of sight at the climax of the story. Nobody else involved in the editing of the book has had a problem with it, but now that Jennifer has mentioned it . . . well, yes, it's unignorable. Lavish is, indeed, flapping in the wind.

Terry is irritated. Someone has pointed out that there is something wrong with the book,[*] and that never makes him happy. Plus he has now officially switched into honeymoon mode and sent his mind off in other directions, and suddenly someone is telling him he's got to reroute his thoughts – and quickly, because the book is about to be typeset. Jennifer is going to need this additional material within 24 hours.

So, does Terry simply sit down and crack on with the task? No. It is clear that Terry would rather think about almost anything else right now. A tree has fallen across the stream, he tells me. So we should probably go out and look at that. Which we do. On the way back, Terry makes an unannounced detour to the greenhouse and attends to the tortoises for a while. Eventually we get back to the Chapel. He sits down at his desk, which is fitted nowadays with an impressive array of six flat LCD screens, in two banks of three, attached to a custom-made bracket that we have commissioned, at surprisingly little expense, from a small company down the road.[†]

('Why do you have six computer screens?' people inevitably ask when confronted by this bristling display of hardware. 'Because I don't have room for eight,' Terry replies. And also because they give the Chapel a slight Mission Control vibe. And also because they look really cool with the green 'raining cipher code' screensaver from *The Matrix* flowing down all six of them at the same time.)

Terry fiddles about at his desk for a while, and then goes up to the gaming computer on the Chapel's mezzanine.[‡] There, he loads up *The*

---

[*] Bravely.

[†] QuadVision of Wimborne Minster – for all your multiple LCD screen bracketing needs.

[‡] The most powerful computer in the office was set aside for gaming, not for writing. Terry made no apologies for that.

Elder Scrolls IV: Oblivion, the year-old computer game which is currently his chosen – as he puts it – 'bubble gum for the brain'. He has been playing this game, as he has always played computer games, immersively and tirelessly and with an absolute refusal to entertain the possibility of shortcuts. I have pointed out to him that I could mod the game for him, if he wants: go into its code and tweak a few things to make it easier for him to get through the trickier bits – maybe increase his access to gold or weapons or put all his health stats to the top. And he has looked at me as if I have proposed throwing bricks through a cathedral window. Terry has no interest in skipping over the surface of this game; on the contrary, he is interested in dwelling as deeply inside the world of *Oblivion* as it will allow him to go. However, he *is* interested in the kind of creative modding that the properly keen players go in for and share among themselves. Indeed, he will quite soon reach out to a modder known only as Emma, who has created and voiced a character for *Oblivion* named Vilja. Vilja is designed to act as a companion on a player's journey through the game. Terry, via email, will thank Emma for creating Vilja, and will suggest to her things that Vilja might be interested in saying or doing. And Emma, who has no real idea at first whether her new online correspondent is actually *the* Terry Pratchett, or just *a* Terry Pratchett, will happily collaborate with him to expand Vilja's character and functionality. When Terry begins to have problems with his memory, having a guide in the world of the game will only become more valuable to him.*

So, on this particular morning, with, as it turns out, a book still to finish, Terry settles down and plays some *Oblivion*. And when he has finished playing some *Oblivion*, he plays some more *Oblivion*. No words

....

* Terry's desire to encounter goblins in the world of *Oblivion* without being required to kill them led, after an exchange of emails, to the creation by Emma of a 'goblin peace amulet', which allowed Terry to move among the goblins and into their dwellings without hatred in his heart. Terry was thinking about this kind of thing a lot in 2010, during the writing of *Snuff*. Terry also promoted the introduction of a 'give a gift' function, so that he could reward Vilja for exceptional service, such as saving his character's life. Players of *The Elder Scrolls IV* – and Pratchett completists – may care to know that much of Vilja's Thieves' Guild dialogue was written by Terry.

get written. He finally saves and quits the game. He then looks at the news on one of his other screens and does some admin on one of his *other* screens. He still writes no words. At lunchtime, we go down to the pub and eat, as ever, bubble and squeak, and Terry talks about a number of things, but about the business, not about the narrative. Returning to the Chapel, he finally sits down at his screen like a man who means business – but then promptly decrees an apparently necessary trip by car to the garden centre to buy something for the greenhouse. That mission absorbs most of the afternoon. When we get back, Terry returns to his desk, reawakens his computer . . . and plays *Oblivion* again.

Still no words.

When it starts to get dark, Terry decides to get up and go out to the observatory for a while. I give up and go home for dinner. I then go back to the Chapel so that, finally, we can get this book finished, as surely we must. When I walk in, Terry is still playing *Oblivion*, and there are still no words. Just before midnight, with no sign of any writing forthcoming, I cave in and tell him I'm going home to bed.

Next morning, I arrive at the Chapel, now properly anxious about the chances of getting these words done in the very few hours that remain before New York wakes up and starts demanding them. Terry isn't around, but there is a Post-it note on my screen. 'Tidy this up and get it across to Jennifer.'

I open the Word file, and there they are: the three pages beginning 'Whiteness, coolness, the smell of starch . . .' exactly as they now appear, entirely unaltered, in the Epilogue at the end of *Making Money*. At some point after midnight, following a day of gaming and dealing with tortoises and fiddling about in the greenhouse and stomping around at the garden centre, Terry has laid down this concluding passage, perfectly answering the brief. Placing Cosmo Lavish in recovery on a ward for the bewildered, it's an exquisite exercise in seamless i-dotting and t-crossing, all the way through to the line, 'And two weeks later, when he won the eyebrow-raising competition, he was happier than he'd ever been before.' It's so exact and tightly knitted that it feels almost aggressive: 'I'll teach those editor types for spotting loose threads in my work.'

No dictation needed, and no tidying needed, either. There is nothing for me to do but forward those pages directly to New York. In my opinion, it's the best ending of any of Terry's books.

Writing those stories was so easy for him, and it came to him so naturally. And that was what was so awful and so wrenching, and so hard to witness, when it eventually became so difficult.

★ ★ ★ ★ ★

You could drive yourself mad going back over little incidents and wondering if they were a sign − picking away at tiny things that happened and asking yourself if that was the first indication you had that something was wrong. Lyn found herself, after the diagnosis, thinking about a time when Terry hadn't screwed the lid back on a jar. Was that something? Or had he . . . just not put the lid back on a jar? Colin Smythe thought back to a time, at least fifteen months before any of us knew what was going on, when he introduced Terry to someone at a convention and Terry didn't so much as turn to acknowledge them. Which felt so odd at the time, but was that a sign? Or had he just been . . . unusually preoccupied?

There were always explanations. Terry had had some minor issues over a number of years with high blood pressure, and took medication for it, so that condition was always in the background as a convenient catch-all for anything that cropped up for him, health-wise. It was just his blood pressure, wasn't it? Or it was just his medication. Similarly, his typing worsened − but then, he had never been the tidiest of typists, had he? And he spilled a few things − but then, Terry was amusingly clumsy at the best of times. It wasn't unusual for him to come into a room and clatter something over − an ornament, a mug, a pile of books. He didn't even necessarily have to touch anything. With astonishing regularity, journalists' tape recorders would break in Terry's presence. Hotel fire alarm systems malfunctioned in the night so frequently during Terry's book tours that we practically stopped saying 'Goodnight' before we went to our rooms, and started saying, 'See you in the car park in your pants with everyone else in a couple of hours, then.' We cheerfully credited him with extensive powers of destruction. Where was the difference, just because he swiped a mug onto the floor again?

He misbuttoned his shirts a couple of times. He came into the Chapel one morning with his T-shirt on inside-out. He came in on another day with his T-shirt on inside-out *and* back-to-front. But even then, these levels of distractedness were not completely out of character, and especially not when there was a book being written, which was pretty much all the time. That was one of the problems for amateur diagnosis in this case. Forgetfulness, preoccupation, being present and yet almost entirely absent at the same time, insufficient attention to T-shirts, buttons, inanimate objects and other people . . . so many of the indications of early onset Alzheimer's turned out also to be indications of full-blown authordom.

And, in any case, the rest of the time he was completely fine, wasn't he?

But then there was the day that Terry arrived in the Chapel and told me about a noise he could hear in the house. It had cost him a few broken nights, he said, and he had been all over every room and he couldn't locate it. Would I come down and help him look for it?

I assumed it would be a smoke alarm or a clock or something – a battery that needed replacing somewhere. We went down to the house and stood in the kitchen, listening.

Terry was facing me, but gesturing behind him.

'Can you hear it?' he said.

I couldn't hear anything.

We went and stood on the stairs.

'Can you hear it now?' asked Terry, again making a vague wave over his shoulder.

Still nothing. We went up onto the landing and stood and listened there for a moment. Terry himself seemed to be looking a bit doubtful now. He opened the bedroom door and we went and stood in there.

More gesturing.

Silence.

After a short while, I said, 'Terry, do you think it's possible that this noise doesn't actually exist?'

Terry thought about it for a moment.

'Yes,' he said. 'I think quite possibly it doesn't.'

We went downstairs and then walked back up to the Chapel.

'Well, that was weird,' I said.

'Wasn't it?' said Terry.

The noise was never talked about again.

The change was incremental. It crept in slowly, and if you were with him all the time, then, of course, you wouldn't even register it. Very often what eventually struck you was not something Terry did, but his reaction to it. On one occasion, dedicating a book during a signing in a shop, he transposed a couple of the letters in the name 'Sarah'. Well, he was signing hundreds of books in quick succession, so why wouldn't that happen every now and again? Except this time, clearly, the jumbled letters bothered him. He looked at what he had written, as if he was trying to work out what was wrong and how to mend it. 'I can't see,' he said, eventually, through a half-laugh. And then he took off his glasses and handed them to me and I cleaned them for him. After that, he went back to signing the books, as before. But it was an odd moment. That seemed to be something that he was saying increasingly: that he couldn't see. Or that something was shining on the page. Or that there was a shadow passing over what he was looking at.

Or what about that time he bumped his car against the gatepost at his parents' house near Hay-on-Wye? He was leaving to come home after visiting his father, who was in the final stages of pancreatic cancer, so this would have been in 2006, at least a year and a half before diagnosis. It was just a scrape, but he didn't even want to see what he had done. He got out, locked the car and walked away from it. He came home in a taxi and I went back later and collected the lightly damaged car. Not that he ever drove it again. 'What if it had been a child on a crossing?' he kept saying – which seemed to me, at the time, to be making something dramatic out of a tiny incident. He only nudged a gatepost . . . But the very next day we put his licence in an envelope and sent it back to the DVLA. Well, Terry had never particularly enjoyed driving, so maybe he was looking for an excuse. But it was such an extreme reaction to what was just a minor mishap, that, with retrospect, you wondered whether it was part of a wider anxiety – a gathering sense he had that things weren't right.

These accumulating incidents took us first to the optician, and then to the GP. This was in August 2007, just after we had wrapped up *Making Money*. I went with him, to keep him company.

The GP asked him if he had been aware of any memory loss.

'Not that I can recall,' said Terry.

Drum roll, cymbal crash. He's here all week, folks.

She gave him the standard cognitive test for dementia – and he sailed through it. Then she sent him off for an MRI scan at New Hall Hospital in Salisbury. Ever the novelist, Terry claimed that he had lain in the MRI machine's clanking barrel, thinking, 'There'll be some material in this, somewhere down the line.' His scan seemed to show patterns on the brain consistent with the death of cells caused by a transient ischaemic attack – a miniature stroke. But the damage looked historical rather than fresh. It was possible, Terry was told, that he could have had this stroke as long as three or four years ago. Terry was much taken with that thought. 'I had a stroke without even knowing,' he said, proudly. There was no reason to fear any lasting effects. He could go home relieved and reassured.

Yet the little incidents didn't stop. They increased in number and became unignorable. Now, just occasionally, there were short periods in the day when everything seemed somehow confusing, or oddly overwhelming – 'Clapham Junction days'. And now, when I passed him a cup of tea, he started reaching for it with both hands, as if to be doubly sure of his hold on it. He would pick the cup off the table with both hands, too, and before he put it back down, he would take a hand off the cup and tap the table with his fingers. The sound of that tapping became part of the soundtrack of the Chapel – a low-level irritant, like a partner's habit that you do your best to ignore. Eventually I asked him about it.

'Just making sure the desk is still there,' he said, quietly.

I was up on the mezzanine level of the Chapel one day. I heard Terry call up: 'Come on, what have you done with it?'

I went down to him.

'What have I done with what?'

He was staring directly down at his keyboard.

'The "S". You've taken the "S". Where is it?'

I was mystified. I went and stood beside him and looked. The letter S was on the keyboard, in between the letters A and D, as usual. I leaned forward and punched it.

He looked at me and held my gaze. There was anxiety in his eyes.

How frightening that must have been for him – his known world suddenly and inexplicably not making sense, utterly disorienting signals emanating from his computer keyboard, of all the familiar places.

Shortly after this, he walked up to the Chapel one morning with his shoes on the wrong feet. He hadn't noticed any discomfort.

We went back to the GP and the GP referred him to a specialist – Dr Peter Nestor, a neurologist at Addenbrooke's Hospital in Cambridge. By now it was the first week of December 2007, a Friday. I drove Terry to his appointment and he spent a day doing tests and having some more scans.

During the afternoon, Dr Nestor came to me as I sat and waited in the corridor and said, 'I think I know what it is.'

I said, 'Can you tell me?'

He said that Terry was doing one last test, and then, when he had seen the results from that, he would sit down with us both.

Which I took to be a bad sign.

A while later, we sat opposite Dr Nestor in one of those anonymous NHS consulting rooms with a sink and a bed with a paper sheet. Dr Nestor said, 'Terry, I think it's PCA – Posterior Cortical Atrophy.'

Terry said, 'What's that?'

Dr Nestor said, 'It's a rare form of Alzheimer's disease.'

The room seemed to fog over after that. Dr Nestor was still talking, but I don't think either Terry or I were listening very intently. Or, at least, we were listening but trying to control our rampaging minds at the same time. Terry said afterwards that, in his mixture of shock and fear, he was practically hallucinating. He saw Dr Nestor in front of him, outlined in flaming red.

Only scraps of what the doctor said came through to me.

. . . the back of the brain . . . visual information . . . motor skills . . . very rare . . . progressive . . . no cure.

We got up slowly and left the room. And then we stood in the corridor outside, trying to gather ourselves. In a little while, the door opened and Dr Nestor came out with his coat on, knocking off for the day. He bent over to put on a pair of cycle clips then and went on his way. Terry said that he saw the cycle clips, too, ringed in fire.

Eventually, we started to make our way out to the car. It was so bewildering. There was no course of action, no golden pathway, no date for the start of treatment – because there was no treatment. There was nothing to cling on to – not even a pamphlet to walk away holding. We left exactly as we had arrived, except that one of us now, at the age of 59, had an incurable degenerative brain condition.

In the car, I said, 'What do you want to do?' The original plan had been to drive back via Colin Smythe's house in Gerrards Cross where Terry was going to sign some books for a charity auction, but now Terry just wanted to go straight home. From the car, he phoned Sandra, a long-term family friend and my partner.

'There was no preamble,' Sandra remembered. 'I picked up the phone and he simply said, "It's Alzheimer's," and then burst into tears.'

Sandra, who had already been through the trauma of Alzheimer's with her father, Gerry, and who knew instantly what lay ahead, burst into tears too.

'He was asking me, "What do I do? What do I tell my wife?" I told him, as best I could, that he needed to get everything into order and that he needed to do it straight away.'

Then Terry phoned Colin.

'Are you sitting down? I've got Alzheimer's.'

'It was just disbelief,' said Colin. 'I simply couldn't believe it. I didn't *want* to believe it.'

As we drove, Terry started talking rapidly. 'I need to finish *Nation*,' he said. 'And I need to do the autobiography . . .' But how much time did he have left? Two years? One year? Six months? We realized that we didn't know. 'We'll clear the diary,' he said. 'We'll get as many books done as we can.' I could hear the rising upset in his voice.

'At least it's me,' Terry said, at one point, breaking a long silence. 'At least it's not Lyn.'

When we got back to the manor, I went into the house with him while he told Lyn, which he had asked me to do. I think he thought I would be able to fill in the gaps if he missed out something important. Lyn hugged him.

'In some ways, it came as a relief,' Lyn said. 'I thought he was going to tell me he had a brain tumour. But then, people can recover from brain tumours.'

'He phoned me that night,' Dave Busby said. 'He said, "I've got something rather unpleasant to tell you." He seemed to think he would have two more years of productive life, if he was lucky. It was very hard to know what to say to him. I just kept saying how sorry I was.'

I rang to check on him later that evening. He said that he and Lyn had had a tearful conversation with Rhianna and that they had then had dinner and put a movie on, like any other Friday night. He was struck by the extraordinary instinct simply to carry on as if nothing had changed, while at the same time being all too aware that everything had. His world seemed somehow torn apart, and yet exactly as it was. It wasn't even as if he was noticeably ill. The next day, a Saturday, he went and worked in the garden and he realized, as he worked, that he was whistling. He wasn't sure where this embedded resilience came from. But he told me he was glad it was there.

The news leaked almost immediately. Over the weekend, I was rung by someone asking after Terry who had found out about the diagnosis from somebody we hadn't told. Clearly it wouldn't be long before we lost control of the story altogether. Terry and I talked about it in the Chapel on Monday morning. 'Who do you think we should tell?' I thought we could make a list: friends, publishers, associates . . . Terry was standing by the Chapel's mullioned window. 'I think we should tell everyone,' he said.

He composed a statement during Monday and gave it the heading, 'An Embuggerance'.

Folks,

I would have liked to keep this one quiet for a while, but because of

*upcoming conventions and of course the need to keep my publishers
informed, it seems to me unfair to withhold the news. I have been diagnosed with
a very rare form of early onset Alzheimer's, which lay behind this year's
phantom 'stroke'.*

*We are taking it fairly philosophically down here and possibly with a mild
optimism. For now work is continuing on the completion of 'Nation' and the
basic notes are already being laid down for 'Unseen Academicals'. All other
things being equal, I expect to meet most current and, as far as possible, future
commitments but will discuss things with the various organisers. Frankly, I
would prefer it if people kept things cheerful because I think there's time for at
least a few more books yet.*

When I had finished typing, Terry read it back to himself.

'Do put a smiley face on that so they know we're deadly serious,' he said.

So I did.

. . . because I think there's time for at least a few more books yet :O)

Terry didn't do social media. Twitter was less than two years old and
hadn't taken off yet, and Terry had nothing to do with the sites he satiri-
cally referred to as 'MyFace' and 'YourTube'.* But he had recently taken
to posting news items on Sandra Kidby's Discworld merchandising website, and that's where, on Tuesday 11 December, we now placed 'An
Embuggerance'.

The response stunned us. Within minutes, hundreds and then thousands of messages of sympathy and support were flooding in, until the site
gave up and crashed. I had to move it all across onto its own dedicated
server, with Terry shouting across the office, not especially helpfully:
'Buy more bandwidth!'

So now the news was public. But the truth was, we were still in the
early stages of framing our own response to it. We were literally in the

---

* Terry's malapropisms in the area of new-fangled social media weren't always satirical or
deliberate. 'I want my own blogger,' Terry brightly informed me one day. 'What do you
mean?' I replied. 'You know,' he said, 'somewhere I can write and post essays on things.' By
'blogger' he meant 'blog'. The idea came to nothing.

office Googling 'Alzheimer's' and 'PCA'. It was as basic as that – playing Dr Google in the hope that, if we looked long enough, we would find someone who would tell us that everyone with Alzheimer's lived in a state of perfect ease and contentment until the age of 110. As it happened, our initial searches took us to Jeremy Hughes, chief executive of the Alzheimer's Society. But Jeremy did not get back to us within the timeframe of Terry's impatience to be cracking on.* Rebecca Wood at Alzheimer's Research Trust, on the other hand, did find herself in the position to pick up the phone immediately, and so it was Alzheimer's Research Trust, and not the Alzheimer's Society, who received Terry's deliberately public and splashy donation of $1 million, announced at the Trust's annual Network Conference in Bristol in March 2008.†

And it was Alzheimer's Research that led Terry to Professor Roy Jones from the RICE Centre, a charity in Bath. Roy had worked extensively in the care of dementia patients and was the founder of one of the earliest memory clinics in the UK, and he agreed to see Terry as a patient. At their first session, in April 2008, Roy asked some questions and did some tests designed to establish how far the disease had progressed. One of his questions was about how well Terry managed to cope in a supermarket. Terry and I looked at each other. Caught on the back foot! This was like the 'How much is a pint of milk?' question used to entrap out-of-touch celebrities.

I stepped in. 'I guess it's been quite a while, really, since supermarkets were a big part of Terry's life . . .'

But, stepping lightly round that one, the tests did cut to the core of the problem. Asked to name as many things as he could in a specified category – animals, countries – Terry delighted in ripping out the examples so fast and so fluently that his examiner, Dr Claudia

. . . .

* By my estimate, Terry gave it ten minutes. Possibly less.

† Why $1 million? For the same reason that trains need to crash into nuclear flasks at exactly 100mph, and sold books need to stretch to the moon. £619,243 just doesn't have the same punchy, headline-generating zing. In 2011 Alzheimer's Research Trust became Alzheimer's Research UK.

Metzler-Baddeley, couldn't keep up. But asked to copy some simple pencil line drawings – two overlapping pentagons, a spiral with three loops in it, a basic house – and to arrange the numbers around a clock-face, he struggled. It was Roy who gave me the smashed mirror analogy: that if I wanted to imagine how Terry was now starting to see the world, I had to think that I was looking at the reflection in a broken mirror – but a broken mirror where some of the fragments were upside down, some were in colour and saturated, some were in black and white, some not there at all. For the sufferer, making sense of the image was, as much as anything, a matter of trying to pick the right piece to look at.

Roy prescribed Terry the drug Aricept. It wasn't going to stop the PCA but it might ameliorate and even slow some of its effects. But Terry would have to pay for it – £120 per month. Apparently he didn't qualify to receive it on the National Health because he was too young to have Alzheimer's. That piece of bureaucratic brilliance drove Terry nuts. 'It's easier to get crack cocaine off dirty Charlie round the back of the bus station than it is for me to get Aricept,' he fumed.

The art was to take pride where you could find it. 'It's going to take years for your brain to deteriorate to normal levels,' one of the specialists told him. Terry loved hearing that. It gave him the same kind of pleasure as talking about having the 'Rolls-Royce version' of the disease – 'the gold standard of Alzheimer's', as he would put it. Professor Jones tutted at him for saying so, but Terry went on saying it anyway: it was too good an opportunity to decline. He returned to RICE every six months for six years, and, odd as it may seem, those trips to Bath were something Terry came to savour. They imposed a structure, a sense, however fleetingly, of control. He got to receive steady care under Roy Jones and his team, and then to walk round the city afterwards and go into Topping & Company, which was possibly Terry's favourite bookshop in the world, with its oak floors and towering handmade shelves and books in signature plastic coverings.

Offers of help flooded in from outside the world of mainstream medicine, too. Many people got in touch with suggestions for dietary cures, homeopathic remedies, and tinctures of turmeric in orange juice.

Very many of these suggestions, though largely anecdotal, were clearly made out of kindness and with the best intentions. But quite a number, we noticed, seemed to come with a request attached for money, framed as Terry's big chance to invest in further research and cure the disease in his name. To that extent, we sometimes felt as though we were drowning in snake oil in those first few months. One day a single pill arrived in the post. It was enormous – about the size of a Lego brick. The accompanying letter said, essentially, 'EAT ME', but also explained that, as it passed through Terry's digestive system, this pill would cunningly realign his ions, significantly improving his condition while leaving the rest of his body unaffected. Oh, and £25,000 wouldn't go amiss . . . Our strict rule on not eating food that came in the post promptly expanded to include not taking Lego-sized pills that came in the post, either.

But Terry did try a few things. What wouldn't you try, if you thought it might make a difference? Because he was hearing from so many quarters that it would be a good idea, he made an appointment with his dentist and underwent the removal and replacement of all his amalgam fillings. Also, we came across an article in a Sunday paper about a British doctor who had developed a helmet which allegedly fired light at an intense wavelength deep into the wearer's head, with beneficial effects, the inventor maintained, for the brain in dementia sufferers. Even in the midst of our scepticism, Terry and I were agog at this suggestion. For one thing, anything involving hats was always going to play well with Terry. For another, the idea of arresting Alzheimer's disease purely by the power of passive electrical components that you could buy off the shelf from Radio Shack spoke profoundly to the lifelong, solder-carrying hobbyist in both of us. We tracked down the helmet's inventor – a GP from County Durham called Dr Gordon Dougal. Dr Dougal came down to the Chapel to see Terry, bringing the helmet. Black and spiky, it was as if Heath Robinson had designed a satellite. We irreverently dubbed it 'the loony helmet'. Unfortunately, it was extremely uncomfortable and, after an initial testing session, it left deep indentations in Terry's head. 'A cactus hat would have been more comfortable,' Terry said, ruefully fingering the new dips in his scalp.

This is where it pays to have your own in-house sculpting team.

Bernard Pearson and Ian Mitchell from the Discworld Emporium stepped in, creating a cast of Terry's cranium which could be used as the basis for a bespoke helmet. The slathering of Terry's head in wet plaster gave everyone a good half hour of entertainment, although the hollow *donk* as Bernard later used a hammer to crack the mould off Terry's new plaster cranium echoed on in all of our memories for some time afterwards.* Dr Dougal wired up the cast in his workshop and Terry now had a properly fitting, light-emitting helmet, such as not even Lock & Co. of St James would have been able to provide for him.

Sitting still was never one of Terry's strengths, but the patient sat in his chair in the Chapel library and solemnly began to submit himself to the recommended 30 minutes of light therapy each day, normally after lunch. In the aftermath of these sessions, he seemed to be no better – but he also seemed to be no worse, and, as Terry pointed out, this was a degenerative disease we were dealing with, so 'no worse' always had to be regarded as a non-step in the right direction. Whatever else those sessions achieved, they obliged Terry to take some time out in the middle of the working day – frequently with Patch the office cat on his lap – which was not something he commonly afforded himself. After a fortnight, though, he decided he had had enough of seeing the light and the loony helmet was set aside.†

Doing *something*, though – this seemed to be the key from here on in: active engagement. It didn't take Terry very long to establish that the disease he had got was undervalued. It was undervalued in terms of the money the government was prepared to spend on research into it – just three per cent of the funding that went towards cancer seemed to be going towards research into dementia. It was undervalued in the sense that the NHS didn't even run to financing a 59-year-old man's drugs for it. And it was undervalued in terms of public perception. 'When

....

* Just to be clear, the mould was not still on Terry's head at this point.

† In the wake of my earlier remarks about the naked opportunism we witnessed at this time, I should like to make absolutely clear that Dr Dougal asked for nothing at any stage of his collaboration with Terry, not even the cost of his bus fare home.

you've got cancer, you're a battler against the disease,' Terry said. 'When you've got Alzheimer's, you're an old fart.' There were fights to be fought here, clearly, for someone with the appetite and the strength to fight them. And the more Terry thought about it, the more he realized that he had that appetite, and the more he realized that he had that strength. 'I intend to scream and harangue while there is time,' he said. 'I'm going to make Alzheimer's regret catching me.'

With that end in mind, having pledged in the car on the way back from Addenbrooke's to clear the diary entirely and devote himself to writing in private, Terry almost immediately took the decision to invite a television camera crew to come and join us in the Chapel for a year.

18

KNOTTED TIES, PASSING SHADOWS AND A TERRORIST IN THE RHYTHM SECTION

The call came within a few days of Terry going public with his diagnosis, just before Christmas in 2007. A producer called Craig Hunter from a TV production company named KEO Films phoned to ask if Terry would have any interest in committing to a fly-on-the-wall documentary about adjusting to life with Alzheimer's disease. He mentioned something about a possible commission from Channel 4. We had heard of neither Craig nor KEO Films, and the commission from Channel 4 didn't exactly sound like it was set in concrete. I assumed Terry would turn him down flat – just as Terry had turned down the six other approaches in this vein that he had already received. But, for some reason, Terry didn't reject this one outright. He said he would at least consider it. 'Let's wait until we've knocked the scab off the new year,' Terry told Craig. 'Call me back a fortnight into January.'

Was that a test? Probably. And it was one that Craig passed with flying colours. First thing in the morning on 14 January, exactly two weeks into the new year, Craig phoned again. It now seemed to be the BBC who were interested in backing this film, and Craig was proposing somebody called Charlie Russell as director. Charlie had made a film for the BBC titled *Looking for Dad*, about a quest he embarked on with his brother to seek information about their father, whom they didn't

360

see in the seven years leading up to his death. Terry and I watched a DVD of it together. There is a devastating moment in the film when Charlie reduces his mother to tears, which I thought would prove too much for Terry and put him off the whole idea. I was wrong, though. Terry thought the film was great: honest, open, unsparing. If he was going to make a film about his condition, he said, then he would want it to be those things. We also watched *Beryl's Last Year*, an intimate portrait Charlie had made of his grandmother, the novelist Beryl Bainbridge, who was convinced that she would die at the age of 71, as had no fewer than nine of her close family relatives.* Terry found that documentary persuasive as well. It was a film about imminent death and about conquering the fear of it, and that would become the theme of Charlie's work with Terry, too – not just in this first documentary, *Terry Pratchett: Living with Alzheimer's*, but in the subsequent two films that we somehow found room to make with him and Craig in the following years, *Terry Pratchett: Choosing to Die* and *Terry Pratchett: Facing Extinction*.

I'm not sure Terry entirely knew what he was letting himself in for with this project. It was certainly a strange feeling when the crew first pitched up at the Chapel. It felt intrusive and embarrassing and stilted, and I couldn't see Terry sticking with it for long. But Charlie was brilliant. He was very good at asking the minimal questions to get what he needed. Indeed, Terry and I ended up teasing him that the only question he knew was: 'So, what do you think about that, Terry?' He was gentle, respectful, and very easy to be around – and right at the beginning of the filming, I couldn't have been more angry with him.

'We need a visual metaphor,' Charlie had said. He wanted a simple scene to paint a picture of what Terry was going through. He decided to film him attempting to knot a tie. I thought that was contrived, given that Terry barely ever wore a tie. But Terry seemed to like the idea and was happy to comply. A tie was fetched from the house. Time and again, as Charlie filmed, Terry tried to pass the ends of the tie over each other in the right order, and time and again he failed. Still the camera rolled. I

---

* Dame Beryl Bainbridge died in 2010 at the age of 75.

found it unbearable. I felt we were watching Terry humiliate himself – which was everything that I wanted to protect him from during all this. And the humiliation was happening in our own office, at our own invitation. I couldn't stand it. I walked out, slamming the door as I did so, and went down to the Studio and locked myself in.

Soon Charlie was outside, banging on the door. I opened up and shouted at him, telling him I thought he was making a fool of Terry. Charlie shouted back. 'Show the man some respect,' he said.

Those words rolled around in my head for a long time. I just hadn't thought about it that way. My desire to jump in and shield Terry was respect of a kind – but it wasn't the respect for the reality of his condition which he now needed. Yes, he was struggling, but there was a value, and even a dignity, in having the bravery to show the struggle. Terry had latched on to this way before I did, and Charlie, too. When the film was up for a BAFTA – and, indeed, at every other award ceremony – the sequence with Terry trying and failing to knot his tie was the clip they showed in the nominees montage.

It was an interesting time to be working on a documentary. Just the previous year, the BBC had been caught red-handed manipulating film of the Queen leaving a room that she was, in fact, entering, and there was an intense spotlight on contrivance and fabrication in the non-fiction realm. This no doubt played to our advantage, in terms of the scrupulous authenticity of the film that got made – as well as setting Terry up for some comedy opportunities that he couldn't resist. 'Good morning!' he would say, walking into a room where the camera was rolling. 'Or should I say, good evening?' And then he would shuffle out backwards.

Anyway, Charlie and his crew were there – and *actually* there – in March for the premiere of Sky TV's *The Colour of Magic*, with Terry again hitting the red carpet in glory at the Curzon Cinema in Mayfair. And they were there in August for the Discworld Convention in Birmingham, catching the simply shattering moment during the traditional 'Bedtime Story' slot, when Terry lost his place on the page and complained of a shadow obscuring the words. It was just too poignant.

Having come for his ability to type, the disease was now heartlessly coming for his ability to read. From this point, I would be doing all his public reading on stage. The cameras also came to Terry's first consultation with Roy Jones at RICE, and we flew to California to see how the research for cures was going and to visit a dementia patient care home – a facility which I absolutely hated but which Terry, much to my surprise, said he rather liked. On account of the travel aspect, we started referring to the documentary, and the subsequent ones, as 'What We Did on Our Holidays' – and when I fondly look back at those films now, they do kind of serve that purpose.

The cameras also filmed a consultation with Professor Charles Duffy at the University of Rochester in Pennsylvania, producing a moment which stood out in the finished programme. Terry and I are sitting opposite the professor shoulder-to-shoulder in a cramped office. At one point, I visibly look across at Charlie, who is crouched out of shot below the camera, and see that he is holding up a handwritten sign saying, 'HOW LONG?'

My initial thought is that he is asking me how long we have got before we need to wind up the interview and head off to the airport, so I don't react. After all, we've got lots of time.

Charlie gestures a little more agitatedly with the card: 'HOW LONG?'

It eventually clicks that he wants me to ask Professor Duffy, as an expert, how long he thinks Terry has got to live.

I draw a deep breath and put the question. But before I can finish, and certainly before the professor can come up with an answer, Terry's arm shoots up: 'DON'T ask that question.'

And fair enough.

What with everything, *Living with Alzheimer's*, which was supposed to be a single hour-long programme, grew into a two-parter. And that's despite the fact that Terry must have pulled the plug on the project about a dozen times – including once, quite dramatically, while Craig was on a plane somewhere over the Atlantic, flying off to Miami with his wife on holiday and assuming all was well. Craig landed and switched on his phone to a torrent of urgent messages.

'We can't pull out again,' I said, tentatively, after about the seventh time this happened.

'I can do what I want,' Terry replied.

But then, for all that he had decided to embrace the virtues of going public, this film was hard for Terry. It wasn't about getting used to being trailed by the camera: that happened with startling speed. It was the fact that, in many ways, even though he was a nationally recognizable figure, Terry had been a substantially private person before this. He had allowed the Terry Pratchett persona out into the spotlight, in the hat and the jacket, in certain relatively controlled environments: the signings, the conventions, the media appearances promoting his books. But actually letting cameras into the Chapel like this, and being filmed going about his ordinary life – this felt exposing enough even without the extra aspect of a slowly encroaching disability. If he eventually stuck at it and allowed the programme to happen, it was because the illness, and exposing the illness, was now the mission. He wasn't going to just shut himself away and endure Alzheimer's privately, as much as that might have suited him temperamentally; he was going to suffer it out in the open, where everyone could see him suffering it, in the hope that doing so would make a difference. And, whatever it cost him in terms of personal anxiety and frustration, a two-part documentary on national television was inevitably going to make a huge contribution to that.

When Charlie and the film crew packed up and left for the last time, the Chapel felt quiet. They had been important company in those difficult first months, while Terry was still feeling his way with this disease and trying to work out what it meant for him, and while I was trying to figure out our new reality, too. And the resulting films would help him define a role for himself in the middle of all this upsetting dislocation. Terry had started referring to himself, mockingly, as 'Mister Alzheimer's', but he knew it was an important job, and it was the job he was now doing. When the documentaries were broadcast, in February 2009, they noticeably raised Terry's visibility, in a way that only appearances on television can. I was a witness to it: literally overnight, Terry moved several rungs up the fame ladder to the 'hooted at by passing vans in Salisbury' level. And to raise the visibility of Terry now was automatically to raise the visibility of Alzheimer's.

Terry's attitude to that? 'Good.'

★ ★ ★ ★ ★

Without the medical complications, 2008 would have been a year of celebration for Terry. It still was. In October, he and Lyn marked their fortieth wedding anniversary. Their gift to themselves was to have a stone bridge built over the River Ebble in the grounds of the manor, and there was a big dinner with Rhianna and several of us at the Castleman, featuring, of course, honeycomb ice cream. And before that, in the spring, a giant party was thrown for Terry's sixtieth birthday, in an enormous marquee on the field near the manor. Friends, family and neighbours came. Dave and Gill Busby were there, and the Table of Eight from the CEGB with their partners.* The live music wasn't too shabby: Rhianna got Steeleye Span to perform. 'It's not often you see a folk group with Osama bin Laden on the drums,' noted a visibly moved and certainly well-refreshed Terry, in his thank you speech. Liam Genockey – for it was he – seemed to take it in good part.

And then, in autumn, Terry celebrated the publication of *Nation* with a launch party at the Royal Society in London. It was his first non-Discworld novel since *Johnny and the Bomb* in 1996, and it had been in his mind for a long time. Terry had always been fascinated by the story of how the tidal wave that followed the eruption of the Krakatoa volcano in 1883 had carried a steamship two miles inland. He had

. . . .

* Terry was, of course, continuing to attend the annual Christmas lunches, which always went down in the office diary as 'CEGB piss-up', despite the fact that a more modest set of drinkers it would have been hard to assemble. Terry's fondness for sprouts on these occasions had by now been folded into the mythology of the lunch. One year when he couldn't make it, the others persuaded Interflora – Interbrassica, as they renamed it – to deliver a stick of sprouts, festively adorned, to the manor. It became the centrepiece of the Pratchett Christmas table. Terry then had tiny silver sprout badges made for everyone, after which the emailed invitations started to include the instruction, 'Sprouts must be worn.'

imagined the dazed sailors looking out to find their ship becalmed in a sea of trees, and wondering if they had gone mad. It had led him to tinker with the famous old English hymn and supply some additional verses: 'For those in peril on the land'. And from these thoughts had come the tale of Mau, the boy on an island whose entire world is crushed by a wave and who finds himself railing against the gods for not existing. Terry started writing the story in 2003, then set it aside when an actual tsunami hit Sumatra in the Indian Ocean on Boxing Day 2004. He did not feel able to take it up again until 2007.

'That book came from deep within him,' Philippa Dickinson said. 'It was an emotional project for him, in a way that was quite different for Terry.' His attitude to the jacket epitomized how separately he thought of *Nation*. In the UK, the sales people were keen to put a comical illustration on the jacket to tie it in with Terry's other books, but he refused to let them: 'No way. It's not a comedy. That's not the book.' For heaven's sake, he kept pointing out: this is a novel which opens with a boy disposing of the corpses of everybody he has ever known. Terry had seen the cover image in his mind's eye almost as soon as the story came to him – a boy alone on a tropical beach, staring across the water to a huge, rising moon – and that, after a short fight, was what he got, painted by Jonny Duddle.

It's true that Terry was now obliged to write every book as if it were his last. Yet it would be too simple to suggest that the passion with which he attached himself to completing *Nation*, and the strength of his feelings about it once it was published, had its roots in his diagnosis. The first draft of the book was completed before his appointment at Addenbrooke's in December 2007, and the novel's structure was almost wholly in place before Terry knew how ill he was. It's more the case that Terry sincerely believed that, with *Nation*, he would finally be able to put a great and career-defining novel for younger readers to his name, which had been the ambition all along, ever since he had sat down to write *The Carpet People*. The tale arrived in his head so mysteriously complete, and fell onto the page so rapidly, that he spoke of not writing it, but 'channelling' it. He would say that it was 'consuming' him, that he was 'possessed' by it. In the acceptance speech he wrote to be read at the presentation ceremony for the Boston Globe–Horn Book Award for Fiction and Poetry in America, Terry said, 'I believe that *Nation* is the best book I have ever written, or will write.' He dedicated it to Lyn.

As well as the Boston Globe–Horn Book Award, *Nation* won the Los Angeles Times Book Prize for Young Adult Literature and the Brit Writer's Award, and was a nominee for the 2010 Carnegie Medal.* It was also adapted and staged at the National Theatre in London, an endorsement which initially pleased Terry enormously, although, sadly, the production itself pleased him much less, as he very much made clear.

Terry had never struggled to speak his mind, and Alzheimer's seemed in no way to be impairing his fluency in that respect. Indeed, at this point in the disease's advance, it was increasing it. I drove Terry to London for a performance of *Nation*. He had seen Mark Ravenhill's script while it was being written, and he had expressed reservations about it. Indeed, he was so anxious about what he was seeing that he sought counsel from Michael Morpurgo, whose *War Horse* had been adapted by the National to fantastic acclaim a year earlier, and from Philip Pullman, whose *His Dark Materials* had gone the same way a couple of years before that. From both those esteemed writers, the message was essentially the same: relax and enjoy it. This is the National, they seemed to be saying: they don't cock these things up.

And now Terry was sitting in the Olivier Theatre with his arms wrapped tightly across his body – his characteristic pose during offences against his vision. After the show, when the audience had left the auditorium, the cast gathered on that famous stage to meet the author. Whereupon a significantly disinhibited Terry greeted them by saying, 'I'm sorry you all had to go through that.'

There was some hesitant laughter. Paul Chahidi, who later played Sandalphon in the Amazon Prime *Good Omens* adaptation, was on stage

---

* On the downside, he didn't win. On the upside, the person he lost out to was Neil Gaiman, with *The Graveyard Book*, and Terry was genuinely happy for Neil. 'The boy done good,' he said. Now they both had Carnegies.

among the National cast as Cox that night. He told me the moment stayed with him. 'It made quite an impression,' Paul said. In an attempt to guard against further disappointments in this area, Terry expressed to Rhianna his fervent hope that if anybody were to write the screenplay of *Nation*, it would be her – someone he could trust.

Meanwhile, what we might call 'Operation Scream and Harangue' continued. In November 2008 Terry handed in a petition at 10 Downing Street, on behalf of the Alzheimer's Research Trust, pleading for more investment in dementia research. Terry's earlier claim, in public, that he would like to 'kick a politician in the teeth' over this funding issue somehow did not dissuade the Prime Minister from having him in his house that day. After photographs at the door, we were invited to have tea with Gordon Brown in the Cabinet Office. Terry looked around the room at the rosewood furniture and the gilt-framed paintings with a mixture of awe and glee: at last he had made it to the very epicentre of political power. Someone wheeled in a tea trolley and left. To our surprise, Gordon Brown got up and went to the trolley, asking Terry, on the way, how he took his tea. He then poured out two cups and handed them across to us, before returning to the trolley to spread some biscuits on a plate. Until that moment, we would have confidently assumed that a British Prime Minister would have someone to do his tea and biscuits for him. It was heartening, if disorientating, to discover otherwise.*

As we said our mutual thanks on departure we were both tempted to give Gordon Brown a knowing wink – 'no, thank *you*, Prime Minister' – because a piece of news had recently reached Salisbury, instantly qualifying as 2008's biggest and most welcome surprise. One Saturday morning, the phone rang in my car and Terry said, 'Where are you?' I was on my way to the framer's in Salisbury, as it happened. 'Turn round and come and see me,' said Terry.

. . . .

* There was a similarly disorientating moment on a later visit to Downing Street for a meeting with the then Chancellor, George Osborne, next door at No. 11. As the door opened to admit us, the unmistakable figure of Bruce Forsyth came out, going the other way. You never know who you are going to find at the epicentre of power.

When I arrived, Terry was flushed with excitement – possibly as excited as I had seen him since the first unveiling of the shepherd's hut. Colin Smythe had rung him that morning, when he was at the kitchen table having breakfast.

'Hello?' said Terry.

'Arise, Sir Terry,' said Colin.

As you do when your client has just been asked if they would accept a knighthood.* For 'services to literature', no less. And this despite Terry once having said that his biggest service to literature was not trying to write any.

'It doesn't fit,' Terry said. 'I just can't put "Pratchett" and "knight-hood" in the same sentence.'

'It sounds like you won't be turning it down though, Terry,' I said.

He smiled broadly. 'There are some good connotations with knights,' he said. 'Damsels, dragons . . . I don't think a fantasy writer should be in the business of turning that down, do you?' He had also already worked out that 'the letterhead will come in useful'. Indeed it did – in his new role as a campaigner, but also for general proclamations and protestations. Thereafter, the cry would go up in the Chapel, 'I think it's time we wheeled Sir Terence out, don't you?', and shortly after that we would be firing off a letter to the editor of *The Times*, or some other august journal.

The knighthood was announced in the 2009 New Year Honours list and the ceremony took place at Buckingham Palace that summer. Terry, Lyn and Eileen, his proud mother, spent the night before at The Langham in Portland Place, Terry's favourite posh hotel. A problem with the plumbing put the bathroom in Terry and Lyn's suite out of bounds. So, no shower for Terry on the morning of the knighthood – but best not mention this to the Queen who would literally, on this occasion, be welcoming the great unwashed to the palace. In the morning, Graham

* And as the Queen *doesn't*, as it turns out. It's a common misconception that the phrase 'Arise, Sir [insert name of newly ennobled person]' appears anywhere in the official knighthood ceremony. It's a tap on the shoulders with the sword, and then up you get – using the thoughtfully supplied handrail attached to the red velvet kneeling cushion, a facility for the older, less flexible knee which Terry said he had been grateful for.

Hamilton picked Terry and Lyn up at the hotel, along with Rhianna, and bore them all to the palace in a vintage Rolls-Royce.

'As we went through the gates,' Lyn remembered, 'one of the policemen on duty shouted, "There he is!" I was really alarmed for a moment. I thought Terry was in trouble. Actually, they had just been looking out for him, knowing he was coming and wanting to get their books signed.'

After the formalities, Terry posed for the press with the Paralympic swimmer Ellie Simmonds, who had just received an OBE. Then, with Lyn, Eileen and Rhianna, he was driven round to the Athenaeum Club on Pall Mall, where Colin Smythe was a member and had laid on a private room for lunch. Among the party of seventeen were me and my partner Sandra, Leslie Hayward, Colin's publishing partner, Dr Jack Cohen and Dr Jacqueline Simpson, Terry's trusty collaborators, and the novelist A. S. Byatt, who had so constantly stood up for Terry and whose loyal approval in the face of so much highbrow disdain meant an enormous amount to him. Also invited was Sir David Jason, who was unable to come but sent, from one knight to another, a poem in his place, which Colin magnificently declaimed to the room:

ODE TO SIR TERRY PRATCHETT
FROM SIR DAVID JASON
I send this message, not as myself
But as a wizard, and then an elf
The first as Rincewind, full of magic
Then Albert, friend of Death so tragic.
Characters of unique invention
So clearly drawn, no need to mention
They're from the pen of Terry Pratchett
If he were a bus you'd want to catch it
As he takes you on a magical ride
Where wizards and skeletons stand side by side.
The Queen has obviously jumped on board
For just this morning she raised her sword
To tell the world a knight so merry

Should now be known as good Sir Terry.
And it's a good knight from me, and a good knight to him.

Terry made a little speech to thank us for turning up, and was promptly overcome and choked up. Terry Pratchett – lost for words. This didn't often happen.

So now he really was Sir Terence Pratchett, a prospect which would have seemed unlikely to his teachers back when he was climbing all over his primary school desk, but which had nevertheless come to pass, ultimately fulfilling, surely, the most outlandish of Eileen Pratchett's aspirational wishes for him. He had his coat of arms – books and a more-pork owl perched on a helmet – and his Latin motto – 'Noli timere messorem', or, as Blue Oyster Cult originally had it, 'Don't fear the reaper'. What he didn't have was a sword. Practically Terry's first question to Colin when Colin broke the news was, 'Do I get to carry a sword?' Colin said he didn't think so. 'Terry thought that was a bit offish,' said Colin.

But Terry could at least make and own a sword, even if there were going to be finicky, pettifogging rules about wielding it in public. And he would make that sword using the ancient ways, too. Not for Terry a careful scan of the latest reviews in *What Sword?* magazine, followed by a trip with the credit card to Swords R Us. On the contrary, here, in Terry's eyes, was the homespun craft opportunity to outstrip all previous homespun craft opportunities – the construction of a sword from the earth itself. He seized it.

He got a local blacksmith, Jake Keen, to join him on the project and help him with the smelting. Terry's first words on meeting Jake were, 'I'm told on good authority that you're completely mad. Are you mad?'

Jake said, 'Of course.'

'Good,' said Terry. 'I like mad people.'

Together they gathered raw iron ore from a field that Jake knew outside Tisbury – 60 kilos of it. They built a furnace in the grounds of the manor, collecting hay and sheep dung from Terry's fields and slathering it with clay dredged up from the foundations of my house, which was conveniently undergoing a two-storey extension at this moment in history. They roasted their ore in a bonfire, lobbing in some pieces of the Sikhote-Alin meteorite, to play the part of Thunderbolt Iron, which folklore insists is highly magical.* Then they crushed the ore, and smelted it in their furnace – making the fire with friction, of course, not shop-bought matches – producing two separate blooms of iron, which they beat into bars on an anvil, or, in the case of the less expert Terry, into something closer to metal Toblerones. The bars were then taken to Hector Cole, the blacksmith and master swordsmith, for fashioning into the required piece of ceremonial weaponry. Terry joined Hector at his forge near Marlborough to help beat the metal for the blade. When Hector eventually showed him the finished item, complete with its hilt, Terry was visibly moved, holding it out and turning it in the light in wonder. For someone whose life was devoted to working with the intangible, the creation of something so emphatically solid – and by properly ancient means – brought immense joy.

Did Terry know how hard Colin Smythe had worked in the background to lobby for his candidature for a knighthood? He most certainly did. Would Colin be expecting Terry to express his gratitude for that work in a touching moment of togetherness between the author and his long-standing agent? Obviously not. Colin knew, probably better than anyone, that that simply wasn't Terry's style.

Or maybe these days it was. One day, not much later, as they walked through Library Square at Trinity College Dublin, Terry took Colin aside and – making sure of course that he was well out of anybody else's earshot – said to him: 'Thank you, Colin. I cannot tell you how much I appreciate that.'

★ ★ ★ ★ ★

----

* The Sikhote-Alin meteorite fell on the mountains of south-eastern Russia in 1947, but this particular piece of it landed, much later, on the shelves of Colin Smythe at Cornerways in Gerrards Cross. Terry, who coveted the item badly, proposed buying it off Colin, but Colin cannot remember whether money ever changed hands. One thing we can say for certain is that bits of it ended up in Terry's sword.

And still there was writing. And while there was still writing, there was still Terry Pratchett. For the first year since 1986, in 2008 there had been no Discworld novel – and in most of the intervening years, of course, there had been two, so the sense of deprivation among Pratchett readers was substantial. In 2009, Terry would do his best to make amends for that interruption to normal service by writing the longest Discworld novel of them all.*

Back in May 1998, while on tour for *The Last Continent*, Terry had found himself waiting at Newcastle airport for the flight home to Southampton. As he wrote in his tour report at the time: 'On the television in the lounge was some kind of football match between men in red shirts and men in black and white shirts. I watched five minutes of it, the longest amount of time I've devoted to football in my life. It seemed obvious to me that the men in red shirts knew a lot more about football, but I decided not to tell anyone.'

A quick scan of the record books reveals that Terry was watching the 1998 FA Cup final in which Arsenal, in the red shirts, beat Newcastle, in the black and white shirts, 2–0 with goals from Marc Overmars and Nicolas Anelka. So, to that extent, the men in red shirts *did* know a lot more about football, and Terry's five-minute analysis, based on a lifetime of committedly not watching the sport at all, was spot on. Maybe it should have been blindingly obvious even then that Terry Pratchett was the perfect novelist to embark on a 540-page examination of the beautiful game and all its ramifications. Whatever, just over a decade later, he did so.

'I've worked it out,' he said, bursting through the Chapel door one morning with a triumphant expression on his face. 'The most important thing about football is that it's *not about football*.' That, of course, was Terry's 'Get Out of Jail' card in respect to this project – but it was also true. Football had a culture of behaviour and affiliation around it that extended far beyond the game which was supposedly its centre. And

. . . .

* It came in at 135,000 words. None of the other Discworld novels gets very much above 110,000 at the longest.

that was certainly the case on Discworld, which is still, as the novel opens, hosting the lawless street game of 'foot-the-ball' or 'Poore Boys' Funne', as the ancient small print has it.* And anyway, the story that follows turns out to be as much about the professors of Unseen University and the journey of self-discovery taken by Nutt the candle dribbler as about sport itself, and to allude as strongly to *Romeo and Juliet* as it does to *Match of the Day*.

Terry's ability to work unassisted at the keyboard had now all but deserted him, but we got hold of some speech recognition software, in the hope that, when I wasn't around to help him, he would at least be able to speak his words into the computer. Having taught our computers to talk, back in the day, could we now teach them to listen? The first package we tried didn't last a day before Terry abandoned it in frustration. He said it was like operating a child's toy steering wheel, suckered onto the back of the driver's seat: you were spinning the wheel but having no effect whatsoever on the direction of the vehicle. In fairness, the program we had picked was mostly intended for surgeons to record brief, hands-free notes, rather than for novelists attempting full-blown works of fiction about the evolution of football in an alternative world. However, after Terry had complained loudly in public about his struggles in this area, we were then contacted by Clive Henson, the technical director of the company behind a package called TalkingPoint, whose program looked as though it might be more fit for our purpose. We tipped the text of all Terry's novels into the software and road-tested it, as deviously as we could, throwing in long words like 'marmalade', 'corrugated iron' and 'Weatherwax' – yet with fairly reassuring results. We felt like true pioneers of the computing age again – albeit that, funnily enough, the system doggedly insisted on translating the word 'pioneer' into prose as 'pie on ear'. But, a few small bugs aside, TalkingPoint served us well, and, most importantly, allowed Terry to continue working entirely independently for a while longer.†

. . . .

* 'Poore Boys' Funne' was, for quite some time, going to be the title for this novel.

† There were some teething issues with switching in and out of the program at the appropriate moments. Philippa Dickinson claims to have received at least one file of text

Mostly, though, *Unseen Academicals* was written – in common with every book since *Night Watch* – by dictation, with Terry energetically rattling out the words, and with me, as ever, barrelling along in his wake. I can report that the construction of the book also involved the first and only use of the 'copy and paste' function in my time as Terry Pratchett's human TalkingPoint program. It came late in the novel, at the moment when the gifted playmaker Professor Bengo Macarona insists that, if the crowd are going to continue hymning him in the traditional football style – 'One Macarona, there's only one Macarona'* – then they must at least have the decency to employ his full title and qualifications, which is to say:

> One Professor Macarona D. Thau (Bug), D. Maus (Chubb), Magistaludorum (QIS), Octavium (Hons), PHGK (Blit), DMSK, Mack, D. Thau (Bra), Visiting Professor in Chickens (Jahn the Conqueror University (Floor 2, Shrimp Packers Building, Genua)), Primo Octo (Deux), Visiting Professor of Blit/Slood Exchanges (Al Khali), KCbfJ, Reciprocating Professor of Blit Theory (Unki), D. Thau (Unki), Didimus Supremius (Unki), Emeritus Professor in Blit Substrate Determinations (Chubb), Chair of Blit and Music Studies (Quirm College for Young Ladies), there's only one Professor Macarona D. Thau (Bug), D. Maus (Chubb) . . .

. . . and so on, for just over one and a half pages.

Now, entertaining though it was to assemble in the first place, there was no way – then or now – that I was going to type out that fiddly word-cluster four times in total if I didn't need to. Instead, I copied and pasted the relevant section. Terry, rather touchingly, worried that this might somehow be looked on by readers as a form of cheating – as if people would somehow be able to hold the finished book up to the

---

from Terry in this period which devolved halfway through into a conversation between the author and his personal assistant about tea and biscuits. Could have been worse, I guess. At least the conversation was only about tea and biscuits.

* To the tune, I'm sure I don't need to tell you, of the 1929 Cuban classic, 'Guantanamera'.

light and see that the words had not been formally typed through in full, but accumulated by a trick of the software. But, as I made clear, that was just a risk we were going to have to take.

The plot of *Unseen Academicals* was complicated and carefully interwoven, yet it seemed to arrive in Terry's head with ease and clarity. For those of us now permanently and painfully alert for signs of the PCA beginning to impact on his work, this was a fantastic relief – and also a source of wonder. The one problem with the book occurred at the end, when Philippa Dickinson – having prepared what Terry referred to pointedly as 'the Timeline of Doom' – pointed out that, strictly speaking, 24 hours seemed to have gone missing somewhere during the plot's linear development. A full working day in the Chapel therefore had to be devoted to going back over the novel, making expansions here and contractions there, until the timeline was properly squared off. It was extremely complex and bitty work, but Terry simply rolled up his sleeves and got on with it. It was astonishing to witness. Here was someone with a degenerative brain disease, merrily scrolling 135,000 words of novel backwards and forwards in his mind. As for his supposedly healthy and considerably younger personal assistant, on the other hand . . . well, I had to get up from my seat at the computer and retire to the Chapel's lavatory midway through the afternoon in order to throw up, all these adjustments to the text having brought down on me the first full-blown migraine of my adult life. But Terry could have gone on for hours.*

Unseen Academicals is not only Terry's longest book, it is also, in my opinion, his funniest: a book in which it is the evil plan of Dr Hix 'to spread darkness and despondency throughout the world by the means of amateur dramatics';† a book in which a character called Glenda

. . . .

* Rising to head for the lavatory, I realized that I hadn't moved once from the desk since I'd sat down first thing that morning, such was the intensity of the task. 'You look a little green around the gills,' Terry remarked blithely as I shot past him. 'Are you all right?' 'Bleeeuuchh,' came my eventual reply, from a distance.

† Dr Hix is another Tuckerization, secured by John Hicks, the chairman of the 2014 Discworld Convention and greatly dedicated to amateur dramatics.

Sugarbean is 'taken aback and affronted at the same time, which was a bit of a squeeze'; a book in which a lingering kiss is said to sound like 'a tennis ball being sucked through the strings of a racket'. Something that Anne Hoppe said rang in my head again and again in this phase of Terry's life: 'How could this white-hot brilliance on paper exist in the same world as Alzheimer's?'

However, if Terry remained as solid as ever in prose, elsewhere little cracks were slowly but surely beginning to appear. When the novel was published, in the autumn of 2009, Terry did an event for press and public at the *Guardian* newspaper near Kings Cross in London. Terry was struggling for focus that day. In the questions session afterwards, a Brazilian journalist stood up and asked a question about football. Terry's reply set off on a long, rambling journey that seemed to trek its way across a number of continents and found room for a brief digression on religious bigotry before returning to the hall in London. When he had finally brought it back home, Terry said, 'Does that answer your question?'

The baffled Brazilian journalist replied, 'No. Not really.'

There would be some tricky moments from here on.

19

FROTHY COFFEE, OPEN WINDOWS
AND THE HAT WITH BLACK FEATHERS

'Imagine that you're in a very slow motion car crash,' Terry wrote, in his Richard Dimbleby Lecture in 2010. 'Nothing much seems to be happening. There's an occasional little bang, a crunch, a screw pops out and spins across the dashboard as if we're in Apollo 13. But the radio is still playing, the heater is on and it doesn't seem all that bad, except for the certain knowledge that sooner or later you will be definitely going head first through the windscreen.'

This was life for Terry now – and, at one remove, life for me, too, as I worked alongside him. That gradually unfolding reality was the permanent context for everything we now did. As Terry also wrote in that lecture: 'The disease moves slowly, but you know it's there.'

Or as he also put it: 'Alzheimer's hovers in the corner of my imagination like a station ident.'

He couldn't deliver his words himself, from the lectern. He was now officially someone who could write a lecture, but not read a lecture. His world seemed to be filling up with these non sequiturs. He was also someone who, as a consequence of problems with his 'visual acuity' and his 'topographical management', would struggle to make his way unassisted through something as uncomplicated as a revolving door, or up a short set of well-lit stairs. Yet he was still someone who could accurately wield the terms 'visual acuity' and 'topographical management'. And the terms 'marmalade' and 'corrugated iron', for that matter. This was baffling for the people who had long conversations with the supposedly 'ill' Terry Pratchett and emerged believing there was nothing remotely wrong with him. Having met Terry during the making of *Living with Alzheimer's*, Professor Simon Lovestone of King's College, London, got on the phone to Professor Roy Jones to express surprise that the Terry he had encountered was in need of Roy's specialist help. Roy said, 'Yes, but did you ask him to draw two intersecting pentagons?' And if it was baffling for other people, how baffling must it have been for Terry, on the inside of this gradual and inexorable disintegration?

'How are you, Terry?' people would ask.

'I'm fine,' he would say. 'For a given value of fine.'

Yet, if he couldn't read the lecture he had written, he could at least introduce it, and he could sit on the stage while Tony Robinson read it for him, and he did so proudly, even defiantly, that February evening, in front of a dignitary-rich audience in the Dorchester Library at the Royal College of Physicians.

The Dimbleby family had approached Terry in the autumn of 2009 about the possibility of him giving the annual televised lecture which they had inaugurated four decades previously in memory of Richard Dimbleby, and Terry felt honoured to be asked. He was a journalist at the *Bucks Free Press* when Richard Dimbleby died, in December 1965, and he remembered the impact, not just of the death of this famous broadcaster and national figure, but of the fact that his family came out and openly said what he had died of: cancer. The term carried a shock because nobody spoke of cancer in those days except in hushed tones. The euphemism – as the journalists of the era well knew – was 'a long illness'. 'Before you can kill the monster you have to say its name,' Terry wrote. And now he was out there, too, trying to kill the monster of Alzheimer's disease by calling it out. And if he could take down the taboo around assisted dying at the same time, then, yes, he would do that as well.

'It was obvious that he would be interested in how things end,' said Philippa Dickinson. 'He was a fantasy writer: everything in his working day was about how the narrative ought to go, how you might bring about the optimal, most satisfying conclusion. It stood to reason that he would think about his life in the same way.'

And he really *did* think about it. He had got it sorted, Terry told me one day, out of the blue. He'd been talking to a local farmer who had a shotgun. They had laid out the plan. At the appointed time, Terry would go for a walk and, somewhere along the path, the farmer would step quietly out of a bush behind him and shoot him in the back of the head. Painless. Easy.

It was a complete fabrication, of course. But this was what he told me. And these were the kinds of plots he found himself working on, now that the question 'How does this end?' was constantly in his mind.

But being Terry, he decided to turn his personal fear outwards, and channel it into something bigger. He would become an advocate for assisted dying – a passionate proponent of the right to follow a good life with a good death, and an ambassador for the dignity of going at the time of your own choosing. And, of course, Terry was a highly persuasive person to have on the side of those things: he was thoughtful, articulate, rational – and now deeply and unquestionably invested. He had also devoted a working lifetime to writing novels in which Death is a thoughtful and dutiful figure on a white horse called Binky. He had worked hard to make the inevitability of death seem just that little bit less frightening – friendly, even, and certainly funnier. Readers wrote to him all the time to tell him how grateful they were for that.* In some ways, this new advocacy for assisted dying was just an extension of what he'd been doing as a writer for years.

Terry began writing his Dimbleby lecture almost as soon as he was asked. He was full of fury about his diagnosis and angry, too, about the lack of choice that people in his position faced over how and when to end their suffering. That fury fired the first draft of what became 'Shaking Hands with Death'. It was during these days that we discovered

. . . .

* Letters came from people who said they had used passages featuring Death at funerals, but letters also came from people who had used passages featuring Death at weddings. 'Thank you for your letter,' Terry could only reply. 'What more can a modest man say?'

some new limits in the TalkingPoint dictation program. The software was by now easily capable of recognizing such key terms in Terry's writing lexicon as 'Vetinari' and 'Weatherwax'. But confronted with the anger in Terry's voice as he shouted into prose his thoughts about the misery of end-of-life care, the change in tone at the microphone was just too much and TalkingPoint practically gave up and melted. Eventually I stepped in and let him shout at me on the keyboard instead.

Terry was pleased with what he put together, but would the BBC, with its tricky commitment to balance and its inherent caution, be ready to broadcast his thoughts in this controversial area? He very strongly doubted it. We showed the text to Phil Dolling, the producer, over cappuccinos in the café of the National Theatre. Both of us were convinced that the piece would glow too hot for the BBC. As Terry sat and drank frothy coffee, Phil read through to the end, silently and with an expression that gave nothing away. Then he put the script down and there was a long pause while he continued to stare at the table. Finally he looked up at us – and a smile spread across his face. That was when we knew the lecture was going to happen.

By the time we turned up at the Royal College of Physicians in Regent's Park for the recording on 1 February, news was out about Terry's intended theme and there were journalists and film crews in the street. Rival networks jostled for exclusive interviews for their lunchtime slots. Terry calmly spoke to all of them, and gave each one something different. Then we got out of the hubbub and went through to the peace of the college's magnificent oak-panelled library, the venue for the lecture, where the formidable ranks of leather tomes, rigidly secured behind iron grilles, could only contrast strongly with the sight of Terry nonchalantly holding his lecture, rolled and slightly scrunched, in his hand.

My biggest concern was how Terry was going to get those words read. It was one thing for him to cope at his own pace with large fonts on the bank of screens in the Chapel, quite another for him to manage a continuously scrolling autocue. At the first rehearsal, it became quickly obvious that this arrangement simply wasn't going to work. No matter how the autocue was adjusted, the words came at Terry too fast. His own words. It was a huge blow for him – another signpost moment as this disease continued slowly to strip him of his powers. And yet he was calm and practical in the face of this setback, and simply proposed his solution: 'a stunt Pratchett'. 'I think Rob should read it for me,' he said. After some discussion, the BBC agreed to give this a go, but wanted Terry at least to say a few words ahead of the lecture. We quickly sat down and wrote some additional opening paragraphs, and then we rehearsed it on the stage – Terry giving his introduction and then handing over to me. The backslapping from the production team after that run-through suggested that our hastily improvised fix had worked.

As the afternoon went on, I can't say I wasn't anxious at what lay ahead. I had read for Terry in public many times, but this was on a different scale: a Dimbleby lecture, for national broadcast, and with Terry's hard-won words and heartfelt message at stake. The pressure was on – and I only had a handful of hours left to work on the performance before recording was due to start.

That afternoon, the actor Tony Robinson came to the library to see Terry. Tony had just flown back into the country so that he could be in the audience for the lecture that evening, and we had arranged for him to drop in for tea and a chat. One of the producers wondered if, seeing as he was there, Tony would give me some professional pointers for my delivery. He was happy to oblige. Tony duly went to the lectern and read the lecture through while I stood next to him and listened. He didn't just give a few pointers – he gave a masterclass in public speaking. All the emotion that had surged through Terry as he wrote those paragraphs emerged in Tony's voice with absolute and memorable clarity. This, clearly, was how 'Shaking Hands with Death' was meant to be heard. I said to Terry, 'I think we've just found our stunt Pratchett.' That night it would be Tony that Terry handed over to.

The lecture was recorded 'as live' early in the evening, and shown by the BBC later that night. By the time it was on the nation's screens, we had adjourned for a celebratory dinner. If Terry had any worry at all, it was that, having recently established himself as 'Mister Alzheimer's', he would now forever be reinvented as 'Dr Death'. That didn't happen. Poignantly harnessing his anger and his dread, the lecture touched its audience and set off a national debate. Terry never expected it to change the UK's end-of-life laws at a stroke, but it did at least provoke politicians to start talking about the subject and it began a conversation that continued, with Terry's participation, for the rest of his life.

That conversation in due course brought Craig Hunter and Charlie Russell back into our lives. After *Living With Alzheimer's*, Terry and I were very clear, both with them and with each other: there was simply no way we were going to make another film. Enough precious hours had been consumed by cameras. Now our days were going to be all about the books, on which the clock was loudly ticking.

So much for that. We now spent much of the latter part of 2010 making the documentary *Terry Pratchett: Choosing to Die*. That film included the most harrowing experience of my working life, and I don't expect to have another to match it. When I joined Terry as his personal assistant, it was not really in my mind that one day the pair of us would travel to Switzerland together to watch a man die. But we did. Together with Charlie and his crew, we stood in a room in the building Dignitas call Blue Oasis, and watched Peter Smedley, an Englishman who had lived for three years with motor neurone disease, sit on a blue sofa with his wife and end his life using a fatal dose of pentobarbital.

No day I ever live through will, I'm sure, be as strange and disorientating as that one. I am haunted by so much of it: the calm ministrations of the Dignitas escorts, Erica and the pipe-smoking Horst; the sight of Peter Smedley, minutes before his death, going over a selection of individually wrapped Swiss chocolates, deliberating over which one he would eat to counter the bitterness of the pentobarbital; the formal words of Erica before giving him the drug – 'Peter Laurence Smedley, are you sure you want to drink this medicament, with which you will sleep and die?' And then, perhaps most of all, Peter's wife, Christine, on the phone to their daughter afterwards: 'Yes, Daddy's gone.'

We were briefed very strictly by the BBC on our conduct that day and it was made very clear to us that we were to do nothing that could in any way be interpreted as aiding Peter. 'Even if he drops his walking stick on the way into the building,' we were told, 'you are not to pick it up for him.' Terry bridled at that. 'I'm an Englishman,' Terry insisted, 'and he is a gentleman. If he needs to take an arm, I will give him mine.'

Terry thought Peter Smedley's act was entirely brave – he considered him 'the bravest man I have ever met' – and he thought his act was right, and therefore that it should *be* a right. I agreed with him that it was brave, but was more sceptical about how right it was – and that's a source of tension in the documentary: Terry's mounting belief in the justice of the cause meets my increasing unease about what we're witnessing. What about the family and friends left behind? They were the ones I kept thinking about. And I guess you didn't need to be a psychologist to unpack why. In the back of my mind was the thought that this, ultimately, would be what Terry wanted for himself – that it would be us, sometime too soon, heading in a taxi through the snow to this house in a grim Swiss industrial estate, with its view directly overlooking a machine shop. I told him, 'I'll do anything for you, but, if that moment ever comes, I'm not organizing for you to come to Switzerland to die.' We argued about it, including, probably most strongly, at the airport in Zurich on the way home after witnessing Peter Smedley's passing. I told Terry he lacked empathy for those who were left. He told me I couldn't possibly understand where he was coming from. When we landed at Heathrow, he went one way, to Salisbury, and I went the other, to Wembley to see Paul Weller in concert and try to shake my mind onto something else.

Yet, of course, the episode at the clinic lingered in our heads. After Peter was declared dead, the nurse had opened the window. Terry asked her why. 'Because I believe the soul leaves the body after death, and I'm allowing it to depart,' she said. That made a huge impression on Terry. After this, he became convinced that he had witnessed the exact moment when the soul left Peter Smedley's body. Now he would often ask me, 'Do you think there's something on the other side?' This, to be clear, was not the same, in Terry's mind, as 'finding God'. When a newspaper article implied in a headline that Terry had become a believer around this time, he felt obliged to issue a correction: 'There's a rumour going round that I've found God,' he said. 'Which I think is unlikely because I have enough difficulty finding my keys, and there is empirical evidence that they exist.' But one of Terry's purposes in going to Switzerland, I realized, had been to see if death could be turned into a construct, a place that you could visit. Making the film seemed to bring him some calm and to alleviate some of his dread. It was enough somehow to know that there were options, even if he never ultimately took them, and the panicked anger went out of the argument after Zurich.

On the night of the broadcast, in the early summer of 2011, we assembled to watch the show go out at Charlie Russell's mother's house in north London, where the decorations included a stuffed water buffalo, once the property of Dame Beryl Bainbridge. I was petrified about how the programme would be received. Well in advance of its screening – and well before anyone had seen it – this BBC programme with its death scene had already generated a scandalized *Daily Mail* front page. Terry and I were in New Zealand at the time that happened – in Mata Mata, to be precise, having just had that great day, mentioned before, visiting the Hobbiton movie set. News from home that the papers were already gunning for our programme made me anxious, but the fuss was of absolutely no concern to Terry. Headlines like 'Pratchett Defends Suicide Doc' were fine by him – all part of the crusade, in fact. What in the end delighted Terry most of all was that the programme received 750 complaints in advance of its broadcast, and far fewer complaints afterwards. That summed it up, for Terry. It was also, he thought, a sign that we were doing things properly.

I needn't have been concerned, in any case. It was the first time we had been connected to social media at a time like this, and able to watch the reactions happen in real time. Deep into the programme, I started tentatively scrolling through Twitter. It was incredible: tweet after tweet of positive reaction, more than one per second. I scrolled on through the timeline, stopping at random: more and more amazing positivity and appreciation for Terry and the programme. I scrolled on again, through reams and reams of approval and once more brought my index finger down.

Bingo.

'Terry Pratchett's assistant is a right knob.'

Ah well. The programme was debated in Parliament, generated count-less articles in the press, and went on to be highly garlanded, winning awards from BAFTA and the Royal Television Society, and also taking an International Emmy. And through it all, Terry remained ... well ... Terry.

'Did you expect to win tonight?' he was asked, in London at the BAFTAs, as we clustered around the trophy in our bow ties.

It was one of those classic TV interview questions expecting the answer no.

'I thought we had a pretty good chance,' Terry said.

He didn't hang around afterwards, either. For Terry, it was all about the film. The fancy, after-show stuff? Not really. Once we had received the award and done our PR duties, we were led to our dinner table by our specially appointed star chaperone, Rob Brydon. We had just sat down – all of us very hungry after a long evening – when Terry decided that he'd seen enough. 'Get the car,' he said. Still clutching the golden mask BAFTA trophy – surprisingly heavy, incidentally – I left the room, and then the building, made contact with our driver, and then went back inside, wav-ing the BAFTA at security by way of a pass on my way through. I returned to the table, fetched the author and, without further ceremony, Terry Pratchett went home.

★ ★ ★ ★ ★

There was a lot of death in those years. There was too much death. But there was a lot of living, too. Gloriously defiant and extra pre-cious living. And an awful lot of that living seemed to get done in Ireland.

Midway through 2010, Dr David Lloyd, the Dean of Research at Trin-ity College Dublin, rang to talk to Terry about the possibility of him becoming a professor there.

Oh that the headmaster of Holtspur Primary School had been living at this hour.

Our contact with David and Trinity went back to 2008, when the college offered Terry an honorary doctorate. Terry, in the middle of writing *Unseen Academicals*, and already in possession of five honorary doctorates, instantly wanted to turn it down. Colin Smythe and I – fans of Irish literature and Ireland in general and, in Colin's case, an actual alumnus of Trinity College Dublin – were devastated. He wanted to turn down the college of Jonathan Swift, Oscar Wilde and Samuel Beckett? Not on our watch. In the ensuing days, we conspired to wage an extremely unsubtle campaign of propaganda until he relented.

He never regretted it. In 2008, ahead of the doctoral ceremony, all three of us checked into the Westin Hotel and then Terry went to meet David Lloyd, who turned out, contrary to Terry's preconceptions regarding university deans, to be startlingly young-looking. Indeed, David was fresh-faced enough to be known around the university as 'Baby Dean'. Early in their meeting, when Terry asked to use the bathroom, David guided him to the nearby Provost's Residence at 1 Grafton Street, a splendid Georgian Palladian townhouse. It was there that Terry encountered the Provost's truly sensational downstairs lavatory – a massive lump of Victorian porcelain with a vast wooden seat, known as the Deluge on account of the torrential force of its flush. Showing Terry into this mighty throne room, David told him, 'You've got to hang on the chain a while to get it going properly.' Terry was enchanted. Few things in life moved him as much as fully functioning Victorian plumbing. Flushing the loo, and activating the Deluge after his ablutions, Terry let out a loud 'Woo-hoo!', slightly startling David who was waiting for him outside. Terry straight away made clear to David that, if the building was ever renovated, he would like to be given the chance, as an honorary doctor of Trinity College, to buy the Provost's lavatory. Alas, that hour never came. But clearly Terry's love affair with Trinity College had already commenced.*

After the Deluge, they went over to the robing room, where Terry was introduced to Mary Robinson, former president of Ireland and the

. . . .

* Terry was almost as impressed by the Provost himself as he was by the Provost's lavatory. Dr John Hegarty had a mane of white hair and a luxurious white beard that Terry could only be jealous of. 'You can't possibly be in academia,' Terry told him. 'You look like a movie star.'

Chancellor of the University, and to Sir David Attenborough, national treasure, who was also being honoured. That was a big moment for Terry. As we know, he didn't much go in for being starstruck, but for Sir David Attenborough, as for Sir Patrick Moore, he made an exception. Then it was on to the Public Theatre for the ceremony. Terry, now thoroughly enjoying himself in a mortar board and his blue and red doctoral robes, had a celebratory oration about him read aloud in Latin. After that, everybody processed across the cobblestones to Front Square and the dining hall, where Terry swapped his mortar board for his fedora and was handed a pint of Guinness.

The following day, we went back to the Public Theatre, where Terry was interviewed by David Lloyd in front of an audience of 400. At the end of the conversation, Terry stood and said, 'Now it is my turn.' He explained that he was in a position to award honorary degrees on behalf of Unseen University and would be proud to bestow one on David. This was my cue to play the Debbie McGee to Terry's Paul Daniels and arrive on stage holding the night's star prize – an Unseen University scarf and a roll of parchment.

'But,' said Terry, 'you'll have to answer a question correctly first.'

David, whose knowledge of the Discworld novels was easily *Mastermind* standard, looked quietly confident.

Terry's question was: what is the Ankh-Morpork city motto?

There was an embarrassed silence. David didn't know. Terry threw it over to the audience. The embarrassed silence continued. None of them knew either.

'OK,' said Terry. 'I'll ask another. What is the motto of Unseen University?'

Again, David could only sit there looking blank. Again, Terry asked the audience to put the contestant out of his misery. Again, the audience couldn't help.

At this point, Terry consented to offer David a clue. 'Now you see it . . .'

'Now you don't?' said a mortified David, hesitantly.

'Correct!' said Terry, and David received the scarf and the parchment.

Subsequently, David would pore over the Discworld books in search of the references that he had failed to summon . . . and not find them. About two years later, he asked Terry about it. 'Those questions you asked me . . . The answers aren't in the books. I've gone back and checked.'

'Ah,' said Terry, blithely. 'It was a test of your *canonical* knowledge.'

After the conferral, two further trips to Dublin had ensued, one for an alumni dinner at which Chris de Burgh was present and gave the room an acoustic rendition of 'The Lady in Red'. Terry sang along loudly. On the second visit, Terry met graduate students, including one whose PhD thesis was on the Discworld novels, and was taken on a behind-the-scenes tour of the Long Room library, where he got to handle, with some excitement, a notebook used by Samuel Beckett, and was shown the Pollard collection of illustrations for children's literature. That was also the trip on which he was introduced to the joys of the Yamamori noodle house on South Great George's Street.* What with one thing and another, Dublin and Terry clicked.

And now here was David Lloyd on the phone, offering Terry an adjunct professorship in the School of English.

'A professor?' Terry shouted into the phone. 'Me? Are you mad? You're mad. You're a mad Irishman.'

David explained what the job would involve: nominally, two trips a year, an inaugural lecture and then masterclasses and some research supervision. Terry thought about it for a long time.

'Is there any type of hat associated with this position?'

David said not officially, but it could certainly be worked on. At that point, Terry, completely satisfied, handed the phone back to me to firm up the arrangements.

That professorship made him so proud – possibly even prouder than the knighthood. When David phoned to get the title of Terry's inaugural lecture, Terry instantly offered, in an allusion to Wilde, 'The importance of

. . . .

* Sushi and plum wine was the standard order. Going for servings of Irish stoup – a soup and stew combo – in the Science Gallery café also became a must-do.

being absolutely amazed by everything'. Or possibly it was, 'The importance of being amazed by absolutely everything'. The title seemed to shift every time anyone said it, and it never got pinned down definitively. Eventually, in a nod to the Discworld novel ~~Faust~~ Eric, invitations to the lecture were issued with the 'absolutely' crossed out.

Terry went over to Dublin for the ceremony, again in the Public Theatre, in November 2010. I read the lecture from the lectern that night, while a gowned Terry sat beside me on a tall wood and leather button-backed throne, heckling furiously and providing footnotes. At the end, David Lloyd produced a white box containing the promised hat, a John Rocha-designed, sensationally gothic mortar board with black feathers. Terry could not have been more delighted.

Our double act that night had gone over OK. 'I suppose you and I are now sharing a brain,' Terry said to me afterwards.

'I suppose we are, Terry,' I replied. From Terry, this was quite the compliment.

The next day, 'Professor Sir Terry Pratchett OBE, Blackboard Monitor, Adjunct of the Oscar Wilde Centre for Irish Writing and the School of English at Trinity College Dublin' – as David Lloyd had introduced him – gave his first creative writing class. He was anxious about it. How do you tell people how to write? Either you do it, and you're good at it, or you do it and you're bad at it, or you don't do it at all. 'How can you *learn* to write?' Terry kept saying.

We went first to the student common room to meet Professor Gerald Dawe, from the School of English, and to be given a cup of tea. Terry almost immediately fell asleep on the sofa. He was nudged awake with the tea and a snifter of brandy. Then he was taken through to the classroom. I remained, nervously, in the common room. It seemed reasonable to wonder: would this be the shortest creative writing class in the history of creative writing classes?

An hour and a half later, Terry had to be practically pulled out of the room with ropes. It appeared he had got into long discussions with the Masters students about writing and motivation. He was lit up by the experience.

He would go to Dublin twice in 2011, and twice in 2012. On the first of the 2011 visits, in May, he met the Queen in the Long Room library during the first state visit to the Republic of Ireland by a British monarch since 1911.* But, as usual, Terry's main business in the city was spending at least 90 minutes explaining to students exactly why it was impossible to teach creative writing. He allowed himself to entertain a fond vision of an alternative future, one in which our twilight years would be spent securely in academe, in some nice college room with a crackling fire, sitting in comfortable armchairs, composing his books and the odd lecture, with three meals left on a tray outside the door each day. The notion very strongly appealed to him.

Another source of inspiration in these years, and an extra lease of life at a crucial time, came in the form of a new writing partnership. It was at Malcolm Edwards' usual pre-London Book Fair dinner that Terry fell into conversation with the sci-fi writer Stephen Baxter. Steve was nine years younger than Terry, had a doctorate in engineering, and was much gilded with science fiction awards, both British and American. The pair of them got talking about 'The High Meggas', the novel about a series of parallel worlds and the voyagers who step between them, which, back in the mid-eighties, Terry had got 40,000 words into before abandoning it to write *Mort*. Those words had sat there, unvisited, ever since. Would Steve be interested in working with Terry to adapt and expand on them? By the end of the evening, the pair had roughed out an approach to what would quickly become the 'Long Earth' series.

What was also concocted was a unique plan to write the first story in the series while in an open-top car speeding along American highways between New Orleans and Madison, Wisconsin. Kind of sci-fi meets Hunter S. Thompson. In the summer of 2011, Terry was going to be in Louisiana to receive the Margaret A. Edwards Award from the American Library Association for his contribution to young adult literature, after which he would be heading over to Madison to make an

. . . .

* As we left the Westin that morning, we noted the exceptionally unusual sight of a Union Jack flying above Trinity College.

appearance at the North American Discworld Convention. So why not combine business with pleasure and a road trip, and get some words done while covering those 1,000 miles in a hired convertible? Terry was up for it, I was *certainly* up for it, and Steve . . . well, I never quite worked out what Steve really thought of the idea. Let's just say that, when the scheme was eventually abandoned on the grounds that it would have been too much of a stretch for Terry, very few complaints were heard from Steve's quarter.

Instead Steve came and stayed at the pub near the manor, and worked with Terry in the Chapel, in and around lunchtime breaks for bubble and squeak. His hardcore SF style made for a beautiful mix with Terry's brand of humour, and the collaboration kept Terry writing and creating and granted him a whole new outlet at a time when his illness seemed to have ideas about him closing down. The series would eventually grow to be five novels long.

★ ★ ★ ★ ★

For Terry, books frequently found their own path in the course of being written. This is possibly not something you can hold out as an exemplary approach to other writers, because it maybe only works if you have a mind like Terry Pratchett's.

Snuff, for example, opens with Sam Vimes putting on a pair of socks that his wife has made him. But she makes socks very badly; they're itchy and scratchy and they require Vimes to have shoes which are one and a half sizes bigger than his feet in order to accommodate them. Yet he loves her, so he doesn't say anything about it. He just puts on the socks. That was the scene that Terry began with – a simple domestic moment in the life of a besotted husband – and that was the departure point for the next scene, which in turn would provide the departure point for the scene after that, and so on until a novel appeared. Or as Terry also put it: 'You throw a stone and you go where that stone lands.'

Published in autumn 2011, *Snuff* was Terry's fiftieth book – the fiftieth time in forty-five years as a published author he had thrown a stone and gone where it landed. It was a remarkable run. Reviewing *Snuff* in the *Guardian*, A. S. Byatt described Terry as 'a master storyteller' and 'endlessly inventive' and observed no decline in his powers.* Other readers felt the same. The book sold 55,000 copies in three days, making it the third fastest-selling novel in the history of British publishing. 'Blimey,' said Terry, when this was broken to him. 'If I'd known what having Alzheimer's would do for book sales, I'd have got it sooner.'†

Snuff also contained one of my absolutely favourite passages of Pratchett. Vimes is relaxing in a luxurious bath, 'feeling as if he was trying to fit all the bits of his brain together'.

> Then Vimes floated again in the warm steamy atmosphere and was
> only just aware of the swish of clothing hitting the floor. Lady Sybil
> slid in beside him. The water rose, and so, in accordance with the
> physics of this business, did the spirits of Sam Vimes.

For *Snuff*'s launch, Terry and I headed to the West End of London – to the Theatre Royal, specifically, for 'An Evening with Terry Pratchett' in front of 2,000 fans. Transworld had considered hiring the Royal Albert Hall, but ultimately settled for something more modest. A shame: who doesn't want to say they've played the Albert Hall? As it happened, the demand for tickets when the event was announced would have filled the Albert Hall twice over. But the Theatre Royal had its kudos, too. The musical of *Shrek*, which Jeffrey Katzenberg had been on his way to see when he met Terry for tea earlier in the year, was in

....

* A. S. Byatt added, 'I think his mad footnotes are there because he can't stop his mind whirring, and our whirring minds go with them.' I'm here in a footnote to tell A. S. Byatt that I think she is absolutely right to say that.

† When *Snuff* won the Bollinger Everyman P. G. Wodehouse Award for a comic novel, Terry had the traditional honour of seeing the title of one of his books bestowed as a name on a Gloucester Old Spot pig. Snuff may not have been the most attractive name for a farm animal, but given that others in that distinguished line had been called 'Zoo Time', 'The Butt' and 'Bridget Jones's Baby', maybe Snuff ought to have been thankful for small mercies.

the middle of its run there – though, to my disappointment, we didn't get to appear on its set, which had been partly demounted for the night and moved to the back of the stage. Terry and I did, however, get to use a dressing room whose paper sign on the door declared it to be set aside for 'Donkey'.

'As it's the two of *us* in there,' Terry suggested, as we stood outside in the corridor, 'maybe it should really say "Ass".'

I needed a shot of brandy for my nerves that night. Terry took a shot of brandy, too, though he didn't seem at all nervous. These events never fazed him. They hadn't before he had Alzheimer's, and they didn't now. From my more agitated point of view, there was the scale of the theatre and the size of the gathering to contend with. My mum and dad, my two brothers, Kevin and Dale, and other members of my family were there. And when your Aunt Muriel is in the front of the dress circle, you feel the pressure. Plus Larry Finlay from Transworld had pressed an envelope into my hands containing a sheet of figures relating to how well *Snuff* was selling, so there were things I needed to work into my spiel. But it went OK, even after I had made the mistake of referring to our recent trip to the US as 'awesome', a term earning me an immedi-ate reprimand from Terry. 'It's not awesome unless God and the Devil and their hosts came down to Earth,' he explained. 'Otherwise, it's just "great".' Point taken.* Near the end, perhaps as a consequence of the brandy, but more likely because the gradual winding-up of everything was constantly in my mind now, I grew a little emotional and thanked Terry for letting me share the ride with him over the past decade and a half. Terry looked at me, held my gaze and, seemingly ignoring the audience, said, 'It's not over yet.'

As indeed it wasn't. The next day, Transworld threw a party for *Snuff* with a boat trip up the Thames on board a booze-laden vessel named *The Wonderful Fanny*.† There were canapés and champagne on the way out, and

. . . .

* The other banned term around Terry: fun. Fun was no fun at all, as far as Terry was concerned.

† *The Wonderful Fanny* is a paddle barge working the Quire which, in *Snuff*, is commissioned

bacon baguettes on the way back and, in between times, there were speeches, with Larry Finlay presenting Terry with a bottle of 50-year-old cognac. Terry spoke, too. He couldn't hold the microphone because he would struggle to keep it in the vicinity of his mouth, so I converted myself into an impromptu microphone stand and knelt in front of him, holding the mic towards him. From my position on the floor, I watched helplessly as Terry got some words out and then dissolved into tears. Everything inescapably carried the weight of a valedictory in this period. It was overwhelming.

After *Snuff*, the writing got harder. Actually, after *Snuff*, *everything* got harder. Things getting harder was simply the path we were on. In 2012, Terry started in on *Dodger*. A non-Discworld tale, aimed at young adults, and set in Victorian London, it was the culmination of Terry's love for Dickens and his fascination with Henry Mayhew's *London Labour and the London Poor*, which had begun all the way back at Beaconsfield Library. The book was a hard slog throughout that year, but he got there. And then *Dodger*'s publication, in the autumn of 2012, took us to New York for what we didn't know, but might have surmised, would be the last time.

Neither of us would forget it.

It was possible to gauge the decline in Terry by thinking back to the previous time we were in New York, a year earlier – in late September 2011. Leaving a packed, evening-long event at Barnes & Noble in Tribeca, an invigorated Terry had insisted on visiting the Occupy Wall Street protest camp, then in position at Zuccotti Park. Terry had heard there was a library in the campsite, 5,000 volumes strong, and he was keen to see it. Anne Hoppe, Terry's US children's editor, slightly uneasily joined us. The fact that we arrived at this anti-capitalist demonstration in an SUV with tinted windows could have been deemed provocative, but nobody seemed to object. We walked around, Terry wearing his bowler hat. The library was largely shrouded in tarpaulin against the

. . . .

to transport iron ore, chickens and goblins from the Shires down to Quirm. This didn't need a spoiler alert, did it? Apologies if it did.

misty rain that was falling, but a woman minding the books was a Discworld fan who recognized Terry and organized a couple of people to give
him a tour. Some chanting was going on and someone was leading a medi-
tation circle. 'Terry was simply charmed and rather elated to find the
sixties alive and well,' said Anne Hoppe. Then we got back in the car and
went to Papillon to eat our respective body-weights in French onion
soup.

A year later, improvised late-night rambles into New York protest
zones were no longer really on the cards. Terry these days was having
some trouble rambling on his own doorstep. A couple of times he had
set off from the manor on impromptu walks and ended up getting lost;
at least once, a neighbour had found him up the road, looking confused,
and had safely returned him. So this US trip was necessarily short and
tightly structured: two events in New York, including an appearance at
New York Comic Con, and one in Chicago. We had posted notice in
advance: 'Terry will not be signing any books or memorabilia on this
tour.' It was touring, then, but not really as we knew it. On the Saturday
we entered the aircraft hangar which is the Jakob K. Javits Convention
Center on Eleventh Avenue, where Comic Con was raging and where
we observed the brutal economy of stardom in action, with signatures
available on a sliding scale from $20 (Lou Ferrigno, the Incredible Hulk)
up to $500 (Carrie Fisher in *Star Wars* mode). But you never know who
you are going to see at Comic Con and this time we were enormously
gratified by a sighting of Adam West, the original – and best – Batman.
We also bumped into Sean Astin backstage – 'Uncle Terry!' he shouted –
and Terry later gate-crashed, and practically took over, Sean's panel.
Then, under the guidance of Jennifer Brehl, we managed a trip to a
Manhattan hat shop, where Terry was keen to acquire a top hat, à la
Fred Astaire, and duly did so. Eventually we ended up back at our
hotel – the Omni Berkshire Place, which was one of Terry's favourites
in New York, mostly because it backed very conveniently onto the
HarperCollins building.

By this point, when we were away on trips our established end-
of-the-day routine was to have a nightcap in Terry's room, where I
would check that he was OK. And then, just before leaving, I would

loosen the bed sheets. We had discovered that, for PCA sufferers, tightly tucked hotel bed sheets can represent a serious obstacle to getting into the bed.

That night in New York, though, I came to the unutterably saddening realization that Terry needed even more help from me, just to cope at this most basic level. Now I didn't just need to loosen the bed sheets. I helped him with his dentures. I took off and folded his glasses. I fetched him a glass of water from the bathroom. I tucked him in.

And then I went back to my own room, lay on the bed fully clothed and burst into tears. Because I realized that this was it: we were done. If this was where we were now, the end could not be far away.

And now it's Sunday – and that most unusual thing, a free day. We aren't travelling to or from anywhere, and we have no events to go to. I cannot remember the last time we had one of these. And we're in New York! So at least there is this.

Around lunchtime, I decide to get out of the hotel and go and see the Freedom Tower. Terry, who has already watched *Men in Black 2* that morning and is now bored, decides to come with me. We take a taxi downtown from the Omni.

We step out on the pavement near the Tower and I get my camera from its bag. I manage to take one photograph before, behind me, Terry makes a sighing noise which is also a groan.

'I think I need to go back,' he says. 'I don't feel so good.'

Our taxi hasn't even had time to move away. I tap on the window.

'Can you take us back?'

At this stage, I'm not concerned. To be perfectly honest, I'm more annoyed at having my sight-seeing trip cut short on this, our one free day, and I'm staring out of the window of the moving cab, looking out crossly over the East River.

Then, next to me, I hear Terry's breathing change.

I look across at him and he is sweating and his colour is high.

I say to the taxi driver, 'How long to the hotel?'

'About twenty minutes?' says the driver.

And suddenly Terry is rigid and throwing himself back into his seat with enormous force and then vomiting bright yellow bile, which is all over me and all over the taxi, and I am yelling to the driver that we need a hospital and fast because Terry is having a heart attack.

Time stops.

I am half on the seat, half on the floor, trying to minister to him in the back of this cramped taxi with its smeared Plexiglass screen, and thinking that it's too late anyway because he is dying in front of me. I clear his mouth and nose of liquid with my fingers and I move his tongue to unblock his airway. I loosen his shirt and I start to give him CPR.

The taxi pulls up at the hospital and it's like a movie – people in scrubs seem to come out of nowhere. Terry is slid from the back seat and put on a trolley and whisked through the doors. I'm taken to a room and given a fresh T-shirt and some things to clean myself, and I remain convinced that Terry is actually dead until someone tells me, 'He's fine, he's not going to die.' They're doing some tests and they will be able to tell very quickly if he's had a heart attack.

The wait seems to go on all afternoon, but is probably only about 40 minutes. Then someone comes and says, 'He hasn't had a heart attack.' But they need to know about the medication he is taking. I carry his prescription with me in my camera bag, so I hand that over to them, and again I'm left to wait. And then a senior doctor comes and calmly explains that there is a conflict between Terry's blood pressure medication and some of his other pills and his blood pressure had dropped dangerously low, resulting, in the taxi, in a bad bout of atrial fibrillation, which is not a heart attack but sure as hell looked like one to me.

Terry is kept in the hospital, for observation, out of an abundance of precaution. Anne Hoppe joins me that night and we sit on the floor by Terry's bed and talk the whole thing out while, above us, Terry sleeps the sleep of the righteous, and while, every two minutes, one of the hospital machines that goes bing unnecessarily goes bing, meaning Anne and I have to take it in turns to get up each time and mute its alarm.

Somewhere around dawn, my phone rings. It's the garage, in England. My sports motorcycle is ready for collection, having had its MoT and a service. Also, would I like to book a test drive of that Harley-Davidson they recently took delivery of? I say that, actually, I'm in New

York, in hospital with somebody, so I can't really book a test drive now, but . . . no, actually, what the hell, I'll just buy it regardless, because if I've learned anything over the last few hours, it's that life is for living.

In the morning, Terry is fine – for a given value of fine.

Actually, he's just *fine*. Like nothing happened.

'Right,' says Terry. 'We're going to Chicago.'

'No, Terry,' I say, firmly. 'This was bad. We're going home.'

We go to Chicago. Terry's one concession, solemnly granted, is that, when we do our talk at the event, we won't mention what just happened – the point being, we have yet to relay to anyone in England just how bad this has been and we don't want the word getting out before we arrive home ourselves to report it in full.

We are less than a minute into the event when Terry, adopting his best comedy patter voice, says to the audience, 'You know what? A funny thing happened on the way to the theatre tonight . . .'

I'm thinking to myself: the man is incorrigible. But at least he is still alive.

★ ★ ★ ★ ★

In December 2012, Sir Patrick Moore died. He was 89. We went to the funeral. There were only fifteen or so people there, and no press – not even the local Chichester paparazzo. Afterwards we went back to Farthings, Patrick's house, where we told stories about Patrick, and where Jon Culshaw read a piece in Patrick's voice. Then, in accordance with instructions left by Patrick himself, we lit a candle. Patrick had promised us that, in the event there was an afterlife, he would blow out a naked flame on the night of his funeral so that we would know.

We stood for a while and watched the candle burn defiantly. So much for the afterlife.

And then, in a sudden puff, it went out.

In the car on the way home, Terry said, 'I've started to think that God might be tempting me to believe in him.' I said that I, too, felt that it was very hard sometimes not to reach that conclusion. At the same time, we both agreed that it was extremely useful to have, as Patrick did, television production people among your closest friends for when you wanted to have a beautifully planned visual stunt pulled off in your absence.

* * * * *

And then, in the spring of 2013 – as you do when you are six years on from a diagnosis of PCA, and in a state now of quite radical physical decline – Terry flew to Borneo to see if he could find an orang-utan.

It was madness, really. He was unsteady on his feet, prone to bouts of confusion and in need of careful monitoring anywhere that was not his entirely close and familiar surroundings. And we were flying halfway round the world and going into the sweltering heat and overwhelming humidity of the jungle to search for an orang-utan that hadn't been seen for months. But Terry wanted to do it. And I could only admire him for that – and go with him to make sure he came back.

Fourteen years previously, in 1999, Terry had made *Terry Pratchett's Jungle Quest*, a half-hour film for the Channel 4 series *Short Stories*, tracking extinction-threatened orang-utans in the Borneo rainforest. He had no record before that as a globe-girdling David Attenborough figure. True, he was the man who had made the librarian of Unseen University an ape, but that was mostly because he was looking for some-one in the role who had very long arms and could climb, assets which Terry realized would have been enormously valuable during his own spell in that line of work. Yet this incidental association seemed to be enough. On that trip, he had come face to face with Kusasi, the king of the orang-utans on the patch that Terry was surveying, and they had looked each other in the eye, and Terry had never forgotten it. Maybe Kusasi had never forgotten it, either. But Terry was passionate about orang-utans and their preservation for ever after. And perhaps the spring of 2013 would be a good time to head back into the jungle – hook up again with the conservationists there, and see what had become of Kusasi and whether he was still around.

Hello again, Craig Hunter and Charlie Russell. After *Living With Alzheimer's*, Terry and I swore we would never make another documentary. After *Choosing to Die*, we swore the same thing again, only twice as hard. And now here we were, packing our leech socks to go and make *Terry Pratchett: Facing Extinction*.

The leech socks were courtesy of the BBC, who had promised a box of essentials for the trip. 'What are you sending us?' Terry asked. 'A banana?' No, they were sending us leech socks and other items of stout clothing and various precautionary traveller's medicaments – and also, of course, now that Terry had mentioned it, a banana.

'I'll need you to get my rucksack down from the attic,' Terry told me. I went up and brought it down. It was quite dusty – also quite *fusty*. I unfastened the flap, upended it, and out came, in a shower of dried soil, the boots Terry had worn to Borneo on that 1999 trip, unworn since.

And so began this crazy and intrepid adventure – although the first stage wasn't really very intrepid at all. We flew to Jakarta on Singapore Airlines Suites, which has to be the poshest airline ever created and is like having your own Pullman railway carriage, but up in the air. Terry's and my flying apartment featured two bedrooms each and a living room with a 32-inch television screen on which we watched a selection of movies.

After that, though, things got distinctly less fancy. We landed in Jakarta and spent the night in the FM7 Airport Hotel, where we hooked up with the crew, who had flown ahead. In the morning, Terry was not in good shape. He had always done well at fighting jetlag, but the Alzheimer's seemed to have removed that skill. With Terry very groggy, we now took a taxi into the centre of Jakarta. The traffic was terrible, the heat was stifling, and the drive took three hours. Moreover we had a cameraman on board with us, so we couldn't use the taxi's aircon, which would have at best misted the lens and at worst completely ruined the hugely expensive camera body. Not a great start. But we met Charlie and went to a restaurant where he was going to go over plans with us. We had not been sitting down very long when Terry literally face-planted on the table. He was utterly exhausted and had fallen asleep with his face on the tablecloth. Rosy Marshall, the production co-ordinator, leapt into action. The restaurant happened to have a small selection of bedrooms, available to hire by the hour. No prizes for guessing what these were commonly used for, but suffice to say it was not normally for sleeping off jetlag. Nevertheless, Rosy hired Terry a room and he went off, unaccompanied, to get some sleep. While he was resting, Charlie sat at the restaurant table and sombrely started crossing lines through his plans.

After a couple of hours, we woke Terry and then took him back to the hotel – a drive which, thankfully, took a lot less than three hours. I was thinking, this is already over: scrap the film. Terry's health must come first. At the hotel, I had a private chat with Terry and said I thought we should go home. But Terry had once again had one of his unforeseeable resurgences. He would hear nothing of it. Ten minutes later we were in Terry's room having hidden cameras fitted into our shirts before heading back into the city to a market where we going to investigate the trade in rare animals.

We spent two more days filming in the city, with Terry now firmly post jetlag and on good form, and then we flew to Pangkalan Bun, where we met Ashley Leiman from the Orangutan Foundation and got some more footage, before taking a Klotok boat deep into the jungle.* By this point Terry was happily storming up and down jungle paths – even blundering about up to his thighs in a swamp at one point. We were out in the jungle for two weeks. Two weeks with no wi-fi or phone signal. Two weeks looking for Kusasi.†

Charlie wanted Terry and me to have a conversation on camera about the end – Terry's end. He wanted it to take place on the boat, and the idea was that we would glide downriver at night to a place where there would be a beautiful backdrop of fireflies and then start talking. As it happened, rain fell and put paid to the fireflies, but we did attempt the sequence. However, Terry quickly shut the conversation down, just as he had done with his outstretched arm in the 'HOW LONG?'

....

*   Klotok boat – named for the noise it makes.

†   Did we find him? Not telling you. No spoilers here, remember. The film can easily be found online.

incident in the *Living With Alzheimer's* documentary. But Terry and I did end up having the chat – in private, back at the Rimba Lodge where we were staying. I had an iPad with me and one evening, near the trip's end, we played music on it and had a beer. At one point, 'Looking for a Destination' by my dear friend Charlie Landsborough started up, and the plangency of the song was not lost on us. We reminisced. We recalled the time when I had just started working for him and I was accompanying him for the first time to the offices of Transworld in London – how I'd shown up on the driveway that morning wearing a suit. Well, I didn't know what you wore to go to a publisher's, and I thought I needed to be smart. I think I had in my mind the image of Patrick Janson-Smith – the only London publisher I had really come across at that stage – mingling at the Discworld Convention in his blue blazer with gold buttons. Alas, my suit was nothing that would have found a hanger in the Janson-Smith wardrobe. It was a Mr Byrite special – khaki in colour, with a slight sheen to it.

Terry looked me up and down on the driveway and said, 'Oh, my god – it's the under-manager.'

The ribbing then didn't stop, all the way to London in the car: 'The under-manager wishes to see you . . . You'll have to run that past the under-manager . . .' I was so mortified that, when we reached Ealing, I ran up the road to Marks & Spencer and bought some jeans, a shirt and a jumper, and changed into them in the car before I went into the building. I wore jeans and a T-shirt to work from that day forward.*

We laughed a lot to recall all that and how far we'd come since then and what we'd been through together. In due course, I asked Terry what he wanted for his memorial service.

'To be there,' he said.

And then he started talking about Graham Chapman, and I knew exactly where he was going. When Chapman died, in 1989, aged 48, his Monty Python colleague John Cleese said, in his tribute, that he had heard Chapman whispering in his ear, urging him 'to become the first

. . . .

* And not, I want to add, M&S ones. That was an emergency.

person ever at a British memorial service to say "fuck" '. Terry now issued me the solemn instruction that, at *his* memorial service, I should use the words 'fuck' and, just for good measure, 'bugger' in front of an audience which he knew would include my parents.[*]

I asked him, 'Do you think you'll still be read in three hundred years' time, Terry?'

He said, 'Good god, no. In three hundred years' time we'll all be eating each other.'

We began a list: 'A dozen things to do before you die.' But we didn't get very far with it. Terry said he wanted to go up in the Virgin Galactic spacecraft; that he wanted to dig a ruby mine in the Congo; that he wanted to go back to the OK Corral; and that he wanted to write a best-seller. He did the last of those. Actually, he wrote two.

Finally, even though it was not somewhere the conversation naturally went for either of us, I told him how much of a privilege it had been to be alongside him over these years.

'A privilege for you?' Terry said, seeming genuinely surprised.

'Yes, a real privilege,' I said.

'Your privilege was all mine,' Terry said.

Which I think was intended as a compliment, but, as with so many of Terry's compliments, it was hard to be entirely sure.

. . . .

[*] I duly complied with Terry's fervent wishes at the Barbican on 14 April 2016. As Cleese also said of Chapman, 'Anything for him but mindless good taste.'

20

A ROGUE RECLINER, TAKE-AWAY SCAMPI AND THE BITTER, BITTER END

I'm sitting in the Chapel one morning, waiting for the call to go down to the house and collect Terry. This is where we are now. He can no longer make even that short journey alone. He needs to walk up to the Chapel on my arm. On dark evenings, he will sometimes need me to take him back in the car.

And in between those guided journeys, there will be a day, of some kind, in the office. Mid-morning, I will fix him his 'glug': coffee with a shot of brandy in it – and brandy, as Terry would gladly tell you, is in the British Pharmacopoeia and therefore qualifies as medicine.* If he has had a bad night, which he often has, he will need to spend some of the day sleeping. And he will probably need at least one change of clothes, which I will go down to the kitchen to collect from Lyn and then bring back up to him.† And then I will help him put on his clean

. . . .

* On some days, depending on how Terry was feeling, coffee with a shot of brandy in it might become brandy with a shot of coffee in it. We called it 'glug', of course, after the noise of the brandy departing the upturned bottle.

† Terry, who was healthily unsqueamish about all bodily functions at all times, was heroically open and unembarrassed by the encroaching incontinence that was another of the little gifts of PCA. 'I think I may need a gentleman's gentleman,' he would say, when he

clothes, and we will go back to work – the work that he is so determined to continue doing. Because the work has always been the most important thing, but it has taken on a whole new dimension now. Work is Terry's last defence against this cruel disease which is stripping him of himself. For as long as he writes, he is still Terry Pratchett.

So, for as long as he needs me to, I will help him to write.

And on this particular morning, I am waiting for the call to go and get him. Instead, there is a bang as the door flies open, and in comes Terry at speed.

'Honey – I'm home!'

I jump out of my chair and propel myself across the room towards him. I am gobsmacked. It's unbelievable – an utter transformation. There has recently been an adjustment to his dose of Aricept, and this seems to be the miraculous result: a Terry who can get himself to the Chapel unassisted; a Terry with a buzz of energy about him, who has clearly been readying that opening line on his way up from the house; a Terry who seems to have been to the other side of Alzheimer's and has now returned to issue his first-hand report from behind the curtain.

He talks mostly about the fog. He sits there in the Chapel, in his chair, and tells me that this was what it felt like, these past months: a fog. And he was trying to punch and claw his way through that fog but not making any progress. He knew there was something wrong, but the fog blew up and overcame him and he couldn't pull himself beyond it.

But never mind that now: he wants to talk urgently about the garden. When did he last sound urgent like this about something that wasn't the writing? He remembers that he has been meaning to change the battery in the meter that measures the volume of rainwater in the sump sunk under the stables for irrigating the garden. Could we do something about that?

. . . .

required help after an accident – quoting, of course, Sam Vimes in *Snuff* on the subject of his manservant Willikins. To be clear, Willikins is not an example of Tuckerization. Willikins was Vimes's righthand man long before I came along to be Terry's. But it is a funny coincidence. Let's call it, instead, then, an act of predictive nominative determinism, if that isn't too many syllables for one sentence.

'Yes, Terry! Of course we can!'

And then, obviously, he wants to work. Because work is what Terry Pratchett does, and work is who Terry Pratchett is. I open the file and the words come, flowing freely in a way that they have not done for months, and we do a full-on day of writing towards the novel *Raising Steam*.

I come to think of it as Miracle Drug Day.* I go home that night, thinking, 'My god, he's back in the room.'

The following morning, I sit in the Chapel and I'm waiting for the door to bang open and for Terry to come in at speed.

'Honey – I'm home!'

I wait.

And I wait.

And then I get the call.

I go down to the house and collect him and I bring him up to the Chapel on my arm.

Today he is not so sharp. We have a slow day.

The day after that he is less sharp still. We have an even slower day.

The disappointment is utterly devastating. The effect of the Aricept, the solitary drug in our armoury, is wearing off. The fog is moving in once more, and rapidly swallowing him, and I know now there is nothing he or I will ever be able to do to prevent him from disappearing in it altogether.

★ ★ ★ ★ ★

At the end of 2012, considering what to write next after *Dodger*, Terry had, as ever, a number of options. There was the idea he had for a Discworld novel called 'Running Water'. This was going to feature Moist von Lipwig in the role of Joseph Bazalgette on Discworld, and centre on the announcement by Lord Vetinari of 'the Grand Under-taking', which at this point would turn out to be the construction

....

* Read *Dam-burst of Dreams* by Irish author Christopher Nolan.

of an underground water and sewage system for Ankh-Morpork. And that work would inevitably involve excavating the city, which would disclose another, older Ankh-Morpork beneath the current one, and another, even older Ankh-Morpork below that, and those excavated Ankh-Morporks would turn out to be not so dead and buried after all.

That was the idea I thought Terry might opt for. He had already spoken, some while ago, to the manager of a sewage farm in Somerset who had happily agreed to show him around. Call it Practical Research 101. And guess who would have been accompanying him. When Terry eventually decided not to go with 'Running Water', I rued a missed life experience.

Then there was 'Raising Taxes', which would also have starred Moist von Lipwig, who, on this occasion, would have been appointed chief tax gatherer and instructed to use his considerable wiles and charm not only to make the reluctant citizens of Ankh-Morpork pay their taxes, but also to be happy that they were doing so. That seemed like a solid idea, too.

Terry had also started talking about the dramatic possibilities of killing off one of his major characters – without specifying which one. Many years previously, Philippa Dickinson had put the notion of this device to Terry and he had seemed appalled by it.

'He looked at me in astonishment and said, "Why would I do that?"' said Philippa. 'Why would he deny himself a good character that he might get some more books out of?'

At this point, though, with time running out, the idea clearly took on a different complexion. But which character would he bump off? My assumption, from things we had discussed, was that it would be Lord Vetinari. Vetinari would die somehow, but then, in the book's closing stages, we would step back and reveal that he had actually been alive the whole time and pulling Moist von Lipwig's strings from afar. Could that have been part of the plot of 'Raising Taxes'? Perhaps. But Terry passed over it.

Instead he decided that it was time for Discworld to experience the industrial revolution. Terry had this theory that steam engines could only happen in a culture when it was time for steam engines to happen – and on Discworld it was clearly steam engine time. We spent the latter part of 2012 and the beginning of 2013 getting the words down for what would be Terry's last adult Discworld book, *Raising Steam*.

It was a tough job. In keeping with everything getting harder, the writing again got harder. Individual sentences were still gleaming, there were flourishes and whole scenes that sang, the carpet squares were still appearing. But where was it all heading? As never before, I found myself worrying about that as we were going along. The scenes accumulated and accumulated, the word-count rose and rose in the bottom corner of my screen, and yet the unifying, crystallizing vision that would have turned these scenes into a novel wasn't emerging. In the writing of these books, there had always been that magical 'Eureka!' moment, where Terry walked through the Chapel door one morning and said, 'I've got it! I've worked it out,' and suddenly the whole thing fell into place and we knew what the novel was. When was that 'Eureka!' moment going to happen this time?

We were going at it seven days a week now, desperately driven to get the book done, and yet somehow with no clear end in sight. I was letting him run because what else was I to do? Terry lived to write, so every day that Terry wrote he stayed alive. And in the past, nothing he produced, however stray or orphaned it seemed at the time, had ever gone to waste. It would go into the Pit and find a home somewhere, at some point. And on top of that, there would always come the great day of reckoning when Terry went back and cut and shifted things around, and planed and sanded and polished what he had written until it was the novel. But this time, in a way that filled me with panic, there was no sign of that day coming. He was just downloading these scenes, beautiful scenes, one after another. The book simply grew and grew. By the end of March 2013, the count stood at 130,000 words – the length of *Unseen Academicals*.

At that point, I said to Terry, 'Let's down tools momentarily, and have a look at what we've got.' Over that weekend I went back over the text, stripped out the scenes that were repeats of each other and the scenes that set off down dead ends, and realized, with a sinking heart, that there was no narrative direction whatsoever.

We were in new territory now. On the Monday morning, I called

Philippa Dickinson. We were going to be extra-dependent on her editorial brilliance from this point in. What we had at that moment was essentially a number of unconnected carpet squares, in an untidy pile. What Philippa was able to do was spread them out, see the pattern in those squares, detect where the gaps were, and then lead Terry to where the holes needed to be filled and the stitches needed to be made. Over the ensuing months, she and I spoke twice a day. Every morning, having reviewed the previous day's progress, Philippa would call me to say where she thought we should try and go that day. And every evening I would call her and report on where, with my coaxing, Terry had gone. Out of this painstaking, laborious and patience-sapping process, *Raising Steam* finally emerged. Without Philippa's overview, and her ability to guide it from above, the book would never have come together in the shape that it did.

'Who do you want to dedicate it to, Terry?' I asked him, when the novel was finished.

'To our fathers,' Terry said.

'To *your* father, you mean,' I said.

'No,' he said, 'to *our* fathers.'

For the front of the book, he wrote:

To David Pratchett and Jim Wilkins, both fine engineers who taught their sons to be curious.

I could not have been prouder. But the book itself continued to worry me.

That autumn I accompanied Terry to World Fantasy Con 2013, at the Metropole Hotel in Brighton. I did an interview with him on the stage – another outing for the Terry and Rob act and, as it turned out, the last. As we came off afterwards, I walked past Malcolm Edwards. 'That was great,' Malcolm said. 'You asked some really great questions.' He paused momentarily. 'And answered them yourself.'

I realized that this was over. It was Terry's final public appearance on stage.

We bumped into Jennifer Brehl at that Con. As she moved forward to greet him, Terry took a step back. 'I was worried that you might want to kill me,' he said, and began to cry. The rights to Terry's American publishing had recently moved from HarperCollins to Knopf Doubleday, depriving us of Jennifer's essential input on *Raising Steam* – depriving us of Jennifer, full stop. It was a grave shame, and a bad decision in my view, but it was just business and there were no hard feelings. We went for dinner, along with Neil Gaiman, ate oysters Kilpatrick and had a good night.*

Outside on the pavement, before we got into our car, Jennifer said goodbye to Terry. 'I hugged him,' said Jennifer. 'I knew it would be the last time I would see him.'

I was in Florida, taking a short holiday, when *Raising Steam* came out. I was sick with anxiety about what readers were going to think of it. Hunched under the duvet in my villa, I looked at the early reviews on Amazon. And right away my worst fears were realized. I scrolled down: one-star review, two-star review, one-star review ... 'The characters aren't themselves ... the writing is different ... not like Pratchett's previous work ... not interesting, not funny, *not Pratchett*.' I closed the laptop and pulled the duvet over my head.

Within 48 hours, fans would come rushing to Terry's defence, never prepared to stand by and see him slated, least of all now, and the book's ratings got boosted to 4.6. Well, bless them for that. But those reviews were the one-liners. The longer, more considered ones tended to see it differently. And, much as it hurt to admit it, I thought the more considered ones had got it right. The book was a missed opportunity. I knew that the real triumph of *Raising Steam* was that it existed at all.

★ ★ ★ ★ ★

And then it was 2014, and we started losing him at 100mph.

We worked on *The Shepherd's Crown* that year – the final Tiffany

-----

* A good night, yes – but it became clear the morning after that Terry, Neil and I had all gone down with food poisoning. 'Do you think Jennifer poisoned us?' Terry asked, darkly.

Aching book, the final Terry Pratchett book. And still the words came, but he was really having to cast around for them now. He would reach out with his closed hand as if trying to snatch the elusive word out of the air. And he would find it eventually. But it would take longer than it ever had, and it was wrenching to witness. Every day there was a diamond, even now. Every day there was something great. But, as with *Raising Steam*, he couldn't seem to do the big picture. The book was struggling to coalesce.

He was sleeping a lot, too. That, also, was hard to witness. Terry had been so much the opposite of a person who took naps – dynamic all day long. Now sleep would overcome him almost at random. I ordered him a two-seater reclining sofa for the Chapel. There hadn't really been a chair in there that he could comfortably sleep on. I put it in front of the mullioned window. Terry wanted to test drive it immediately. He sat down on it and I pulled the lever at the side. Maybe I pulled it a little hard, but the reclining mechanism went off faster than either of us expected. Terry's legs shot forward on the footrest, and as his head rocketed back, his hat dropped down over his eyes. He didn't flinch. Just like that, in the fully reclined position, he went to sleep and slept for two solid hours.

There were still good days. That spring, the Story Museum in Oxford put together an exhibition of photographs called '26 Characters', with authors dressed as their favourites from their childhood reading. The esteemed photographer Cambridge Jones came to the Chapel, and Terry, who thoroughly approved of the Story Museum, agreed to pose – rather convincingly, as it happened – as Richmal Crompton's William Brown, complete with catapult and bare knees.* He attended the exhibition's opening night, too, and enjoyed himself so thoroughly that he instructed me to pick up the bill on his behalf for Olivia Colman's table on the other side of the restaurant where we ended up afterwards.†

. . . .

* Neil Gaiman appeared, equally convincingly, as Badger from *The Wind in the Willows*.

† Just to be clear, Terry instructed me to pick up the bill for our table that night, too. At least, so far as I remember he did. Maybe we only picked up Olivia Colman's bill. It was that kind of night.

Another good day: the one in March when Dave Busby came to see him. 'At the end, Terry said, "That was so good, I really enjoyed this, we'll have to do this again,"' Dave said. 'He kept putting me off, though. He didn't want me to see the decline.'

Yet another good day: 27 May. That was when Terry had his tenth and final honorary doctorate bestowed upon him, by the University of South Australia in Adelaide. David Lloyd had left Trinity College Dublin, to take up the post of Vice Chancellor there, and we were working together on setting up a bursary in Terry's name that could fund a student exchange programme between Dublin and Adelaide. Terry clearly wasn't going to make it to Adelaide for the doctoral ceremony, so we decided that Adelaide would come to Terry, and the doctorate would be conferred in the Chapel. A couple of weeks beforehand, David sent me an email: 'Is it okay if Kryten from *Red Dwarf* attends the conferral on 27 May?' Naturally, Terry had no problem with that, even if the exact reason for it remained opaque. So David duly turned up on the day in a brand new electric Tesla S with the actor Robert Llewellyn.[*] As well as a cast member from one of Terry's favourite television shows, David had also thoughtfully packed the essential doctoral bonnet – with corks hanging from it, naturally. Terry had composed an address to the graduating class of 2014 which I read to camera and which was screened at their graduation ceremony in August. It was a warm and jolly few hours.

But Terry's behaviour was growing gradually more eccentric – and sometimes, there is no denying, that was funny. Terry's foraging around the grounds for kindling for the Chapel's two wood-burners, in as much as he could manage it, took on an unpredictable dimension. He once entered the Chapel bearing a sizeable bough from an apple tree. I'm not sure where he got hold of it, but it was still so fresh that it had fruit on it. Terry then stood and stuffed this groaning bough into the

....

[*] Robert Llewellyn was an early-adopting electric car advocate, hence the Tesla. The party called at my house on the way to the manor, and I asked Robert if I could take a picture of him beside my fridge. Which was a bit tacky, I know, but *Red Dwarf* fans will understand: the fridge is a Smeg.

stove, apples and all, folding bits of it over to fit it in. Or, at least, he stuffed in as much as he could: when he had finished and the stove was full, about 90 per cent of the branch was still hanging out on the floor.

Then there was the day he announced to me that he was going to pledge £50,000 to the Orangutan Foundation. He picked up the phone and I heard him say, 'Hello? This is Terry Pratchett. I have decided to give you £50,000.' There seemed to be, understandably, some gasps of surprise and appreciation at the other end, and then Terry hung up.

Unfortunately, instead of ringing Ashley Leiman of the Orangutan Foundation, Terry had just rung Audrey Swindells of the Bath Postal Museum. Ashley and Audrey were right next to each other on the alphabetical speed-dial. Close, then, but not what Terry intended. This slip of the fingers only came to light some days later, when Audrey from the Bath Postal Museum rang for further discussions, and after Terry's cheque had already gone off to Ashley at the Orangutan Foundation. I had to explain that there had been a little mistake. By then Audrey had excitedly revealed news of Terry Pratchett's generous gift to her museum's trustees. Everyone was very understanding about it, in the circumstances, but we decided it might be a good idea to limit Terry's unsupervised use of the phone after that.

But then there was the eccentric behaviour that was simply distressing. One Saturday night, Terry rang me at home from the Chapel at about 11.00 p.m. 'There's a beeping. Can you hear that?' I felt as though we had been here before with the phantom noises. I couldn't hear anything over the phone and I told him he should call it a night and get Lyn to take him down to the house. We could sort the noise out in the morning, assuming there was a noise, which I doubted. The next day, at 7.20 a.m., my phone rang again. 'I'm still in the Chapel,' Terry said, 'and it's still beeping.' I doubted that as well, but I drove in at speed. A battery from the computer's back-up power supply had been beeping randomly. Terry had spent the entire night fretting about it and failing to locate it. He had tried to nap on the mat in the Chapel.

He told me about a dream he had had about us both. 'You were standing behind me,' Terry said, 'and my brain was made of grey sand.

And you were trying to hold it all together, but this grey sand was slipping through your fingers, and you couldn't.'

Trying to hold on to to Terry's brain as it slipped inexorably through my fingers . . . that was exactly what these months felt like.

We sought refuge in the reliable pleasure of going to buy a hat. It was an unfailing truth with Terry: 'any day with a new hat in it is a very good day indeed'. We got a driver to take us to Elm in Burford, a shop we knew from experience to be the stockist of authentic Australian Akubra hats. We had just got out onto the pavement in the High Street, and were getting ourselves together, when Terry suddenly took a step in the direction of the busy road. I grabbed him, thinking he was about to walk into the traffic, and he swung an arm to steady himself, catching me in the face with great force. So now we were two grown men wrestling on the side of the road. What must we have looked like? Terry was getting recognized everywhere now, so how could I protect his dignity in a moment like this? Eventually we straightened ourselves up and went into the shop. And we bought a hat and that was a pleasure. But it was dark and pouring with rain when the driver brought us home and the oncoming headlights were refracting through the wet and the thrashing windscreen wipers. Terry, in the front seat, became terrified. He thought he was being strafed by laser beams. We were in *Star Wars*, on board the Millennium Falcon, getting shot at by Imperial Tie Fighters. It could have been funny, except that Terry was howling in his confusion and terror – proper, animal howling – and throwing his arms up to protect himself, and I was reaching round from the back to try and hold his shoulders and calm him and reassure him that it was nothing, just headlights and rain.

Somehow we got home, and somehow we went on.

That year, Terry finally agreed to the publication of a collection of his non-fiction, *A Slip of the Keyboard* – the book he had thrown out eight years previously because of the publishers' presumption in offering too large an advance. Neil Gaiman sent over his introduction. It was fantastic – more so than I could have ever expected. It described Terry in ways that nobody had thought to describe him before, with intimacy and obvious fondness. And it boldly addressed Terry's anger, head-on, locating in it the fuel that powered the engine that drove Discworld.

But there was also no getting round the fact that the essay was an obituary – a valediction. I sat on the steps that lead up to the Chapel mezzanine and read it aloud to Terry, and when I got to the line 'I rage at the imminent loss of my friend,' I choked up. I waited for Terry's reaction. 'Well, I don't think it was *exactly* like that,' he said. What had caught his attention was Neil's story of Terry making them both late for a radio interview during their US tour to promote *Good Omens*. 'You'd better go and run it past my wife,' said Terry.

So I went down to the house and sat in the kitchen and read the piece to Lyn, revisiting those thoughts about Terry's anger, and once again choking up at the line 'at the imminent loss of my friend'.* Lyn sat and thought for a while, clearly testing Neil's words against her own lifelong experience of Terry. Eventually she said, 'I suppose he *can* be a little bit grumpy.'

In August, I went to the Discworld Convention in Manchester without him. It was the first time Terry hadn't attended since the UK Cons in his honour began, back in 1996. It was awful. He cried when I left without him. But getting him there – the four-hour drive to Manchester, the overnight in a hotel – and getting him through the public exposure without risking his dignity, just seemed like an impossible task in the circumstances. I have reflected anxiously on that decision a lot over the years since, and wondered whether I should have taken him. No doubt the event itself, and the warmth and love of the fans, would have given him an energy, as it always did, and maybe that energy would have been sufficient to propel him through the difficulties of being there. But at the time, with Terry in front of me, and with the situation as it was, it just seemed unworkable and fraught with risks. It hurt him so much not to go, though. I was doing my best to ignore the bigger implications, but he must have known he wouldn't see another convention. The fans in Manchester knew it, too. The atmosphere was warm,

. . . .

* I have never been able to read that piece in public without choking up. Not once.

but also subdued. It was a party without a host. It was hard to escape the feeling that people were already starting to do their mourning.

When I got back to the Chapel, we carried on with *The Shepherd's Crown*. While he was working, he was still Terry Pratchett. And there were still sentences that unfurled from his mind that you could only marvel at. But there were whole patches of time when he was stuck.

'Terry,' I said one day, as we wrote. 'We're going inside a shed – what do we see?' I knew that Terry loved a shed as much as I did: jam jars nailed under shelves, carefully painted silhouettes of tools on the walls, all those shed smells . . . This was all delicious territory for Terry and I was anticipating him really letting fly here. But there was practically nothing. He couldn't do it. He couldn't visualize space any more.

It was the same when we were writing a passage towards what would have become *The Turtle Stops* and needed to take the reader inside Great A'Tuin.

'Terry, we're inside the star turtle. What do we see?'

'It's as big as a cathedral.'

'Bigger, surely . . .'

'It's as big as a city.'

'Bigger than that, too, surely . . .'

In *The Shepherd's Crown* he wrote the same scene over and over. It was the scene, near the beginning of the story, in which Granny Weatherwax contemplates death. And every time he rewrote it, he thought the book was finished.

'Terry, we've done this scene already.'

'Have we?'

The book was agony. Once again, Philippa Dickinson was amazing. We were back in the routine of twice-daily phone calls. Every morning she would suggest where we might go, every evening I would tell her where we had been. Again she found threads and made suggestions for ways that Terry might tug at them. The book nudged forward by degrees, painfully slowly. But every day that Terry stuck at it was another day that Terry was still a writer. And every day that Terry was still a writer was another day that Terry was still alive. So we stuck at it.

'When did you realize that I'd lost it?' he asked me suddenly one day, out of nowhere.

'What do you mean, Terry?' I said. 'You haven't lost it. You're the great Terry Pratchett. Of course you haven't lost it.'

He looked at me.

'When did you realize that I'd lost it?' he said again.

He didn't want flattery. He didn't want soft soap. Not now. He wanted honesty. And I owed him that, at the very least. So I thought about it. And I told him about a moment, quite recently, when he had left me to tidy up a passage that he had dictated. As usual, he had asked me to read it back to him when I had finished. And I read the passage to him, and he didn't pull me up once to correct something or change something – not once for the whole passage. And that had struck me at the time. Because Terry *always* wanted to correct or change something in those moments. Always.

He thought about that for a while.

'That wasn't when I lost it,' he said, eventually. 'That was when YOU finally got BETTER!'

And then he laughed loudly. And I laughed too.

I remember the last weeks in the office as an endless succession of farewells – silent farewells, a long string of last visits that could not really declare themselves to be last visits.

Bernard Pearson came, using a walking stick now, and at the end of his visit the pair of them walked out, a little way down the slope from the Chapel, Terry on Bernard's arm. 'Terry said to me, "You know, Bernard, I used to be Terry Pratchett." And I said to him, "You know, Terry, I used to be able to walk."'

Colin Smythe came, with his partner Leslie – Colin who had been with Terry for forty extraordinary years. He brought a picnic lunch: Scotch eggs, pork pies, tracklements . . . We spread the feast out in the Chapel and then I closed the door and left them to reminisce.

Neil Gaiman came. I went to pick him up from Salisbury station. There had been a huge decline in Terry even in the short time since Neil had last seen him, and I didn't quite know in what terms to warn him about it. Neil had last been at the manor in the early autumn of

2014, when Dirk Maggs was producing a radio version of *Good Omens* for BBC Radio 4. Neil and Terry had a cameo in that dramatization as two policemen – appropriately named 'Neil' and 'Terry' – chatting in a squad car, a scene which they recorded that day. I assumed Dirk would have a button on his mixing desk that made people sound as though they were talking inside a car, but no: the way you make people sound as though they are talking inside a car is by making them talk inside a car. We used mine, parked outside the Chapel, with Terry and Neil in the front seats and Dirk in the back, recording them.

Terry couldn't read his lines that day, but he could repeat them when they were fed to him. That, I knew, would now be beyond him. This time when Neil walked in, Terry barely seemed able to acknowledge that he was in the room. I set up a small table in the library so that they could sit opposite each other. Neil talked, delving back into the past, pulling out memories, recalling the time when they toured together with *Good Omens*. Still Terry seemed unresponsive. I was going to leave the two of them together and go down to the pub to pick up lunch. Maybe an order of take-away scampi would bring Terry back into the room. It had been known to do so before.

I was in the doorway on my way out when I heard Neil begin to sing. What he sang was the first lines of 'Shoehorn With Teeth' – his and Terry's favourite They Might Be Giants song. And Terry joined in. He raised his voice with Neil's and 'Shoehorn With Teeth' rang around the Chapel.

I left them singing. When I got back with the food, the noise that greeted me was the sound of Terry's voice, animatedly chatting to Neil. I set down the food and left them to it, two multi-millionaire authors eating out of polystyrene boxes at a flimsy card table. In the car on the way back to the station, Neil told me that Terry had asked him to make sure that he wrote *Good Omens* for the screen. It hadn't happened in Terry's lifetime, but maybe it could happen after. 'And nobody loves the old girl like you,' Terry had told him.

Friday, 5 December 2014: that was his final day in the office. *The Shepherd's Crown* was finished. Given another month, would it have been a better book? Most likely, yes. But as Terry always said, 'In a month, I could make the book three per cent better. But in a month I would also tell you that in a month I could make the book three per cent better.'*

What he hadn't managed to incorporate was one final twist that he had conceived during the book's writing. Terry had a notion that it might emerge that the deceased Granny Weatherwax had, in fact, temporarily placed her consciousness in You the cat, enabling her to reappear at the end of the book, in the manner of Yoda, Anakin Skywalker and Ben Kenobi in *Return of the Jedi*. Death would then only collect her in the Epilogue, with Granny declaring, 'I am leaving on my own terms now.' But there wasn't time. You had to stop somewhere: that was just a fact of life.

Shortly after 5.00 p.m., we closed the file. Terry made two phone calls – to Rod Brown and to Mark Boomla, his accountant. Then I took him down to the kitchen, where Lyn now had cushions spread on the floor to catch him when he fell. In the kitchen, he rang Rhianna. 'I hope I was good,' he told her. 'I could have been better . . .' He cried.

After that, I sat with him and we had a conversation about which book might come next. Maybe 'Raising Taxes'? Possibly. But there were so many other options . . .

He had a fall that weekend. Lyn wrapped him up and put him to bed downstairs in the sitting room. But he didn't get up. On the Monday, Lyn called out Dr Nodder, our friend and the village GP. Dr Nodder arrived and examined Terry. She said he had pneumonia and called an ambulance. She was in tears when she came away from him. We had a drink in the kitchen and I talked to her about *The Shepherd's Crown*, and how it was coming out in the autumn and at least Terry could look forward to that. Dr Nodder said, 'Rob, Terry isn't going to be here in the autumn.' I had been so deep in denial, shovelling the end off into the future. But the end was happening now.

He went into hospital. I went to see him on the first three days and each time he was unconscious. On the fourth day, I went in and his bed

* Terry's other favourite drawing-the-line expression: 'It's good enough for folk music.'

was empty. My stomach dropped. I went rushing round the wards, crashing through swing doors, trying to find out what had happened to him. Eventually someone directed me to the dementia ward. 'Don't worry,' they said. 'He's been moved there.' When I burst into the room, he was sitting up in bed holding a plastic beaker of tea.

'Hello, Rob,' he said. 'Is that you?'

He then leaned towards me and began to talk in a conspiratorial tone about how we needed to take the ducks up the hill. Then he stopped and laughed.

'That was a load of bollocks, wasn't it?'

'Yes, Terry,' I said, 'but it was *our* bollocks.'

That was the last proper conversation we had.[*]

He remained in hospital over Christmas. And then, in late January 2015, he came back home and Lyn appointed a team of carers to help us look after him.

These were the final weeks. Sometimes he would get out of bed in the middle of the night, triggering the alarm in the mat on the bedroom floor. Rhianna, who had moved back into the house to be near him, went to him one night. 'He looked like a bewildered gnome, standing in the middle of the room,' Rhianna said. 'He was very confused. He said, "Oh, Grump – you've found me!" He was often waiting for trains at those times. "Will we need tickets?" he'd say. I said, "I think we will, Dad, yes." He said, "Don't they know we're *Pratchetts*?" '

More last visits. Maddy Prior from Steeleye Span came to sing to him. She sang 'Thomas The Rhymer'.[†] Philippa Dickinson came with the jacket for *The Shepherd's Crown*. 'He was in a bed on the ground floor by then,' Philippa said. 'He was non-verbal. The carers were damping his lips with sponges. I showed him the jacket and I told him about it. I so wanted him to like that cover, and I wasn't even sure that he could see it. But he gave me the impression that he did like it.'

. . . .

[*] It's possible that Terry's ducks were a confused memory of the manor's chickens who, at the end of the day, would need to be herded up the ramp into their coop.

[†] It was utterly beautiful, but I have not been able to listen to that song since.

Dave Busby came. 'Lyn said, "You'd better come down." It had been a year of just talking on the phone. He had made such a huge effort to conceal his condition from me. In our calls, there had often been long hesitations on his side of the conversation, but he always sounded rational and humorous. He didn't discuss his condition much – his mind was on future projects. He always said he was still writing. I would come off those calls, and Gill, my wife, would say, "How was he?" And I would say, "He's OK, you know – not too bad, all things considered." I didn't realize how much he was deteriorating physically. I was shocked to see him. He was in bed, and there were two carers attending to him. But he wasn't there. There was no Terry. He had already departed.'

Terry went into a coma on Monday 9 March and the doctor told Lyn and Rhianna to prepare for the end. 'Mum asked the carers, "Can you raise the bed so I can cuddle him?"' Rhianna said. 'That was the hardest part: seeing my mum and realizing what she was losing.' Late on Wednesday night the carers reported that Terry's breathing was slowing. Lyn and Rhianna sat with him, Rhianna fetching Pongo the cat, who curled up at Terry's feet and went to sleep. 'I took his hand,' said Rhianna, 'and at 3.30 a.m. on Thursday morning he was gone. Mum, Pongo and I were all with him. I think he waited until we were all in place.'

Rhianna phoned me soon after and Sandra and I went over. We sat with Lyn and Rhianna as it got light, and through the day. We talked and cried and comforted each other. We drank tea, we ate lemon drizzle cake. Terry's body remained in the house until the evening, so, when we needed to, we could go through to him.

'I must have gone to see him about two dozen times that day,' Rhianna said. 'It didn't seem weird or scary. There wasn't that much difference between how he was and how he had been just before it happened. That was comforting, somehow.'

I went to him, too, at one stage, and closed the door so that it was just me and him. And I told him that now he was going to have to listen to me, and this time he couldn't cut me off when I tried to thank him and tell him what I felt – that he would just have to lie there and take it. And I told him that it had been the most amazing time, an incredible ride, and that he had changed and enriched my life so much, and that I felt honoured to call him my friend, and that he was a phenomenal writer – a genius, actually, which was not, he had taught me, a word to go throwing around lightly – and that he would never be forgotten, and that it had been an absolute privilege, and in fact a dream, to sit in a room and get told stories by the great Terry Pratchett and to be able to call that my job, so thank you, thank you, thank you.

Oh, and mind how you go.

And then I opened a window for him.

There was something very calming about those hours in the house, when the news had gone no further. Partly we held on to it so that it remained ours and ours alone for a little longer, which we knew it could not be for ever. And partly we felt as though we were protecting people from it – this sad thing we had to tell people which we knew would upset them. But we also knew that eventually we had to open the door and let the word out and the world in.

Rhianna and I decided to do it using Twitter, in three consecutive tweets.

AT LAST, SIR TERRY, WE MUST WALK TOGETHER.

Terry took Death's arm and followed him through the doors and on to the black desert under the endless night.

THE END.

Rhianna and I tapped them into our phones, and sat with them at the kitchen table, all set to go. It was just after 3.00 in the afternoon, twelve hours after Terry had died. We understood that from the second we touched those buttons, Terry's death would stop being ours and become everyone's. Which explains why we lingered, with our forefingers poised, for as long as we possibly could.

'Ready?' I said.

'Ready,' said Rhianna.

'OK,' I said, '. . . go.'

EPILOGUE

There were fewer than ten minutes between Rhianna and I pushing the button on the Twitter announcement and Lyn running into the kitchen and saying, 'Dad's on the telly!'

'*The author Sir Terry Pratchett has died at the age of sixty-six . . .*'

The news was out and an international outpouring of love and respect for the life of Professor Sir Terry Pratchett OBE, Blackboard Monitor, Adjunct of the Oscar Wilde Centre for Irish Writing and the School of English at Trinity College Dublin was underway.

And it was only a few minutes after that when I took a call from a journalist, Nick Higham from the BBC, who offered his condolences and asked carefully, 'Was Terry assisted?' I admired him for that because it was the obvious question, and yet he was, strangely, amid all the media attention around Terry's death, the only journalist who rang me up and directly asked it. And I was able to tell him that, no: this fervent proponent of the right to die with dignity at the time of your choosing had himself died quietly and naturally at home with his family around him and his cat curled up at the foot of his bed.

At 7.00 p.m., Mr Adlem, our area's esteemed local undertaker, came to take away Terry's body. That's Mr Richard Adlem MBE, to be precise, the man who organized the burials of Lyn's mother, father and step-father, and also of the former Prime Minister Anthony Eden, and society photographer Cecil Beaton. When he had performed his duties and driven away, I walked up to the Chapel. It was after nightfall now. Entering the headquarters of Discworld on Roundworld for the first time since Terry's death, I felt entirely hollow. His desk, his empty chair . . . It was too much. I went and stood at the mullioned window and looked out into the dark. The blue light from the office's alarm key-pad was casting a double reflection in the glass which, as I stared at it, became two electric blue eyes – the unmistakable eyes of Discworld's Death. I had probably looked at that reflection more than ten thousand times before now and never seen it that way.

The funeral was ten days later, on 25 March 2015. In accordance with Terry's wishes, his body was carried in a wicker casket. Lyn wanted to deck the casket with wild flowers, and that morning Rhianna went out and gathered an armful from the grounds of the manor. Again in accord-ance with Terry's wishes, the casket travelled the last part of the journey to Salisbury crematorium in a black, glass-sided carriage, drawn by two black horses with plumes. *Not* in accordance with Terry's wishes, but def-initely something he would have asked for if he'd thought of it: when the carriage moved off, its back doors flapped open, creating a brief moment of slapstick in which the horses had to halt again while one of the under-takers jumped down and secured the load. Further along the way, in another touch that Terry would certainly have scripted given half a chance, a plume fell off one of the horses and was run over by the follow-ing car. Further along again, one of the horses took a moment to empty its bowels – and at this point we were thinking that the day actually *was* being scripted by Terry.

At the crematorium, Rhianna carried Terry's sword behind the cof-fin, having taken advice from her friend Sámhlaoch, a sword fighter, on the correct positions: under the chin on the walk behind the coffin (a salute to the leader) and across the heart (a personal salute) as the coffin was laid down. 'And I did it with Jimmy Choos on,' said Rhianna, 'which Dad would have been pleased about.' Seven pieces of music were played: Steeleye Span's 'The Making Of A Man', Queen's 'These Are The Days Of Our Lives', Abba's 'When All Is Said And Done', 'MLK' by U2, 'Nimrod' from Elgar's *Enigma Variations*, Thomas Tallis's 'Spem in Alium', which Terry had always imagined as the elevator music one might hear in heaven; and then, as the coffin was lowered and we all departed, the full-length version of Meat Loaf's 'Bat Out Of Hell', 9 minutes and 50 seconds. Neil Gaiman spoke, and I tried through tears to read the opening chapter from *The Shepherd's Crown*. And then we went to the Castleman Hotel to eat and drink, where our small gathering included Pete Lucas, the bass player from The Troggs, a regular drinker at Terry's local and, in fact, arguably its cornerstone.

In as much as these occasions can ever 'go well', it went well. Indeed, I can think of no greater accolade for the funeral of Terry Pratchett than the one Rhianna came out with: 'Had it been for someone else, and Dad had been attending, he'd have wanted one just like it.'

★ ★ ★ ★ ★

After the funeral, I was shattered. That final year, in particular, had taken its toll, and I was full of grief. I needed to clear my head a little. In April 2015, we took a family holiday, flying out to New Zealand, via Dubai, and then going on to Australia where, in Sydney, I went to the Australian Discworld Convention. Stephen Briggs was also there and at the worst of times it was good to be among friends.

And then I returned to England and went back to the Chapel to start work again. I had the leather top of Terry's desk overlaid with glass, thereby encapsulating and preserving for posterity the mug rings, the patches of spilled tea and coffee, the pen marks and the scars from where he would sometimes idly whittle at it with a wood-handled penknife. Terry was no great respecter of that leather, all in all, but I felt the need to respect it now; Terry Pratchett made those marks.

And then I opened the letter he left me in the safe – which is where this book began – and started to follow its instructions. I had the fine pieces of jewellery cast to his design: the necklaces for Lyn and for Rhianna and for Sandra, the signet ring with a bee for me, the gold bee pins for Terry's friends and colleagues in what Terry called the Venerable Order of the Honeybee – his collective name for the team who helped him with the business throughout his life. I chose gifts and sent flowers. I did not learn to fly, but one day maybe there will be time. I certainly raised a brandy to his memory and to happy days.

And I turned my mind to looking after the business – to managing Narrativia, in partnership with Rhianna, and minding the Terry Pratchett estate and its legacy, and to getting his stories off the page and onto the screen in the ways he would have wished, beginning with *Good Omens*.

And then, of course, in April 2016, there was his memorial to organize. We held it in the Barbican Theatre. Contrary to his most fervent wishes, Terry himself could not be there. But his sword and his hat made it along, brought to the stage by my son Louis, and so did Steeleye Span, who played 'Thomas The Rhymer', and so did the Epiphoni Consort, who sang 'Spem in Alium'. And so did Rhianna, who read the tribute she had written to her father, while Lyn and Sandra watched from the audience. And so did Colin Smythe and Larry Finlay and Paul Kidby and Tony Robinson and Neil Gaiman and Philippa Dickinson and Jennifer Brehl and Anne Hoppe and Bernard and Isobel Pearson and Dr Pat Harkin and every member of the Venerable Order of the Honeybee. And Stephen Briggs was Lord Vetinari for the night, and Dave Busby and the Table of Eight from the CEGB were in the audience, and Eric Idle sang 'Always Look On The Bright Side Of Life' and I, as compere, said both 'fuck' and 'bugger' in front of my parents, exactly as Terry decreed.

Afterwards, when I had jumped down from the stage and was standing among everyone, exhausted and not a little bewildered, John Lloyd, the creator of *QI* and the producer of *Spitting Image*, *Blackadder* and so much else, came up and gripped me by the arms and spoke some words that have stayed with me ever since. 'Of all the dead authors in the world,' John said fervently, 'Terry Pratchett is the most alive.' It felt entirely true to me at that moment, and it feels entirely true to me now.

No more Terry Pratchett novels, though. In August 2017, in accordance with Terry's further wishes, I extracted from the main office computer the hard drive containing all his unpublished fiction, took it to the opening of the Great Dorset Steam Fair, and had it ritually run over by a vintage John Fowler & Co. steamroller called Lord Jericho. Prior to taking on the job of crushing Terry's extant fiction, Lord Jericho had metalled the road at the top of the manor's drive, so was clearly the right steamroller for this important ritual of closure – a symbolic gesture to indicate the placing of a big, rumbling full stop on Terry's writing career and to make it clear that there would be no further novels.

Which is deeply saddening, of course. All those books he never got to write! All those books we never got to read! How many of them might there have been? Several were already underway: 'Raising Taxes'; 'Running Water'; 'The Turtle Stops'; a second volume of adventures for the Amazing Maurice; 'What Dodger Did Next'; 'Twilight Canyons', in which the elderly patients in a home for the bewildered solve the mystery of the missing treasure and defeat the rise of the Dark Lord despite the fact that many of them don't entirely know whether it's Tuesday or a lemon; 'The Dark Incontinent' about the secret of a crystal cave thick with carnivorous plants; a whodunnit starring Constable Feeney, briefly entitled 'The Feeney', in homage to the great 1970s TV cop show *The Sweeney*, and set among the goblins; 'Up School!', where Susan Sto Helit becomes the headmistress of Quirm College for Young Ladies; 'Cab's Well', about the poor forsaken chap at the bottom of the wishing well whose job it is to make the wishes come true when the lucky coins get tossed in; and 'Clang!', a story of revolution on Discworld, with campanology as the main medium of communication from place to place.

'But Terry,' I said, when he had got me to jot down the initial thought for that last one on an A4 pad, with 'Clang!' written, at his insistence, ten lines tall at the top of the page, 'haven't we already done revolutions in *Night Watch*?'

'Ah, but that's the thing about revolutions,' Terry replied. 'They do tend to come round.'

And then, of course, there was his autobiography . . .

But how much writing Terry did manage to cram into his foreshortened life; as I sit here in the Chapel library, I look along the shelves of books that he did produce, and I remember what Neil Gaiman wrote, in an introduction to his favourite Terry novel, *Mort*: 'This is the loophole writers get. If you read our books, we aren't dead.'

So, yes, that's our consolation. Terry *is* still alive, and somewhere all of us can always find him when we need to: in those millions of words in those many, many books.

But is he still alive in any other form, in any other place? Well, Terry told me, before he died, that if there turned out to be anything on the other side, he would ring me and let me know.

No call as yet.*

. . . .

* But a good personal assistant's phone is always on.

'No one is finally dead until the ripples they cause in the world die away – until the clock he wound up winds down, until the wine she made has finished its ferment, until the crop they planted is harvested. The span of someone's life is only the core of their actual existence.'

Terry Pratchett, *Reaper Man*

PICTURE ACKNOWLEDGEMENTS

The publisher would like to thank the following for kind permission to reproduce images. While every effort has been made to trace the owners of copyright material reproduced herein, the publishers would like to apologize for any omissions and will be pleased to incorporate missing acknowledgements at the earliest opportunity.

All photographs are courtesy of the Pratchett Estate, except for the following:

First plate section

Page 2, top left:	*Science Fantasy* magazine Vol. 20, No. 60, from the Pratchett Estate archive
Page 4, top:	Terry's customized ZX81 © Kismet Photography
Page 5, top:	Terry and Colin Smythe at the launch of *The Carpet People* © Paul Felix
Page 6, top left:	Terry and Rhianna © Alexander Caminada
Page 8, bottom left:	silver locust © Kismet Photography, with kind permission of Colin Smythe

Second plate section

Page 1, top:	Terry in the Chapel © Roger Elliott

Page 2, top right: Sir Terry being knighted by the Queen © Alamy Stock Photo; below right: Terry and Lyn at the *Hogfather* premiere, from the Pratchett Estate archive

Page 4, second
from top: sword photo © Kismet Photography

Page 7, top: Terry and Rhianna © *The Sunday Times Magazine* / News Licensing Online

Page 8: Terry portrait © Roger Elliott

Text

Page 439: Childhood doodle of an airship by Terry Pratchett

Terry Pratchett was the acclaimed creator of the global bestselling Discworld series, the first of which, *The Colour of Magic*, was published in 1983. In all, he was the author of over fifty bestselling books which have sold over 100 million copies worldwide. His novels have been widely adapted for stage and screen, and he was the winner of multiple prizes, including the Carnegie Medal. He was awarded a knighthood for services to literature in 2009, although he always wryly maintained that his greatest service to literature was to avoid writing any.

www.TerryPratchettBooks.com

Rob Wilkins worked with Terry Pratchett for more than twenty years, first as his personal assistant, and later as his business manager. He now, in partnership with Terry's daughter Rhianna, manages the Pratchett literary estate and Terry's production company, Narrativia.

www.ALifeWithFootnotes.com

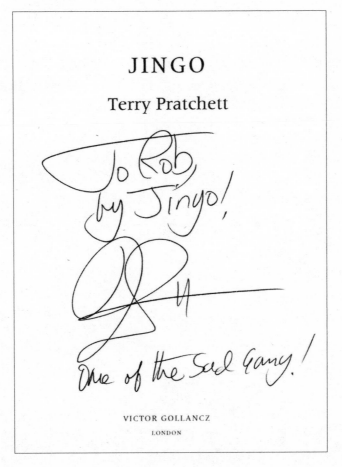

JINGO

Terry Pratchett

To Rob,
by Jingo!

One of the Sad Gang!

VICTOR GOLLANCZ
LONDON

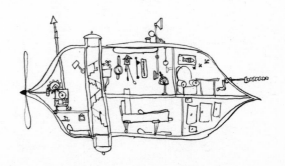